The
FOOD & WINE
PAIRING
Guide

Published in 2009 by Struik Lifestyle
(an imprint of Random House Struik (Pty) Ltd)
Company Reg. No. 1966/003153/07
Wembley Square, Solan Road, Cape Town 8001
PO Box 1144, Cape Town, 8000, South Africa
Reprinted in 2010, 2011, 2012

www.randomstruik.co.za

Publisher: Linda de Villiers
Managing editor: Cecilia Barfield
Editor: Gill Gordon
Designer: Ilze van der Westhuizen
Proofreader: Glynne Newlands

Reproduction: Hirt & Carter Cape (Pty) Ltd
Printing and binding: CTP Book Printers
Cape Town

ISBN 978-1-77007-787-4

For more information on food and wine pairing, visit
www.katinkafoodwine.co.za

Contents

Part I: Grapes, wines and food **5**
Introduction: First, a bit of this and that 7
The matter of preference 11
From the past to the present 13
How to pair food and wine 18
Likeness and contrast 28
'No order' is in order 30
Sauces and their impact on wine choices 32
Cooking with wine 44
Putting your wine fears to rest 46
Wines and their food matches 54
Wine as an apéritif 112
Serving temperatures for wine 114
Sharing wine in a restaurant 117

Part II: Matching food and wine **119**
Starters 120
Soups 141
Salads 144
Fish and seafood 147
Eggs and egg-based dishes 159
Pasta, pizza, risotto and vegetarian 164
Matching meat and wine 170
Beef 172
Lamb 191
Pork 198
Veal 205
Venison and ostrich 209
Offal 211
Chicken and other birds 214
Indian cuisine 227
Japanese cuisine 237
Chinese cuisine 242
Thai cuisine 249
Desserts 254
Cheeses and cheeseboards 270
Glossary of wine and cheese terms 306
Selected bibliography 311
Index 313

About the authors

Katinka van Niekerk has developed food and wine matching courses which she presents both locally and abroad. A career in the wine industry was followed by a stint as a lecturer for the Cape Wine Academy and she is currently a consultant to chefs and winemakers as well as a visiting lecturer at many hotel schools and catering colleges.

Katinka's interest in food and wine pairing began when she was the young wife of a New York-based diplomat. At the time, formal dinners often ended with chocolate mousse, the fashionable dessert of the day, accompanied by champagne. She found this combination jarring, as the sweetness of the dessert ruined every subtle nuance of the champagne. When she wanted to challenge the food and wine practices of the time, she was gently told to follow convention and that she would soon 'get used to how things should be done.' But she didn't, and her taste buds remained unconvinced!

Ultimately, this experience turned into a passion for discovering what works and what does not work when it comes to pairing food and wine. Building on the opportunities that came from living in the USA, Germany, Israel, the UK and South Africa, Katinka has, over the years, refined and developed this passion, constantly tasting, testing and investigating, all the while compiling an extensive database of notes and a prodigious 'tasting memory' of flavours and sensations.

Brian Burke is a passionate foodie with a specific interest in food and wine pairing. During his years in the corporate arena, he hosted numerous business lunches and dinners and keenly felt the lack of a guide to assist him, at a glance, to select wines to accompany those meals. The problem was not a lack of wines to choose from, but rather, which wine would best enhance the food without losing its own character. Being a marketer with a passion for identifying customer needs, Brian realized that many diners could find themselves with the same dilemma. Meeting Katinka was a 'light bulb moment'. At the time, she was offering courses for people in the hospitality industry who needed to learn the principles of matching food and wine and how to choose the best wines for a meal.

She had the practical knowledge, he had the research and marketing skills and it wasn't long before they realized that there was a way they could share their expertise with **all** wine and food lovers wanting to discover the key to matching wine and food, and *voilà!*, the concept for *The Food and Wine Pairing Guide* was born.

Part I:

Grapes, wines and food

Introduction: First, a bit of this and that

In recent years, we have started paying more attention to food and wine pairing. Thirty or forty years ago, this concept was a European phenomenon, in which the instinctive pairing of regional foods with regional wines was very successful. For example, a roast leg of lamb, studded with rosemary, a classic Bordelaise dish, is excellent when paired with a Bordeaux blend. Similarly, pasta with a hearty tomato sauce, so common in Tuscany, pairs unequivocally with Sangiovese, the food-friendly Italian grape, and its Tuscan incarnation, Chianti. Many regional pairings, like these, have withstood the test of time and are still unbeatable today. Over time, the concept of pairing certain foods and wines spread to non-wine producing countries in Europe and the New World, and it wasn't long before people were discovering that kangaroo steak pairs well with Shiraz, a wine that Australia has virtually adopted as its own; that Malbec goes well with an Argentinian beef barbeque, or that our own Pinotage partners happily with a springbok potjie.

But regional foods are no longer exclusive to their original domain. Thanks to the ease of global travel and the prevalence of the Internet, the world has become a village. Even your local convenience store now stocks foods and ingredients from all corners of the globe that we hadn't heard of a decade or two ago. At the professional level, chefs no longer stick to the tried-and-tested, and their patrons are revelling in new flavour combinations, thanks to mould-breaking experiments in food preparation.

In the same time frame, there has been a worldwide revolution in wine production and an increase in the availability of wine styles and cultivars. All this experimentation with food and wines naturally led to a curiosity about how the two would work together in the modern idiom. It was just a matter of where to begin.

Soon, restaurants began holding 'gourmet evenings', where the chef designs a menu to show off his creativity and skills and invites a winemaker to present wines to match and, hopefully, complement the food. This can prove tricky, however, as a winery may only have four or five wines in its range and a dish on the special menu might require a wine that falls outside that range of wines.

Lifestyle and cooking magazines soon followed suit, with a food editor, chef or wine fundi suggesting one or more wines to match various dishes. Similarly, many wine club members are no longer satisfied with winemakers leading them through a straightforward tasting, but frequently request food and wine pairings, or at least some tips, to get to grips with the perennial question: How do you go about selecting a wine to go with a particular dish?

The back labels of wines are also awash with pairing suggestions: 'Good with pasta' or 'Goes well with cheese' are typical examples, but **which** pasta dish would that be? One with a meaty Bolognese *ragù*, or a creamy sauce, such as a *fettuccine all'Alfredo*? Or maybe they meant a bowl of pasta dribbled with nothing more than olive oil and basil pesto? This is very puzzling to those among us who find it difficult to read minds, as no wine could possibly cope with three such divergent 'pastas'. And **which** cheeses were they referring to on that back label? No single bottle can please a salty Gorgonzola, an acidic goat's-milk cheese and a creamy Brie all at the same time.

Despite some excellent writing on the subject of matching food and wine, most of us remain unsure of how to go about selecting a wine to accompany a specific dish, or vice versa. Although we may come across often-helpful pairing suggestions, understanding how they were arrived at appears to be the prerogative of a privileged few. Why certain choices are made and why there is synergy between a specific dish and its accompanying wine remains hidden in shadow.

For the wine aficionado, this can be particularly puzzling. He or she attends wine shows, reads up on all the ratings and delights in buying and cellaring fabulous prize-winning wines. The hitch is that, most often, those highly rated prize-winners were scored alongside other wines of the same style, and seldom, if ever, tasted with food. If the wine-buff later has one of these showpieces with dinner, it may taste quite different from his memory of tasting it on its own. 'Is this the wine I bought?' he may ask, often humorously concluding that 'it didn't travel well...'. What he has discovered, however, is that, sure as dammit, food changes the taste of a wine.

It is one thing to sip a wine while socialising, but quite another to combine that same wine with some food because, undoubtedly, its character and flavour will change. That rich, wooded Chardonnay you fell in love with when you tasted it solo and purchased for a special dinner will have every bit of character knocked out of it by the salad starter with its lemony vinaigrette. You were probably unaware that this was going to happen; if you **were** aware, you would certainly have chosen a different wine or prepared a different dish.

Until now, an easy-to-use guide for those of us who enjoy drinking wine along with our food has been missing from the scene. Book-shelves are weighed down with cook books and wine books, but there is very little that brings the two topics together. We think it is time to demystify the subject of food and wine matching and pare it down to the basics in a format that is not only suited to the chef or winemaker, but also to the restaurant-goer, dinner-party giver, wine club member, wine steward, food and beverage manager, collector of fine wines and, most importantly, the everyday wine drinker.

'How ambitious', you might say. But there are not different food and wine pairing criteria for different people; the celebrated chef and the novice cook use the same guidelines. Food and wine pairing is rather simple; there is nothing high-brow about it. All you have to do is to take a bite of food, followed by a sip of wine and consider whether the combination works or not. It is as basic as that.

There **are**, however, reasons why particular food and wine combinations work or don't work. Where appropriate, we give reasons for the recommendations we make, so that they will make sense to you. But this is not a book of rules; treat it as a guide towards a greater understanding of basic principles of food and wine pairing.

How to use this guide

Whether you want to make a study of food and wine pairing, or just casually glance at what wine to enjoy with your pizza tonight, this guide should meet your requirements. For ease of use, it is compiled in two parts. The first part deals, among other things, with the theory behind this food and wine pairing 'thing'. It challenges old dictums such as only serving 'white wine with white meat and fish' and 'red wine with red meat', and addresses the orthodoxies of serving a white wine before a red wine or a dry wine before a sweeter one. But this may be more detail than you wish to run with.

If so, turn to Part II, **Matching Food and Wine** (see page 119), where we get down to business. In this section, dishes are listed in alphabetical order in chapters that cover everything from Starters, Fish and Seafood, Pasta and Vegetable dishes to Meat, Desserts, and Cheese, as well Indian, Japanese, Chinese and Thai cuisines. Once you are in the relevant chapter, you can look up the name of the dish you intend to serve to see what wine will partner best with it.

To ensure that we are all singing off the same song-sheet, a short description is given of each dish so that you know exactly what tastes and flavours we have based our wine recommendations on. Chefs and recipe writers love to give classic recipes a twist that can change the flavour profile of the finished dish, and these variations might lead you to choose a different wine.

For example, you may order the line fish of the day, say, grilled kabeljou, only to discover that this menu-staple arrives at the table accompanied by a ginger parsnip purée, mangetout in apricot-and-sparkling-wine foam, lemon mascarpone, caper-stuffed raspberries and vanilla caramel. Surprises such as these 'garnishes', each with its own foot-stamping personality, may influence your wine selection far more than the now-swamped central ingredient, the kabeljou. While we can give you a wine suggestion to match the basic fish, we could never anticipate every costume change in its cross-dressing line-up, or presume that you will only stick with 'classic' dishes. This is where experimentation kicks in.

If, in the food pairing suggestions, you come across wines you have never heard of before, turn to the chapter on matching wine and food (see page 54), where you will find a brief discussion of each grape variety produced in South Africa, along with the tasting descriptors usually associated with its wine, and notes on what to serve with it. This is also the chapter to consult when you want to start with a wine and select a dish to show it off to its best advantage; to 'cook for the bottle', if you like. If you come across a wine term that is unfamiliar to you, refer to the brief glossary of wine and cheese terms on page 306.

Few pleasures in life are as universal as eating and drinking. Worldwide, national cuisines may differ and favourite drinks may vary, but how they work together has a common thread in terms of finding ideal matches between food and beverage. For instance, the committed beer drinker may find that his favourite tipple goes better with foods having a hint of sweetness than with savoury dishes, but beer has grave limitations when paired with many other foods. In general, beer is fairly monotone in flavour and is incapable of rising to meet food even halfway. Whisky can be a good accompaniment to some foods, but its 'heaviness' limits it to dishes that are equally heavy. 'Brandy 'n Coke' is quite happy with sweetish coffee and chocolate creations, while brandy on its own fares better with creamy vanilla-flavoured desserts. However, despite these, and other, options, we mostly reach for a glass of wine when eating. When it comes to food, wine is undoubtedly the anointed choice. So go for it.

Use this guide to get you started, and then experiment further. Soon pairing foods and wines will become intuitive and you will not have the least difficulty in choosing a wine that will happily match our ever-evolving and, often daring, modern eating trends.

Bon appétit, and cheers!
Katinka van Niekerk and **Brian Burke**

The matter of preference

We all have preferences. Some of us love rock, while others listen to classical music. Some enjoy game-watching in the Kruger Park, while others go surfing at Jeffrey's Bay. Some eat meat, others don't touch it, and some of us like red wine, while others stick resolutely to white. There is nothing wrong with any of this; after all, preferences and likes and dislikes add a bit of spice to life.

But this book is not about **preferences**. It is about **pairing** food and wine, about selecting a specific wine to match a particular dish to the best advantage of both. It is for those who love food and want to enjoy it with a wine that will do it justice. It is also for the wine drinker who, while having a meal, wants to savour everything a bottle of wine has to offer. For it is one thing to enjoy a glass of wine while you're pottering around at home or socializing with friends, and quite another when you're having food with it.

When it comes to food and wine pairing, it is of no consequence what wine you prefer to drink on its own. This book is not about recommending specific wines or wine styles, because that is a personal choice. **We intend to show you how to choose the best wine for whatever food you are going to eat with it because, when you make a happy match, both the food and the wine will benefit**.

Picture the scene: you are quaffing your preferred wine while preparing a barbecue sauce, making a salad and grilling the steak. But when you get down to eating that steak with its sweetish sauce, the wine that was so moreish a few minutes ago seems to have turned to diluted vinegar. We bet you were drinking Sauvignon Blanc... (and that, most probably, you are a white wine devotee, which is why you were drinking the Sauv in the first place).

Examples of other nasty wine and food combinations that might be in store for you are a vinaigrette-dressed salad with Chardonnay, rare roast beef with a special late harvest (or any semi-sweet white, for that matter), and chocolate mouse with a dry Chenin Blanc. Or perhaps you're a red-wine-only drinker who has encountered more than your fair share of unhappy combinations, such as smoked mackerel with Cabernet Sauvignon, prawn curry with Shiraz, and fresh fruit salad with Merlot.

If you have had these, or any other 'unconventional' food and wine combinations and thought nothing of them, you certainly are not 'wrong', for there is no such thing as 'right' or 'wrong' when it comes to food and wine pairing. But, as in all relationships, there are certain combinations that are happy together and complement each other, and those that are very unhappy and at great odds with their partner in the glass or on the plate.

If some people find the combination of chocolate mousse and Chenin Blanc, or prawn curry with Shiraz horrendous, but it works for you, that's fine. And if you have not noticed a clash between your rare roast beef and a semi-sweet wine, or you fancy a glass of lightly chilled Merlot alongside a tropical fruit salad, who are we to argue? However, the one time when this won't be fine is if you decide to serve an 'unhappy' food and wine combination to people who may not share your preferences.

On the plus side, there is no doubt that certain food and wine combinations have stood the test of time because they are, to use a well-worn cliché, marriages made in heaven. So, regardless of whether you tend towards the traditional Old World wine-producing and wine-drinking countries with their centuries-old cuisine and practice of pairing regional foods with local wines, or whether you prefer to follow the boisterous and brave New World, free of any restrictive 'traditions' to guide your food and wine adventures, we can probably all agree that some food and wine combinations are incontestable. Some of these classic pairings are:

- Crayfish (rock lobster) with Chardonnay
- Classic fish pie with Semillon
- Goat's-milk cheese (Chevin) with Sauvignon Blanc
- Olives with pale dry (fino) sherry
- Peppered steak with Shiraz
- Roasted lamb with Cabernet Sauvignon
- Roquefort cheese with noble late harvest
- Stilton cheese with tawny port
- Venison with Mourvèdre
- Oysters with dry sparkling wine.

But why do these particular food and wine combinations work so well? To understand the magic (and a little of the science), read on.

Style note: Throughout this book, we have used an initial capital letter to denote wine varietals (e.g. Cabernet Sauvignon) and lower case letters for wine styles (e.g. special late harvest).

From the past to the present

We are not born with a natural 'wine palate', but learning to enjoy and evaluate wine is a skill that we can all acquire. However, there are degrees of evaluation, and not all of us seek the same outcome. For some, a quick slurp is all that is needed to determine that a wine is fine to drink; for others, the swirling, sniffing with a quick intake of breath, holding the glass up to the light to study the wine's colour or examine its 'legs', then tasting it while rolling it around in the mouth, before spitting into the nearest receptacle, is an essential precursor to enjoying a glass of wine. And who is to say who is right or wrong?

In the food world, the concept of sensory evaluation is pretty much unique to wine. Few other food products elicit such a degree of ritual although, perhaps, a traditional Japanese tea ceremony comes close... Whisky, olive oil, beer and chocolate are just a few food products that we have begun to evaluate in recent times, but all of them have taken their cue from the wine geeks who have honed their rituals down to a fine art. If you move in these circles, you'll be familiar with the whole tasting rigmarole; perhaps you've even done it yourself, without pondering the notion that no other consumer product demands such consistently bizarre behaviour as wine.

Sure, we all love the aroma of just-baked bread, but do you give every loaf you cut a good sniff? Do you swirl your glass of orange juice at breakfast, or reflect on the colour of the fruit in the flan at tea time? When you first take a bite of grilled chicken do you bounce it around in your mouth to determine what the depth of its flavour is, before spitting it into the bin? Anyone not familiar with wine tasting procedures would think you'd gone quite mad.

So, let's set aside all the rituals and affectations surrounding wine and remember that, at heart, it is there to be drunk and enjoyed. It is sad that many people are intimidated by wine and avoid drinking or ordering it for fear they might get it 'wrong'. As we've already said, there is no 'right' or 'wrong' when it comes to choosing a wine to drink on its own, but there are better and worse combinations of wine and food. This book will help you to learn what tastes good when consumed together and what is best kept well apart.

Old rules of colour coding

You probably grew up with a rule-of-thumb that dictated: 'serve white wine with fish or white meat; red wine with red meat'. And, while it might be rather charming to have red wine to go with the red meat that matches the red candles and red roses on the table, these days, that's about as far as the value of this advice goes. Over time, we have come to realize that, when it comes to food and wine pairing, colour has nothing to do with it.

So where did this 'colour rule' come from? Prior to the late 1950s, when South Africans spoke of classic food and wine combinations, we meant the cuisines and wines of Europe. At that stage, we had no real food or wine culture of our own, but we were not alone; while we drank beer or brandy with our braaivleis, Americans quaffed 'Bud' or bourbon around the barbecue, and the Brits downed 'flat' ale or gin-and-tonics with their pies and gravy.

In those days, to the 'civilised' world, *haute cuisine* meant France, and remnants of those classic rules still pop up regularly, such as the advice to 'serve red wine at room temperature'. Oh yes, and where might that room be? The average summer temperature in a *pension* in Paris might be 18°C, ideal for a decent bottle of *rouge,* but in Paarl, Pretoria or Pietermaritzburg it is likely to hover around 28°C, at which point your fine red wine will certainly lose its lustre. Let's throw out the rule books! Once upon a time, we blindly followed the herd, but now we need to adopt what works for us.

So, how do you teach an entire country to drink wine? You launch an easy-drinking semi-sweet wine, that's how. South Africa did it in 1959 with *Lieberstein*, a white wine that came in a gallon flagon with a handy carrying 'ear' which meant we could pour it from over our shoulders. Although we were not natural-born wine drinkers, we thought we were quite cool and took to it with great enthusiasm. *Lieberstein* sales rocketed, from 30,000 litres a year in 1960 to an astounding 31 million litres by 1964, thereby claiming an entry in the Guinness Book of Records.

This simple, semi-sweet Chenin Blanc certainly taught us to drink wine and suddenly, there was wine all over. You could have it with soda at breakfast, well chilled at lunchtime and party with it all night long. But, as a committed braai nation, we must have struggled desperately to drink 'stein' with the *wors en tjops*. Although *Lieberstein* has long-since disappeared from the local scene, it left behind a certain stigma to opening a bottle of semi-sweet wine, and that's a pity, because semi-sweet whites certainly have their place at the table.

This backlash against semi-sweet has an echo in today's 'ABC club' – which stands for 'anything but Chardonnay' (or Cabernet) – and where, all of a sudden, a once-popular wine becomes unfashionable and a new 'flavour of the month' takes over. But we maintain that much of this fickle behaviour comes from repeatedly pairing a wine with food with which it is greatly unhappy.

Despite its flaws, the 'white with white, red with red' rule of thumb was a good starting point in our learning process at a time when there were very few local wines to choose from but, as the range of available wines grew, this rule got altered.

The evolution and expansion of quality wine in South Africa has been phenomenal in the last 50 years or so. Here, as elsewhere, winemaking technology has progressed exponentially, bringing great changes wherever wine is made. One positive result is that, today, very little wine is really badly made, and buying inexpensive wine is no longer a risk. However, another change, and one that is relevant to the food and wine pairer, is that the taste of wine has altered. Across the price spectrum, modern wines taste fruitier and riper than their counterparts of old. This does not only hold true for South Africa and other New World producers (see page 308), but also for the traditional European producers, including France.

Nowadays, white wines taste fresher and crisper, even when they undergo some bottle maturation. Red wines, whether they are young or matured, taste softer and rounder and are less tannic. In the past, some red wines were undrinkable unless they were at least five years old. Now, many reds are made with lower tannins so that they can be enjoyed earlier. For the most part, home cellaring has disappeared. We live in a world where we can pop into the supermarket on our way home to buy ingredients for tonight's supper and, at the same time, grab a bottle of wine to go with it.

The introduction of large stainless steel fermentation tanks has also resulted in changes to the taste of wine. As the tanks can be temperature-controlled, they allow the winemaker to ferment the grapes at lower temperatures, thereby eliminating those cooked, 'jammy' flavours that can come from fermentation at high temperatures. For local winemaking, it meant that the era of rough, clumsy *dikvoet* wines was behind us.

New World winemakers also started to use oak barrels differently from their counterparts in France and elsewhere. It didn't take them long to discover that flavoursome new oak imparts very seductive overtones to wines, both white and red. In some older European winemaking traditions, oak barrels were used as handy vessels for fermentation and storage rather than as a part of the winemaking process itself. In the New World, however, the flavours of coconut, vanilla, spice, toast and smoke that oak barrels imparted charmed the winemakers so much that, in the 1980s, they started to use oak barrels extensively; in some cases, to an excessive level, so that when you smelled the wine you thought you were in a lumberyard. Thankfully, these incidences are on the wane.

Locally, cuisine has undergone a revolution since the 1970s. In the last few decades, Mediterranean, Indian, Mexican, Japanese, Thai and other cuisines have arrived at the southern tip of Africa, where they have merged and mingled with everyday local fare such as chicken pie, bobotie, macaroni cheese and fish cakes, and with each other. Nowadays, we sprinkle Asian spices over Mediterranean-style roasted vegetables, and accompany our traditional meat cuts with Oriental dipping sauces.

By the late 1990s, a new trend had emerged for mixing different national food styles within the same menu, even within the same dish. No wonder those age-old food and wine recommendations based on colour needed updating; they fall very short when it comes to contemporary eating.

So, in the true South African fashion, we not only updated our thinking on food and wine pairing, we also threw out the old rules and decided, in the spirit of 'anything goes', to drink whatever wine we fancied with whatever food we were eating. This fitted our pioneering spirit and showed our disdain for traditions and rules.

But the problem with this unbridled freedom in pairing wine with food is that it can be a hit or miss affair. You can stumble upon combinations that are simply awful or, if you happen upon a good match, you probably won't know why it works. This *laissez-faire* approach serves neither the chef nor the wine drinker. Unless you have an unlimited budget and can afford to experiment, failing to get the best out of your food and wine seems a bit foolish, as these commodities are not inexpensive.

But we can go too far with food and wine pairing. Many pairers make it more complicated than it needs to be, even taking it to a point of manic precision. In the introduction to their book *The Right Wine with the Right Food*[1], Jeffrey Benson and Stuart Walton tell a delightful story of meeting an eminent eye surgeon at a smart dinner party:

> As though the world of opthalmology were not demanding enough, this gentleman had managed to find time to pursue a side line in gastronomic studies with singular fervour. He was of confirmed opinions as to which wine made the perfect fit with practically any classic dish, but one match had for many years continued to elude him. What was the best wine to drink with spaghetti Bolognese?

---

1. Author's note: As we believe that there are no 'rights' and 'wrongs' when it comes to food and wine pairing, only happy or unhappy partnerships, we find the title of this otherwise well-researched book a bit misleading.

Although it may not seem like the most difficult of dishes to please, nothing quite met with the doctor's unqualified approval. Oh, there were wines that just about worked, if you were prepared not to think about it too closely, but then he did think about it closely. The problem all but kept him awake at nights until, one day, in the kind of sweet serendipity with which the history of scientific investigation is strewn, revelation happily dawned. There was only one wine, ultimately, just as he knew there would be, that properly went with spaghetti Bolognese. And it wasn't an Italian grape, as one might have expected, given the provenance of the dish. No, it was Château Lafite [a top-notch, exorbitantly expensive Bordeaux blend], and not any old Lafite either, but specifically the 1953 vintage.

And the good doctor, apparently, was not pulling anybody's leg. He was deadly earnest in his belief that only the 1953 Lafite (not the 1952 or 1954) could match this humble dish. The point, of course, is that you can overdo it. No wonder an eminent chef at a restaurant on the Stellenbosch wine route was quoted in a 2008 *Wine* magazine article as saying something to the effect that food and wine pairing takes all the pleasure from eating and drinking wine.

We agree. If you have to 'think about it too closely', it is simply not worth it. In the next chapter, 'How to pair food and wine', we provide you with a straightforward framework, a guideline, if you like, to help you make these decisions so that you don't have to 'think about it too closely'. Working within this framework, and after one or two practice runs, you will soon find that pairing food and wine becomes as intuitive and natural as driving a car.

How to pair food and wine

The primary aim of this chapter is to provide a structure, or foundation, for how we go about pairing food and wine without having to think too deeply about it. There are just three things to consider when you are selecting a wine to accompany a dish: **weight**, **flavour intensity**, and the role of the **five primary taste sensations**. But we don't call them 'rules', because we believe that the moment you come across a food and wine pairing rule, you should do your best to break it. Instead, we prefer to call them 'tips', and each of them is discussed in more detail below.

WEIGHT

The weight of a dish is the most important thing to take into account. But what do we mean by 'weight' in this context? Consider the difference between a piece of grilled hake and a grilled sirloin steak – the fish is 'light', while the steak is 'heavy'.

Similarly, wines can be light or heavy. A dry Chenin Blanc and a wooded Chardonnay have very different 'weights'. In general, light-bodied wines tend to be lightly fruity, with low alcohol levels (in South Africa, 10–12% by volume), while heavy- or full-bodied wines will be deeply fruity, with ample alcohol (>13%).

You should always aim to balance the weight of the food with the weight of the wine, so that neither overwhelms the other. For rich, hearty food, select robust wines (for example, a full-bodied Shiraz with an oxtail casserole); for medium, not-too-rich food, a medium-bodied wine is best (a young, fruity Merlot with roast chicken); and for light food, choose a light-bodied wine (such as a delicate Sauvignon Blanc to accompany grilled kingklip).

To come back to the 'colour coding' discussed previously (see pages 13–15), let's look at another example of matching weight with weight. Meat-lovers often choose a creamy pepper or mushroom sauce to top the grilled steak of their choice. Together, this makes for a heavy dish that needs to be paired with an equally heavy wine. In fact, the creaminess of the sauce begs for an equally creamy wine, which immediately points us towards a white. A buttery, velvety, oaked Chardonnay or Semillon would provide both the weight that the steak needs and the creamy texture that the sauce demands. Forget the colour of the meat; you are no longer eating just red meat – you are also eating sauce, and it is the sauce that throws its weight around now and which must be matched.

FLAVOUR INTENSITY

By flavour intensity we mean the degree of flavour that a dish has. For example, when it comes to fish, a plain sole has less flavour than a plain piece of mackerel. Similarly, different flavour intensities are also apparent if we compare a pan-fried fillet steak with an aromatic roast leg of lamb. White meat, such as chicken breast, pork fillet or veal schnitzel, has a very different flavour profile to red meat, and the added ingredients used in the preparation of white meats have a much bigger role to play than those used for more robustly flavoured meats. Similarly, vegetables, pulses and grains can be grouped into different flavour categories.

Wines also vary in flavour intensity. Consider the flavour profiles of an unwooded Chenin Blanc, a Weisser Riesling or a Gewürztraminer. The latter two are produced from highly aromatic grape varieties that are much more assertive in flavour than Chenin. Likewise, among the reds, a lighter-bodied Cinsaut will not have the flavour intensity of a Shiraz, for instance.

You should always try to match the flavour intensity of your food to the flavour intensity of your wine. For example, ethnic dishes, such as those from Mexico, North Africa, India, Thailand and Japan, are highly aromatic, and are best when paired with equally aromatic wines. Conversely, you should match food that is not very aromatic with wines that have a similar profile.

THE FIVE PRIMARY TASTE SENSATIONS

Wines and foods share some basic tastes. Physically, we have taste buds that give us the intrinsic ability to 'register' five primary taste sensations in the mouth: **sweetness**, **acidity**, **saltiness**, **bitterness** and **umami** (or 'savoury'). Each of these five tastes is present to some degree, and in various combinations and permutations, in all foods. For example, roasted shoulder of pork stuffed with prunes is both salty and sweet.

Wine is also a combination of primary tastes, usually three: sweetness, acidity (sourness) and, in the case of red wine, umami. These combinations define a wine's profile and determine with what food it is best served. An educated guess, then, would be that a stuffed pork shoulder will meet its match in a wine that is both sweet and acidic. But let's take a closer look at how the five taste sensations can distort or influence the taste of wine.

Sweetness Sweet foods need to be matched by wines that are at least as sweet, if not sweeter, than the dish. If the wine is not as sweet as the food, it will taste sour, a little bitter, and will appear sharper, less fruity and less sweet (that is, drier than it really is). In a nutshell, dry wines are nasty with sweet foods. Anyone who has attended a wedding where a dry (brut) champagne or sparkling wine was served along with the wedding cake (whether a traditional iced fruit cake or the more modish profiterole-pyramid swirled with spun sugar), will be familiar with just how nasty a wine can become. That expensive champagne, for which Papa has mortgaged his house, turns into a lemony, effervescent antacid remedy. Even the sweetest bubbly will not be sweet enough for the wedding cake, and Papa would have been better advised to save the bubbly for the toasts and serve a sweet, still wine with the cake.

Generally though, matching wines with sweet desserts is a very good start. Simply pitch the level of sweetness of the wine to that of the dessert. The richest chocolate and toffee creations, fruitcakes and ice-cream are all well-matched by the sweetest of wines, such as muscadels and fortified wines. Less-sweet desserts, like crème caramel and cream- or fruit-based desserts, pair well with special or noble late harvest wines.

When it comes to savoury food that has a touch of sweetness, the match is not so obvious. Rich duck and pork dishes, typically served with sweet fruit-based sauces, or other dishes where fresh or dried fruits are an integral part, are best matched with off-dry to medium-sweet wines, depending on just how sweet the dish actually is.

However, there is a second route when trying to match wine with savoury food that has a touch of sweetness: red wines with 'sweet' fruit flavours. These give the perception that they are sweet when, in reality, they are not. However, not all red wines have this profile. Choose a full-bodied Shiraz, Grenache (or a blend of the two), Tempranillo or Pinotage that has been produced from very ripe grapes.

Acidity Acidity in food needs to be matched by a wine that is equally acidic. If a wine is less acidic than the dish it is accompanying, it 'thins out' and can taste flat and dull. You will be hard pressed to find a wine that is too acidic for most tart dishes. You may often have found a still wine or a dry sparkling wine that is mouth-puckeringly acidic when drunk on its own but, put it with a tart dish, and it begins to boogie. Foods that are high in acidity decrease the perception of sourness in a wine, making it taste richer and mellower. A word of caution though; if the wine has a touch of sweetness alongside its acidity, such as an off-dry Weisser Riesling, the wine and food will appear to taste sweeter than you might have wished for.

Something the home cook often overlooks is that the acidity of certain ingredients can raise the sharpness of the finished dish.

Here, tomatoes share the top spot on the list with capers in vinegar, but less-obviously acidic ingredients include leeks and spinach.

So how acidic must food be to warrant an acidic wine? Consider this example: a butternut soup that includes orange juice and zest will have perceptible acidity and it will need a wine with a similar degree of acidity, whereas a vegetable soup with just a teaspoon of vinegar added to give it a lift will not be perceptibly acidic, nor would it insist on an acidic wine.

While it may be quite straightforward to determine how acidic a dish is, it is less so for wines. Wine labels are often no help either. The most you can expect are cue words on the back label, such as 'crisp' or 'zesty', and hope that the producer is right. Generally though, white wines have higher acidity levels than reds.

The white varieties with natural acidity are Sauvignon Blanc, Chenin Blanc, riesling (Cape, Paarl or South African, aka Crouchen Blanc), Weisser Riesling, Pinot Blanc and Pinot Gris/Pinot Grigio. If the grapes were grown in a cool climate, such as Cape Point, Constantia, Durbanville, the Helderberg, parts of Stellenbosch, the Overberg, and pockets on the West Coast, you can expect the wines' acidity level to be higher than those made with grapes from a warmer climate.

Acidic food points us towards young wines, as acidic wines will often soften with bottle maturation or oak (barrel) maturation. If you want wood, seek out very lightly oaked white wines that had acidity to start with, such as a wooded Sauvignon Blanc (blanc fumé) or Chenin Blanc. Steer clear of warm-climate Chardonnay, or one that is heavy-bodied, rich, ripe, buttery and oaky; the same applies to Semillon and Viognier.

Red wines, generally, lack acidity. Those that do have acidity are young, light-bodied reds from cool climates and, crucially, they have low tannins. Acidic food and tannins clash with the intensity of cymbals clattering onto a tiled floor – something to be avoided whenever possible. Look to Cabernet Franc, Gamay or a light-bodied, cool climate Pinotage, Italian varieties Sangiovese and Barbera, and that old standby, Pinot Noir, which always comes to the rescue when we're in a spot of bother with making the right choice.

Even when they are young and fresh, blanc de noir and rosé are often too soft for very acidic food, although they can show a bit of spunk if they have been produced from Pinotage.

An unexpected bonus of an acidic wine is that it can bring out the flavours of a gentle, subtle dish, just as a squeeze of lemon does on a piece of pan-fried hake.

Saltiness Saltiness in food has a significant impact on wine. Overly salty foods can make a wine seem more alcoholic ('hotter' in wine-speak) than it is. What we want is for the wine to harmonize with the food, not come at it like a shot of *witblits*. Salty food is also greatly unhappy with tannic wines. Just as salt enhances the flavour of food, it emphasizes the tannins in red wine, often to an unpleasant level.

The good news, though, is that salty food does have an affinity with certain wines. Salt has an ongoing love affair with wines that have some sweetness. We already eat that way: think Parma ham with melon or ripe figs, roast pork with apple sauce, and so on. The saltier the dish, the sweeter the wine can be. It's no wonder that South Africa is famous for its *soetes*; we had to have something to go with all that biltong! Similarly, when it comes to salty blue-veined cheese, we intuitively reach for a port. This love affair extends to wines that have very little residual sugar, but seem to be 'sweet', as they have spicy-sweet flavours and aromas, like a dry Gewürztraminer, with its rose-petal and litchi aromas. However, bear in mind that salty foods can make sweetish wines taste even sweeter.

Saltiness has a second affinity, and that is with acidity. Wines with good acidity, such as Sauvignon Blanc or dry sparkling wine, lessen the perceived saltiness of a dish. In general, white wines are inherently sharper than red wines, and therefore pair better with salty dishes than red wines do. One obvious example is our instinctive choice of a dry white wine or brut sparkling wine with pre-dinner savouries. Another is pale dry (fino) sherry, which seems to mirror salty flavours, pairing well with the intense saltiness of olives and their tapenades, which are often further salted by the addition of an anchovy fillet.

Because of salty food's affinity with both sweetness and acidity, it is not surprising that if you treat it to a wine that has both, such as a semi-sweet Chenin Blanc or an off-dry Weisser Riesling, the food wil be in clover.

However, red wines are not off the list for partnering with salty food, but they must have a certain profile. They need to be generously fruity and low in tannins, or their tannins need to be ripe, soft and rounded, like those found in reds from warm growing areas. Ruby Cabernet from the Breede River Valley would fit the bill, while reds with natural acidity, like Pinot Noir, are also ideal candidates.

Bitterness Bitter foods accentuate any bitter elements in a wine. Examples of food with varying degrees of bitterness are curly leaf endive, chicory (also known as Belgian endive or witloof), radicchio, rocket leaves, asparagus, sautéed broccoli, olives, Seville orange and lime marmalades, grapefruit and dark chocolate. A bitter note is added to a dish by adding ingredients such as citrus peel and some bitter herbs and spices. Bitterness is also inadvertently added to many foods during cooking, especially at high temperatures. Chargrilled, oven-grilled or blackened foods develop a perceivable bitter edge. In order to avoid the accentuation of any bitterness in wine by bitterness in the food, we call in the help of acidity, either in the food or in the wine, or better still, in both.

Why is asparagus often dressed in lemon butter? Why do artichokes always land in a hollandaise sauce? We maintain that it is to save the wine, but you may find the odd chef or two who disagrees. Either way, the acidity masks the tannin in the wine, just as it masks the bitterness of the food. Therefore, if you are having bitter salad leaves, or a dish containing bitter vegetables, go wild with the vinaigrette on the salad or sprinkle your vegetables liberally with lemon juice, then pour yourself a glass of wine with good acidity.

Bitterness in wine comes from tannins which, in turn, come from grape skins (fruit tannins) or from the oak barrels (wood tannins) in which the wine is matured. An example of tannin is Ceylon tea that has been boiled on the leaves, becoming astringent, bitter, furry and gritty. Wine tannins share these unpleasant attributes, yet a red wine without them lacks structure, firmness and complexity. New winemaking techniques enable winemakers to 'manage' tannins so as to make them accessible sooner, but tannins are as necessary in reds, to enable the wine to age, as acidity is for bottle-maturing a white wine. By nature, certain reds, such as Cabernet Sauvignon, Shiraz and Nebbiolo, are more tannic than others, while Gamay and Sangiovese are lower in tannins.

No food holds out a begging bowl for tannins, and they can spell trouble. A tannic red wine is unpleasant with fish, especially oily fish, and very bitter with salt, but with eggs it becomes downright nasty. Certain cheeses, such as Gouda or goat's-milk cheese, turn a tannic red into heavy metal, and it's not music we're talking about!

However, if tannin has one friend, it is meat. Rare steak, and other red meats with discernable texture, are its biggest ally. Those harsh tannins are literally tamed and counterbalanced by the protein in red meat. Many red wines, but especially Cabernet Sauvignon, can taste a bit dry and hard on their own but, when they are paired with red meat, they become bright-eyed and bushy tailed. There is simply nothing quite like the combination of a charcoal-grilled steak along with a full-bodied, tannic Shiraz.

Two final thoughts on tannins. If you are faced with a very tannic wine and there's no red meat in sight, reach for the salt cellar.

You will find that a sprinkling of salt on food will suppress the bitter taste of the wine. But, if you are serving a gammon with its inherent saltiness, accompanied by a sweet-and-bitter-orange sauce (sauce bigarade), then play to the sweetness, bitterness and saltiness in one go by pairing the dish with an off-dry Weisser Riesling or fruit-cored Gewürztraminer.

Umami This a Japanese word formed from 'umai' meaning 'delicious' and 'mi' meaning 'essence'. It is the term for the fifth taste sensation that describes deliciousness, savouriness, meatiness, relishlike or just plain *lekker*. In Japanese, 'umami' is pronounced 'oo-MOM-ee', but in our English-speaking, rugby-and-cricket-playing country, we pronounce it as we write it, 'OO-maa-mi'.

The term 'umami' has been around since 1907, when a Japanese scientist, Mr Ikeda, discovered the taste. He did not believe that the savoury nature of a traditional Japanese seaweed broth could be formed by the four accepted tastes: sweet, sour, salty and bitter. Being a scientist, he then successfully isolated a fifth taste 'sensation', but he was by no means the first. There was a reference to the savoury nature of certain foods in a science book published in Paris almost a hundred years earlier and it seems that the Chinese have been talking about it for 1200 years. Mr Ikeda also discovered that the ingredient in seaweed that makes the broth so savoury and delicious was glutamic acid, or glutamate, and he started to ponder whether he could reproduce this taste. One thing led to another and soon he was able to formulate a flavour enhancer which we now know as monosodium glutamate (MSG).

At the mere mention of MSG, alarm bells start going off as, apparently, in concentrated form, it is bad for your health. But glutamate does not only appear in MSG, Worcestershire sauce, soy sauce, oyster sauce, Marmite, Bovril or Aromat; it also appears naturally in many foods, from beef and lamb to ham and seafood (abalone, crab, scallop, shrimp and lobster), tomatoes (and in most tomato products from ketchup and marinara sauce to tomato-based pizza and pasta), asparagus, and cheeses such as Parmesan and Roquefort. Oily fish (sardines, mackerel and tuna canned in oil) seem to have more of an umami taste than lighter fish. The 'sweet' taste associated with many shellfish is actually the umami taste. Shiitake mushrooms also have umami, especially when they are dried.

Indeed, when foods are dried or when they ripen, their umami levels rise. For example, a ripe tomato has ten times the glutamate of an unripe one. The same happens when food undergoes other transformations, such as curing, ageing and fermenting. That is why cured leg of pork (gammon) is much more moreish than when it is just plainly roasted. Biltong is another example of a meat that is much tastier when dried than if the same cut were roasted.

How often don't we jazz up a 'mac 'n cheese' by adding grated Parmesan, a mushroom or six, or some truffle oil, and serve it topped with sliced tomato or a good dash of tomato sauce? No doubt, we need to pump up this rather bland dish with umami's razzmatazz.

Likewise, a basic chicken stew can be rather unexciting unless you add some tomatoes, mushrooms and a dash of wine; layering it with these umami-rich ingredients turns an ordinary dish into a savoury and robust creation.

Because wine is produced by fermenting grapes, it has a natural umami component. So does beer and cider. Unsurprisingly, the level of umami is higher in huge, rich, deeply fruity red wines, such as blockbuster Shiraz and Pinotage, and big, fat, creamy Chardonnays with extended lees contact. Wines that have been made from very ripe grapes, as these examples are, simply have more of everything in them, including umami.

Of all the taste sensations, umami not only sounds the most intriguing, it is also the most seductive. But, for all its sexiness, it does have a downside: umami hates tannin, and can make a huge, full-bodied tannic wine taste bitter and metallic.

Furthermore, umami in any food will increase the perception of bitterness in the accompanying wine. A little bit of acidity and salt in the food helps somewhat, but avoid that blockbuster red wine as a partner. Imagine what might happen if you have a double dose of glutamate coming at you from both the food and the wine. If you've ever had this experience, you may recall the sensation of the enamel being stripped right off your teeth.

Well then, which wines would be the least harassed by umami-rich food? Of course we would choose one low in tannins, but the real clue is in that drop of acidity which we alluded to. A wine with good acidity is just what we need, and we have learned this from the Italians. Alongside pizzas laden with glutamate-rich toppings (think tomatoes and mushrooms), they drink Chianti, a wine produced from Sangiovese, a grape that is low in tannin and has good acidity. The oft-given advice that we should drink 'red wine with pizza' somehow got mangled in translation. It didn't mean **any** red wine, it specifically meant a wine like Pinot Noir, Barbera, a quaffable Pinotage or Cinsaut, or the aforementioned Sangiovese.

SECONDARY CONSIDERATIONS

The three primary considerations discussed above (weight, flavour intensity and the primary taste sensations) form the backbone of a framework to use as a guide to food and wine pairing, but there are a few other considerations to take into account when selecting a wine to accompany a dish.

Sauces In principle, we match our wine to the main ingredient of a dish, such as the beef in a stew, not the onion, celery or carrot added for flavour. Similarly, we select a wine to match the roast beef, not the accompanying Yorkshire pudding, roast potatoes or vegetables. However, once you add a sauce or condiment, the picture can change. As some additions can run the show when it comes to wine selections, we deal with sauces at length later on (see pages 32–43).

Cooking methods Marinating the main ingredient of a dish may change its taste, but the cooking method will also play a part. **Steaming**, **poaching** and **boiling** impart very little flavour and do not have a big impact on the taste of the finished dish. **Stir-frying** is another gentle cooking process that imparts minimal flavour, allowing the ingredients to speak for themselves. Going up the intensity scale, **sautéeing** is also fairly neutral but can add a mild sweetness, especially if there are vegetables present. **Frying** and **grilling** may add a slight bitterness and an outer crust, which **char-grilling** amplifies. **Smoking** adds a whole new flavour dimension, giving not only an obvious smoky taste, but also sweetness.

In this guide, we have covered the effect of cooking methods, if they are pertinent to the choice of wine, in the alphabetical listings of the dishes. For example, the effect of roasting a cut of beef is dealt with under 'Roast beef' in the chapter dealing with beef dishes.

Pepper Lock up the pepper mill before you dust off the cobwebs from that prized, well-matured, complex vinous treasure you've been saving for a special dinner. Although black pepper does not have salt's ability to harass a wine, it will mask some of a fine wine's subtleties. However, if you are pouring a glass of something quaffable from a box, by all means grab the pepper mill and *laat waai*! A grinding of black pepper over your food will bring out the best in a simple wine; it literally gives the wine more body and flavour.

The echo factor Many producers use their back labels to describe their wine as 'minty', 'citrusy', 'spicy', 'floral', 'buttery' and so on, and recommend that you pair this particular wine with dishes with the

same food flavours. Er, no. Using the 'echo factor' as your sole consideration for pairing wine with food does not ensure a good match.

Rather follow the 'tips' given in this chapter for weight, flavour
intensity and the effect of the five taste sensations on wine.

A sixth taste sensation? Prevailing theory allows for five food
tastes, as discussed above: sweet, sour, salty, bitter and umami.
However, scientists have long debated whether there aren't more
than five 'tastes'. The present debate is whether there is a receptor
that resides in our taste buds for sensing fat. If this is found to be
the case, it would probably explain why fat-free foods just don't taste
quite as good as their full-fat counterparts. Until more research has
been done, we treat fat, for the purposes of this guide, as providing
texture to food and not as a sixth taste sensation.

Likeness and contrast

Likeness and **contrast** are two terms used to describe what is known in the food and wine tasting business as **horizontal pairing** and **vertical pairing**.

Traditionally, food and wine combinations are made on the principle that **likeness attracts** and, in food and wine pairings, this is certainly true. In this type of matching, known as a **horizontal pairing**, both the food and the wine are of equal importance. In fact, some of the very best food and wine pairings are based on shared characteristics: when the main elements of the dish and its accompanying wine are on the same plane, they resemble each other, luxuriate in each other and flow into each other so that you don't know where the wine ends and the food begins; each element becoming perfectly acquainted with the other.

Examples of tried-and-tested horizontal pairings include a tannic Cabernet Sauvignon with a rich lamb roast, an off-dry Weisser Riesling with sweet-and-sour pork, or tawny port with a salty Stilton. Just like being in a room full of mirrors, the food sees itself in the wine and the wine sees itself in the food – and both the diner and the wine aficionado are content.

In the early 1980s, a few adventurous souls (at the time, some called them mavericks) started to maintain that horizontal pairing was not the only way to go. They suggested that food and wine should be paired on the basis of **contrast**, not just on likeness, using the rationale that **opposites attract**. Their objective was different and, in this type of matching, called **vertical pairing**, a wine is selected specifically to show off the food, or vice versa, with either the wine or the food being sacrificed in the process.

Vertical pairing is often done by chefs who want to show off a particular culinary creation. For example, they might select a crisp, nervous little Sauvignon Blanc with good acidity to serve with the smooth, creamy sauce they have created. In reality, the sauce would work better with its obvious partner – an equally rich and creamy Chardonnay without any discernable acidity. But the chef knows that the Sauvignon Blanc's natural acidity will present his signature creamy sauce in all its glory, even though the sauce is going to knock out every bit of flavour the wine may have had. Fortunately for the chef, the maker of that particular wine is safely tucked away in his cellar, blissfully unaware that his wine has become a casualty.

This does not mean that the winemaker cannot have his own say in the kitchen, though. He (or she) could just as easily select a dish to show a wine to its best advantage, leaving the food to play second fiddle. A piece of grilled hake, adorned with nothing more than a pat of parsley butter, will spotlight the winemaker's rich, judicially oaked Chardonnay, but the chef will find few opportunities to show off his creativity with such a 'plain' meal.

Today, vertical pairings are common, and no longer confined to the mavericks among us. But bear in mind that although a vertical pairing can produce an ideal balance of flavour, either the food or the wine will have the upper hand. So, if you've cooked up a storm and plan to hold a vertical pairing to show off your culinary skills, don't spend too much money on the wine – although the chances are that you've blown your budget on the food anyway!

Another point to remember is that, in a vertical pairing where the food dominates, you can't expect success with just any old wine. You'll need a wine that is light- to medium-bodied, fruity, and with crisp acidity in order to provide a sharp contrast. And the merest hint of sweetness in the wine will be a bonus, especially if you want to show off a rich, flavourful dish.

In this guide to matching food and wine, you will encounter mainly suggestions for horizontal pairing, as we have the interests of both the chef and the wine drinker at heart.

'No order' is in order

It used to be customary to serve wines in a formal order that went as follows: **White before red, light before heavy, dry before sweet, young before old, and not-so-noble before noble.** Why was this so? Let's look at these traditional serving guidelines one at a time to answer the question.

The reasoning behind the suggestion to serve white wine before red was that white wine was lighter than red wine in body; therefore, if you started with a red wine and followed it with a white, the latter could taste insipid. This may have been appropriate in traditional European wine-producing countries where the white wines were inevitably lighter than the red wines, but today, many New World producers, particularly, make 'blockbuster' whites that would knock many a red for a six.

The idea of serving a light wine before a heavy one, even if they are the same colour (for instance, a Colombard before a wooded Chardonnay), is that after a heavier wine, a light one could taste watery.

'Dry before sweet' was based on the premise that drinking a dry wine after a sweet one would make the dry wine taste astringent. This applied not only to the obvious example of serving a dry wine before a dessert wine, but also to serving a dry Weisser Riesling before an off-dry version, for instance. However, by the time the dishes are cleared and the next course is served, the pH in the mouth will have returned to normal levels, so this is actually not an issue.

'Young before old' comes from the notion that if you drink a young wine after an older one, the tannins of the youngster will seem more pronounced than they really are, as the tannins of the older red would have mellowed. While this may hold true for classic Bordeaux reds, which need at least five years of bottle maturation, New World wines are mostly accessible at the time of bottling. Although they will undoubtedly develop further and become more mellow with a bit of bottle maturation, more often than not they are ready to be enjoyed when they reach the retailers' shelves. The bottle maturation that they undergo during the journey home is more than enough!

Serving a not-so-noble wine before a noble one comes from the assumption that if you consumed a not-so-noble wine after a fine, complex one, the former will probably taste even more simple or one-dimensional. What a pity! Let's rather look at it this way: if, after finishing a not-so-noble bottle, and a slight tipsiness has set in, it would make most of us quite oblivious to the fine qualities of the noble one-in-waiting. Rather drink your noble beauty first so that you can fully appreciate its complexity.

In the past, hosts used to struggle to draw up a menu that would accommodate these rigid principles of the order for serving wines, and the logistics of 'formal' menu planning could be formidable. But those days are over.

Perhaps it was some of the legendary 'good marriages' between certain foods and certain wines that helped to turn the old rules on their head. For example, the combination of dense, smooth liver pâté and rich, opulent sweet wine is quite irresistible, but it introduces 'sweet wine' at the start of the meal. Does this mean we must serve an even sweeter wine with the main course that follows? Similarly, should a fino sherry, whose fresh dryness makes it an ideal appetizer in combination with olives and typical tapas dishes, be followed by a wine of even higher alcohol levels? And is there any reason why we should not end a meal with the delicious combination of crisp Sauvignon Banc and tangy goat's-milk cheese? Even in the days of the classic rules, meals were often finished by serving a light demi-sec sparkling wine alongside fresh fruit or fruit salad.

Thankfully, nowadays we can embrace a whole new way of serving wine with food, choosing the best combination irrespective of the sequence. So, 'no order' is in order.

Palate-scrubbers As a result of our freedom to enjoy wines in any order with a meal, bread has undergone a name change: it is called a 'palate-scrubber'. In the past, bread would be removed from the table after the starter or soup course, but it now often remains until the end of the meal. This allows the diner to clear his or her palate by munching a piece of bread between each course and its complementary wine. This plain, unflavoured palate-scrubber is handy when you switch from the Cabernet Sauvignon you're having with your starter of fish with rosemary butter (Cab Sav is crazy about rosemary), to the Chardonnay you've selected for the main course of chicken breast smothered in a creamy sauce.

If you're not keen to nibble on too much bread, just wait for seven minutes and four seconds between each course and its matching wine (don't forget the four seconds!). This profound tip comes from a sommelier who maintains that this is exactly the length of time it takes for the pH in the mouth to return to normal after the last sip of wine. And who are we to argue? Just have a three-minute conversation with the dining partner on your left and an equal-length chat with the one on your right. This leaves you a whole sixty-four seconds to preen your feathers before starting the next course with *its* wine.

Sauces and their impact on wine choices

Food is seldom served without being moistened with, or enhanced by, cooking juices, sauces, gravies, dressings or relishes. These play an unequivocal role when it comes to matching food and wine and often have the dominant say. There are oceans of sauces out there: basic sauces and compound sauces, cold ones and hot ones, egg-based or eggless, smooth or chunky... Some sauces are made with cream or butter while others are based on stock. They may contain herbs, spices, fruit or any combination of these, and they may be sharp and acidic or sweet and sticky.

In order to choose wines that would match the various sauces, we first analysed their ingredients to determine the overall taste components. This led us to a classification which is based on the core principles of food and wine pairing: the **weight** of the sauce balanced against the the weight of the wine; the **flavour intensity** of the sauce against the flavour intensity of the wine; the **texture** of the sauce versus the texture of the wine; and whether the sauce is **acidic**, **sweet**, **salty**, **bitter** or **savoury**. A chef may see it differently but, in terms of food and wine pairings, this works for us.

To illustrate the point: a creamy cheese sauce (mornay) on a piece of grilled line fish will require a different wine to that same piece of fish served with a tomato-based sauce (Provençale). In the first case you will need a creamy wine, such as a lightly wooded Chardonnay, whereas it will take a Sauvignon Blanc with good acidity to match the acidity of the tomato-based sauce.

To take this a step further, if any proportions of the taste components change, one to the other, your wine choice will also change. For example, if you reduce, by boiling, a cup of white wine to almost nothing and emulsify it by adding butter to make a sauce, the overall taste components will be richness and acidity. For this sauce, called a beurre blanc, you will need an equally rich-textured wine but, crucially, the wine must have the other component, acidity, that became so concentrated in the sauce when the wine was reduced. In this instance, a lightly wooded Chardonnay with good acidity will fit the bill nicely.

On the other hand, if you make a similarly rich sauce by reducing the white wine only slightly and then combining it with cream, you can become less fanatical about whether that Chardonnay has the good acidity it required for the beurre blanc. And if you add a splash of unreduced white wine to a creamy sauce, the result will be only mildly savoury and it then becomes irrelevant whether or not there is good acidity in the Chardonnay. Here the 'match made in heaven' is the result of creaminess meeting creaminess.

Although sauces run the show when it comes to wine and food pairing, you also need to consider what the sauce is served on. To return to the creamy cheese- and tomato-based sauces mentioned above, serve them on a piece of grilled sirloin and the picture changes. Cheese sauce on steak increases the overall **weight** of the dish. You are still looking for an equally creamy wine, but its weight should increase accordingly and you will have to move on from that lightly wooded Chardonnay to one with more powerful fruit and the buttery complexity achieved from oaking. There's no room for frivolity now; your wine requirement has turned more serious.

The same thing happens when a tomato-based sauce is served with steak. You can still get by with the Sauvignon Blanc from our previous example, but now you'll need a plumped-up version with enormous fruit and balancing acidity. Or you could simply increase the weight of your wine by switching to a red. However, the acidity of the sauce still has to be taken into account, so *that* red wine will have to have matching good acidity: in this case, choose a Pinot Noir, Barbera or Sangiovese.

Sauces are either an integral part of the dish, such as in a chicken curry, or an optional add-on, such as a red-wine sauce on a piece of meat. Add-on sauces are often minefields for the food and wine pairer as they can be sharply acidic, fruity sweet, chilli-hot or deadly salty. For example, some popular sauces and condiments, notably vinaigrette, cranberry sauce, harissa paste and soy sauce, need kid-glove handling if they are not to ruin your wine. Other sauces, such as tartare, horseradish and mint, not to mention yoghurt-based sauces, are beyond the pale when it comes to wine, and it is often easiest to just admit defeat. However, despair not – most sauces are simpler to match to wine. When dining out, just keep an eye open for those heavily reduced, intensely flavoured puddles that became so fashionable in the nouvelle cuisine era; they are still around, albeit under a new name, normally something-or-other *jus*.

We live in intriguing 'food' times. You may innocently have ordered what you assumed would be a run-of-the-mill roasted pork belly, only to be served a jaw-dropping creation that a voguish chef has done his number on. After peeking and prodding a bit, you might vaguely recognise the pork belly that has taken a backseat among Picasso-like swirls of compelling sauces. Perhaps you delayed choosing a wine until you'd decided what to eat but, even so, you could not have been prepared for this sort of surprise, which can send your well- but innocently-chosen wine into orbit. To avoid a similar scenario, always ask exactly what a sauce consists of before ordering your wine.

In this chapter, we only deal with sauces that are **added**, normally after cooking. Dishes with integrated sauces are listed alphabetically in other chapters of this guide.

The lists of sauces in the tables that follow are not exhaustive; they are merely examples tabulated according to their ingredients and styles. If you cannot find your favourite sauce in these lists, then simply use the broad category in which it would fall in order to find a wine suggestion. Once you have analysed whether your sauce is creamy, buttery, eggy, herby, garlicy, sharp, sweet, sweet-and-sour, reduced and meaty, spicy or salty, you'll be able to determine where it will slot into the tables.

WHITE, BUTTER, CREAM AND EGGY SAUCES	ESSENTIAL FLAVOURINGS	WINE MATCHES
Basic white sauce + added ingredients	White (béchamel; velouté) Avocado Cheese (mornay) Chicken stock & cream (suprême; ivoire) Mushroom Onion	The silky, rich textures of these sauces pair well with similarly rich-textured wines. Medium-bodied to full-bodied wooded Chardonnay, Semillon or Chardonnay-Semillon blends, and Viognier, are good choices when these sauces are served on fish, chicken or pork. Even when served on red meat, your best bet is still a white wine. A well-oaked Chardonnay or Semillon, with some acidity, is an ideal counterpoint to red meat topped with these creamy sauces.
Acidic flavours	Butter and white wine (beurre blanc) Butter and red wine (beurre rouge) Creamy lemon or orange Lemon butter Hollandaise, mousseline	Chardonnay, unwooded or lightly oaked, but one that has some acidity, such as those from a cool climate. A full-bodied Pinot Gris/Pinot Grigio or a wooded Chenin Blanc would also work well. These sauces do not pair very well with red wines.
Added flavours	Horseradish (Albert) Mustard (moutarde)	**Horseradish** is very hard on a wine, even when hiding in cream. If you want to have it, choose a white wine, but keep it inexpensive. Horseradish is dreadful with red wine. **Mustard sauces** are the complete opposite; they love red and white wine. Stay with Chardonnay, Semillon and Chenin Blanc; or Merlot or Pinotage, but keep them medium-bodied.

	ESSENTIAL FLAVOURINGS	WINE MATCHES
Cold 'white' sauces	Mayonnaise Garlic (aioli)	Choose lightly wooded Chardonnay or Semillon for plain mayonnaise-dressed food; Viognier for aioli.
BROWN SAUCES		
Basic brown sauce + added ingredients	Rich brown (brune; espagnole) Red wine (Bourguignonne) Onion & white wine (Lyonnaise) Truffle (financière; Périgueux; périgourdine) Beef marrow & red wine (Bordelaise)	Malbec, Pinotage, Shiraz, Tempranillo and Zinfandel are the five musketeers for these sauces, especially when served with lamb. When they are served with beef, crack open a bottle of Cab, but choose one with generous fruit. A Viognier, Sylvaner or very fruity Sauv Blanc or Chenin Blanc would be ideal with the onion and white wine (Lyonnaise) sauce. With truffle sauces, Viognier wins hands down.
With a touch of sweetness added	Madeira wine (Madère) Port (porto)	Go for a top-notch Merlot or a sweet-fruited Shiraz that is not too peppery.
Game-stock based	Rich brown sauce Pepper with white wine or vinegar (poivrade) Pepper with red wine (chevreuil) Pepper sauce thickened with blood and with redcurrant jelly and cream added (grand veneur)	Shiraz, Pinotage and Mourvèdre are all ideal matches for richly flavoured game sauces.

FISH- AND SEAFOOD-BASED SAUCES	ESSENTIAL FLAVOURINGS	WINE MATCHES
Creamy, eggy or buttery	Crayfish (Américaine; diplomate; Nantua) Truffle and crayfish (cardinal) Anchovy (anchois) Bercy Shrimp sauce (Joinville) Mussel (marinère) Mushroom (Normande) White wine (vin blanc, dieppoise)	Lightly wooded Chardonnay is your best choice, although generally, the richer the sauce, the more wood you can have on the wine. A dry blanc de noir is equally good, while Sauvignon Blanc or dry to off-dry Weisser Riesling are good counterpoints to the creaminess of these sauces. If you must have a red wine with these sauces, your only choice is an easy-drinking Pinot Noir.
Wine-based	Red wine (Genevoise)	Pinot Noir is the wine for this sauce.
FRUIT AND NUT SAUCES	**ESSENTIAL FLAVOURINGS**	**WINE MATCHES**
Sweet to sweet-and-sour	Apple, cherry, cranberry, chutney, Cumberland, plum, pomegranate, redcurrant	Off-dry Weisser Riesling, Chenin Blanc or Gewürztraminer (dry- or off-dry) are ideal, but consider the main ingredient. Sweet-and-sour fruit sauces go well with poultry and pork but, if the sauce accompanies red meat or game, white wine may not be everyone's preference. Then, a light- to medium-bodied red with upfront sweet-berry flavours is a better choice. If you insist on a dry white, choose a very young wine with ripe fruit flavours; a Viognier should save the day, although not in every instance.

Citrus-flavoured sauces	Lemon (not creamy) Orange (not creamy) Bitter orange (bigarade)	Gewürztraminer is a particularly good choice, as the wine and sauce affirm each other's core fruity character. Other options are off-dry Weisser Riesling, off-dry to medium-sweet Chenin Blanc, or Viognier.
Nut-flavoured sauces	Peanut Walnut (tarator)	Peanut sauces work particularly well with Fernão Pires, but wooded Chardonnay is the nut-sauce wine *par excellence*.
HERB OR SPICE-BASED SAUCES AND BUTTERS	**ESSENTIAL FLAVOURINGS**	**WINE MATCHES**
Creamy herb sauces	Parsley Tarragon (béarnaise) Mixed herbs (chivry; vénitienne) Herb butters (garlic, maitre d'hotel, etc.)	Wooded Chardonnay or Semillon, or a blend of these, pair well with the rich textures of these sauces and butters, as does Viognier.
Brown herb sauces	Tarragon (à l'estragon; Colbert) Mixed herb (fines herbes) Mixed herbs with mushroom (chasseur)	Flavourful red wines carry the day: medium-bodied Shiraz or Pinotage or a flavourful Merlot. However, if your sauce or gravy is thyme or rosemary infused, it is hard to beat Cabernet Sauvignon (with Viognier coming a close second in this instance).

	ESSENTIAL FLAVOURINGS	WINE MATCHES
Spice-based sauces	Coriander Cumin Cinnamon with ginger	For lightly spiced sauces, choose Gewürztraminer, Viognier, Pinot Noir or blanc de noir, especially when made from Pinotage grapes. The spicier the sauce, the more difficult pairing becomes. You need young, spicy red wines with good fruit flavours, low to moderate alcohol and moderate oaking; try Shiraz, Pinotage, Malbec, Tempranillo or Zinfandel. Take into account what the sauce is being served on.
SHARP AND PIQUANT SAUCES		
Creamy and buttery sauces	Creamy tomato (aurore, Choron) Curry	These sauces may have a sharp or spicy edge, but at heart they are creamy and smooth. Pair them with similarly rich-textured wines such as lightly wooded Chardonnay or Chenin, or with Semillon or Viognier. (Don't miss the sublime experience of Viognier with a lightly curried cream sauce.)
Creamy and acidic sauces	Caper Niçoise (mayonnaise, red peppers, tomato purée, lemon juice, herbs) Rémoulade (mayonnaise, capers, gherkins and anchovies) Tartare (rémoulade with mustard and egg yolk added)	Amber lights flash when it comes to creamy sauces with an acidic sting in the tail. Unlike the category above, here, the scales tip towards the acidic note of these sauces, which play havoc with most wines. Sauvignon Blanc comes to the rescue for the whites; for a red wine, stick to Pinot Noir, Sangiovese or Barbera, and pray.

SHARP AND PIQUANT SAUCES (cont.)	ESSENTIAL FLAVOURINGS	WINE MATCHES
Dairy-based creamy and acidic sauces	Yoghurt sauces (Indian raitas)	Raw yoghurt sauces are instant death to wine. You may think that a wine with good acidity will pair with these sour sauces, but there is something very nasty about the combination of wine and the yeast cultures of uncooked yoghurt. No amount of praying will get you past this one. (Note: when yoghurt is added and cooked, as in many Indian curries, or used to replace cream in a dish, it ceases to be a problem.)
Tomato-based sauces	Tomato sauces (Portugaise; Provençale) Chilli Salsa (Mexican-style, raw)	These acidic sauces cry out for wines with equally good acidity. The sharpness of Sauvignon Blanc goes very well with tomato, as does Chenin Blanc, Pinot Noir, Barbera and Sangiovese. The concentration of the tomato will determine your choice. Mexican-type raw **salsas** are sharp and acidic to varying degrees and are best with Sauvignon Blanc. Consider Pinotage for less-concentrated tomato sauces, such as the popular **tomato and onion braai relish**, especially when the sauce is served on red meat, but keep it medium-bodied, lightly wooded, if at all, and with soft tannins.

| With added flavours | Horseradish (raifort)
Mustard (Robert) | **Horseradish** is very hard on a wine. Accept the fact that *sauce aux raifort* will strip a wine of all its flavour. If you don't want to drink water, go for any two-for-a-penny wine.
Mustard sauces, on the other hand, love both white and red wine. Bottle-aged Chenin Blanc, unwooded or lightly wooded Chardonnay or Viognier are good choices for white wines. Pinot Noir, Grenache, Cabernet Franc and Merlot are all great red wine choices. |
| Vinegary sauces | Mint
Vinaigrettes
Salsa verde | Traditional **mint sauce**, which combines vinegar and sugar, is instant death to a wine. Skip the sauce, skip the wine or compromise. Go down, down, down in the quality of your wine so that nothing will be lost.
Match the acidity of a **vinaigrette** with a wine that shows equally good acidity, such as a Sauvignon Blanc, Chenin Blanc, Weisser Riesling or Pinot Blanc.
The tartness of **salsa verde** is well-matched with the same wines as for vinaigrette, although the main ingredient of your dish will play a decisive role. |

Fiery sauces	Brown sauce devilled with cayenne (diable) Salsa picante Harissa Peri-peri	The hotter the sauce, the more difficult the pairing, as your taste buds are knocked for a six and any wine will suffer. Consider what the sauce is being served on (seafood, meat, poultry, etc.). If you choose a red wine, opt for a young one with moderate alcohol and minimal wooding. An off-dry white or rosé is much better than a dry white wine.
SWEET & SALTY SAUCES	**ESSENTIAL FLAVOURINGS**	**WINE MATCHES**
Very sweet sauces	Barbecue	Sweetness in food needs a sweet echo in the wine. Sweet barbecue sauces lead us to whites often made in sweetish styles: Bukettraube, Gewürztraminer, Colombard, Chenin Blanc, Weisser Riesling and rosés. You may not want to drink these wines with braaied red meat, so look to Viognier or full-bodied reds that are packed with concentrated, generous, ripe fruit, such as Shiraz, Pinotage or Zinfandel.
Sweet-and-sour sauces	Monkeygland Raisin Chinese Japanese Thai	Match a wine with sweet and acidic notes to sweet-and-sour sauces. Off-dry to medium-sweet Chenin Blanc, off-dry Weisser Riesling or Gewürztraminer are successful. If the sauce is on red meat, try Viognier or a red with low tannins, low to medium alcohol, light oaking and sweet-berry-fruit flavours: Sangiovese, Pinot Noir, Merlot, Ruby Cabernet, Cinsaut, easy-drinking Cab Sav, quaffable Cab-Merlot or a Cab-Shiraz blend, all made in this style.

Sweet and salty sauces	Soy-based (teriyaki)	The sweetness in soy-based sauces points to wines with similar sweet notes. You have a double whammy here, as salty food also likes sweetish wines. Off-dry to medium-sweet Chenin Blanc, Colombard, stein, off-dry Weisser Riesling, Bukettraube or Gewürztraminer are all good choices. If you want a red wine, limit your choice to easy-drinking, up-front, fruity Merlot, a Merlot-Cab or Merlot-Shiraz blend, a Cinsaut or a Ruby Cabernet. However, an off-dry rosé is perhaps the most delightful partner to this style of sauce.
Sweet and spicy sauces	Chocolate chilli Sweet chilli Tomato sauce (ketchup)	Go straight for the spicy wines. For white, select a wine that has some residual sugar: Weisser Riesling saves the day on all fronts, with Gewürztraminer close on its heels. For a ketchup-type sauce, consider Sauvignon Blanc, but a ripe, fruity version rather than a crisp, herbaceous one. **Chocolate-chilli sauce** needs the depth of a red, such as a spicy Shiraz or chocolatey Pinotage, that will echo all the flavours of the sauce.
Salty sauces	Soy-based	Low to moderate alcohol, some sweetness and good acidity in a wine are what we look for to pair with salty sauces. This leads us to the life-saver, dry or off-dry Weisser Riesling. The sharper dry rosés and blanc de noirs also work, as does a dry (sec) sparkling wine, with its inherent acidity and sweetness, as even the driest (brut) sparkling wine has more residual sugar than any dry still white wine.

Cooking with wine

Using wine in the preparation of food is probably as old as wine itself. It would not have taken *Homo sapiens* very long to discover that the juice gathered from fermented grapes has a knack for transforming even the simplest, blandest of foods into delectable dishes and giving them added depth and flavour.

Wine can be used as a marinade, a flavouring agent or a cooking liquid. In South Africa, our favourite way of preparing a haunch of venison is to marinate it in red wine before roasting. Or, if venison is not available, we'll opt for *'n nagemaakte wildsboudjie*, a mock leg of venison, by marinating a leg of lamb in red wine to masquerade as the real thing. Often, the marinade is discarded when the meat is roasted; sometimes, some of it is added to the gravy.

When wine is used as a flavouring ingredient, such as in wine-based sauces (beurre blanc or beurre rouge), it is often reduced by boiling to intensify its flavour, but wine can also be added at the last minute without any further cooking.

Wine can replace all or part of the cooking liquid, such as in *coq au vin* (chicken cooked in red wine) or a Belgian-styled mussel-pot. White wines should always be added with a bit of caution, as their acidity becomes concentrated when they are cooked, especially if they are reduced. Consequently, white wine is usually added in an equal amount with another liquid, such as stock or water. Red wine, on the other hand, may constitute all the cooking liquid.

The 'rule' that you should cook with only the best wines – certainly nothing less than you will serve with the dish – is excessive. If you are going to serve a top-quality wine, you really don't have to cook with it as well. Regardless of whether you use wine as a flavouring agent or as a cooking liquid, once you have finished cooking, the wine will bear little resemblance to what was in the bottle in the first place, as most of its alcohol and water will have evaporated. This is particularly so if the dish is cooked for a long time, such as a *boeuf en daube* (beef braised in red wine.) The only time you can justify using an expensive wine for cooking is when you add it to a dish at the last minute, without cooking it any further.

But, a good rule to retain is to only cook with a wine that you are prepared to drink. It is a mistake to use 'corked' or otherwise-tainted wine for cooking. The cooking process will accentuate any 'off' or unwelcome flavours and spoil your dish. Oxidized wines that remind you of port or sherry, or wines that have started turning into vinegar, are never suitable. And don't try to get rid of unwanted sweetish wine by cooking with it; the sugars in the wine will be concentrated by the cooking process, which may not be what you intended for a savoury dish. Also, be particularly careful when cooking with a monster red wine; those huge fruit or oak profiles can add an acrid or burnt flavour to food. Young, tannic wines should not be a problem, but heavy oak flavours are not desirable.

So, what wine should you use for cooking? In almost all cases, just select a simple, but tasty, medium-bodied wine that will give its all to the food. And, if you only need a glass or two for the dish, you'll probably find that your chosen wine makes an ideal drinking companion as you stir the pot!

Putting your wine fears to rest

Wine aficionados often worry that certain foods or ingredients in dishes have the potential to spoil their carefully selected and well-cellared vinous treasures. Certainly, there are some foods, flavours and textures that have the potential to modify, amplify, distort or simply destroy the accompanying wines. But there are fewer of these taste assassins than you might imagine. Some of our food and wine matching fears are simply false alarms and, frequently, there are simple solutions. Food and wine are truly natural partners. It is quite astounding how few foods actually ring alarm bells for wine drinkers. This will become apparent from a quick read of what follows.

ARTICHOKES

Fear: Artichokes make a wine taste metallic and sweeter than it is.
Solution: This is true, but you will probably eat them with a dressing or a sauce of some description, usually either creamy or acidic, or creamy and acidic, such as a hollandaise sauce. Just up the amount of lemon in the sauce and reach for a Sauvignon Blanc. If you prefer a sauce on the creamy or eggy side, a lightly wooded Chardonnay, with some acidity, will be just the thing.

ASPARAGUS

Fear: Selecting wines to serve with asparagus is extremely difficult as the sharp and powerful flavour is overpowering.
Solution: Asparagus has such a sharp, powerful flavour that it battles with a number of wines. But there are two wines that sidle up so close to asparagus when it is served plainly, that it is a waste of time to search for others. Sauvignon Blanc echoes the flavours while Cabernet Franc amplifies them, so you can take your pick from white or red. When asparagus is served with melted butter, Chardonnay comes alive; choose a young, unwooded or lightly wooded Chardonnay to latch onto the puddles of butter. Of course, there are those who maintain that the success of this combination lies in the butter, not in the asparagus – but, if it works, so what?

CAPERS

Fear: The sharpness of capers plays havoc with all wines.
Solution: It is not the berry itself, but the preserving vinegar that causes problems with wine. See **Vinegar and vinegar-based salad dressings** on page 53.

CHILLI

Fear: Chilli's ferocious intensity is no friend to a decent wine.

Solution: As surprising as it may seem, chilli does not change the taste of wine at all. It may numb the mouth a bit or burn the taste buds, but it does not deserve all the abuse hurled at it. (Here, we are not referring to those incendiary dishes created for fire-eaters, but to moderately intense ones.) Chilli's mouth-numbing character *will* prevent you from appreciating the nuances of a fine wine, so save it for another occasion. No wine specifically cries out for chilli, but we can approximate a wine profile that will match it: a feisty, young white to withstand chilli's onslaught and which should be served well-chilled to cool and refresh the palate. A tannic red wine will overload taste buds that already have their hands full coping with a chilli-attack.

CHOCOLATE

Fear: Firstly, the extreme sweetness of chocolate desserts and, secondly, their mouth-coating textures will assassinate any wine.

Solution: For once, the fear of 'death by chocolate' is grounded, and wine is the casualty! There are different levels of sweetness and weight to chocolate creations; the weight of an instant pudding made from a packet is poles apart from the weight of a dense, heavy chocolate mousse. A special late harvest will certainly cope with a light chocolate pudding; a noble late harvest with a richer creation, and a tawny port will come to the rescue of the heaviest ones. There is, however, one wine that will cope with all chocolate weights: red muscadel which, in a nutshell, is the key to chocolate. But, if all else fails, which can happen with those seriously decadent chocolate desserts, you can always fall back on a good brandy; it acts both as a solvent and refreshes the palate.

CHUTNEY

Fear: The sweetness and sharpness of fruit chutney decimates wine.

Solution: South Africa is awash in chutney. It is available everywhere, from supermarket to road-side farm stall, church bazaar and Saturday morning-market. We use chutney as a sambal for curry and rice, spread it on Cheddar cheese sandwiches, and serve it with slices of cold roast meats. South Africans abroad are forever asking their visiting relatives and friends to bring a bottle of Mrs You-Know-Who's chutney along. So there really is no point in suggesting that you not have your chutney and eat it. We'd rather give you a solution for enjoying this relish with wine, such as when you just have to add a dollop to your mother-in-law's meatloaf to give it a hint of flavour! Matching the wine to the main ingredient, such as the meat in the curry, or the Cheddar cheese on the sandwich, will diminish the decimating effect of chutney. Alternatively, simply water it down with some H_2O after each mouthful before taking a sip of wine.

CRANBERRY SAUCE AND JELLY

Fear: Faced with cranberry sauce, wine simply fades away.

Solution: This is true, especially in the case of a fine, well-matured Cabernet Sauvignon or Bordeaux blend. Like chutney, cranberry sauce has a concentrated sweet-sharp character, but the cranberry-with-Christmas-turkey enthusiast can take heart that it is, at least, less punishing on a wine than chutney. A top-quality Weisser Riesling with precocious sweetness, or a semi-sweet Chenin Blanc, will handle cranberry sauce admirably, but not everyone wants to drink these wines with meat. Therefore, many food and wine pairers rely on the upfront, fruity character of a full-bodied Shiraz, Pinotage, Mourvèdre or Zinfandel to meet the sauce head-on. Of course, to make it easier on the wine, you could just add a touch of sauce; if you drench your meat, you'll be having nothing but cranberries, anyway.

EGGS

Fear: The texture of hard-boiled egg yolks coats the taste buds and all the flavours in a wine are lost. If the yolk is still runny, the wine becomes simply nasty.

Solution: We don't contest this, but the chances of having eggs on their own, as we did in the days of padkos and picnics, are slim. Anyway, you'd be drinking tea or coffee, not wine, while travelling, so matching wine and hard-boiled eggs wasn't an issue. Nowadays, we might include eggs as an ingredient in a salad or as a garnish, but mainly we serve them in sauces, such as mayonnaise, hollandaise or curry (as in that Sunday supper standby, curried eggs on rice), and therein lies the solution. It is the sauce that diverts the attention and which the wine latches on to. A Burgundy speciality is eggs poached in Pinot Noir (*oeuffs en meurette*) and they serve the same wine with the meal. Now there's a way to have your wine and eat it.

FENNEL

Fear: The intense flavour of fresh fennel, which is so popular with vegetarians, overpowers a wine.

Solution: Yes, many wines are overpowered, but not Sauvignon Blanc with its equally robust flavours. Vegetarians will most likely sauté the fennel in butter, in which case a lightly wooded Chardonnay with an equally buttery profile will be a good match. If fennel is served as a vegetable to accompany meat, opt for a Pinotage or a Viognier.

GARLIC

Fear: Garlic is a real enemy of wine.

Solution: If garlic is used as an ingredient in a **cooked** dish, it will happily fuse with the other ingredients and present no problem to any wine. Just as garlic enhances the flavour of a cooked dish, so it can enhance the flavour of many wines, especially when they have herbaceous undertones. However, a mountain of **raw garlic** included in a dish can become an obstacle course for the taste buds.

GINGER

Fear: As an ingredient, ginger is hard on a wine.

Solution: This depends on whether it is fresh ginger or ginger that has been crystalized or preserved in syrup. Surprisingly, fresh ginger is not a problem for wine; it is very wine friendly and there is a whole range of wines that are matches, depending on the main ingredient of the dish: Weisser Riesling, Gewürztraminer, Pinot Gris/Pinot Grigio, Sauvignon Blanc and, at the top of the list, Viognier. Ginger desserts, cakes and cookies are very happy with both red and white muscadel and so are those pieces of crystalized or preserved ginger used as toppings or garnishes for desserts or in sweet sauces. A common South African after-dinner treat is Cheddar cheese served with preserved ginger. Muscadel will sing in this scenario.

GRAPEFRUIT

Fear: No wine goes with grapefruit.

Solution: There's truth in this. However, not wanting to admit defeat, we suggest that you select a wine with the highest acidity you can lay your hands on. Think Crouchen Blanc, which you may know as Cape, Paarl or South African Riesling, or look for a crisp Vinho Verde from Portugal, which is now available in South Africa.

HERBS AND SPICES

Fear: An over-use of herbs and spices will detract from showing off a top-notch wine.

Solution: Sure, the simpler the food, the better wine will show as it has no competition on the taste buds. Sure, the spicier the food, the more difficult it is to find a match in wine. However, no one, not even the most fervent wine aficionado, wants to eat only poached chicken breast or boiled beef... In fact, herbs are very wine friendly. Rosemary and thyme are a case in point; they are crazy about Cab Sav and vice versa. The only herb to use with discretion is sage, which can be overpowering to both wine and food. Just as herbs enhance the flavour of food, they also enhance and amplify the flavour of wine. But, having said all this, you should not choose a wine based on the herbs you have used, but rather on the main ingredient of the dish.

Spices are also not a threat to wine in either savoury or sweet dishes. Many spicy flavours and aromas find an echo in wines such as Gewürztraminer, Pinot Gris/Pinot Grigio, Hanepoot and Viognier. Once again, select the wine to match the main ingredient and final effect of the dish, not on the basis of its spices.

HORSERADISH AND WASABI

Fear: These relishes strip a wine of all its flavour.

Solution: Er, yes. However, there is one wine that stands up to **horse-radish**, Viognier, although it is too spicy for roast beef or smoked fish – the foods horseradish is traditionally served with. A quaffable red will also be fine with the beef, if you do not mind the knock it will take. Similarly, you could try a lightly wooded Chardonnay with the smoked fish, but choose one that you won't shed any tears over.

Wasasbi, which resembles horseradish, and is served with sushi, sashimi or raw fish dishes, is even sharper than horseradish – and crueller on wine. An equally sharp Sauvignon Blanc, or a Weisser Riesling with good acidity, will do the trick.

ICE CREAM

Fear: Even if we match the sweetness of a wine to the sweetness of this frozen dessert, the coldness acts as an anaesthetic, numbing the taste buds and wiping out the flavours of the wine.

Solution: Not even ice cream can wipe out a muscadel. See **Ice cream and sorbets**, pages 263–264.

LEMONS AND LIMES

Fear: Most wines shudder at the thought of coming face to face with lemon or lime juice.

Solution: Weisser Riesling, Sauvignon Blanc or Chenin Blanc don't even twitch. Weisser Riesling, in particular, has as an affinity for lemon and lime. In savoury dishes, match the acidity of the dish to that of the wine. Serve a special or noble late harvest with lemon- or lime-based desserts, depending on the level of sweetness in these dishes.

MINT SAUCE OR MINT JELLY

Fear: The combination of sugar and vinegar in both the sauce and the jelly ruin a wine, especially a red.

Solution: Crank down the quality of that red wine by several notches so that nothing is lost, and keep the good bottles for another day.

An alternative solution is simply to serve fresh mint, finely chopped, with your leg of lamb. Red wine, especially a Cabernet Sauvignon, will be totally at ease with mint, provided there is no added sugar or vinegar to put up with.

MUSTARD

Fear: Mustard is so flavour-intense that it overpowers any wine.

Solution: Er, no. The opposite is true. Mustard loves wine and goes very well with both whites and reds. It does not even blink an eye in the presence of fierce tannins. There are many styles of mustard but, unless they are overly strong, vinegary or sweet, mustard is the food and wine pairer's dream. The wines that go best with it are full-flavoured, well-rounded whites in the Chardonnay camp, or those with balanced acidity and sweetness, such as Weisser Riesling. When it comes to red wine choices, anything goes: from medium- to full-bodied and from well-rounded and accessible to tannic. And yet it would be out of sync to drink a precious old bottle with, say, rare roast beef with lashings of home-made hot English mustard, or even with the mildest mustard of all, Dijon.

Here's a tip that might come in handy: you decide to finish the leftover roast beef that has now gone cold, so you pour a glass of the same red that was so good last night when the meat was piping hot from the oven. With the first sip you realize that something is different. The meat's texture has changed as the fats have coagulated, and the wine no longer pairs well with it. You wonder if a white wine would have fared any better, but you are sitting with an open bottle of red. No problem; add a dollop of mustard to that cold roast beef, and the mustard will fight a double dual: with a sabre on the left it slices through the beef's cold fat, while on the right, rapier in hand, the wine's tannins are pierced.

OLIVES

Fear: Saltiness, which is so pronounced in olives, is very hard on a wine, especially a red. Salt amplifies the tannins in red wine and makes them taste bitter.

Solution: When eaten on their own, olives are simply magical with pale dry (fino) sherry, which has its own salty echo. When olives are included in cooked dishes, such as stews or a puttanesca sauce, match the wine to the main ingredient, such as beef or tomatoes. When olives are added to salads, consider the other ingredients; the salad has probably been tossed with a dressing, so a dry white wine or a blanc de noir, both with good acidity, will be a good match.

SALSA

Fear: As with all pepper-hot sweet and sour foods and condiments, salsas spell danger to any wine.

Solution: Danger is what you may expect from hot, insistent flavours, but salsas are add-ons and never served solo. Sauvignon Blancs are their biggest allies, especially when the salsa is served in quantity as a topping to otherwise bland main ingredients. Whether we're talking Mexican salsa verde or the voguish tropical fruit versions, they all have a sharp profile that Sauvignon Blanc happily latches on to.

SOY SAUCE

Fear: Soy sauce makes wine taste bitter and metallic.

Solution: Whoever said that must have been drinking a red. The saltiness of soy sauce and its concentrated umami flavour calls for a white wine with notable acidity and, if it has a touch of sweetness as well, so much the better. Choose from Sauvignon or Chenin Blanc, a dry (brut) sparkling wine or an off-dry Weisser Riesling and you'll have found your perfect sushi wines.

If you add soy sauce to a beef stir-fry or to the marinade for a piece of steak, bear in mind that salt hates tannins. Select a red wine with a generous, sweet-fruity character, but one that is low in tannins.

SPINACH

Fear: Spinach, like artichokes, makes a wine taste bitter or metallic, especially in the presence of a red wine's tannins.

Solution: Yes, it does, but you can use this vegetable's acidic nature to advantage. Increase the acidity by sprinkling spinach with a bit of lemon juice and then haul out a white wine that is crisp, young and not too feisty. Or there are two other, equally good solutions: if you've cooked your spinach to perfection and you don't wish to go at it with hammer-and-tongs lemon juice, switch to red wine with an equally gentle acidity, such as Sangiovese, Barbera or Pinot Noir. If you want to properly harness that metallic taste, add butter, cream, or cheeses such as Parmesan and Ricotta, to cooked spinach and opt for an unwooded or lightly wooded Chardonnay or Semillon.

TARTARE SAUCE

Fear: The sharpness of a tartare sauce can send shivers down a wine's spine.

Solution: But not down the spine of a Sauvignon Blanc, as its own sharpness is not in the least bit intimidated by a little tartare sauce. Actually, they play on the same side of the game.

TOMATOES

Fear: Be cautious when selecting wine for a tomatoey dish, as the acidity in tomatoes can ruin a wine.

Solution: It's quite easy: just follow the basic food and wine pairing principle of matching the acidity in food with equal acidity in wine. Chenin Blanc will cope, Pinot Noir, Sangiovese or Cinsaut ought to cope and Pinotage may cope, but two wines stand head-and-shoulders above the pack: Sauvignon Blanc and Barbera. These should be dubbed the 'tomato wines', because their pronounced acidity pairs seamlessly with that of tomatoes.

Sun-dried tomatoes in oil are intensely flavoured, with smoky overtones, and pair well with acidic wine that also has a touch of smokiness. You'd be hard-pressed to find a better match than a wooded Sauvignon Blanc (blanc fumé), but Weisser Riesling with a touch of sweetness and natural acidity comes a close second.

VINEGAR AND VINEGAR-BASED SALAD DRESSINGS

Fear: All wine cries blue murder when it is paired with vinegar and acidic dressings.

Solution: Sauvignon Blanc, Chenin Blanc or Weisser Riesling, with their good acidity, will not let out even a squeak. If there is also a touch of sweetness in the wine, such as occurs in an off-dry Weisser Riesling, so much the better. An acidic salad dressing will completely annihilate a Chardonnay but, if you absolutely insist on Chardonnay with your salad, then make your dressing with the same wine you have opened to drink, and blend it, in place of the vinegar, with some walnut oil to mirror the wine's nutty flavour. Although this is not as good a solution, you can also consider using verjuice in place of vinegar or choose a softer-styled vinegar, such as the vogueish berry ones, but use them in moderation. If you want to drink red wine with your salad, go for one with good natural acidity, such as Pinot Noir, Barbera or Sangiovese. However, if these wines are not on hand, omit the vinegar from the dressing and blend the olive oil with a splash of the same wine you are going to drink.

YOGHURT

Fear: Wine clashes with the yeast cultures in uncooked yoghurt.

Solution: A cucumber and yoghurt relish (tzatziki) or Indian raita are seldom served on their own, so the yoghurt is tamed by the dishes they accompany. Match your wine to the main ingredient and pause for a moment after you've scooped up a mouthful of tzatziki before sipping your wine. Yoghurt added to a dish and cooked, as in many Indian curries, or used to replace cream, ceases to be a problem.

Wines and their food matches

When people discuss food and wine pairing, or how to select a wine to accompany a specific dish, the following remark is often heard: 'Oh, I know nothing about wine. I just drink it'. What a brilliant comment! This is precisely the point. When pairing food and wine, you do not need any wine knowledge; you do not need to know how grapes are grown, or how wine is made and matured. Brush aside the wine-speak such as malolactic fermentation, microclimate or racking. All you require is a pair of eyes (just one will do too) to read the label and see which grapes are in the bottle. Of the four main factors that influence the flavour and character of wine – soil, climate, viticulture (the growing of grapes for wine) and grape varieties – it is the latter that leaves an indelible imprint. Certain dishes, sauces, ingredients and seasonings just seem to cry out for certain grape varieties.

In South Africa (as in other New World wine-producing countries), we produce many varietal wines – those that are made from a single grape variety – with great emphasis placed on the characteristics of the particular variety and its associated fruit flavours. We also name these wines after the principal grape variety used, such as Cabernet Sauvignon, Chardonnay, and so on.

Not all South African wines are made from single grape varieties, though; winemakers also make blends from two or more grapes. However, the names given to the resulting blended wines may not necessarily reflect the varieties used. Some of the country's finest wines are blends, and many of these are indispensable when it comes to food and wine pairing. You may wonder how blending will affect food pairing but, generally, one of the grape varieties in the blend will be dominant, and it is to this dominance that we look when we pair food and wine.

This is not 'yet another' book on wine. Our purpose is to write about food and wine pairing, not wine, so we are not going to give you lengthy descriptions of the wines we recommend in our pairing suggestions. We do not discuss the regions in which the grapes are grown, how they are vinified and matured, or the winemakers' special quirks or philosophies. Instead, we give you an idea of what the varietal wines would smell or taste like and, more importantly, what types of food they have an affinity for. If we suggest, for example, a Barbera, and give you a reason for the choice, but you are not sure what a typical Barbera tastes like, then this chapter will enable you to find out a bit more about the wine. First of all, what scents or flavours you could typically expect from it, and secondly, what type of food is best suited to it. (Where relevant, we also note the effect of different cooking methods such as grilling, frying or stewing.)

Sometimes, we have given wines certain human characteristics – with tongue firmly in cheek, of course – based on how the wines usually respond when paired with particular foods, which was our only focus when we compiled the content.

Tips for using this chapter: We have listed the wines **alphabetically**, paying no heed to distinctions between the grape varieties or any other traditional classifications. Just run your finger through the pages to find what you are looking for. We have also indicated whether each wine is a **varietal wine**, such as Merlot or Chardonnay, or a **wine style**, such as blanc de noir or sparkling wine, as well as the wine's **colour** (red, white or pink).

BARBERA   Varietal wine; red

This productive, versatile grape is widely grown in Italy, its country of origin, but not in South Africa. It delivers medium-bodied, low tannin, firm and fresh red wine with a sour cherry flavour and a high level of natural acidity. It retains this acidity even when fully ripe or simmering under a scorching sun. It is somewhat surprising that there are so few Barbera producers in South Africa, as its tendency towards astringency makes it suitable for growing in a hot climate. With many of the varieties that are grown in hot climates, the viticulturist is faced with the problem of the grapes' sugar levels (Balling) rising too quickly while the natural acid levels lag behind – so much so that the winemaker often has to make adjustments in the cellar.

Barbera's natural acidity is of great value when it comes to food and wine pairing, as there are few red wines with an acidic profile. Barbera takes well to oak, which gives the wine a smoky intensity and acts as a balance to its high acidity. This makes Barbera very kind to grilled or char-grilled foods, which often have a squeeze of lemon as a final touch, such as grilled prawns, kebabs or sardines.

Lemon, which is the death of most fine red wines, especially Cabernet blends, and which flattens most white wines with low acidity, holds no terror for Barbera, as it lends a sympathetic ear to acidity.

Barbera's acidity makes it a 'tomato wine' *par excellence*. Actually, it is a toss-up between which of the two Italian red grapes, Barbera or Sangiovese, is the leader of the pack when it comes to tomato-based dishes. In addition, it is the only red-wine partner to smoked salmon and the ideal choice for the more plebeian, but equally fatty favourite, bangers and mash. It copes admirably with most pasta dishes, from spaghetti Bolognese and *spaghetti alla carbonara* to vegetable-sauced ones. It is equally good with charcuterie and prosciutto crudo (or 'Parma ham', as we call it in South Africa) and lamb's liver and kidney dishes, such as kidneys in a sherry sauce.

BLANC DE NOIR	Wine style; 'pink'

In France, the term 'blanc de noir' has a specific meaning and refers to a champagne made from the two red grapes, Pinot Noir and Pinot Meunier exclusively, without the addition of Chardonnay in the base wine. In South Africa, we use the term to describe a style of wine – that is, a still white wine produced from dark-skinned grapes. (The name is a literal translation of the French term, 'white from black'.)

To make a blanc de noir, the skin of the grapes, which contains the colour, is kept in contact with the juice for a short period only to extract the typical blush of pinkish colour often described as 'onion skin' or 'partridge eye'. (Those who are not in the habit of looking a partridge in the eye can perhaps relate more to the eye of a bantam or *kapokhoendertjie*, which many people had as a childhood pet.) Once the pale juice has been run off the skins, the rest of the wine-making process is the same as for making a white wine.

South African blanc de noirs are often made from Cabernet Sauvignon or Shiraz grapes, but it is Pinotage that delivers an especially fruity, spicy blanc de noir of good intensity. Blanc de noir wines can be made dry, off-dry or semi-sweet.

This is the ideal wine for a fish dish, and it is absolutely in love with salmon, trout and crayfish, plainly served. It is a great companion to chunky bouillabaisse and similar fishy soups and stews – provided the wine is dry, medium-bodied and herby without too much fruit or floral character. Blanc de noir does not have the weight to accompany red meat but pairs well with cooked ham or rabbit stew. It is spot-on with mildly dressed salads, but even a fresh and lively blanc de noir has a tendency to be a bit too soft for acidic foods.

Vegetarians could easily serve blanc de noir with ratatouille, a vegetable moussaka or *melanzane alla parmigiana* (baked brinjal/ eggplant). Oaky white wines normally work well with flavoursome rice dishes, but when saffron is added, for instance to a paella, the tables turn towards blanc de noir. Another Spanish dish, piperade, a combination of scrambled eggs, ham, tomato and sweet peppers, can be very hard on most wines, but not on blanc de noir.

Generally speaking, blanc de noir fills the gap when you need a white wine with the bolder flavours you'll find in red wines. Many ethnic dishes, such as teriyaki or hot Thai noodle dishes, which are flavoured with soy sauce and ginger, play into the hand of a blanc de noir.

Blanc de noir is often described, with flourish, as the ideal picnic or alfresco wine to be enjoyed outdoors, preferably in brilliant sunshine, with a backdrop of majestic mountains, or on the beach next to the roaring ocean, under endless blue skies. Sentimentality aside, the pertinent factor should be the food, not the setting! With an array of picnic dishes ranging from sandwiches to fruit salad via stuffed eggs and cold chicken, you need the unobtrusiveness of a blanc de noir that will simply play a bit of concertina music in the background – provided it's not a *vastrap*... So, when you are looking for the ideal aperitif and you're up to your eyeballs in tart Sauvignon Blancs and effervescent bubblies, choose a blanc de noir – this is one of its finest hours.

BLANC FUMÉ   Sauvignon blanc style; white

In South Africa, Sauvignon Blanc that has been wooded is often labelled 'blanc fumé'.

BORDEAUX BLENDS   Wine style; red

In the Bordeaux region of France, red wine is made by blending a number of different grape varieties: Cabernet Sauvignon, Merlot, Cabernet Franc, Petit Verdot and Malbec. When blended, the resulting wines have a characteristic and identifiable taste. Frequently, the aroma reminds us of blackcurrants, cedar wood, lead-pencil shavings, mint or the inside of a cigar box (and if you don't habitually shove your nose into cigar boxes and don't know what we're talking about, you'll just have to take our word for it!).

The result of this blending exercise produces everything from easy-drinking, everyday red wines to complex, concentrated wines of enormous éclat and depth, with a tannic structure that can last up to 20 years. The exact proportion of the varieties used varies from producer to producer; for example, it could be 70% Cabernet Sauvignon, 10% Merlot, 10% Cabernet Franc, 5% Petit Verdot and 5% Malbec, or it could be 60% Merlot, 30% Cabernet Franc, only 10% Cabernet Sauvignon and no Petit Verdot or Malbec.

There are several reasons why blending is done. In the first place, it ensures uniformity in quality and character from year to year, it adds complexity, and it produces a more harmonious wine. The Bordelais say that 'the whole wine is greater than the sum of its parts', by which they mean that a plummy Merlot can round out the angular structure of Cabernet Sauvignon, or that a less tannic, raspberry-ish Cabernet Franc adds a fruity note. However, in Bordeaux, the unpredictable climate is perhaps the main reason for blending. Cool weather can set in before the Cabernet Sauvignon grapes are ripe, and this will have a huge influence on their quality, not to mention the possibility of a failed harvest. Merlot, which ripens much earlier, comes to the rescue. For the winemaker, having several grape varieties to juggle with, mitigates potential climatological disasters.

Cabernet Sauvignon and Merlot, which are rather similar in taste, are wonderfully complementary. The budding food and wine pairer will be cheered by this discovery, as Cab and Merlot behave similarly when enjoyed with food. If you think about it, there is only a shade of difference between these two varieties: where Cab Sav is the strict schoolmaster, Merlot is the contemporary educator who shares a cigarette with the students during break.

Some of the best red wines in the world are Bordeaux blends, and it is little wonder, therefore, that the New World, including South Africa, tries to emulate these blends by attempting to match the high standards set by Bordeaux's complex, elegant wines. South Africa's winemaking regions are generally blessed with a reliable climate but, like the French, many local winemakers blend their wines for consistency, complexity and harmony.

When it comes to food, the finest partner for a Bordeaux blend is lamb. This is especially true when Cabernet Sauvignon dominates in the blend. Again, we marvel at the phenomenon of regional wines matching regional foods: lamb that has been reared on salt marshes (*pré-salé*) and roasted in the French manner, with garlic and rosemary, is as traditionally Bordeaux as can be. Cabernet Sauvignon is madly in love with rosemary, so you have a double whammy of lamb and rosemary pairing with these stunning blends. It may be a grossly overused cliché, but this really is a marriage made in heaven.

A Bordeaux blend is also good with beef, particularly when the Merlot element is high. Although it turns up its nose at venison, it is a very versatile wine with other red-meat dishes. When very fruity, full and herbaceous, it matches duck (especially duck confit) and other full-flavoured food like calf's kidneys and lamb's liver. When made in this rich style, it is much more tolerant of game dishes. When very blackcurrant and minty, it is good with turkey and its traditional sweet trimmings.

When medium-bodied, lighter in style and mellow (not tannic), as Bordeaux blends from cooler climates often are, it is the perfect match with roast chicken or Irish stew (made with lamb, of course). Fine, old Bordeaux blends are decadently good with rare roast beef served hot or cold.

BUKETTRAUBE   Varietal wine; white

South Africa is about the only country that has adopted this German grape, although there are only a few producers as it is not a variety that makes headlines. It is used mainly for off-dry to sweeter wines with delicate Muscat aromas. Although the grape is not a high-flyer, it can sometimes produce commendable varietal wines with a good sugar–acid balance and a range of floral and perfumed aromas, with honey, cumin, peach and Turkish Delight undertones.

Bukettraube's accessible, uncomplicated, unintimidating and straightforward character is very food-friendly and never rocks the boat, even if it tries to. Wine aficionados, geared towards fireworks in a wine, may ignore it, but the food and wine pairer does nothing of the sort. It has a prominent place at the table as there is an amazing array of foods and ingredients which Bukettraube accompanies with aplomb, from obvious sweetish dishes to the less obvious, including pork, veal, duck, smoky-meat-and-cream pastas and sweet-potato-based soups. It often comes to the rescue when a wine is needed as an unobtrusive backdrop to a food that is too challenging for most wines. It is most successfully used to show off sweet spices (clove, cinnamon, ginger, allspice) in a dish, or to flirt with preparations that are high in salt. Serve Bukettraube with glazed pork roasts, fish with fruity salsas or barbecued chicken. It is delicious with smoked foods such as salmon, mackerel or kassler, or in recipes in which they feature as a main ingredient.

Bukettraube's food-friendliness seems to know no boundaries. To list a few more of its allies: quiche Lorraine, sweet shellfish such as prawns and crab, tuna-mayonnaise sandwiches, sweet-and-salty marinades and sauces with sweet notes, pâtés, salty cold meats, chicken in a honey and mustard sauce, or cold chicken with coleslaw. It is quite good with sushi, but even better with raw fish served with sweet-vinegared rice (nigiri sushi).

CABERNET FRANC   Varietal wine; red

Cabernet Franc, first cousin and namesake to Cabernet Sauvignon, is considered to be less aristocratic, even though it produces wine that is rather similar. It yields a lighter, less tannic tipple with a green vegetable character as opposed to Cabernet Sauvignon's exuberant berry fruit. Its main flavour profile is green peppers, raspberries and, if you've ever come across one, the leaves of a blackcurrant bush.

The reason that Cabernet Franc does not have the flavour, the colour intensity, or the tannin structure of its famous cousin, is that it is less thick-skinned, literally. For the food and wine pairer, it is not important that Cab Franc is less aristocratic than Cab Sav; we are mainly concerned with how the wine responds when it is paired with food. And this it does admirably in the company of very diverse dishes, ranging from asparagus to fish, charcuterie and lighter red meat dishes, such as pan-fried lamb chops, cottage pie, savoury mince or rabbit. The three star-partners this wine is famous for are beef carbonnade (beef braised in ale), which is a difficult food for wine, cheese fondue and rillettes de porc (a delicate potted pâté with pieces of shredded pork added for texture).

If asked which red wines best accommodate both a starter and a main course, thereby obviating changing wines, Cabernet Franc would be one – provided it is medium-bodied and slightly chilled.

Although Cab Franc is almost always blended with its cousin, Cabernet Sauvignon, it has gone solo in South Africa – although with only a few local producers – as well as in other New World wine-producing countries that have the warmer climate needed to bring it into its own. It yields wines of depth with chocolate, green pepper and raspberry flavours and, when bottle-matured, with even a hint of potato peelings. When produced in this style, it copes with all the same dishes that its cousin, Cab Sav, so adores.

There is another Cabernet Franc characteristic that the food and wine pairer particularly values: its good natural acidity. As with Pinot Noir and Barbera, this natural acidity comes in very handy when we wish to pair a red wine with an acidic dish, for instance, Indian food cooked in yoghurt.

CABERNET SAUVIGNON   Varietal wine; red

Plant this noble variety in Bordeaux, Stellenbosch, the Maipo Valley in Chile, California's Napa Valley or in Coonawarra in South Australia, and Cabernet Sauvignon will still taste of itself, yielding the familiar aroma and flavour of blackcurrant, cedar wood and lead-pencil shavings, with perhaps a whiff of sweet-vanilla oak. When grown in some South African *terroirs*, you may detect additional aromas and flavours of green pepper, mint, dark chocolate, tobacco and cloves. And, as it matures, Cab Sav takes on the aroma of a forest floor.

You will find all styles of Cabernet Sauvignon in South Africa: huge wines that are all power and upfront fruit, medium-bodied wines with well-integrated fruit and supple tannins, and easy-drinking, quaffable ones. When it comes to food, Cab Sav is rather snooty. In fact, it has a stiff little back and a toffee-nose. Bring out the voguish berry or chocolate-chilli sauces and it digs its heels in. If it could speak, it would say, with a raised eyebrow, 'You know what, I'll sit this one out'. What it wants is uncluttered food: that Châteaubriand, pink, juicy and done to perfection, or the plainly grilled, lazy-aged steak for which you've paid an arm and a leg. If you really want to show off a valued bottle of Cab Sav of excellent quality, serve it with fine quality food, but keep the preparation simple.

Cabernet Sauvignon, whether blended or solo, is a wine for red meat, especially lamb, for which it has a particular affinity (see **Bordeaux blends**, page 57). It is less successful with game, except when the wine is full and ripe in style, as some Stellenbosch wines are, when it can cope with richer flavours. Serve it with poultry, especially roast turkey and quail, steak and kidney pie or meaty casseroles such as boeuf bourguignonne, Salisbury steaks (made with 100% minced beef) and, of course, lamb's liver.

This may come as a surprise, but toffee-nosed Cabernet is more than happy with Indian curries, especially those from the northern states of that country. (However, this love affair does not extend to Cape Malay curries served with sweet, coconutty sambals.) When the British made India part of their empire, they brought 'home' the fine cuisine of north India, serving up these dishes in their gentlemen's clubs in London, along with fine Cabernet Sauvignon-based wines from Bordeaux. If you come from the mindset of having a beer with curry, or even a lush, sweet wine, like a hanepoot, you may wonder at the 'Cab and curry' combination, but it seems that these two like each other just fine.

Two herbs are madly in love with Cab Sav: rosemary and thyme. Whatever is infused with these, whether it is fish, olives, chicken, pork or lamb, the dish simply cries out for Cabernet Sauvignon.

Three hard cow's-milk cheeses also pair exceptionally well with the wine: Gruyère, Caerphilly and matured Gouda/Mimolette, which is now freely available in South Africa.

Cabernet Sauvignon is not happy with delicate, subtle dishes, strong cheeses, most fish dishes or spice-hot foods (except, of course, for its one-and-only 'hot' love, curry). It also does not work well with most chocolate creations. And, no matter what you have heard about chocolate and Cab Sav pairings, most chocolate is simply too sweet for any dry red wine. Where a Cabernet Sauvignon and chocolate match can work, however, is with a very lightly-sweet mole sauce (dark chocolate-chilli) in which a savoury ingredient, such as chicken, is served. You could also try to get away with a slice of plain chocolate cake, without any icing, and a deeply-fruity, lusciously-rich Cabernet Sauvignon, but it's a risky business.

CAPE BLEND   Wine style; mostly red

The jury is still out on what constitutes a 'Cape blend'. Our wine-makers happily produce Bordeaux blends (we just have to call them something else) and, like the Australians, we merrily blend variet-ies like Shiraz with Cabernet, which would be unthinkable in France with its strict wine regulations, but there are no official regulations in South Africa to stipulate which wines a 'Cape blend' should consist of. Broadly, the thinking is that to make a unique local blend – one that is identifiably different from typical French or Australian blends – a percentage of Pinotage, South Africa's 'own' grape, should be included. At the time of writing, this is still under discussion.

CAPE RIESLING

See **Crouchen Blanc**, page 68.

CAPE RUBY

See **Port**, page 88.

CAPE VINTAGE

See **Port**, page 88.

CARIGNAN   Varietal wine; red

Although it originated in Spain, these days Carignan is most widely grown in the south of France, where it is used as a blending partner with Shiraz and Grenache. This prolific grape yields robust, fully ripe, fruity wines with pepper, ginger, leather and game aromas. It is rather similar to Shiraz in these aromas, but its profile is much softer and more velvety. It is therefore no surprise that it pairs well with carpac-cio, whether made from beef, ostrich or venison.

Carignan loves pork dishes infused with herbs, and will boogie with a spit-braaied suckling pig (or lamb or goat). If you'd like to show off your Carignan, do as the Sardinians do; they spit-braai a suckling pig using fragrant myrtle wood for their famous *porceddu*. We, of course, will reach for the *kameeldoring* or *sekelbos*. Seafood-lovers will find that rich, aromatic calamari and octopus stews (like the Greek *htapo-thi krassato*), made with red wine, onions and tomatoes and flavoured with origanum, come exuberantly to life with Carignan.

CHABLIS

See **Chardonnay**, opposite.

CHAMPAGNE

See **Sparkling wine**, page 98.

CHARDONNAY   Varietal wine; white

Wine drinkers either love or hate Chardonnay. Members of the 'ABC Club' (who, when asked what wine they'd like to drink, inevitably respond 'anything but Chardonnay'), complain that they don't like 'wood' in their wine, nor excessive butteriness. What a pity for them! Food and wine pairers have no such qualms. If we abandoned it, what on earth would we drink with our beloved 'tjicken maynays'? We are sure that such anti-Chardonnay feelings came about for two inadvertent reasons: either the ABC Club member was exposed to one of those early New World Chardonnays where the winemaker had a heavy hand with the wood, which left the wine drinker feeling as if he (or she) was 'chewing on oak', or they had the unfortunate experience of pairing Chardonnay with inappropriate food.

This is not a wine to match with hot and spicy dishes, sweetish food, or sharp ingredients (such as vinegar or sharp fruit sauces). Oaky or buttery flavours in a wine, especially in combination, cannot tolerate acidity at all. We can think of few things worse than a sip of Chardonnay with a typical South African mixed salad containing cherry tomatoes, Calamata olives, feta, capers or chopped gherkins, all on rocket leaves and dressed in a lemony vinaigrette.

But, with or without the support of the ABC Club, Chardonnay is still the darling in the vineyard as it is easy to grow and is a generous cropper in most climates and soil types. Winemakers love it, because it is putty in their hands from which they can mould a whole range of different styled wines: from light-bodied and austere to fat and powerful. They can emphasize its tropical fruit flavours or play them down and enhance its buttery profile. The food and wine pairer is also smitten with Chardonnay, as a happy combination of this wine with appropriate food is instantly appealing and satisfying – more so than with any other cultivar. No wonder it is one of the three traditional champagne grapes. We call Chardonnay the 'maiden aunt'. There she sits, ankles crossed (nothing so crass as crossed knees), hands neatly together on her lap, her head held at an angle with an ever-so-slightly raised eyebrow at anything approaching exuberant behaviour. The bite of vinaigrette is not her forté. This maiden aunt is, no doubt, partly to blame for the existence of the ABC Club; it is gentility that she's after and there is a whole range of dishes fitting this description. Oh, Aunty, what would life be without those comforting dishes with lots of cream and butter in them?

Despite being appreciated for the full-bodied flavoursome wines that it mostly produces, Chardonnay has a rather neutral personality (that maiden aunt, again). However, its character can be completely altered by maturing it in oak, responding so well to the influence of wooden barrels that its buttery, smoky, sweet-vanilla character is often the result of flavours it has picked up from the oak. Its other flavour profile includes apple, citrus, pear, pineapple, peach, melon, wax, honey, butterscotch, toffee and mixed spice. This very spicy, but non-confrontational, character encourages pairing Chardonnay with spicy food, such as schindlbraten, an Austrian dish of pork with paprika. It is less friendly towards herbs, though, and does not want to come near rosemary, which turns it into a medicinal taste reminiscent of the cough mixtures of our childhood. The food and wine pairer considers Chardonnay's neutral personality a virtue as this is the main reason why it goes so well with a wide range of food.

Three styles of dry Chardonnay are produced in South Africa. The first – when lightish, appley, crisp and unoaked, often from a cool climate (the warmer the climate, the more the wine fills out) – is particularly good with foods that can be overwhelmed by too much flavour in the glass. These include gently flavoured risottos and pastas, such as spaghetti dribbled with nothing more than good olive oil and garlic or pesto. Other dishes for this style of Chardonnay are light salad starters dressed with mayonnaise, fresh oysters, and plainly cooked fish dishes, especially freshwater fish.

This style also plays a very useful role when you are confronted with the dilemma of choosing a wine to serve with mixed canapés at a cocktail party; Chardonnay may not be overly successful with acidic or very rich canapés, but it boils down to doing the best you can under the circumstances. It is also a very handy wine for vegetarians who often have vegetable terrines and creamed vegetables in their repertoire. Another bow in its arsenal is that it can be comfortably used for a 'one-wine only' meal as it can stand up to fish, meat and vegetarian dishes.

The second style, when lightly wooded, can stand up to richer foods, such as pasta, poultry and fish in creamy sauces. It is also good with asparagus and melted butter, snails in garlic butter, Caesar salad, mild Indian korma or other creamy, coconutty curries, guacamole and shellfish stews. Also with eggy dishes, particularly those containing cream, butter or cheese, and with soufflés and quiches.

The third style is a fat, powerful Chardonnay, full-bodied, packed with tropical lusciousness and butterscotch richness. The fruitiness is so pronounced that the winemaker can wood the wine to his heart's content as it just absorbs the oakiness while becoming more and more complex. This style can take strongly flavoured food, such as duck à l'orange, and rich sauces, such as a walnut or hollandaise sauce, provided that it is not too lemony. It is particularly good with crayfish thermidor or smoked haddock in a creamy, saffron sauce.

It is equally good with salmon (fresh or smoked), scallops, crabs and with fish, seafood or corn chowders enriched with egg yolk and cream. If you're feeling extravagant, try the wondrous combination of a crab risotto topped with truffle shavings. If you're feeling slightly less extravagant, or just prefer meat, go for a blanquette de veau, which mirrors the wine's creamy complexity exactly.

This third style of Chardonnay can also happily stand up to red meat, such as a plainly grilled steak or roast beef (but omit the horse-radish sauce); or pork casseroled in a creamy sauce, but go slow on the addition of mushrooms, because none of the Chardonnays are mushroom tolerant. It is very good with the lavish marinades made from mustard, grilled red peppers and onions that we often use for braaied pork or chicken kebabs. This style of Chardonnay has a nat-ural affinity for braaied food, anyway, as its own smokiness simply echos the char-grilling. Although it doesn't like lean lamb that much, it doesn't blink an eye at braaied fatty Karoo lamb – fat meets fat and smoke meets smoke. The fat content of cured hams (prosciutto crudo), provided they are not too salty, is the constituent that re-sponds to this wine. However, you can overdo the fat-meets-fat story. Mackerel and sardines, for example, are simply too oily to pair with this Chardonnay as it becomes too much of a good thing.

In most guises, Chardonnay loves all the creamy, fatty cheeses; not just the Bries and Camemberts, but also some of the hard cow's-milk cheeses, like Caerphilly, Cheddar and Parmesan. It is not happy with pungent cheeses, such as the blue-veined ones, or with acidic goat's-milk cheeses.

CHENIN BLANC   Varietal wine; white

This grape variety has been present on our shores since 1655, when it was one of the original selection of grapevine cuttings received by Jan van Riebeeck for planting at the Cape. It subsequently became the work-horse of the budding wine industry in the Cape Colony. It is still the most widely planted white grape variety in South Africa for various reasons, not least of which is that you can make any style of wine from this versatile berry, from dry white to medium sweet, to botrytised or fortified wine, and even spirits.

Chenin Blanc used to be made into plenty of easy-drinking, soft, crisp and fruity wines. These days it is taken more seriously by a number of winemakers, many of whom produce concentrated and interesting wines, often carefully wooded, that are attracting attention from wine drinkers in the UK and Europe. The Chenin Blanc grape has a high natural acidity and some European versions, particularly, can produce wines with the potential for great longevity.

South Africa's climate provides favourable conditions for Chenin Blanc, which needs a lot of sun to ripen properly, bringing its intense fruity flavours to the fore and softening its nerve-tingling acidity. It is this bracing acidity that, incidentally, makes Chenin Blanc so useful in the production of dry sparkling wine.

Chenin Blanc displays aromas and flavours of apples, apricots, honey and nuts, especially walnuts, hazelnuts and almonds (which also manifests as marzipan). It is this nuttiness that recalls the smell of a wet woollen jersey drying on the back of a chair in front of a heater – an often-used description of Chenin.

When it comes to pairing with food, Chenin Blanc's acidity is very useful to serve alongside a dish with a lot of fat to cut through, in the same way as a squeeze of lemon does on a piece of fried fish. This is also why it is so good with avocado and with brandade (a pâté-like purée of salt cod, olive oil and milk). It also works very well with the sharp, lemony flavours in dishes that require a wine with good acidity, whether the main ingredient is fish, poultry or vegetables.

Serve a dry Chenin with salads, plainly grilled fish, especially the milder freshwater species (such as trout and tilapia), with shellfish, and with stuffed baby marrows (courgettes).

A semi-sweet style is particularly good with savoury dishes that have a touch of sweetness to them, like gammon glazed with honey and fruit, duck in fruity sauces, Peking duck with its brush of hoisin sauce, dim sum, gravlax/gravadlax, and fish in creamy sauces.

Either a dry or a semi-sweet Chenin Blanc will pair well with hot and sour Indian vindaloo curries, or with a Cape Malay curry that incorporates lemon juice and zest.

A wooded Chenin Blanc is the exact match to French onion tart, as the fruitiness of the wine works exceptionally well with the sweetness of the onions, while the butteriness from the oak complements the rich, creamy, savoury custard of the filling.

For late harvest, special late harvest and botrytized Chenin Blanc (noble late harvest), see those listings elsewhere in this chapter.

Chenin Blanc is not happy with classic red meat dishes or with bold and robust preparations, which would overpower it. When made in the dry style, it will not go well with sweet food.

CINSAUT (CINSAULT)   Varietal wine; red

Because this grape is drought resistant and a prolific bearer, it is not surprising that Cinsaut was the most planted red wine variety in South Africa until the mid-1960s. If you're of a certain age, you'll no doubt remember the red wine that got you started: Tassies. Cinsaut was the grape variety that supplied legions of young South Africans with their favourite, affordable tipple. In South Africa, at that time, through some confusion, the Cinsaut grape was called Hermitage, a well-known grape variety of the northern Rhône. Pinotage, which originated in South Africa, is a crossing of Pinot Noir and the so-called Hermitage (Cinsaut); the name being a combination of its parentage (see **Pinotage** later in this chapter for the whole story).

Unless the Cinsaut vine is prevented from over-bearing, it produces light, unremarkable wines. At its best, it makes soft, delicate wines and, immediately after bottling, it has a very aromatic profile, which is short-lived. This profile is one of jammy fruit, and the rather attractive whiff of fresh paint. It can also be peppery and sometimes reminiscent of fresh ginger. Cinsaut's lack of structure is the reason why it is mostly blended with red varieties that have some backbone; it immediately adds suppleness, berry-fruit and floral-like perfume aromas to red blends. Cinsaut also produces some delightful rosés.

This easy-drinking wine enjoys everyday, straightforward food, such as a Margherita pizza, 'spag bol', cottage pie, chorizo and pepperoni. It is the answer to braaied spareribs with their sticky, sweet sauces. As it seldom picks a fight with food, Cinsaut can be paired successfully with many fish and seafood dishes that are generally difficult to match with most red wines.

CLARET   Wine style; red

Claret is an English term used to describe the red wines of Bordeaux. Locally, it is used, albeit infrequently, for wines made in the style of a typical Bordeaux blend. There are two theories on the origin of the word. One is that it could have been an Anglicized version of 'clairet', a wine produced in medieval France that had a very pale colour, rather like our modern rosés, as these wines were the result of a short fermentation of only two to three days. The other theory holds that the wine was named after the Earl of Clare, who held a position of power at the time when Henry II married a French woman, Eleanor of Aquitaine. See also **Bordeaux blends**, page 57.

COLOMBARD   Varietal wine; white

Not the most exciting grape variety, Colombard (sometimes written as Colombar) is rather reticent and demure. It was previously extensively used for making brandy in South Africa, and for cognac and Armagnac in France, but its star has waned as other varieties that deliver higher acidity have overtaken it. In South Africa, as in Australia and California, it became popular for producing inexpensive, light, soft and gently fruity off-dry white wines. With the aid of modern winemaking technology, such as temperature-controlled stainless steel tanks, and typical *boer-maak-'n-plan* ingenuity, South African winemakers have pulled a rabbit out of the hat by producing some very pleasant, easy-drinking wines from Colombard.

Although neutral in character, our Colombards have lemony flavours with a drop of tropical fruit and, often, an attractive, richer note of steamed mielies (sweetcorn). It is this neutrality that the food and wine pairer welcomes with open arms. You don't always want a wine that shouts from the rooftop, but you may need one that has no particular flavour, blending into the background and leaving just a general impression of a refreshing, lightly flavoured beverage. You know, the sort of bottle you would choose to enjoy with gently seasoned, informal meals, such as a salad dressed with a drop of olive oil, a lunchtime sandwich or a Chinese take-away. Colombard has its moment in the spotlight when paired with prosciutto crudo (or Parma ham) and fresh ripe figs, with wasabi-enlivened sushi, or with pan-fried fish or vegetables that need a light wine. Another attribute that the food and wine pairer welcomes is Colombard's ability to take a knock from prominent spicing, making it able to stand up to Thai food without suffering too much. Its 'star status' moment is when it is paired with Thai fishcakes (tod man).

CROUCHEN BLANC   Varietal wine; white

You will not find a bottle labelled as Crouchen Blanc in South Africa, although this may change in the future. Currently, the wine made from this grape is labelled Riesling, Cape Riesling, Paarl Riesling or South African Riesling. (Wines made from the German Riesling grapes are labelled Rhine Riesling or Weisser Riesling, see later in this chapter.) We are a country that likes diversity in our nomenclature, despite the confusion it causes! Crouchen Blanc is now more widely grown in South Africa and Australia than in its place of origin, the western Pyrenees of France, where it has faded into obscurity.

Crouchen Blanc produces a light, easy-drinking, neutral wine with a cut-grass and hay or straw-like bouquet. Sometimes, floral notes and tropical fruit flavours are also present. When grown in cooler areas, it takes on a delicate herbaceous character with a touch of lemon zest and, amazingly, a hint of earthiness. This wine benefits from a bit of bottle-maturation that allows it to flesh out a bit and develop a hint of honey.

Despite its neutrality, Crouchen Blanc has excellent acidity and will come to the aid of the food and wine pairer on occasions when he or she needs a wine to match the acidity of a dish. Not that a neutral wine needs to take a back seat, but we often need a wine that is not so in-your-face with its flavours that it would overpower gently flavoured foods. Crouchen Blanc's place at the table is with light, informal dishes. In South Africa, we love to make a salad with crisp iceberg lettuce as the base. Never mind what you add to it, if you use some lemon juice in the dressing, a Crouchen Blanc, never mind what you call it, will bring that plain old lettuce to life. But it's not only at the table that this wine has its place – you'll search far and wide to find a better still wine to serve as an aperitif.

CRUCHEN BLANC

See **Crouchen Blanc**, above.

FERNÃO PIRES   Varietal wine; white

Although there are few producers of Fernão Pires in South Africa, we are one of the only countries outside of Portugal that have adopted this variety, albeit on an experimental basis. It resembles Chenin Blanc in more than one way, being a versatile grape that lends itself to all styles of white wine, from crisp, dry quaffers to oaked versions, botrytized sweet wines and sparkling wines. Like Chenin, it has good acidity, and it likes the same food that Chenin is attracted to. The grape delivers an attractive white wine with spicy, muscat, honey, lemon, pepper and, often, vegetative aromas.

Known in the food and wine pairing fraternity as the 'peanut wine', it has a great affinity with spicy peanut sauces, such as those accompanying satay, but it is also very good with a rocket and walnut salad. It likes most mildly spiced dishes, and with it, you can't overdo the freshly ground black pepper on a creamy *fettuccine all'Alfredo*.

GAMAY NOIR   Varietal wine; red

In France, exuberantly fruity Gamay is used to produce Beaujolais, the well-known gluggable, young (nouveau) red wine that is released in November every year, shortly after the harvest. In general, wine made from Gamay is light and bursting with juicy strawberry and cherry fruit flavours. It is naturally low in tannin and has relatively high, fresh acidity.

The world-renowned wine geek, Oz Clarke, maintains that 'Gamay makes wine you can drink whenever, wherever, however and with whatever you want'. We agree. A light, breezy style of Gamay, slightly chilled, is good with salamis, hams (smoked, unsmoked, cured or dried), salmon and tuna, and guinea fowl. When fuller-bodied, it can take bigger flavours such as brown mushrooms on toast, pan-fried calves' liver, roast chicken, cold roast beef, pork chops, especially when served with a mustard sauce, and bangers and mash. Gamay is the ideal choice as a cooking liquor for poaching fish in red wine.

It is simply delightful served with prosciutto crudo (or Parma ham) and figs. With a bit of bottle-ageing, it develops a gameyness that pairs well with venison, with or without the traditional sweet accompaniments. Vegetarians will go far by matching Gamay to many non-meat dishes. Additionally, it is very good with two soft cow's-milk cheeses that originated in France, Brie and Pont l'Evêque.

An interesting observation we have made is that people who like a lot of salt in their food prefer red wines with low tannins. The reason is that salt, which enhances the flavour of food, does the same to the wine, that is, the bitterness of tannins are unpleasantly overemphasized. Gamay's sweet-fruit character can cope better with salty food than most other red wines, provided the salt is not over-the-top, as salt has an affinity with some sweetness in a wine.

A wonderful alternative to strawberries and cream is to serve bowls of unsweetened, ripe, juicy red berries with a glass of Gamay on the side. It's a heavenly experience.

GEWÜRZTRAMINER   Varietal wine; white

'Gewürz' is the German word for spice and 'traminer' refers to a geographical area in Europe, so the name literally means 'spice from Tramine', and this good-looking, pink-skinned grape lives up to its name. It is, without doubt, the most distinctively aromatic white grape, delivering an exotic, spicy, perfumed wine that has a taste of litchees and seems full-bodied, even if it isn't. It can have a slightly oily texture that emphasizes its tendency to low acidity. Once you are familiar with the exploding, voluptuous aromas of cinnamon, ginger, cloves, cardamom, nutmeg and rose petals, you can pick it out blindfolded. Gewürztraminer is made in many styles: dry (actually off-dry as they are seldom bone-dry), medium-sweet, or as a late harvest, special late harvest or intensely sweet noble late harvest.

With all these flavours and almost overwhelming aromas, this wine may sound like a trip-wire for the food and wine pairer, but it seamlessly complements similar food flavours. Spicy foods containing cinnamon and ginger find an echo in this wine. Of course, this is not the main consideration when selecting a wine to accompany a dish, as we should concentrate first and foremost on matching the wine to the main ingredient(s) and final weight of the dish.

The traditional food and wine pairer's primer would hold that Gewürz is the ideal accompaniment to smoked salmon. While we understand this sentiment (the spicy aroma and flavour of a wine that seems sweet even as it finishes dry would, theoretically, love the saltiness of the fish), we advise you to take care. This particular combination can be overwhelming.

Another listing you may find in that European-orientated primer is the combination of foie gras with noble-rot Gewürztraminer (see **Noble late harvest**, below). However, we find that a special late harvest Gewürztraminer is a much better match, simply because our South African produced noble late harvests are heavier and sweeter than their European counterparts.

An oft-repeated suggestion is to pair Gewürztraminer with spicy dishes, especially those from India and the Far East. Once again, we raise a note of caution, as many dishes from these cuisines are much too subtle for Gewürz. What does work, though, are spicy, but not very hot, Indian and Thai curries, and sweet-and-sour Chinese duck and pork dishes that are accompanied by hoisin sauce.

In our own cuisine, Gewürz comes in very handy when we need a wine for sweetish-savoury South African dishes. First to mind is our much-loved braaied chicken basted with barbecue sauce. Grilling meat in the oven or over open coals imparts a smoky, caramelized flavour to the browned surface that responds very well to a wine with equally emphatic flavours. It comes as no surprise, then, that Gewürztraminer with its spicy, sweet aromas pairs so well with grilled foods, as smokiness can be equated to spiciness. Hence a dish of smoked German sausages served with sauerkraut ('choucroute' in French), flavoured with juniper berries or cumin, with Gewürz on the side is so good, as it forms a spice-smoke-spice triangle.

Serve Gewürztraminer with richly flavoured pâtés, pork rillettes and fish in creamy sauces. The sweetness of onions, leeks and red peppers is particularly good with this wine: think onion tart, leek and ham bake, or stuffed peppers. Gewürz is happy accompanying strong cheeses with a powerful pong, such as Munster, and equally happy with smoked cheeses. It's that smoky, spicy thing again!

For pairing sweeter styled Gewürztraminers with food, refer to **Special late harvest** and **Noble late harvest** in this chapter.

Gewürztraminer is not happy with very spicy, hot dishes, acidic dishes with sharp-tasting ingredients, or with dishes that are too sweet for that particular style of Gewürz. For instance, if you try to match an off-dry Gewürztraminer with a lemon meringue pie, it will fall short as the wine won't be sweet enough. It is very easy to overestimate a Gewürztraminer's level of residual sugar as its extrovert flavours often suggest sweetness, whereas the wine may be dry or just off-dry. Gewürz is also not good when matched with plain or delicate dishes. You wouldn't think of putting a loudmouth next to a wallflower at your dinner table, would you? It would be a recipe for failure.

GRENACHE (NOIR)   Varietal wine; red

This drought-resistant grape thrives in warm climates and in inhospitable terrain, so it is no wonder it is widely grown in the south of France and the north of Spain (where it is known as Garnacha). Grenache has also been successfully planted in the Cape in small quantities. Unless the vine yields are severely constrained, the wine has a tendency to lack structure and, therefore, is often blended with Shiraz or Cabernet Sauvignon to give it some backbone. These blends, which are medium-bodied, moderately tannic and not very subtle, have lots of strawberry and cherry fruit flavours, spice, especially black pepper, and some ginger. Although we do not have many local producers who bottle the wine as a single variety, it happily comes into its own when it goes solo, producing full-bodied, concentrated, warm wines that are quite alcoholic, with peppery and jammy fruit flavours (rather similar in style to Shiraz). Rosé produced from Grenache has a prominent strawberry character.

Not surprisingly, it likes the same food that Shiraz does. Briefly, it is those highly spiced dishes, and food marinated in or served with sweetish sauces and relishes, that meet Grenache's bold, spicy and fruity flavours halfway. It's the same refrain of pepperoni, chorizo, chilli con carne, oxtail, Sichuan beef, teriyaki, peppered steak, Indian lamb dishes, vegetarian moussaka, cauliflower gratin, and so on, (see also **Shiraz**, page 96). Grenache also likes the same cheeses as Shiraz, in particular, a mature Gruyère.

HANEPOOT   Varietal wine; white

The Afrikaans name for Muscat of Alexandria is 'Hanepoot', the most planted grape variety from the Muscat family in South Africa.

For food pairing notes, see **Muscadel**, page 76.

JEREPIGO (JEREPIKO)   Wine style; red or white

Produced in South Africa in either a red or a white style, jerepigo is an unfermented dessert wine. It is made by adding alcohol to very sweet grape juice, usually from one of the Muscat family of grapes. The name is probably derived from 'jeropiga', a Portuguese term for grape must that has been prevented from fermenting by the addition of spirit. The wines are richly toffeed, with intense ripe fig and Muscat flavours.

For food pairing notes, see **Muscadel**, page 76.

LATE HARVEST   Wine style; white

'Late harvest', a term used to describe the level of sweetness of a white wine, irrespective of the cultivar, falls after semi-sweet and before special late harvest in the sweetness spectrum (see below). Serve a late harvest wine with Peking duck, duck with olives, most dim sum morsels, goat's-milk cheese soufflés, fruit salad, apricot tart and apple pie.

South African winemakers have to conform to very clearly defined levels of sweetness in order to label a wine 'dry', 'semi-sweet', 'late harvest', etc. The current permitted levels of sugar per litre for still wines are shown in the table below:

Maximum permitted sugar levels for still wine

Dry	5g/l (grams per litre)
Off-dry	5–12g/l
Semi-sweet	5–30g/l (often more than 12g/l)
Late harvest	20–30g/l
Special late harvest	>20g/l Bigger-bodied (with more concentrated fruit) than a late harvest
Natural sweet	>20g/l Bigger-bodied than a special late harvest; with no or very little botrytis
Noble late harvest	>50g/l The wine must have sufficient botrytis to be labelled noble late harvest

Note: the sugar levels for sparkling wines are different to the levels for still wine. See **Sparkling wine**, page 98.

MALBEC   Varietal wine; red

Although it is one of the five traditional grape varieties in Bordeaux, Malbec is today more associated with Cahors, in southwestern France, and with Argentina. In South Africa, where it does extremely well, it is used in blends and as a single varietal wine. In its own right, it is a rich, velvety, lush-textured, fairly robust, plummy wine with medium tannins, a hint of spice and a touch of liquorice.

If Cab Sav is the wine for lamb, then Malbec is the wine for beef, which it adores in all shapes and styles: grilled, braaied, roasted, poached, casseroled or stewed.

Matambre (literally 'to kill hunger'), Argentina's famous dish of rolled beef stuffed with spinach, carrots, hard-boiled eggs and onion and then poached in beef broth, is a case in point; as is the Argentinian beef stew, *carbonada criolla*, with its pumpkin, corn, peaches and pears. Staying in South America, the slightly spicy character of a Malbec goes well with beef empenadas, a fold-over pie filled with a mixture of spicy minced meat and raisins (picadillo).

Across the ocean and into France, we encounter cassoulet, which combines haricot beans with a selection of traditional meats: pork, lamb, sausages, game, beef and preserved goose – an example of the hearty, nourishing, rustic fare that Malbec pairs so well with. Duck confit is another example, especially when mushrooms are added. It also leaves its calling card with those 'knife, fork and spoon' soups, such as garbure, a thick, satisfying vegetable broth, with cabbage the predominant ingredient and sometimes incorporating ham, as well as with thinner, but equally flavourful soups, such as tourin, made from onion, garlic and egg yolks.

We have many similar dishes of equal weight and flavour in South Africa – like boontjiesop, lentil soup, pea and ham or goulash soups, and our own hearty, rich stews, such as oxtail. Lighter dishes, like beef hash, or anything incorporating red peppers, are equally good with Malbec. And, of course, this is a wine that can be invited to every steak braai. It will even cope reasonably well with the creamy pepper sauce poured over your char-grilled steak, although this is really Shiraz territory.

MERLOT   Varietal wine; red

Although very similar to Cab, Merlot is softer, less tannic, juicier and seemingly sweeter. It also has a distinctive, but less pronounced, blackcurrant aroma. Merlot is plummier and spicier, with clear fruitcake aromas and less of Cab's minty or lead-pencil characters. Sometimes, it can be more floral than fruity. Clear blackberry and chocolate aromas with a touch of smokiness are very typical of Merlot. Merlot's soft-toned character is the reason why it is most often the wine of choice to blend with Cabernet Sauvignon, as it softens the characteristic edges of that variety – a clear case of 'good-cop, bad-cop'. Cabernet Sauvignon may be the most admired member of the partnership, but Merlot is the more loveable one.

Producing Merlot is not without its headaches; coaxing all those soft, purple-fruit flavours from the grape takes some doing. It is also particular about climate, preferring a warmer one, and particular about what happens in the cellar, preferring a soft touch.

Foods for Merlot are similar to those that pair well with Cabernet. For instance, it has an affinity for the curries from northern India, but chill the wine slightly. Its 'sweeter', softer character suits pork, oxtail, rich quail dishes and turkey much better than Cab Sav. Unlike Cab, it can partner fresh grilled tuna, provided the Merlot is not tannic.

Where Cabernet Sauvignon has a 'thing' for lamb, Merlot's penchant is for calves' or lamb's liver (especially when it is pan-fried with onions, as these add another layer of sweetness).

One significant difference between the two is their attitude to a tangy barbecue sauce: Cab wouldn't be seen dead in its company but, provided the Merlot has low tannins, it is more accommodating.

Generally, Merlot pairs very well with beef carbonnade (beef braised in ale), pulse-based stews, and everyday home-style dishes such as cottage pie, goulash, steak and kidney pie, sausage and leek hot-pot, corned beef hash and, especially, moussaka. It has a special affinity for mushrooms and truffles or dishes flavoured with truffle oil. An unexpected gastronomic delight is Merlot paired with roast chicken (or any other poultry) and a sage and onion stuffing.

When the Merlot is light-bodied or showing very little tannin, it is an excellent choice as an aperitif or to serve with charcuterie and pasta dishes containing tomato. When it is full-bodied and fleshy, it works well with vibrant Mediterranean dishes, especially when spices are added, as happens in fusion cooking.

Of all the red wines, Merlot is among the most accommodating of cheese (with Sangiovese hot on its heels). Pair it with hard cow's-milk cheeses, such as Cheddar, Caerphilly, Red Leicester and Emmenthal. And, with Merlot, at last, we have an unfortified red wine that can be trusted with Stilton and the creamy blue-veined cheeses!

Merlot is not happy with delicate dishes, very spicy or hot food, or cheeses high in acidity, such as feta or chevin (goat's-milk cheese).

MOURVÈDRE   Varietal wine; red

This grape, which is starting to make its presence felt locally, has enormous structure. It offers pepper and ginger spices, gamey overtones and intense fruit, with blackberry aromas bordering on the intensity of an aerosol room-freshner. The wines are heady and high in alcohol, tannin and flavour. With all these great qualities, it is no wonder that it is often blended with Shiraz and Grenache to give these wines even more structure.

When produced as a single variety, Mourvèdre, which originated in Spain as Monastrell, falls right into the lap of venison. It has two defining moments: an exact gastronomic match takes place when this wine is paired with roast springbok served with cranberry jelly or sauce; its gamey character and ability to stand up to the tart, sweet berries in the accompanying sauce, results in a match made in heaven. However, it is equally heavenly with char-grilled venison steaks served with mushrooms, either as a vegetable or incorporated into a sauce. Mourvèdre is one of the wines whose intense flavours, big structure and complexity leads it to be paired with robust dishes and not with lighter food, such as plainly roasted beef, which it would completely overwhelm. Mouvèdre is also a perfect match to robust, flavourful Spanish stews and casseroles, typically incorporating red onions, tomatoes, green and red peppers, bacon or chorizo, paprika and saffron – again, the concept of regional wine matching regional food comes into play.

MUSCADEL	Muscat-varietal wine; red or white

Bizarrely, there is hardly a wine grape in the world that produces wines that actually taste of the grape itself; instead, they taste of a wide range of other fruits! But here, finally, we have one that exuberantly presents itself as a grape. Muscadel is produced from any of the Muscat family of grapes. In South Africa the two main varieties are Muscat of Alexandria (muscat d'Alexandrie, commonly known as **Hanepoot**) and Muscat of Frontignan (muscat de Frontignan).

If the wine is fortified, it takes place before or during fermentation. The latter production method adds weight and gives another dimension to the wine and, when muscadels are aged in wood (as a few are), the magic happens. (Out of interest, the world-famous historic wines of Constantia were produced from unfortified, dark-skinned Muscat of Frontignan. Not only Napoleon, but also Jane Austen, Charles Dickens and King Frederick the Great of Prussia were fans.)

If Portugal is indelibly associated with port, and Spain with sherry, then muscadel can surely be considered as South Africa's national fortified wine; affectionately known to locals as a 'sticky' or a '*soete*'. We produce red and white muscadels that hold their own with the best of the world's fortified Muscats. The ones from the Klein Karoo and Breede River regions are quite magnificent. You are not only aware of the perfumed grapes, but also of raisins, oranges, brown sugar and roses. It is as if the wine is infused with muskiness.

Muscadel is the ideal partner to the richest, sweetest of desserts. The flavours it prefers are orange, banana, ginger and nuts, whether they appear in the form of cakes, tarts, custards or creams, and it is wild about mincemeat – the mixture of raisins, sultanas, currants, spices and sugar used in Christmas cakes, pies and puddings.

Ice cream, which is normally a headache for the food and wine pairer, meets its match with muscadel – which is the only wine to successfully pair with ice cream. If you have neither the time nor the inclination to prepare an orange, berry, fudge, ginger or any other sauce to serve with ice cream, a glug or two of muscadel will do brilliantly. The wine already has all the flavours you could ever desire.

Next to ice cream, chocolate is the food and wine pairer's other problem child, but muscadel is a godsend when it comes to this otherwise impossible match. It sits comfortably with anything chocolatey, from a slice of the lightest sponge cake to a decadently rich Sachertorte or even to a Black Forest cake, with its kirsch and black cherries encased in cream and decorated with chocolate shavings.

Combining muscadel's favourite aromas in any concoction is like getting two for the price of one. Think banana split, with its melange of banana, ice cream, chocolate sauce and nuts; baked Alaska, with vanilla cake, fruit, ice cream and meringue; sherry trifle, irrespective of its recipe and, especially, a rich chocolate dessert incorporating orange flavours. Simplest, though, is to serve a glass of muscadel after dinner with a couple of almond biscotti alongside for dunking.

NATURAL SWEET   Wine style; red, white or pink

The term 'natural sweet' on a wine label indicates its residual sugar level, which South African regulations stipulate should be more than 20g/l. You will find, though, that wines labelled natural sweet tend to be bigger-bodied than those labelled special late harvest, but less sweet than a noble late harvest, with no or very little botrytis.

For food pairing notes, see **Late harvest**, **Special late harvest**.

NEBBIOLO   Varietal wine; red

A *terroir*-sensitive, thick-skinned grape that produces dark coloured, massive, dense and full-bodied wines that can be very tannic and acidic and are long-lived. The Italians use this variety to make their famous Barolo and Barbaresco wines. Nebbiolo is intriguingly perfumed and supple, with complex flavours ranging from tar through to cherries, violets, Turkish Delight and dark chocolate.

Full-bodied Nebbiolo likes robust, meaty stews, such as bollito misto (various meats boiled together and served with a sharp, pesto-like sauce), osso buco, sauerbraten, wildspotjie and rabbit stews. Because of its slight smoky character, this wine pairs very well with grilled and braaied meats, provided there are no sticky barbecue marinades or sauces present.

When lighter in style, Nebbiolo likes lighter food, such as chicken breasts wrapped in Parma ham and napped with a tomatoey sauce, pasta with meaty, anchovy or broccoli sauces, cauliflower in a cheese sauce, charcuterie and offal. It has a special affinity for mushrooms, truffle oil, or real truffles, if you're in that league. Because of its good acidity, it can even cope with smoked salmon. Nebbiolo also likes sheep's-milk cheeses such as Manchego or Pecorino.

NOBLE LATE HARVEST   Wine style; white

Noble late harvest is a viscous, very sweet wine with excellent acidity, produced from white grapes affected by a benign fungus, *botrytis cinerea*, commonly called noble rot. Under certain conditions in the vineyard, this fungus attacks fully ripe grapes, feeding off their juice and dehydrating the berries, which shrivel up into '*oumensgesiggies*', the wizened faces of the elderly, while turning brown and mouldy. The chemical chain-reaction that takes place dramatically changes the flavour of the wine and the resulting product is an extraordinary concentration of sweetness and acidity – an opulent, rich, almost oily texture with upfront fruit flavours in a honeyed *jus*. The taste is easily recognizable, as it also has a faint hint of penicillin (you know, that mouldy smell of the apple that you forgot at the back of the fridge) or an attractive overtone of boiled leaf vegetables. Noble late harvest wines have the highest extract of most wines; they are certainly the most complex and they also have the longest shelf-life of the whole range of sweet wines.

If you have even the slightest hint of an inquiring mind, you will no doubt wonder why on earth someone would use such unappetizing-looking grapes to make wine. In fact, three countries are famous for producing exceptional wines from these 'mouldy' grapes, and each has a different story to tell.

The oldest tale comes from Tokay in northeast Hungary. In 1650, the winemaker at a certain estate had to postpone harvesting his grapes, as all efforts were diverted by an imminent attack by the Turks of the Ottoman Empire. While they were under siege, the noble rot took over in the vineyard. When the threat had passed, the winemaker, who was also a priest, decided to vinify the grapes anyway (who knows why?) and the resulting wine was much admired for its unexpected lusciousness. The rest, as they say, is history.

The second tale comes from Germany where, by 1820, they were already doing selective picking of whole bunches of grapes to produce their auslese (late harvest) wines. When, where and how they stumbled upon the benevolent effect of noble rot is uncertain, but it is held to have been in the Rheingau area, as its climate is ideal for noble rot to set in. The famous Schloss Johannisberg claims to have discovered the phenomenon much earlier than the 19th century, though. The story goes that in 1775 a messenger, who annually delivered the permission to begin the harvest from the owner (the prince-abbot of Fulda) to the workers at Schloss Johannisberg, was unexpectedly detained. During the delay, noble rot developed in the vineyard. As with our Hungarian priest, the winemaker decided to make his wine anyway, despite the presence of this unsightly rot and the first of what is now one of the world's most famous noble late harvest wines, Germany's Trockenbeerenauslese, was produced.

The third 'discovery' of noble rot comes from Sauternes in south-western France, again from a specific estate, Château d'Yquem, which maintains that it produced the first French botrytized wine in 1847. Truth or fiction, to this day, this highly prestigious estate produces the most sublime sweet wine in the world.

Although South Africa produces brilliant noble late harvests, we have no similar romantic tales to tell. In the 1970s, we simply began following European traditions in those areas and vineyards that were conducive to the development of noble rot.

It is very difficult to produce a noble late harvest wine, as the winemaker is completely at the mercy of the elements. In order for the spores of the *botrytis cinerea* fungus to develop, the winemaker needs dampness, often in the form of misty mornings but, here's the rub – he does not want dampness all day long; he wants warm afternoons, to prevent the spores from developing too quickly, which results in the grape skins bursting and the juice being lost. Some producers admit that they must be crazy to subject themselves to this nerve-racking undertaking. In some years, not enough spores develop, in other years the cool weather of autumn arrives too soon, before the grapes are sufficiently nobly rotted. In any event, grapes infected by noble rot ferment with great difficulty. In winemaking, you face these difficulties or you back out. 'Not so!', said some Californians, who attempted to simulate the process artificially. They grew botrytis spores in a laboratory, sprayed them onto healthy, picked grapes and completed the process by exposing them alternatively to damp and warm conditions in the cellar. But, after their experiment failed, it was back to nature; either you have it, or you don't!

Grape varieties that are particularly susceptible to infection by the botrytis fungus are Semillon, Weisser Riesling and Chenin Blanc, but Gewürztraminer, Sauvignon Blanc and Furmint also succumb. Noble late harvest wines are mostly made from single varieties, often with a dollop of something else; the little-known Furmint combines well with Weisser Riesling and Chenin Blanc.

It is important to note that South Africa's botrytized wines are far heavier and sweeter than their European counterparts. This is partly due to our warmer climate, which results in higher sugar levels and therefore higher alcohol levels, as well as more intense flavours. These differences come to the fore when pairing savoury foods with our noble late harvests. What works traditionally in Europe, like the combination of noble-rotted wines and foie gras or sweetbreads in a creamy, sweetish sauce, may be less successful with local versions.

However, our noble late harvests pair equally well, if not better, than European versions, with very salty food, like Roquefort cheese.

Noble late harvest's happiest hunting ground is sweet desserts; this is its finest hour. As generalizations go, there are exceptions, as these wines are less happy with chocolate, toffee- or coffee-flavoured desserts. For the rest, go for it, from crêpes suzette, Bavarian cream and île flottante (floating islands) to apple crumble and stewed dried fruit with custard (if you don't have boarding school memories!).

Noble late harvest wines produced from Semillon are fatter and more opulent than those made from Weisser Riesling, Chenin Blanc, Sauvignon Blanc or Gewürztraminer. The intensity and richness of botrytized Semillon matches all eggy, cream-based or cream-dressed desserts, and it loves soft vanilla desserts such as crème brûlée. It is equally happy with lemon- and lime-based puddings, especially when cream is added, with ginger-flavoured sweet dishes and with classic cheesecakes. Remember bread and butter pudding from your childhood? Noble-rotted Semillon must have been invented for it. But, while it will cope with some chocolate- and coffee-flavoured deserts, such as a chocolate mousse made with milk chocolate, or a tiramisu, don't waste your prized or aged Semillon-based noble late harvest on anything deeply chocolatey.

Botrytized Chenin Blanc, on the other hand, gives us gloriously honeyed sweet wine with a vibrant, but completely harmonious, acidity. It is this acidity that makes it suited to fruit-based desserts like tarte Tatin, fruit tarts and flans, especially when they contain apple. It is also very good with cakes, pastries, biscuits and lightish creams based on almonds and hazelnuts.

When the noble late harvest is produced from Weisser Riesling it is, like the Semillon-based versions, very friendly towards cream-based desserts. It likes crème brûlée equally well, but absolutely sparkles when a citrus flavour is present. This is the wine for lemon meringue pie, caramelized orange tart and orange-and-sultana fruit salad. It is not too enthralled by chocolate, unless cream is present, as in pears belle Hélène, where there is only a smattering of choco-late sauce on top.

Nobly rotted Gewürztraminer pairs well with the same desserts as a noble late harvest made from Chenin Blanc, but it has a special affinity for pancakes sprinkled with cinnamon sugar and will happily accept an added squeeze of lemon juice as, like all the noble late harvest wines, it has excellent acidity of its own. Having a natural cinnamony character, it is no surprise that it loves any apple-based dessert that incorporates cinnamon.

PAARL RIESLING

See **Crouchen Blanc**, page 68.

PETIT VERDOT   Varietal wine; red

We associate Petit Verdot with Bordeaux, as it is one of the classic grapes used to add extra power to that region's world-famous blend. It is not planted in any great quantity in South Africa but, in recent years, a few producers have started to bottle Petit Verdot as single-varietal, age-worthy wines of excellent quality although they need time to settle, to enable the taut tannins to mellow. Like Cabernet Sauvignon, the Petit Verdot grape is capable of delivering concentrated, tannic wines, deep in colour, with ripe berry fruits. On top of this, it brings a whole range of extra flavours to the table: strawberry, blueberry, black olive, liquorice, violet and origanum. It displays an expressive individuality as a solo varietal wine.

Petit Verdot is not always easy to match with food, as its bold personality can crush almost any dish that is light and delicate. Choose dishes with considerable weight and character, such as ostrich, beef or wildebeest steaks. Lamb chops and other red meats are prime candidates, especially when they are grilled or braaied, as the charred flavours that come from these cooking methods mirror the slightly bitter edges of the wine's tannins. Hearty sauces, such as those made with brown mushrooms, wine reductions, fresh herbs, and red or green peppers, are fine with Petit Verdot. It also has an affinity for black pepper, which will tame its tannic bite. Use pepper as a crust to meat or simply add it generously to a dish.

Not all Petit Verdots are big and tannic, though. When you come across a softer, lighter-bodied wine, pair it with dishes such as roast chicken or quail, flavourful fish like snoek and maasbanker, and meaty game-fish, such as tuna or marlin.

PINOT BLANC   Varietal wine; white

Although it is less glamorous than unwooded Chardonnay, the wine it seemingly resembles, Pinot Blanc undoubtedly has a place at the table, as it seldom, if ever, picks a fight with the food. It may not be the most exciting grape, as it produces straightforward, rather one-dimensional and perhaps quickly-forgotten wines, but they are refreshing and can be beautifully appley, with a buttery texture similar to Chardonnay. What a pity that Pinot Blanc is so under-produced in South Africa, as it could be the ideal white house wine for most restaurants and an ideal all-purpose white wine at home.

When Pinot Blanc is at its most flavoursome, it is very good with dishes that have just a touch of spice. Not the complex spice blends of Indian dishes, but an aromatic whiff, for example, of nutmeg in a light cream sauce. It is also very good with herbs, such as in a sauce chivry, a tarragon cream sauce. A classic match is with blanquette de veau, a dish that has only a mild meaty flavour and a creamy sauce slightly sweetened by onion and carrots, with a touch of spice from nutmeg and cloves. Pinot Blanc has the ideal matching profile for this dish, as it is never too fruity, buttery or sharp. It is equally good with fish pâtés, terrines and mousses. In fact, most plain fish dishes benefit from Pinot Blanc's neutrality.

You can also pair it with crudités, the plainer risottos and pastas, such as spaghetti with olive oil and garlic (*olio e aglio*) or pesto, with cheese and egg dishes, such as quiche Lorraine, with onion tarts, Thai green curry, sashimi, and prosciutto crudo (or Parma ham). It is fine with salads where a protein has been added to create a light meal (but hold off on chicken livers). Vegetarians might choose Pinot Blanc to serve with a nut roast or couscous salad. It can be paired with goat's-milk cheese, although a Sauvignon Blanc or Weisser Riesling would be a better choice.

PINOT GRIS/PINOT GRIGIO   Varietal wine; red

Although Pinot Gris/Pinot Grigio is very established in Europe, it was a 'laatlammetjie' to the New World. Although the grape is the same, some of our local producers use the French term, Pinot Gris, on their labels, while others prefer the Italian, Pinot Grigio.

Whichever name you choose, this grape produces light, crisp white wines that can be rather neutral with relatively low acidity. However, with good grapes and tender loving care, a winemaker can coax out some complex flavours to produce a nutty, fat wine with spicy notes and a creaminess, almost like Chardonnay. When medium- to full-bodied, this wine hovers somewhere between Pinot Blanc and Gewürztraminer in character, being richer than Pinot Blanc but much less fruity than Gewürz. It is a versatile grape and you can make any style of wine from it, from bone dry to richly sweet. In South Africa, you will mostly come across the dry style.

When Pinot Gris/Pinot Grigio has good body, it is heavenly with smoked salmon. It is equally good with other meaty fish, such as monkfish and yellowtail and goes well with fish pâtés and terrines, and pan-fried trout garnished with almonds. It is also a good accompaniment to a lunch of cold meats and salads, to quiche, courgette or onion flans, pork with juniper berries, any dish containing smoked bacon, Thai green curry, and pasta dishes, such as mushroom ravioli or linguine with cream and Parmesan. Mildly-spiced food will find its echo in Pinot Gris/Pinot Grigio's own spicy character.

Additionally, it is a good partner to poultry in cream-based sauces that incorporate mushrooms, onion and white wine; a good example being chicken à la King, which has herby green peppers as an ingredient. Reach for a Pinot Gris/Pinot Grigio when cooking with bacon, mushrooms, onion, red, green or yellow peppers (particularly when these are stuffed and baked), or even when cooking with a touch of ginger, such as in stir-fries with pork and chicken.

It is very friendly towards vegetarian dishes, especially oven-roasted vegetables. A typical vegetarian dish of parsnip, onion, carrot, garlic, courgette, sweet potato, red peppers and butternut is made even sweeter by oven roasting, as their moisture evaporates and their natural sugars caramelize. A Pinot Gris/Pinot Grigio, with good fruit and some acidity, partners this dish to a T.

Italian cheeses, such as Asiago and Fontina, are good matches, as are Emmenthal and our own Natal Green Sage.

Pinot Gris/Pinot Grigio is not happy with red meats, such as a classic roast of lamb or beef, or with robust, bold preparations that would totally overpower the wine.

PINOT NOIR	Varietal wine; red

This red grape, originally from Burgundy, is as pernickety as a maiden aunt when it comes to the climate in which it is grown. It is also sensitive to the way in which it is handled in the winery where 'as little as possible' is the order of the day.

Generally known as the 'heartbreak grape', Pinot Noir has a history of resisting emigration to new climes and, when it is grown outside its ancestral homeland, the resultant wines never quite manage to reach the ethereal quality of those elegant Burgundies.

Pinot Noir presents the winemaker with two headaches: it either fails to ripen sufficiently in cool climates, resulting in a pale, weedy, thin wine or, in hot climates, it easily over-ripens, imparting cooked, coarse, jammy flavours to the wine.

Pinot Noir has a bit of an identity crisis: it is a red grape variety that thinks it's a white one. However, if you can crack its code, this turns out to be one of the world's great red wines, with a heady, red-berry fruit character, a silken texture and gamey complexity. When the wine is light- to medium-bodied, it has a medium-deep colour. Even when full-bodied, Pinot Noir never really presents the dark, dense, ox blood-like colours of some red varieties.

Pinot Noir is, arguably, the only red wine that succeeds in combining elegance with a whole spectrum of upfront fruit flavours. When young, it is all raspberries, strawberries, cherries and cranberries, as well as violets and roses.

As the wine matures, however, it becomes gamey, with an under-tone of compost or a well-hung leg of lamb. The description of Pinot Noir resembling raspberries soaked in beef broth is not inapt.

With its good acidity and low tannin structure, Pinot Noir is one of the varietal wines that jumps to your aid when you need to pair a red wine with acidic food. Most red wines lack acidity and their tannins clash resoundingly with acidic foods, but a supple, young Pinot Noir from a cool climate, low in tannins, light-bodied, and served lightly chilled, is the saving grace. It is the most reliable red wine to serve with fish, not just tuna and salmon, but also the less-meaty fish types. In fact, this is the perfect wine to serve for a 'one-wine only' meal – in other words, Pinot Noir will happily cope with your fishy starter and your meaty main course.

And, if ever there was such a thing, this is the 'poultry wine' *par excellence*. It loves chicken in every way, from roasted to Southern fried, casseroled and even microwaved. It also likes duck, especially when smothered in fruity sauces. If you want to serve a red wine with charcuterie (cold meats based on pork), then Pinot Noir is one of very few red wines that you could choose from.

Lamb is not Pinot Noir's first choice, it leaves that to the Cab Sav gang, but it happily partners most other red meats, including those served in a classic red wine sauce or basted with barbecue sauce. It has a special affinity for game, which echoes its own gaminess.

Pinot Noir is kind to vegetarian dishes, especially when based on mushrooms. It also pairs well with the dishes we grew up with, such as hash, meatloaf and cottage pie. On the ethnic cuisine side, it is a good choice for rhogan josh, even though it is made with lamb, and teriyaki. It is an absolute hit with soft, creamy white cheeses, like Brie and Camembert, which don't want to come near most red wines.

For a party trick, serve a bowl of ripe raspberries or strawberries (without sugar or cream) with a Pinot Noir. On analysis, it is not such a surprising combination, as it is simply a matter of fresh raspberries meeting the raspberry wine.

Pinot Noir is not happy with dishes that are too bold, or with strongly-flavoured fish and seafood (avoid mackerel, sardines and mussels). You should also avoid very rich dishes with lots of added cream and butter, heavy mayonnaise-based sauces, or any fiery hot preparations. Pinot Noir is all about subtlety. Therefore, it stands to reason that if a dish burns your mouth, it will also burn out every bit of subtle fruit the wine has ever had. Pinot Noir is usually on the expensive side anyway, so why also burn your money?

Of interest, Pinot Noir is a major component of champagne and top local and international sparkling wines made in the traditional way.

PINOTAGE   Varietal wine; red

Pinotage, a uniquely South African grape, was created by a series of planned actions and happy coincidences. Although well known in wine-making circles, the Pinotage story is relevant to the food and wine pairer as it gives a better understanding of why this wine works so well with certain dishes. So, let's tell it one more time.

In the mid-1920s, Professor Perold, of the Faculty of Agriculture at Stellenbosch University, cross-pollinated two grape varieties, Pinot Noir and Cinsaut (which was known as Hermitage in South Africa at the time). Why did he try this when he had one in 10,000 chances of success? The generally accepted theory is that he was trying to create a new variety with the good qualities of the Pinot Noir grape, which he admired, but better suited to the climate. Pinot Noir was not doing well at the Cape as the warm climate was playing havoc with plantings. He chose Cinsaut, which had been successfully growing in the Cape since the 1880s, as the other grape for the crossing, because it is disease-resistant and easy to grow.

How did this enterprising viticulturist do this? You may remember from your schooldays that some plants need the birds and the bees to complete the cross-pollination process. Grapes, however, are self-pollinating. In order to prevent pollination from occurring naturally, Perold physically removed the stamen from some Cinsaut flowers and brushed Pinot Noir pollen against the ovaries remaining in those flowers. The timing had to be precise, as the stamen of the Pinot Noir flower had to be ripe and ready to burst, while the seed-vessel of the Cinsaut plant had to be ready to receive a dose of pollen. Lo and behold, this cross-pollination took and grape bunches formed. When the grapes were fully ripe they were harvested and the seeds dried. He then planted these in his home garden. Only four seeds germinated – and the odds kept going down. Of the four seedlings, only one survived, but it gave usable cuttings. So, when next you enjoy a glass of Pinotage, think of that one 'lonely little seedling' that gave us all the Pinotage vineyards that exist in the world today; for Perold's pollination process has never been repeated.

The good Professor simply compounded the two parental names to arrive at a name for his 'child': 'Hermi+not' was considered, but it was 'Pino+tage' that stuck; it just has a better ring to it.

To create a new grape variety is one thing, but to create one that is sufficiently worthwhile to vinify and that will also be a commercial success is another. Although wine from the crossed grapes was first made in 1941, at Elsenburg Agricultural College in Stellenbosch, the first formal recognition came in 1959 when a red wine made from the Pinotage grape was designated the champion wine at the Cape

Wine Show. In 1961, the name 'Pinotage' first appeared on a label, under the Lanzerac brand. And the rest, as they say, is history.

Pinotage has taken on some of the characteristics of its parents, but it most definitely has a personality of its own. It is a variety that produces a range of styles: from light, gluggable wines through the elegant medium-bodied ones to full-bodied, hugely structured wines with plump berry-fruit and concentrated flavours; it also yields rosés, blanc de noirs and even sparkling wines. In the blockbusters, there are layers of fruit, spice and herbs that only Pinotage can deliver with such generous abandon. For the most part, the wines are rather like South Africans: open, friendly and unquestionably hospitable. Juicy red plums in a spiced, reduced redcurrant sauce is how 'killer' Pinotages are often described.

Generally, Pinotage has great depth of colour, with a vibrant blue or purple tinge. It ages better than most other red wines, developing a meaty complexity (like its daddy, Pinot Noir), strong raspberry scents with a hint of bananas, a robust pepperiness and, when aged in oak barrels, developing chocolate and coffee flavours. However, one characteristic the food and wine pairer celebrates is Pinotage's astringent character – an underlying savoury note – that is present even when the wine is brimming with fruit and has a lingering aftertaste. The wine may not have above-average acidity, yet it presents itself as if it does, reminiscent of a crisp white wine. This is very handy to the pairer who often searches for a red wine that won't be totally destroyed by the acidity of a dish.

When pairing Pinotage with food, it is no surprise that it likes more-or-less the same types of dishes that Shiraz favours, as both wines are spicy, peppery, densely textured and chunky. If we call Shiraz a slutty wine or 'the best stripper in town', then Pinotage is constantly sunbathing in the nude. It is even more uninhibited than Shiraz, presenting layer upon layer of fruit flavours without any hint of shyness. Both like robust meat and/or bean casseroles, or rich stews thickened with oats, barley or stampkoring. Both are totally at home with grilled food or at a braai and cope handsomely with a sticky, sweetish barbecue sauce. On the point of a bit of sweetness in the food, both Shiraz and Pinotage like smoked pork chops (kassler) with sweetish red cabbage, or any deboned roast stuffed with dried-fruit, like prunes or apricots, or that very South African creation, smoked snoek with *korrelkonfyt* or apricot jam. Likewise, both favour home-style dishes, like moussaka and goulash, and are equally happy with whole roast chicken, chicken portions glazed with honey and mustard, or with stuffed quail. And don't forget the vegetarian dishes based on mushrooms.

Similarly, Shiraz and Pinotage are brilliant with spicy food but they have the same response to curry, in whatever form: they baulk. As much as they like spice, they shy away from curry, which strips both wines of their fruit, leaving the drinker – rather unpleasantly – with pepper on pepper, which does not happen with other spices.

This is a pity, as it would have been great to pair a home-grown grape with one of our traditional dishes, bobotie. But, no matter how much we try, this is not to be. We need to look at other, non-curried dishes in our culinary repertoire to illustrate the concept of regional food pairing well with a regional wine. And there are many, foremost of which are our game dishes, such as springbok or kudu casseroles, guinea fowl pies, ostrich steaks and a *wildsboud*, often served with maroela jelly or stewed dried peaches. But we can look even further: Pinotage falls right into the lap of boerewors, *skilpadjies* (sheep's liver wrapped in caul fat) or, for that matter, any liver cooked with bacon and onion, and more contemporary creations, such as *Kalahari kreef* (venison or pork fillets wrapped in bacon) or *pofadders* (braaied stuffed sheep's intestines).

Pinotage not only pairs well with our local dishes but, like its soul mate, Shiraz, is also happy with ethnic dishes, such as Sichuan beef, chilli con carne and teriyaki. Both also pair with the same type of cheeses, those that appear to be spicy or with a touch of the barnyard, like our local Witzenberger (similar to Appenzeller). However, Pinotage is one up on Shiraz when it comes to mild Gouda. No wine but Pinotage pairs as well with an unaged Gouda.

When it comes to meat, Shiraz has the edge over Pinotage with rare, plainly roasted beef, which over-emphasizes Pinotage's seemingly acidic character, but Pinotage differs from Shiraz in its greater tolerance of lamb. Pinotage's underlying savoury ('acidic') note, which Shiraz does not have, can cut through copious amounts of fat, butter, cream or oil, so you can happily lard that piece of lean venison and needn't hold back on the cream in the accompanying sauce. And, just as Shiraz has a moment of glory when paired with a kangaroo steak, Pinotage takes its moment in the spotlight when sitting alongside a wildebeest steak. Talk about matching regional food with regional wine!

Pinotage is unhappy with most delicate food, with most types of fish and fish dishes (apart from the aforementioned snoek), and with fiery, hot food. Full-bodied Pinotages can be high in alcohol; in winespeak, the term used is 'hot'. The combination of seriously spicy food and alcohol actually can be painful in the mouth.

PORT	**Wine style; red or white**

Port, that characterful liquid, may no longer call itself by that name unless it was produced in Portugal, according to bilateral agreements between the EU and other port-producing countries. South Africa uses the name 'Cape' to replace the forbidden word on labels: Cape Ruby, Cape Tawny, and so on, depending on the style of 'port', oops!, in the bottle. Port, by whatever name, is a sweet, fortified, heavy, flavourful red (sometimes white) wine of distinction. As many a port producer would say, 'all wines would be a port, if they could!'.

In days of yore, especially in the UK, sherry was the classic aperitif and port was the tipple you drank later, after the pudding, when the cheese was served (and no wonder, for Stilton and Cheddar are madly in love with port). Of course, the port sipping could continue late into the night, especially once the ladies had withdrawn and the cigars were lit. The 'passing of the port' ritual at the end of a meal endures in some quarters, even if the drinkers don't always remember if it should be passed from left to right or from right to left.

Although the classic Portuguese grape varieties, such as Touriga Nacional, Tinta Barocca or Souzão, are being used more frequently to produce port in South Africa, Shiraz is often still used. The grapes are crushed and fermented, and the moment the desired level of sweetness and colour extraction have been achieved, the fermenting juice is pressed from the skins and a fortifying spirit (normally brandy spirit) is added to stop fermentation and preserve the wine. The wine is then aged in wood, with the length of maturation being determined by the style of port the winemaker wishes to produce.

So, who thought of adding brandy to wine? Well, it happened by accident. In the early 18th century, England and France weren't getting along too well (nothing new there) and the French stopped shipping their wines to England. This was a blow to the Brits, who were great wine drinkers, so they had to look elsewhere. They'd been importing Portuguese wines, but were not overly enthusiastic about them – irrespective of your relationship with the French, once you've enjoyed their wines, you're spoilt for life. After a particularly hot harvest one year, the Portuguese red wines, which had unusually high sugar levels, did not complete fermentation before they were due to be shipped to England. To ensure that his wines reached their destination without turning into red bubbly, one of the shippers had the bright idea of adding some brandy to his casks in order to stabilize the wine for the journey. *Voilà!* Port was born. This sweet wine, with its kick of added alcohol, was a spectacular success among the English and, ever since, the port trade has been in British hands, hence the English brand names on so many bottles of the 'real thing'.

We discuss five styles of port in our pairing suggestions: ruby, vintage and vintage reserve, late bottled vintage, tawny and white.

Ruby This aptly named ruby-coloured wine is made in a lighter style, often blended from different vintages and aged in wood for at least six months. Ruby is the fruitiest of all the ports, reminiscent of flambéd Christmas pudding, with its raisins, cherries and preserved citrus peel. Clear floral notes are often present.

For years, food and wine pairers recommended ruby port, sweet sherry or muscadel to pair with curries, and it is easy to understand why they did so, as the most aromatic curries are at their best with equally aromatic wines, which ruby port certainly is. But we are not convinced, and there are better wines for curries. When paired with curry, ruby port becomes overpoweringly aromatic and too spirity, spoiling both itself and the curry.

However, this port happily participates in the salt-sweet harmony that exists between most food and wine. Try it with salted nuts or strong, salty cheeses to experience this partnership.

Ruby's port of call is also very much dark chocolate, desserts and cakes made with dark choclate, caramelized orange segments with raisins, and Christmas pudding, cake and mince pies. Avoid non-chocolate cream- and egg-based desserts and fresh fruit.

Vintage and vintage reserve As the names suggest, these are ports made in a particular year (or vintage), which appears on the label. When a winemaker has good-quality grapes in a single year, he would 'call', or declare, a vintage, or even a vintage reserve, if the grapes have ripened to perfection, and then mature the wine in wood for at least two years before bottling it. Vintage ports are rich, deeply coloured, very sweet, intensely fruity with blackcurrants, plums and dried figs, and often chocolatey. When pairing vintage port with food, three things come to mind: salt, chocolate, and dried or candied fruit. Hard cow's-milk and blue cheeses, plain chocolate, chocolate cakes and desserts, and desserts incorporating sweet dried fruits are ideal choices to pair with vintage ports.

Late bottled vintage Again, the name says it all. This is vintage port that was bottled after four to five years in wood. It is similar to vintage and vintage reserve port, but the flavours are doubly intense. As the flavour intensity of the port increases, so the flavour intensity of the foods mentioned above can increase.

Tawny This is a port that has received lengthy ageing in wood, anything from 8–40 years. There are no regulations to compel the winemaker to indicate the maturation period on the label; often he will simply bottle the wine the moment he is satisfied that the port has reached the required character of a tawny. But what's in the name? A tawny is pale rather than brown: in fact it tends to be an orange-brown colour, with a mellow, nutty, toffee-like, slightly woody, dried fruit character. Unlike a vintage or late bottled vintage port, a tawny is best served lightly chilled. This aged port can survive an encounter with the heaviest chocolate desserts or saltiest of hard cow's-milk and blue cheeses. English Stilton and tawny port is an exact gastronomic match. But then, so is a tawny with a ripe Pont-l'Évêque (a washed-rind cheese from Normandy in France).

White port Often made from Chenin Blanc in South Africa, white port is the lightest and least-sweet of all the styles. It has a nutty, creamy character with floral whiffs. If you like something sweet before a meal, this is the only port that works as an aperitif, but chill it well. White port is an ideal partner for sweet-and-sour dishes, as well as light, cream- and egg-based desserts, such as milk tart, or sweet morsels containing almonds, such as macaroons, or coconut, such as Hertzogkoekies (jam tartlets with a coconut meringue topping).

PRIMITIVO

See **Zinfandel**, page 110.

RHINE RIESLING

See **Weisser Riesling**, page 108.

RIESLING

In South Africa, the term 'Riesling' denotes a wine made from **Crouchen Blanc** grapes (see page 68); whereas wines made from the German riesling grape are labelled Rhine or Weisser Riesling.

ROSÉ   Wine style; pink

The difference between rosé and blanc de noir is in the production method, resulting in slight differences in colour and taste. Rosé can be made by simply blending finished red and white wines to produce a pink wine, or by allowing a brief fermentation on the skins of red grapes. The alcohol created during this short fermentation extracts the desired colour. Rosés are mostly dry, off-dry or semi-sweet.

When blanc de noir is made, fermentation does not take place on the skins. Instead, the red grapes are crushed and the juice is slowly drained away. The depth of colour of the juice will determine the depth of colour of the wine.

However, these different production methods are of little interest to the food and wine pairer. Rosé and blanc de noir both have the same affinity for the same food and, when it comes to food and wine pairing, they can be used interchangeably. See **Blanc de noir**, page 56.

RUBY CABERNET Varietal wine; red

In 1949, quite a few years after our own Pinotage made its debut into this world, a Californian oenologist similarly crossed two grape varieties – Cabernet Sauvignon and Carignan. This was an attempt to combine the profiles of two different grapes to see whether the sum would bring more to the cellar than the individual parts. The aim was to fuse Cab Sav's fine, noble qualities with Carignan's higher productivity and heat tolerance, in the hope that the new variety would perform better in warm climates. It did, but unexpectedly, the grape also proved to be successful in cooler regions. It just goes to show, you never know what surprises an offspring can come up with!

Ruby Cabernet had its hey-day in California in the 1960s, but it has become more obscure as a varietal wine since then. It was first planted in South Africa in 1982, and has done well in the Breede River Valley and other irrigated areas. An original aim, to achieve higher productivity, has been achieved, as it produces up to four times more grapes per hectare than Cabernet Sauvignon.

Ruby Cabernet produces a juicy wine with berry and plummy fruit, laden with chocolate, toffee and spice. When medium-bodied, it fits the mould of an easy-drinking, food-friendly red that can be partnered with a wide range of dishes. When chilled to bring out its fruit flavours, it is very enjoyable, especially in warm weather.

Serve Ruby Cab with barbecued meats, chicken, sausages, liver, aromatic Cape curries, prosciutto and home-style dishes such as cottage pie or slow-cooked beef and lamb stews.

SANGIOVESE Varietal wine; red

Italy's famous red grape reaches greatness in Tuscany, where it is the main component of Chianti. It is also blended with Cabernet Sauvignon to produce wines known as 'Super Tuscans'. Being a late ripening grape, Sangiovese does well in South Africa, where there is less chance of the winter cold setting in early, as can happen in Tuscany for, when Sangiovese grapes are not fully ripe, the resulting wine has huge acidity and hard, unpleasant tannins.

The name, which derives from the Latin *sanguis Jovis*, or the blood of Jove, indicates its ancient lineage; there are theories that the Romans made wines from this grape.

When Sangiovese is made in a light style, it is lively, pale and freshly fruity, with prominent acidity. Serious versions have much more depth, and can be medium- to full-bodied, firm, rich, dry and slightly spicy, with intense flavours of cherry, plum, herbs, tobacco and a twist of tea leaves. Sangiovese is often blended with other wines as, on its own, it can be too lean, tannic and astringent.

Sangiovese is a food and wine pairer's dream. When light, young and fruity, it washes down pasta, sausages and anything that loves acidity. It is gulpable with spinach and ricotta cannelloni, 'spag bol' and all tomato-based pasta dishes. It is great with cold meats, especially carpaccio, meaty risottos and lighter meat dishes, pasta with a creamy rabbit sauce (*pappardelle al coniglio*), cottage pie and snails in garlic butter. It is the only wine that really works with pizza.

When full-bodied, it would be hard to beat a Sangiovese with a char-grilled steak. It's quite surprising, then, that South Africa, Texas and Argentina haven't adopted this wine as our national tipple, but perhaps the time will come. Apart from char-grilling, Sangiovese works magnificently with all grills and roasts: chicken, pork, beef (roast sirloin with Yorkshire pudding is a winner), game and quail, plainly cooked or bathed in herbs. It is also very good with pasta with porcini mushrooms or truffle shavings (if you are that fortunate).

When eating acidic food, the trick is to match it with a wine of equally good acidity; conversely, when enjoying a red wine with some astringency, it is a good idea to pair it with food that has an acidic profile. Ever wondered why the Italians are so fond of squeezing lemon juice over their roasts, and sprinkling gremolata (a mixture of parsley, garlic and lemon zest) over so much else? We speculate that this is to match the acidity of their Sangiovese! Staying with acidity, let's move across to Greece and Cyprus where their *stifadho*, a sweet and sour stew, pairs well with Sangiovese. Or move north and match it with a German sauerbraten, which is also spicy, sweet and sour. Way down south, we have our own Sangiovese signature dish: tomato bredie; the combination is lip-smackingly good.

This food-loving wine will not be happy with just one cheese – like Merlot, it favours a hoard of them: Pecorino, young Parmesan, Pont-l'Évêque, Camembert, Cambozola and mild Gouda, to name a few.

Sangiovese is unhappy with spicy or fiery hot food. And, apart from tuna, swordfish and salmon, it is not at its best when paired with fish or seafood.

SAUVIGNON BLANC   Varietal wine; white

This is a wine to enjoy when fresh and young, when it is still intensely aromatic and crisp. When left too long, the freshness fades without the benefit of an increase in complexity, as with so many other wines. In the first place, the attraction of Sauvignon Blanc is its direct flavours and brilliant acidity. Should these fade, you can be left with a tired, unexciting little tipple.

Sauvignon Blanc is not without its demands on the climate in which it is grown. If these grapes see too little sun, they become tart and thin. If they are exposed to too much sun, often the case in South Africa, they develop a clumsy character with unattractive flavours of tinned asparagus and green beans instead of its intrinsic racy, fresh herbaceousness. It is also fussy about its soil types, preferring limestone and flinty soils, while not performing well in rich, fertile ones. In addition, this little number keeps the winemaker on his toes, as it is not an easy-going grape.

Although they are in the minority, some South African producers do oak their Sauvignon Blancs. The varietal characteristics of this grape disappear under oak and the result is a wine that, although crisp, has a definite overtone of smokiness and cream. Although the traditionalists raise an eyebrow to this, for the food and wine pairer, this 'blanc fumé' style adds another option. It certainly suits *groen mielies* (corn on the cob) and other sweet vegetables, such as leeks, whatever you do to them.

Under the right conditions, Sauvignon Blanc produces wines with a strong, easily recognisable personality: it is a 'nervous little number', with noticeably high acid, and flavours of newly cut grass, apple, tropical fruit, blackcurrant, green fig and green pepper.

A common flavour description is 'gooseberry'. Most South Africans find this confusing as, to us, gooseberries mean Cape Gooseberries, not the European variety, which is being referred to. When grown in its homeland, the Loire Valley in France, Sauvignon Blanc has a stony, flinty or smoky undertone. An oft-repeated textbook description of Sauvignon Blanc as 'cat's pee on a gooseberry bush' is so prevalent in Sancerre and Pouilly-Fumé (two French regions where Sauvignon Blanc is made) that if you order a glass of 'cat's pee', you'll automatically get a glass of Sauvignon Blanc. Just make sure you can do it in French, *non*!

For the food and wine pairer, Sauvignon Blanc comes in handy when foods with sharp flavourings or racy acidity need a wine with a bit of a bite and an equally sharp texture. If you need a wine with good acidity to act as a foil to rich or fatty foods, it acts like a squeeze of lemon. This acidity, and the wine's herbaceousness, means it can cope with bitter salad leaves such as rocket, chicory and radicchio.

When it comes to food, Sauvignon Blanc's strong points include salads dressed with vinaigrette, goat's-milk cheese, lemon-garnished fish dishes and Thai food – if Thai food carried a banner, it would surely depict the Sauvignon Blanc grape in one form or another.

It is the tomato's closest ally, whether accompanying a tomato-based soup, salad, pasta sauce, mutton bredie or rhogan josh curry; no wonder it is referred to as the tomato-wine. Sauvignon Blanc is also delicious with fresh asparagus or asparagus quiche, with fish, including oily ones such as mackerel, with seafood salads, oysters, mussels and other shellfish, particularly tempura-battered prawns.

It likes vegetables too, especially parsnips and fennel, but here's a word of caution for the vegetarian: go carefully when combining Sauvignon Blanc with green vegetables such as broccoli, spinach and baby marrows (courgette), as they tend to overaccentuate the wine's herbaceous character. This is particularly applicable to the blockbuster style of Sauvignon Blancs that are now appearing in South Africa. These have explosively intense, vividly grassy, crunchy, concentrated green fig flavours, which are delicious, but can be over-whelming when paired with certain foods.

When it comes to cheese, densely-textured Lancashire and crumbly Wensleydale cheeses are excellent partners, but nothing is as good as goat's-milk cheese with a glass of Sauvignon Blanc on the side. For a decadent experience, try warmed goat's-milk cheese, what the French call *chèvre* and we call chevin, on a salad dressed with lemony vinaigrette.

Sauvignon Blanc is unhappy with savoury food that has a touch of sweetness to it, as well as with classic red meat dishes. You can try to force your palate to accept Sauvignon Blanc with red meat by squeezing a lemon over your grilled steak or serving lamb with a citrus sauce (a bigarade, say), but Sauv is a hard wine to fool.

One of the accepted ways of matching food and wine is by a vertical pairing (see page 28), but Sauvignon Blanc is not happy with very rich food. Although the food flavours will be amplified and taste good, the wine will be totally overpowered, which is what a vertical pairing does; so, if you care about your Sauvignon Blanc, don't do it.

SEMILLON   Varietal wine; white

Semillon, or *Sémillon* in French, known universally as 'the old work-horse of Bordeaux', is an important variety for the food and wine pairer as it yields a rather unusual dry white wine that is, generally speaking, very food friendly. If there were such a thing, this would be the 'ultimate food wine'.

Semillon is appreciated for its rounded, lanoline-like quality and its honey and citrus tones. It responds well to being oaked, which brings out its character even more. When young, it often displays herbaceous, grassy flavours that are rather similar to those of the much sharper Sauvignon Blanc, with which it is often blended. In fact, it takes on a prominent role as a blending partner, also with Chardonnay and Viognier. Semillon has the ability to age with grace, becoming rich, luscious, even more lanolin-textured and increasingly honeyed and toasty, as if it had been oaked.

As in Australia, which has adopted Semillon in a big way, it has carved a niche for itself in South Africa as a solo variety in two main styles: dry white, and ultra-sweet, botrytized noble late harvest. For food pairing with botrytized Semillon, see **Noble late harvest**.

Dry Semillon is the ideal partner for risotto, particularly when flavoured with mushroom, Parmesan and truffle oil, or with crab meat. It is equally good with prawns, black mussels (such as mussels à la mariniere), but not oysters, and with meatier types of fish, such as monkfish or yellowtail. It goes well with richly sauced fish dishes, and is simply marvellous with a traditional fish pie – what a good combination that is! It is also very successful with omelettes, spicy pork dishes, roast turkey and with guinea fowl pie or casserole. It shines with the ever-popular honey and mustard bastings on fish, poultry or pork. It is mad about maize in whatever form: from *mieliebrood* (corn bread) to Chinese sweetcorn or Mexican corn soups. It pairs well with creamy Indian curries (such as korma) and coconut-rich dishes (such as Vietnamese chicken curry). An aged, reserve-quality South African Semillon even stands up beautifully to red meat dishes, as its weight equals many full-bodied red wines.

Semillon is unhappy with hot or spicy dishes, with very sharp and acidic ingredients, even if the wine has good acidity of its own, with savoury food that borders on slightly sweet, and with blue cheese or goat's-milk cheese (chevin).

SHERRY   Wine style; from white grapes

Sherry is a fortified wine of Spanish origin. A dry base wine, made from white grapes and slightly fortified, is stored in casks for about two to three years in a 'nursery' (*criadera*), during which time a specific yeast, called *flor*, covers the surface. It is this *flor* yeast that gives sherry its characteristic flavour and bouquet. After the wine is fortifed to full strength, it passes through the solera, which is an ageing and blending process. Not all sherries are subjected to *flor* yeast, but all, except old brown, are matured in wooden casks.

South Africa makes sherries of Spanish quality but, according to EU legislation, we may no longer use the word 'sherry' on the labels. (Although we use the 'new' product names in this guide, we also use the word 'sherry', as we don't distinguish between the Spanish and South African products for pairing purposes.)

Fino and Pale dry (Fino: less than 20g/*l* sugar; Pale dry: less than 30g/*l* sugar). These are both crisp and dry with yeasty tangs of the *flor* yeast, and delicate flavours of almonds. Serve with gazpacho, Thai tom yum and Japanese miso soups, grilled sardines, chicken with cashew nuts, and ripe Camembert (but catch it before it runs!).

For many people, fino is synonymous with tapas, those savoury snacks of anchovies, chorizo, cured hams and olives. Indeed, fino is the only tipple that really works with green or black olives, as the wine has an uncanny salty flavour that echos the saltiness of both olives and tapenade.

Medium cream (between 80 and 115g/*l* sugar). This sherry does not have the yeasty notes of *flor* and is nuttier, darker and sweeter than pale dry or fino, with a recognizable wood character. Serve it with sherry trifle and blue cheeses.

Full cream (at least 115g/*l* sugar). Fully sweet, without the yeastiness of *flor*, but with discernable fig, prune and wood flavours. Serve with pecan-nut pie, fudge, sticky toffee or malva pudding, mince pies, or, at a push, with chocolate ice cream. It is good with Parmesan, if you like to nibble it on its own, or with 18-month or older Cheddar.

Old brown (at least 100g/*l* sugar). This dark sherry does not have the *flor* yeast character. Instead it is very musky, nutty and woody. Serve with the same foods as full cream sherry. And try sloshing some over chocolate ice cream for a different experience.

SHIRAZ   Varietal wine; red

Worldwide, Shiraz is gaining popularity, even presenting itself as a sparkling wine or an Italian-styled, full-sweet, red dessert wine. And no wonder, as this grape delivers a wine that is probably the most exotic of all the reds, with immense concentration and complexity. It thrives in warmer climates, which is why there are so many local producers. Australia, with its warm climate, has done something similar, to the point where Shiraz has almost become their national drink.

In cooler climates, Shiraz tends to be raspberry-ish, slightly lighter, more one-dimensional and more peppery than those from warmer countries, and often displays an undertone of violets and roses.

Our full-bodied Shirazes are powerful wines, headily rich, with gamey and ripe-berry fruit flavours, and considerable alcohol levels. They are multi-dimensional with layers of raspberries, blackberries and blackcurrants, full of mixed spices, evidently leathery (think luxurious leather seats in expensive motor cars), with dark chocolate flavours, rich and smoky oakiness and, sometimes, a hint of tar.

If you have a home cellar in which you lay down red wines for maturation, you will find that your Shirazes will reach maturity much sooner than your Cabernet-based wines.

It is self-evident that the exuberant character of Shiraz would lead us to pair it with equally exuberant food, and it does this with glee. In fact, we call it the 'slutty wine', complete with fish-net stockings. As in Chris De Burgh's famous song about Patricia (who calls herself

Delicia), Shiraz is the 'best stripper in town'. It bends over backwards to be accommodating and can often stay the night. Sometimes, it takes a couple of seconds before the wine realizes that it is out of tune with the music of the dish, but it will always try first.

Food to pair with Shiraz roughly falls into four quadrants. The first includes those intensely flavoured, slow-cooked casseroles, usually made with less-tender cuts of meat, which are already brimming with flavour. The casserole theme spans the globe, from Spanish cocido Madrileño (Madrid stew) to the French boeuf en daube, to Moroccan tajines and our very own potjies made with lamb neck, oxtail, waterblommetjie-bredie or soutribbetjie. Also in this quadrant are other non-casserole dishes that are strongly flavoured, such as herb-roasted or spiced meats and vegetables. An unbeatable combination is steak au poivre (pepper meets pepper).

In general, Shiraz works with a whole range of robust foods. Like our favourite stripper, Patricia, Shiraz undoes 'all her clips', and 'with a swing of her hips', happily touches sides with ethnic dishes from all over the world, from Jamaica's jerked chicken to South Africa's boerewors, Lebanon's merguez sausages, Mexico's chilli con carne, Thailand's beef satay, Japan's teriyaki, China's Sichuan beef and Turkey's shami kebab. With their moles, the Mexicans have taught us to enrich our savoury sauces with a little dark chocolate. Shiraz, already chocolatey, latches on to these sauces, including chocolate chilli sauce. However, this is not a generalization or intended to imply that Shiraz pairs well with all chocolate dishes – here, we are specifically talking about a savoury sauce enriched with dark chocolate and flavoured with chilli.

The second quadrant includes game, in all forms: hoofed, furred and feathered, ranging from pan-fried kudu or ostrich steak, roasted springbok haunch and venison pie to rabbit with prunes, stuffed quail and roast duck. Shiraz, with its inherent gaminess, laps it all up, like Patricia/Delicia, 'with a lick of her lips'.

The third quadrant includes grilled, braaied or barbecued foods. The pronounced 'browning' flavours that develop with these cooking methods are very happy with a wine that is intensely fruity, oaky and smoky. Shiraz seamlessly finds a match here – more so than with gentler cooking methods, such as roasting – as braaied food is happier with a tannic wine rather than a soft-centred one. Shiraz does not bat an eye at a rack of braaied spareribs with a sweet, spicy or sharp basting sauce.

This brings us to the final quadrant, which includes the sweeter sauces, jellies and relishes that accompany many savoury dishes. Shiraz's 'sweet' berry-fruit flavours, particularly in those full-bodied wines made from fully-ripe grapes, work beautifully with these sweet trimmings. Shiraz remains unflustered by cranberry jelly or sauce served with roast turkey, or the traditional sauces served with game birds.

As if it has not covered enough territory, and outside of the four quadrants, Shiraz also pairs very well with everyday dishes such as cottage pie, bangers and mash, beef cooked in red wine, mushrooms on toast, and a mild, rare pan-fried steak.

The pairing of Shiraz with three of the hard cow's-milk cheeses is unbeatable: Swiss Appenzeller (a local equivalent is Witzenberger), French Tomme, and a mature English Cheshire. With Shiraz, strong cheese with a whiff of the barnyard is a plus. It also stands up to a hard, matured goat's-milk or sheep's-milk cheese, but the combination may be too powerful for the faint-hearted.

Shiraz is unhappy with acidic food, with fiery hot dishes (which will increase the perception of its alcohol), light and delicate dishes, strongly-flavoured fish, and mild cheeses.

SOUTH AFRICAN RIESLING

See **Crouchen Blanc**, page 68.

SPARKLING WINE	Wine style; white, pink or red

In this guide, we use the terms 'sparkling wine', 'sparklers', 'fizz' or 'bubbly' for all wines with a bubble, irrespective of their origin or production method. When we discuss sparkling wine and food matches, we do not differentiate between production methods, nor between locally produced sparkling wines and imported ones. For the food and wine pairer, the most important things are a sparkling wine's levels of acidity and sweetness, and the grape variety used.

How is sparkling wine made? Champagne, the French sparkler, is made by a very specific method, called *méthode champenoise* or *méthode traditionelle*. South African producers use this same method but call it méthode cap classique (MCC for short) as they are barred from using the word 'champagne', or any term that sounds remotely champagnish. Champagne is made only in the Champagne region of France, and *basta!* with the rest. (French producers of sparkling wine made outside this small area of their country may also not call their products champagne.)

Without going into laborious details, méthode cap classique is a labour-intensive production method, as the second fermentation, which produces the tiny bubbles, takes place in the bottle and the resulting sediment has to be removed, bottle by bottle, to provide us with an exquisite hand-crafted product that is predictably expensive. However, the bubble can also be created in large containers, such as a pressurized steel tank, by a less-costly method called charmat. Even easier and cheaper is to slowly pump carbon dioxide into a base wine, called the carbonation method or, snootily by some, the 'bicycle-pump' method. It goes without saying that these three methods produce sparkling wines with different bubble and flavour qualities.

The **sugar levels** in sparkling wines are different to still wines. They are indicated on the label using traditional French terms. (For the sugar levels in still wines, see page 73.)

Maximum permitted sugar levels for sparkling wines

Brut (bone dry)	Although called 'bone dry', there is quite a bit of sugar in the wine, up to 15g/*l* (grams per litre).
Sec (dry)	This is called 'dry', but there will be more than 15g/*l* and less than 35g/*l* sugar.
Demi-sec (semi-dry)	This has between 35g/*l* and 50g/*l* sugar.
Doux (sweet)	The sweetest bubbly has more than 50g/*l* sugar.

Whose idea was it to jazz up wine with bubbles? Legend has it that sparkling wine was 'invented' by the wine-making monk, Dom Perigon, in the 17th century. The Champagne region of France is quite far north and fairly cold, and what often happened in those days was that the wines would stop fermenting if the winter set in early. The winemaker would unsuspectingly bottle his wine, not realizing that the halted fermentation would begin again with the arrival of warmer spring days. When fermentation takes place, carbon dioxide is released, and this resulted in bubbles forming in the bottle instead of being released into the air. And *voilà!* champagne was born. At first, this was not seen in a favourable light as the flimsy bottles of the time were bursting all over the cellar due to the pressure of the gas build-up.

As the story goes, Dom Perigon stepped into his cellar one evening just as one of the bottles popped. Rather daringly, he tasted the wine, and his reported comment was 'I am tasting the stars'. But this is the stuff of legend; the reality is more prosaic. The transition from still wine to sparkling wine was a natural process rather than the result of any discovery by a single winemaker.

And the problem of those popping bottles? It was solved thanks to advances in glass-making techniques by the Brits, resulting in the production of stronger bottles in which the wine could withstand the rigours of travel. The new 'sparkling' wines soon became the rage of London's café society.

So what do you serve with sparkling wine? Although it is generally considered to be a 'special' or luxury drink, to be hauled out at celebratory occasions or when a toast has to be made, sparkling wine certainly has its place at the table, and not only at the high table. Because of its reputation for opulence, it became associated with the kind of luxury foods that are served on special occasions, such as foie gras, caviar, black and white truffles, oysters and the finest smoked salmon. Apart from the smoked salmon (see **Smoked fish**, page 138), it certainly does pair happily with these luxury foods, but it also goes with more mundane dishes.

Even at its richest, sparkling wine is a delicate style of wine and you have to pussy-foot around it when pairing it with food, despite what the Champenois would have us believe. This lightness in style dictates the type of food that it can be paired with, within clearly defined parameters. Overstep these parameters and your sparkling wine will taste thin, mean and sharp, or the food will become like a bull in a china shop, breaking every fine nuance in sight. And why do this when you may have paid an arm and a leg for that bottle that now tastes like nothing special? One of sparkling wine's finest hours is when it is enjoyed on its own.

Brut and sec sparkling wines These wines work well with asparagus and artichokes served with their traditional accompaniments, with shrimps and other shellfish, seafood in light, creamy sauces, lightly dressed seafood salads, plainly cooked chicken, guinea fowl and quail, and savoury food served with almond- and walnut-based sauces. It also goes well with Chinese and Thai dishes, and with Japanese sushi and raw-fish dishes.

One of the reasons why these sparkling wines are served as an aperitif is that they counterbalance the slightly salty canapés and snacks often served at cocktail parties or with pre-dinner drinks. However, a fizzy wine can easily be overpowered when the canapés are too spicy, too rich (go slow on the mayonnaise) or too heavy. Step outside of those parameters, and you are in trouble.

Demi-sec and the sweetest sparkling wines A demi-sec is great with duck à l'orange, mild, creamy curries containing coconut, and light desserts. Wimbledon's tradition of serving strawberries and cream with champagne is a good example. They even get away with a brut or sec because champagne's good acidity and sweetness (in all styles) latches on to the strawberries' natural acidity and sweetness. Other light desserts you can consider for demi-sec sparkling wines are fruit salads, fruit-based mousses or fools, and light cream cakes. A note of caution though, even the sweetest sparklers are seldom sweet enough for the sweetest and heaviest desserts.

How does champagne differ from cap classique? The French product is complex with an underlying intensity and lingering flavours in the aftertaste, with three flavour profiles that New World producers (including South Africa) cannot readily achieve. The first is champagne's subtle, but very rich, biscuity brioche-like, yeasty flavours that are obtained from ageing the wine on its sediment (the lees). Secondly, champagne has a toasted, nutty character that develops when Chardonnay, one of its components, ages. Lastly, Pinot Noir, another grape component, performs brilliantly in the Champagne region of France, and the gorgeous, but very subtle, raspberry notes it imparts are unequalled.

Most local sparklers, and those from most other New World producers, for that matter, are heavier, sturdier, fuller and more overtly fruity, with less structure and softer acidity. But New World sparkling wines shouldn't attempt to be copies of champagne – they simply don't have the same *terroir* (those chalky French soils definitely play their part). If you want the real thing, just go out and buy it! New World bubblies should be appreciated for themselves and enjoyed for their own fine qualities. *Vive la difference!*

Should champagne and cap classique be served with different food? Generally, all sparkling wines work the same way with food. The prime considerations are acidity and sweetness levels. Thereafter, weight and flavour variations come into play. Certainly, there are occasions when champagne pairs better with a particular dish than cap classique and vice versa. Because South African sparkling wines tend to be fruitier than champagne, they are less successful with game birds, but they pair better than champagne with slightly weightier dishes, such as crayfish thermidor, guacamole, mushroom or truffle risottos, vegetable terrines and lightly spiced dishes. Our sparklers are also less successful than champagne with fresh oysters (served with nothing but a squeeze of lemon), but pair better with more elaborate treatments, such as oysters Rockefeller (grilled oysters topped with a buttery spinach-based topping).

Which grape varieties are used for sparkling wine? In France, a blend of three grape varieties, Chardonnay, Pinot Noir and Pinot Meunier, is used in the production of champagne, but single varietal champagnes are also made (most often Chardonnay on its own, with the resulting champagne being called a *blanc de blancs*). In South Africa, we use the same three varieties and make single varietal sparklers, but we also use non-traditional varieties, such as Chenin Blanc, Sauvignon Blanc, Pinotage and, more recently, Shiraz.

Sparkling wines made from different grape varieties are described below, with reference to their food pairing characters.

Chardonnay When made entirely from Chardonnay, the wine matches lightly dressed seafood salads and plain fish dishes, but not when richly sauced. The signature dish for this style of sparkling wine is undoubtedly a mixed seafood platter, which the French know as a *plateau de fruits de mer*, served simply with lemon or garlic butter. It also pairs well with gravadlax (gravlax), avocados filled with a seafood mix and even with avocado Ritz with its sweetish pink sauce. As a consequence of the sparkling wine production method, Chardonnay in this form shows good acidity, which finds a match in acidic and salty cheeses, such as goat's-milk cheese, Lancashire, Wensleydale and feta. It is also very good with Japanese raw-fish dishes and lime-flavoured Thai food, even if it makes the wine taste a bit sweeter and blander than it is (choose only a brut or a sec for this reason). Go straight to the demi-sec to pair with Chinese food, although a brut or sec would be good, too, as they also have some sugar (*see* page 99). Steer clear of red meat.

Pinot Noir and **Pinot Meunier** These classic varieties give us the 'pink' sparklers that the French call *blanc de noirs*. They are an absolute hit with rich creamy soups and dishes that have an inherent 'toasty' character, such as puff-pastry dishes. They are also very good with mixed canapés, especially those based on seafood. But steer clear of red meat as it is way outside a pink sparkler's parameters. Well within the parameters, though, are nuts. A selection of walnuts, almonds and pistachios are very enjoyable served with a pink demi-sec at the end of a meal instead of a dessert.

Pinotage and **Shiraz** Mould-breaking red sparklers made from Pinotage and Shiraz are something of a head-scratcher – not quite what you'd expect, but delightful nonetheless. As can be expected, there is a firmness to these wines that is not found in sparklers made from other varieties. They are densely structured, dry and often tannic. And no wonder, as Shiraz is one of the red grapes that is inherently more tannic than the others.

At last, a sparkling wine to match red meat! And it is red meat that is these new-age sparklers' closest ally – a braaied T-bone steak, served rare, with its chewy texture, partners them as well as the still versions of these varieties. But, be warned, the bubbles can get in the way, particularly after the second glass... If your steak has a brush of barbecue sauce, these sparklers won't blink an eye, as they are more deeply fruited than their still counterparts and, like all other sparkling wines, have higher residual sugar levels, so sweetness simply meets sweetness. Roast turkey with its traditional sweet trimmings, rich pâtés and mature goat's-milk cheese are also good with red sparkling Pinotage or Shiraz.

Fizz throughout the meal? The Champenois would have us believe that champagne is the one wine that can be served with a meal, from starter to dessert and cheese. Fair enough, but what they failed to mention, or we misunderstood, is that it is not the same bottle of champagne from start to finish, but a different style of sparkling wine for each course. The menu planner needs to work within sparkling wines' food parameters. For example, serve an ethereal Chardonnay-based sparkler with asparagus as the starter, switch to a more grounded one that includes Pinot Noir to accompany a main course of poached fresh salmon, napped with a dill-flavoured sauce and some fresh veg (but not broccoli, as it will make the wine taste metallic). For dessert, swop to a sweet sparkling wine to accompany apple crumble served with custard and, finally, open up a bottle of Sauvignon Blanc-based bubbly to go with a piece of crumbly Wensleydale cheese to end off the meal.

While on the subject of the Champenois, it is worth noting that their traditional cuisine is at loggerheads with their delicate, refined champagnes. The traditional food of the region is robust, stick-to-the-ribs fare based on root vegetables, game, hearty sausages and meaty terrines but, as these foods completely annihilate sparkling wine, restaurant cuisine underwent a change, resulting in lighter dishes more in tune with champagne's limited parameters. This is a modern example of how the phenomenon of matching regional wines and foods must have come about.

And what about the 'champagne breakfast'? We suspect that the gastronomically precise match of creamy scrambled eggs garnished with smoked salmon slivers, and accompanied by a sparkling wine, inadvertently got carried over to any old breakfast food, resulting in the ubiquitous 'champagne breakfast'. Serve a delicate bubbly with grilled boerewors, bacon and fried pork sausages, baked beans on toast, fried lamb's liver and kidneys? Um... no, we don't think so. Once again, our frequently repeated refrain applies: step outside of a sparkling wine's parameters and you're in trouble.

It makes more sense to finish that bottle of fizz before you start your breakfast, and then crack open a bottle of Chardonnay when the eating starts. No wonder orange juice is added to the fizz as they are like peas in a pod: they both have good acidity and sweetness, but mixing them intensifies the problem with, say, bacon and eggs. However, if you change the menu and serve the Buck's Fizz with fruit salad and yoghurt, ham with fresh pineapple, stawberry-filled pancakes (sans syrup), etc., you'll have a match.

What not to serve with sparkling wine? Spicy, strong-flavoured, rich dishes, sweet food, bitter vegetables and any red meat.

SPECIAL LATE HARVEST   Wine style; white

'Special late harvest' is a term used to describe the level of sweetness of a white wine, irrespective of the cultivar. It falls after late harvest and before natural sweet wine in the sweetness spectrum. In South Africa, winemakers have to conform to very clearly defined levels of sweetness in order to label a still wine 'semi-sweet', 'late harvest' or 'special late harvest'; see page 73.

A special late harvest wine pairs very well with the lighter egg- and cream-based desserts, such as milk tart, cheesecake, bread and butter pudding, crème caramel and baked custard. It is very good with fruit-based desserts, such as tarte Tatin, apricot and peach tarts and glazed fruit tartlets. It is nuts about nuts: think almond tarts, marzipan, pecan nut pie and Italian-style soft nougat pudding (*torrone molle*). Make life easy, skip the dessert and serve a medley of three nuts (walnut, hazel and pecan) with a glass of well-chilled special late harvest wine. Even simpler, do as the Italians do, and dip a biscotti or a chunk of panettone into that glass of nectar. Or go local and opt for a soetkoekie or a home-made ginger snap.

If the special late harvest is made from Chenin Blanc, with its good acidity, it seamlessly meshes with the acidic punch of lemon meringue pie. For another great experience in matching, serve a glass of special late harvest wine with a slice of Gorgonzola.

STEEN   Varietal wine; white

'Steen', the old South African name for the Chenin Blanc grape, was a widely used term in the past but is less so nowadays. Do not confuse Steen with Stein, which can easily happen as the spellings and pronunciations are so similar. See **Chenin Blanc**, page 65.

STEIN   Wine style; white

Stein, not to be confused with Steen (see above), is not a grape variety, but denotes a semi-sweet white wine of any single cultivar or a blend of several cultivars.

This useful wine pairs happily with a wide range of dishes, particularly when there is an obvious bite of sweetness to a savoury dish, such as glazed gammon garnished with cherries and pineapple. It is good with chicken, duck and quail in fruity sauces, and likes mustard sauces, especially when a drop of honey is added. Roast beef, when cold, needs a different wine from when it is served hot, and a stein fits the bill. It is good with scallops, crab mousse, grilled trout, smoked fish, and fish or shellfish napped with exotically flavoured dressings.

Vegetarians will find that a stein pairs well with oven-roasted vegetables, stuffed red peppers and dishes incorporating sun-dried tomatoes. And, when you are searching for a wine to thoroughly enjoy with Chinese food, grab a bottle or two of stein.

SYLVANER   Varietal wine; white

This rather neutral wine, which originated in Alsace and Germany, has a vegetal quality, rather like steamed cabbage and, sometimes, an appley or floral note. Characteristically, it has an attractive, earthy taste and, although it lacks a specific flavour profile, it can have good body and acidity. Sylvaner is often gainsaid by wine geeks as not being very distinguished or distinctive, but the food and wine pairer welcomes it with open arms. If a key principle of pairing food and wine is to match the flavour intensity of a dish with the same flavour intensity in a wine – aromatic food with aromatic wine, less aromatic food with less aromatic wine – what shall we turn to for a simple chicken stir-fry with no exotic flavourings, for rice-stuffed peppers, a pork and vegetable stew, plainly stir-fried calamari, or a gentle fresh-water fish, such as poached trout with a hint of butter and garlic? We turn to a wine like Sylvaner, which is not going to blow the roof off, but will meet these dishes head-on without overpowering them.

Like many wines, Sylvaner also has a signature dish from its homeland: eisbein with potatoes and sauerkraut. A close second is a gentle bratwurst (a pale-coloured German pork sausage), also often eaten accompanied by potatoes and sauerkraut. It also works well with frankfurters and with weisswurst (a greyish-white veal and bacon sausage). It is no surprise that we stay in Alsace and Germany when pairing Sylvaner with cheese: it sets the stage for Munster like no other wine would.

SYRAH

The French synonym for Shiraz. Some South African producers prefer this term and label their bottles accordingly. *See* **Shiraz**, page 96.

TEMPRANILLO   Varietal wine; red

Tempranillo, Spain's most important grape, is often thought of as their answer to France's Cabernet Sauvignon. It is the main component, blended with Grenache and other varieties, of the famous Spanish red, Rioja. Although the grape takes well to oak, there are unoaked versions of Tempranillo and Rioja.

On its own, Tempranillo shows sweet, rounded strawberry, blackberry and blackcurrant fruit combined with soft, buttery toffee-like flavours. When wooded in American oak, as it often is in Spain, it picks up a distinct vanilla flavour, which could be overpowering if it were not for the grape's good balancing acidity.

Oaked or unoaked, this is a very useful variety to the food and wine pairer, as it matches a variety of foods, ranging from medium flavourful to highly flavoursome. Tempranillo pairs as well with lamb dishes (whether plainly roasted or rich casseroles) as the *de rigueur* 'lamb wine', Cabernet Sauvignon. The lamb stew from Saragossa, *cordero en chilidrón*, with its tomatoes, red and green peppers, smoked ham, chillies, paprika, garlic and black olives, is a good example of the complex lamb stew flavours that Tempranillo happily copes with.

It also clicks its heels at spicy meat dishes such as kebabs, or at herb-infused dishes, like roasts under a herby breadcrumb crust. When not too heavily oaked, it partners Indian curries just as well as Cab does. Because of its sweet fruit flavours, it is perfectly at home with sticky barbecue or berry sauces and sweet condiments, and even more so when a sweetish ingredient forms an integral part of a venison dish. It loves not only the sweetish taste of kidneys in sherry sauce but also kidneys in a creamy mustard one.

But Tempranillo also pairs well with less intense flavours, as in stuffed red peppers, roasted chicken or pork, homely dishes such as cottage pie and bangers and mash, or composite meat salads and that typically Catalonian dish of snails stewed in a tomato, red and green pepper and chilli mixture.

We would be remiss in not mentioning Tempranillo's huge affinity for mushrooms, an ingredient that can be hard on many wines. This extends to dishes containing truffles or truffle oil. When it comes to cheese, we're right back with sheep: Tempranillo is mad about sheep's-milk cheese, so try a local Pecorino or, if you want to stay ethnic, go for a Spanish Manchego.

TINTA BAROCCA — Varietal wine; red

This was the most popular port grape in South Africa for years, but it is also used to produce a red table wine. As in Portugal, its country of origin, Tinta Barocca does very well in arid, hot conditions, delivering sturdy, dark-skinned grapes that are all cherries, pepper, blackberries, spice and plum jam. Herbs abound, quite opposite in character to the 'greener' flavours of Merlot and Cab. The wine also displays a juicy acidity, like that of verjuice.

As a red table wine, it is treasured by the food and wine pairer as a well-rounded, full-bodied, immensely fruity red wine, with an uncanny delicacy and striking purity.

As dishes that pair well with Tinta Barocca are similar to those that pair with **Touriga Nacional**, see that entry, opposite, for recommendations on food and wine pairing.

TOURIGA NACIONAL   Varietal wine; red

More and more South African wine producers are experimenting with Portuguese varieties, which are suited to our climate. Touriga Nacional, the most revered port variety, is used to produce red table wines, even though the grape is more suitable for port. As a red table wine it shows all the flavours, concentration and richness of port: spiciness, dark, ripe berry fruit, but without port's sweetness, alcohol and tannins. As in Portugal, which produces some exciting, 'new' red wines, South African winemakers also conjure up some full-throttle Touriga Nacionals that roar like a souped-up racing car. Needless to say, this wine likes the same souped-up foods, not the more dainty dishes that are more at home with a family sedan.

Serve Touriga Nacional with caldo verde, the Portuguese vegetable soup made with potatoes and cabbage and pepped up with olive oil and chorizo, with rustic, spicy, garlicky stews such as a pork and bean casserole, or with Mexican refried beans.

VIOGNIER   Varietal wine; white

This difficult to grow variety has been a bit of a cult wine since it became rather fashionable in South Africa in the 1990s. Even in a good year, its yields are low, which is partly the reason why it is a relatively expensive wine to purchase. It has an exuberant character: head-spinningly perfumed and opulent, but dry, in spite of lowish acidity, full-bodied, and with seductive flavours of apricot, peach, musk and lime blossom. Some people feel it is a wine that should be enjoyed when young, as this is when its extraordinary scented spiciness is at its peak, but it all depends on what you pair it with.

As is often the case with gloriously lush, aromatic wines, Viognier is not that easy to match with food. Predictably, it does best with spicy food, such as an Indian korma, and other mild to medium aromatic curries, extending even to the hotter Thai red curry and Indian vindaloo. Viognier is at home with these ethnic cuisines, as well as with those of China and Vietnam; often, of its own accord, it will echo the aromatic spices used. Depending on the main ingredient, it will latch onto ginger with enthusiasm (but, of course, you would not serve Viognier with ice cream topped with preserved ginger, as the wine will not be sweet enough). Its muskiness also leads to an affinity with mushrooms (and truffle oil or truffles, if you're in that league), depending on the dish to which the mushrooms or truffle shavings are added.

Viognier is very good with the rich, sweet flavours of crab and crayfish, and likes fish and seafood in creamy sauces, particularly when flavoured with saffron. It is quite unbeatable with a mushroom or crab risotto, with koftas (those meatballs from central India) and with a soup or salad that features carrots and oranges. Viognier has a love affair with rosemary, so much so that, if you're set on having a bottle of Viognier at all costs, you could manipulate almost any food, from meat and poultry to vegetables, by adding sufficient rosemary. Despite its lowish acidity, Viognier is also fine with sushi, provided you are dipping the portions into soy sauce flavoured with wasabi. It also has a place at the vegetarian's table, as it likes most vegetables, especially when spiced.

Perhaps not surprisingly, the fact that Viognier is so in vogue is because it works well with fusion food. The conglomeration of acidic, spicy, fruity and sharp flavours that we are confronted with all at the same time is overboard for most other varieties, but we can reach gratefully for Viognier, and it will save the day.

Viognier is an absolute winner with Cantal cheese and can be exquisite when paired with salty cheeses. As we do not understand this flirtation with salt, we are at a loss to explain it, but it works remarkably well with Feta and Roquefort-styled cheeses. Could it be that a full-bodied, ripe and fruity Viognier implies sweetness, just as a late harvest does? Whether this is a credable explanation or not, Viognier certainly does work magic with salty cheeses.

Viognier is unhappy with light and delicate dishes, with acidic food, sour dressings and vinaigrettes, olives, capers and other sharp ingredients, fiery hot dishes, and with strongly flavoured fish; avoid mackerel, snoek, sardines and marlin.

WEISSER RIESLING   Varietal wine; white

South Africa is the only country that needs a qualifying noun before the word 'riesling'. Way back when, the wine produced locally from the grape variety Crouchen Blanc was inadvertently called Riesling, or Cape or Paarl Riesling, and more recently, South African Riesling. Even now that we know better, we need a qualifier to identify the real thing: Weisser or Rhine Riesling. To the rest of the world, this quintessentially German wine is called, plainly and simply, Riesling.

For once, there is a lot in a name. Weisser/Rhine Riesling and Cape Riesling are as different as the proverbial chalk and cheese. Crouchen Blanc, even when masquerading as 'Cape Riesling', is a lesser grape, whereas Weisser Riesling is, arguably, known as 'the greatest white grape variety' in the world.

We like to describe Weisser Riesling as the 'metrosexual grape': it has the self-assurance to be made into any style and carries it off with aplomb without ever needing the aid of oaking. From bone dry to off-dry, to semi-sweet, late harvest, special late harvest and finally, to immensely rich noble late harvest, it will join the party in any guise. Similar to Sauvignon Blanc, it has a strong personality and equally good acidity. But, it is very much more adaptable than Sauvignon Blanc, thriving in both cool and warmer climates. And, as if all this isn't enough, it also has the potential to age well. A unique characteristic is the tug-of-war between its acidity and its sweetness: it is as if the wine is balancing on the edge of a sword. Is it sweet or is it sour? No other wine displays this dichotomy.

With all its fine qualities, it is sad that Weisser Riesling's image was rather tarnished in the past when huge quantities of bland, semi-sweet German wines, such as Blue Nun and Liebfraumilch, were dumped onto the international market. The irony is that these wines seldom contained a drop of Riesling, but were erroneously perceived as such, simply because they were from Germany. Fortunately, Weisser Riesling's merits are being rediscovered worldwide, albeit slowly. The food and wine pairer particularly welcomes this wine, as it is indispensable at the table.

Weisser Riesling's flavours and aromas bring to mind a patchwork quilt made up of anything from a scrap of tartan to a square of chintzy floral or a candy-stripe. Depending on style and age, you will find that it's very appley, from fresh Granny Smiths to spiced, baked apples. There are also quince, orange and granadilla flavours, not to mention spice, honey and geranium. This melange of flavours and the wine's racy acidity and balanced, delicate sweetness lead us to a similar patchwork of food, a veritable cornucopia, packed with olives, sun-dried tomatoes, capers, kedgeree, smoked salmon, cold roast meats, beetroot, mustard, fresh berries and many more; almost anything works as a partner to Weisser Riesling.

For local food and wine pairers, this wine is of particular interest. Its affinity for a touch of sweetness in savoury dishes and its generous, sweet-fruit character suit typical South African dishes where there is often added sweetness in one way or another, from dried apricots in sosaties, to cinnamon and sugar on pumpkin fritters, to *korrelkonfyt* with snoek, and Mrs Ball's chutney on the rest. It is also the answer to those hard-to-match salads where a wine must cope with both the acidity of the dressing and the addition of something sweet to the salad, like diced apple, pineapple or plums. Weisser Riesling's sweet-sour character meets these salads head-on.

When young, Weisser Riesling displays vivid fruitiness and lively acidity. With age, it develops a honeyed depth of ripe apricots and peaches. With bottle-maturation, particularly in the sweeter-styled wines, mineral notes and the aromas of petrol and toast emerge.

Most South African Weisser Rieslings have a pronounced lime

character, which is why they pair so well with lime-flavoured Thai dishes. It also has a strong attraction for lemon-flavoured dishes. When dry or off-dry, it has 'a thing' for Thai green curry. In fact, this 'thing' actually extends to other ethnic cuisines, such as Indian, Chinese and Japanese (it is the sushi wine *par excellence*). The list for the dry to off-dry styles seems endless: ceviche, gravadlax (gravlax), calamari, scallops, trout, mackerel, herring, fish pâtés, fish in cream sauces, stuffed red peppers, cold roast duck and quail, roast vegetables and avocado salad. Weisser Riesling also enlivens many rather bland poached dishes, such as poached hake or sole.

Another cooking method that it takes under its wing is stir-frying, which allows the ingredients to speak for themselves.

When Weisser Riesling is made in a late-harvest style (with noticeable sweetness), it is simply brilliant with roast pork served with apple sauce or stuffed with prunes, and roasts such as game birds or warthog, which are often served with fruit-based sauces.

A special late harvest Riesling (a sweet wine) makes an excellent partner for fruit tarts and fruit-based desserts, and it is unbeatable with apple puddings in any size or shape, especially if a touch of cinnamon, ginger or almond is present. It also pairs well with lighter desserts, such as caramelized lemon tart, crème caramel and profiteroles. When the Riesling is a noble late harvest, it will cope with the sweetest and richest desserts, from pecan nut pie to tipsy tart and steamed puddings with their golden syrup sauces. When fruit is present, such as in pears belle Hélène, it is still lip-smackingly good. *See also* **Noble late harvest**, page 78.

Dry or off-dry Weisser Riesling is unhappy with dishes that are very peppery. They become totally miserable when paired with red-meat dishes such as roast lamb, beef or venison. An off-dry version is also not happy with green vegetables in vegetarian preparations, unless they are served with a slightly sweet sauce.

ZINFANDEL   Varietal wine; red (in SA)

California and its most famous grape, Zinfandel, are virtually synonymous; mention the one and you think of the other. Actually, California is only its adoptive home, as the grape is the same as southern Italy's lesser-known Primitivo grape, which comes from Apulia. Zinfandel is now also grown in South Africa by a small number of producers who have taken advantage of the suitability of our climate for this variety. It prefers a warm, but not too hot, climate, and revels in the top reaches of mountain slopes, of which we have many.

Zinfandel may not have Shiraz's hoity-toity image, and it is not in the same 'noble' class of grape varieties as Shiraz but, oh boy, just let it loose! Given half a chance, it produces world-class wines with enormous extraction and power, packed with ripe berry fruit and supple tannins. Although the berry flavours (blueberries, blackberries and raspberries) dominate, Zinfandel also prominently displays cherry flavours, along with 'sweet' spices, freshly ground black pepper and an unexpected whiff of tea leaves.

It is a very versatile grape; in California it is turned into 'blush' (pink-tinged) wines and the mass-produced 'jug wines' so popular in the USA. California also produces a white Zin; actually, it's a very pale pink (paler than the 'blush' wines), made by leaving the juice in contact with the skins for only a brief period.

In South Africa, we've preferred to mould the grapes into serious, ripe and velvety reds; well, thus far anyway. Zinfandel becomes accessible soon after bottling, but it has an optimum lifespan of only four to eight years in the bottle.

Zinfandel is a life-line for the food and wine pairer, and there are two instances where it comes to the rescue: Firstly, when you want to enjoy a red wine with the sweet sauces, jellies and relishes that often accompany poultry, meat or game dishes. Late harvest (which has both sweetness and acidity) would normally be the best match, but sometimes you just want a red. Secondly, when you need a red wine that will not fall apart when whatever you are braaiing is covered in a sweet basting sauce. No wonder Zinfandel is known as the 'spare rib' wine. When paired with sticky spareribs glistening with sweet, spicy, sharp barbecue sauce, a 'killer' Zin triumphs every time.

Zinfandel also meets its match with antipasti, especially if olives and anchovies are present, with a salad containing pomegranates, and with ratatouille, stuffed peppers or a casseroled vegetable medley. A powerful, ripe, cherry- and blackberry-flavoured Zinfandel will be too vigorous for plain roast beef, but will match spicy dishes, from sausages to casseroles and pies, honey- and mustard-flavoured meats, strongly seasoned lamb, steak with mustard or soy sauce, and peppered steak with garlic. On the poultry side, think Cajun-style or barbecue sauce-laced grilled chicken, or duck with black cherries or hanepoot grapes. Game dishes include grilled ostrich steaks or casseroles, and roasted kudu served with quince jelly. A generously flavoured Zin is brilliant with red cabbage and sausages cooked the German way, with red wine, apples and smoked bacon. It can even cope with curries, especially those from northen India.

And here, at last, is a still, dry, unfortified red wine that can cope with dark chocolate, although this is taking a risk.

Zinfandel is unhappy with light and delicate fare, with fiery hot foods and with most fish.

Wine as an apéritif

The purpose of an apéritif is to stimulate the appetite before a meal. In French, it means 'opener' and you could say that is a 'preparation' for what is to follow. Wine is one of the best apéritifs you can choose. However, South Africans often drink a beer before lunch or dinner. 'I'll start with a beer,' a guest will say, 'and move onto the wine a bit later.' The beer-before-food devotees say that there is nothing to beat an ice-cold tipple when the temperature is 30°C in the shade. Beer undoubtedly quenches a thirst and it suits our hot climate, but it tends to dull rather than whet the appetite. Of course, a well-chilled glass of white wine can also quench a thirst, but that is another point of view. Fortunately, there is room for both.

Sparkling wine is an unbeatable pre-lunch or pre-dinner drink. Any of the various styles will be a success, as their good, natural acidity hones the appetite. Sparkling wines based on only a white grape variety, such as Chardonnay, and the brut styles work particularly well. There is something about bubbles on the palate that prepares you so well for food to follow...

The best **still wine** to drink before a meal is a dry white, as its acidity primes the appetite. Choose one that is light- to medium-bodied, fresh and aromatic without too much texture, and light on the wood flavours (if it has no wood, so much the better).

Oaking provides both richness and depth to a wine, which has a satiating effect on the palate, but try telling that to the dedicated wine-with-wood drinkers! And, if they are used to having a well-oaked wine before dinner, then why ever not?

Generally, the most successful wines to serve as an aperitif are Sauvignon Blanc, Pinot Gris/Pinot Grigio, Pinot Blanc, Chenin Blanc, and unwooded Chardonnay and Semillon. A word of caution, though; many people find a wine with discernable acidity too intense as a cocktail sipper, but they will usually be comfortable if there is some food to accompany it. Fortunately, the savoury things we like to nibble on with our pre-lunch or -dinner drinks suit acidity in a wine well.

But what if you prefer a sweeter wine? Then go ahead and enjoy one. The sweetness in a wine may spoil your appetite a bit, much as a few sweets might do, but that is called 'compromise'. An off-dry or medium-sweet Chenin Blanc, with its good natural acidity, is an ideal choice for the sweet-toothed wine-drinker.

Red-wine drinkers looking for a pre-dinner drink should choose a wine that is light, fruity and not too tannic, leaving the blockbusters for the meal, to match a heavier main course.

Sherry, the classic appetite-whetter, is less popular with the young generation but is still served frequently in winter. However, we should learn from the Spanish and chill a pale dry (fino) sherry for a delightful summer apéritif – especially when olives and tapas-style food are being served. The 'saltiness' of a dry sherry seamlessly matches the saltiness of the olives. You would search far to find a better combination than salty snacks and dry (fino) sherry.

But what if you prefer a medium-cream sherry? Go right ahead and pour yourself a glass. The sweeter sherries are equally successful with salty snacks and, in this case, the saltiness of the olives will openly flirt with the sweetness of the sherry.

Cocktails based on sparkling wine, such as Kir Royale and Buck's Fizz, and **fruit punches** made from either still or sparkling wines, are popular as summer apéritifs. Although the wine aficionado may have a fit at the thought of adding anything to wine, if you're into these drinks, you'll have no such qualms.

SERVING WINE AT A PARTY

At cocktail parties or other receptions, it is a smart move to serve only one white and one red wine, otherwise the guests invariably end up with a blend from different bottles – especially if waiters are walking around and topping up glasses, or when bottles are plonked on a table for people to serve themselves and someone else, helpfully, offers to get you a refill!

No single wine, white or red, can cope with a varied assortment of canapés and cocktail snacks that can range from smoked salmon and horseradish to blue cheese and green fig preserve, via mini samoosas, spring rolls and cocktail sausages with mustard dip.

The simplest solution is to choose two good all-rounders, such as an unwooded Chardonnay or Semillon for the white, and a young, medium-bodied, light-on-tannin Merlot for the red. If you have no budget restrictions, you could consider Pinot Noir instead, as this food-friendly wine works like a charm with most canapés.

Serving temperatures for wine

A wine's temperature makes a considerable difference to the way it smells and tastes. The ideal serving temperature will enhance the good qualities of a wine and mask some of its bad ones. The warmer the wine, the more readily its volatile flavour compounds evaporate when it is opened, with the result that the wine's aroma will be more pronounced. This happens when a bottle of wine reaches a temperature of between 16° and 18°C. If a wine's temperature rises above 20°C, the alcohol will start to evaporate, which can cause it to become unbalanced.

The other side of the picture is equally undesirable. Serving a wine very cold can prevent its volatile compounds from evaporating and you can land up with a wine that has hardly any aroma or flavour at all. This makes the decision easy on what the ideal temperature for serving a wine should be. Simply divide your wine into categories, as indicated in the accompanying table.

The recommended serving temperatures shown in the table are not hard and fast rules, merely guidelines. We take the view that wine should be approached in a relaxed manner. If you like to drink your wine as cold as possible, then go right ahead and add ice cubes to your glass, as many South Africans do. If you want to add some soda water, then do that too. Wine should be served in a way that is most enjoyable to you, and not according to someone else's 'rules'.

Of course, if you add ice or soda water, you will dilute your wine and its charm will most definitely be lost. Therefore, you may decide not to do that to a special bottle or to a wine that is full-bodied, complex and rich. After all, you bought it in the first place so that you could enjoy its qualities to the full, not so?

Here's a tip: why not consider freezing leftover wine in ice-cube trays to add to your glass when you serve the same wine again? But there is one hitch; it has to be exactly the same wine, from the same producer and the same vintage. You would most definitely not add Sauvignon Blanc ice cubes to a glass of barrel-matured Chenin Blanc; or Chardonnay cubes from one producer and vintage to a glass of Chardonnay from another producer and a different year. You will probably chill your white and sparkling wines in the fridge, but a handy emergency stand-by is to pop an unchilled wine into an ice-bucket filled with ice cubes and water, to which you have added a handful of salt. But you do need to put the bottle back into the ice-bucket, or into the fridge, after pouring the first round, as a bottle of

IDEAL SERVING TEMPERATURES FOR STILL AND SPARKLING WINES		
White, pink and sparkling wines	Young, light- to medium-bodied, austere or fruity/lightly spicy; unwooded or lightly wooded Dry (crisp), off-dry or semi-sweet Late harvest, special late harvest, noble late harvest Sparkling wine (all styles: white, pink and red) Rosé and blanc de noir	8°C	These wines taste best when they are cold.
	Complex, deeply fruity, full-bodied; with or without bottle maturation; wooded or unwooded	10–12°C	These wines come into their own when served relatively warm.
	Inexpensive, one-dimensional, humdrum	8°C or below	Chill well; you cannot lose anything, as there was nothing to lose before you started!
	Tired and a bit flabby from too much bottle maturation	6°C	Serve as cold as possible, without giving yourself the shivers.
Red wines	Light-bodied, soft and fruity	10–14°C	These wines are best when served slightly chilled.
	Huge and complex with ample fruit, body and tannin	16–18°C	Do not chill below 16° (even on the hottest day); these wines are so opulent that you don't want to inhibit them in any way.
Fortified wines	White port, white muscadel, hanepoot; dry (fino) sherry	10–12°C	These wines shine brighter when slightly chilled.
	Port (ruby, vintage, LBV, tawny); Red muscadel Sherry (medium-cream, full-cream, old brown)	16–18°C	When served too cold, these wines lose their flavour; if too warm, they become 'hot' (alcoholy).

wine very soon returns to room temperature if you leave it standing out. This is the reason why white wine glasses are usually smaller than red wine glasses. You might have thought it a bit unfair, but there's every reason why smaller quantities of white wine than red wine are served in one go. In the blink of an eye, the white wine warms up, so it is better to enjoy a smaller quantity at its optimum temperature, with several refills if required, than to sit with a glass of warm white wine just for the sake of 'fairness'.

Speaking of 'room temperature', you may be familiar with the old advice to 'serve red wine at room temperature'. Er, no. Not if the room temperature is above 18°C. As mentioned elsewhere, this 'rule' is a relic of the past when we mimicked Britain and Europe. Over there, in the days before central heating, they may well have had rooms with an ambient temperature of below 18°C, even in summer. In southern Africa though, our summer and winter daytime temperatures are often way above that rather cool mark.

And don't forget that, on the coldest winter days, a blazing fire or other form of heating can soon warm a room up to 'summer' levels, so take your home's heating arrangements into account when considering whether or not to chill your red wines before serving them.

Sharing wine in a restaurant

Although certain food and wine combinations undoubtedly work better than others, it is not always possible, when eating out, to order a different wine with every dish; not only is this expensive, but it can be impractical. The dilemma of what wine to drink with a range of dishes really only comes up with restaurant dining as, when we entertain at home, we control the choice of both food and wine (and any left-over wine can always be saved for the next day!).

A typical scenario at a restaurant is that you are presented with the wine list as soon as you have taken your seat, before you have even looked at the menu or given half a thought to what you might want to eat. What are you meant to do with the wine list at this stage? Why don't restaurants present an apéritif list instead? The ideal list would offer a range of pre-dinner options – cocktails, beers, spirits, coolers and so on, as well as wines by the glass.

Furthermore, restaurants should offer a selection of decent wines by the glass that aren't priced into the stratosphere! Inevitably, when the price per glass is too high, we tend to order a bottle instead, and that 'starter' bottle will probably still be going when the meal arrives. And, even if it is a bad match with our meal, our inclination is to finish the first bottle before ordering another wine that might be more in harmony with the food. So, we battle on with an unhappy food and wine match, wondering why our dining-out experience is not quite what we anticipated. Then, chances are that when the first bottle is finally empty and the wine steward asks if he can bring another, more often than not, we agree without giving it a second thought. It seldom occurs to us to order a different wine.

When it comes to eating out, there is no doubt that wine by the glass is the way to go. Although they are still few and far between, some restaurants that offer wines by the glass have gone to the trouble to select specific wines for each dish on the menu. Sadly, this is not yet a general practice, and it will only become widely accepted if restaurants do not charge exorbitant prices for a single glass of wine. In the meantime, we have to look for other solutions.

When there are only two or three diners, and a poor selection of wines by the glass, finding a solution is not as easy as if there are four or more of you (and/or the restaurant offers a good range of 'by the glass' options). Most often, two people will share one bottle for the whole meal and that single wine must be able to cope with their different food choices.

When there are four diners, however, it is more likely that they will share two bottles during the meal (working on the basis of about half a bottle per person). A solution is to wait until everyone has decided what to eat and then order two different wines, selecting ones that will best match all the food choices.

As the number of diners increases, so does the potential to order a greater number of wines of varying styles, which makes mixing and matching so much easier. When a group of diners each orders a very different dish, the best solution is to select wines that are 'multi-faceted' and can cope with a variety of tastes and flavours.

When it comes to a white wine, this means one that is medium-bodied, with elegant fruit, and not too dry. An unwooded Chardonnay fits the bill, as it has a firm but subtle personality and will work with almost any food, from fish to chicken, pork and beef, especially if the dish is accompanied by a rich, creamy sauce. Pinot Gris/Pinot Grigio is another option.

For the red wine, choose one that is medium-bodied, with forward, but subtle fruit (not a blockbuster). We immediately think of Pinot Noir, the great leveller at the table, as it also matches fish, chicken, pork and beef. Pinot Noir's unique combination of both red wine and white wine characteristics endows it with great flexibility to pair with a wide range of ingredients and preparations. Merlot, another flexible wine, is not far behind, provided it fits the profile mentioned above: medium-bodied and gently fruity.

To illustrate this by way of an example, let's imagine four diners who order: Grilled calamari with tartare sauce; chicken cordon bleu; rump steak, cooked medium-rare, with a monkey-gland sauce; and pizza Margherita (tomato, mozzarella and basil).

Each of these dishes would have loved a wine specially selected for it: Sauvignon Blanc for the calamari and its tartare sauce; a wooded, buttery Chardonnay for the chicken cordon bleu, Shiraz for the steak and its sauce, and Sangiovese for the pizza. But, if our four diners, who are all white wine drinkers, want to order only one bottle to share, an unwooded Chardonnay will do the best for them. If they were all red wine drinkers, then a Pinot Noir or lighter-styled Merlot would cope admirably. If there are both red and white wine drinkers present, then a bottle of each wine is the obvious answer. You get the picture...

Part II:

Matching food and wine

Starters

Ah, food, at last! We are the most hungry when starters are served. But, isn't that what starters are all about – to take the edge off our hunger so that we can enjoy the main course at leisure? Unless you had an hors d'oeuvre with your pre-lunch or -dinner drink, this is the first time you'll be enjoying food and wine together and, if the starter and its wine companion are unhappy with each other, you will be more keenly aware of it now than if you had a mismatched wine at a later stage of the meal.

Unless you have especially prepared a meal around one wine, and have chosen one that will go well with the entire meal, you'll almost certainly need different wines for the starter and the main course. If you are entertaining at home, this is easy, as there will be a common starter and, if you don't finish the bottle, you can set it aside for later. However, at restaurants, with their prohibitive mark-ups on wine, this is not always feasible or affordable.

If four diners each order a different starter it would be ludicrous to order four different wines, especially if the restaurant's liquor licence does not allow you to take your unfinished wine home. If all four diners have the same starter, or choose starters that are happy with the same wine, they could probably finish a bottle, whereas two diners probably won't. For a solution to this predicament, see **Sharing wine in a restaurant**, page 117. Thank goodness for the slowly evolving custom of restaurants offering a variety of wines by the glass. Now, if more proprietors offered a decent selection of wines by the glass, without charging the earth for them, we'd be in clover...

In this section, we have only listed dishes that are commonly served as starters. If you are having a starter portion of something that could also be a main course, refer to the appropriate section of this guide for pairing suggestions.

ANTIPASTO

Antipasto (or, in plural, antipasti) is the Italian word for 'starter'. 'Anti' means 'before' and 'pasto' means 'meal' (not to be confused with pasta, which means 'dough'), so it is 'before the meal'. Typical antipasti include savoury cold or hot foods such as olives, raw or marinated vegetables, cured meats such as prosciutto and salami, garlic prawns, or grilled tomatoes. A mixed platter of antipasti needs a wine with high acidity. This is Chenin Blanc's territory, so choose a nutty, yeasty version.

A dry Weisser Riesling or dry, young rosé are also very successful. If you want to drink a red, choose an easy-drinking one, such as a Cinsaut/Cabernet Sauvignon blend or a Sangiovese, and make sure it is juicy and young with ample red-berry flavours. For individual antipasto dishes, see separate alphabetical listings, below.

ARTICHOKES

Globe artichokes don't play ball with wine, making it seem metallic and bitter, or strangely sweeter than it really is. However, serving artichokes with a squeeze of lemon juice or a vinaigrette usually saves the wine. Artichokes served with a lemon butter sauce call for a young, somewhat assertive white wine with high acidity, which is why Sauvignon Blanc is a good partner. Artichokes are perfect partners for eggs, and when served with an eggy, rich hollandaise or mayonnaise, they prefer a medium-bodied, wooded Chardonnay.

ASPARAGUS

The powerful, earthy flavours in both green and white asparagus battle with many wines, but respond well to wines of a particular profile. Wines with a distinctive flavour, such as Sauvignon Blanc, find a companionable echo with asparagus. A light red wine with low tannin levels would also work, particularly if the wine is from a cool climate, and Cabernet Franc leads the way here.

When fresh asparagus is simply steamed and dressed with a bit of melted butter, an exhilaratingly fruity Sauvignon Blanc is the ideal partner; still so when a squeeze of lemon is added to the butter. Even when served with a hollandaise sauce, a Sauvignon Blanc with good acidity works well, especially if the sauce is distinctly lemony.

If the sauce is more eggy or creamy than acidic, a rounded, young, unwooded or lightly wooded Chardonnay shines brightly. This is a clear example of the sauce determining the choice of wine, even when served with such a powerful, earthy flavoured vegetable.

AUBERGINE PURÉE

See **Brinjal purée**, page 123.

AVOCADO

The richness of ripe avocado needs a wine with a good acid bite to counteract it. A crisp Sauvignon Blanc works, as does a fruity Chenin Blanc. When 'avo' is served with lemon juice, a simple vinaigrette or lemon-infused olive oil, Chenin Blanc is hard to beat.

Avocado accompanied by prawns, either pan-fried or grilled, needs a wine with some opulence, such as a Weisser Riesling, but

Chardonnay, dry sparkling wine or any dry, flavoursome white wine will work. Avocado Ritz has been a popular starter since the 1980s. A half avo is filled with shrimps in a seafood sauce, often made of shop-bought mayonnaise blended with a dollop of tomato sauce. This combination can be hard on a wine, so keep it simple with an inexpensive Chenin Blanc with some acidity and a touch of residual sweetness. An avocado mousse, heavily laced with mayonnaise and cream, takes on a different complexion, so serve this dish with an unwooded Chardonnay.

BILTONG AND DROËWORS

These national treasures had their origin in pioneering days as a method of preserving meat and have stayed with us ever since. What was once everyday fare has become very expensive, but remains a firm favourite, nevertheless. Snacking on biltong and droëwors while watching the game, serving them with pre-dinner drinks, or wrapped up in a crusty bread roll for lunch, they have become as ingrained on the South African social and food scene as olives have in Spain.

Biltong and droëwors are salty and rich in umami flavours (see page 24), both of which have a great impact on wine. The classic partner for both salt and umami is a wine with good acidity and some sweetness. Invariably, this leads us to an off-dry Weisser Riesling or a medium-sweet Chenin Blanc but, while these are ideal choices for a dedicated white wine drinker, not everyone wants to drink white wine with biltong and droëwors.

Red wines can be a touch problematic, as salty and umami-rich food have an unhappy effect on tannin. This is easily overcome by choosing a red that has a bit of acidity, a generous, sweet-fruity character and low tannins (or the soft, ripe tannins found in reds from warmer climates). Stick with these styles rather than heavy-bodied, complex wines with tannin-structures that are made to last.

This is the time to crack a quaffable Pinotage, Shiraz-Merlot blend, Ruby Cab or Pinot Noir. Or, to fit right in with our mixed heritage, try a Tempranillo, Mourvèdre or Nebbiolo, provided they fit the biltong-wine profile. A pale dry (fino) sherry would also work well.

BRANDADE

Brandade is a fish 'paste' made by pounding dried or smoked fish with olive oil and milk into a creamy purée. As with pâté, it is served with Melba toast or bread. If it is made with dried fish, a firm, full, bone-dry white wine is the order of the day, as the paste-like texture of the dish is beautifully set off by the wine's acidity in a vertical pairing. This is Chenin Blanc's 'ah-ha!' moment.

If the brandade is made with smoked fish, such as salmon, snoek or trout, the same Chenin is still a very good combination, although a wooded version would be even better but, hold onto your hat – a lightly chilled Pinot Noir will blow you away.

BRINJAL PURÉE

Melintzanosalata, hatsilim, baba ghannouj, baba ganoush

A purée of brinjals (aubergine or eggplant) is called a 'salad' in some countries. While it often forms part of a mezze platter, it is also served on its own as a starter, with pitta bread. Brinjal loves red wine, particularly an aromatic and herby one, and Merlot, Shiraz or Pinotage answers the call. When yoghurt is used in the preparation, a Sauvignon Blanc matches the sharpness of the purée, but a brut sparkling wine is also highly successful. This comes as no surprise as Middle Eastern food, in general, loves a bubbly.

BRUSCHETTA

Bruschetta [broos-KET-tah] is, technically speaking, just plain grilled or toasted bread, rubbed with a clove of garlic while still hot and then drizzled with good-quality olive oil. Any wine will pair well with this simple starter but, ideally, you want one that will show off the olive oil, so select an unwooded Chardonnay. If the bruschetta is enhanced with a simple topping, such as fresh tomato and basil, sautéed mushrooms, grilled brinjals (aubergines or eggplant) or roasted vegetables, the unwooded Chardonnay will still cope admirably.

For more elaborate toppings, see **Crostini**, page 127.

BUFFALO WINGS

Named after the city of Buffalo (USA), where they originated, these are chicken wings that are deep-fried and coated in sauce (or with the sauce served on the side). The traditional sauce has three main ingredients: vinegar, cayenne pepper and butter. The vinegar, which cuts the richness of the chicken skin, butter and the frying oil, needs a sympathetic wine partner with good acidity. This is Chenin Blanc territory, and a wooded Chenin is best, as it latches onto the butter in the sauce. Alternatives are wooded Sauvignon Blanc or dry Weisser Riesling. If you want a red, choose an easy-drinking Pinotage.

CARPACCIO

Carpaccio is named for a Renaissance painter who used a certain shade of red, reminiscent of these wafer-thin slices of raw beef. It is traditionally served dressed with olive oil and topped with Parmesan shavings. It will come as no surprise that the soft, almost-creamy texture of beef carpaccio is very happy with an unwooded or lightly wooded Chardonnay. However, if there is an abundance of Parmesan with it, a red wine is safer; but, like Signor Carpaccio favouring a specific hue, this dish likes specific red wines – it has an affinity for Carignan, but settles down nicely with Pinot Noir and Sangiovese, or with Pinot Noir-based sparkling wines.

Carpaccio is sometimes made from meats such as ostrich and springbok, or even tuna, but these variations should not alter the wine choices. However, if the carpaccio (of whatever meat) is dressed with lemon juice, mustard and capers, a Sangiovese is the best partner. Capers are very hard on any wine and the best way to accommodate them is to match them with a wine that has, or seems to have, an acidic note.

Tuna carpaccio dressed in olive oil, and flavoured with garlic and basil, will be happy with any of the wines mentioned above.

CAVIAR

You can't beat the tradition of serving caviar with a shot of ice-cold vodka, which has the weight and flavour caviar requires.

The other classic pairing, caviar and champagne, probably originated as a marketing ploy to link champagne with luxury foods like caviar, truffles, foie gras and oysters. Even at its richest, sparkling wine is delicate and easily overpowered by most foods. Compounding the difficulty is that not all caviars are alike. Sparkling wine may hang on by its fingernails when served with the gentle osetr (osetra, oscietra) or beluga caviar, but when it comes to powerfully flavoured sevruga, no sparkler, produced in whatever way, can stand up to it.

A neutral white wine (with the emphasis on neutral), such as an unwooded Chardonnay or Semillon, is a better match for all types of caviar. We are, of course, talking about the real thing: the roe from sturgeon found in the Caspian and Black seas.

Historically, caviar was served in its original container or in a non-metalic bowl set on a bed of crushed ice, accompanied by slices of lightly buttered toast or blinis (small pancakes made from buckwheat flour), sour cream and, sometimes, chopped hard-boiled eggs. The ice on which it was served has a practical explanation: as it is highly perishable, caviar should be kept at zero degrees. Consequently, it is also a good idea to serve your tipple of choice well chilled.

For a more modern take on caviar, skip the sour cream, which masks the beauty of this rare experience, and stick to blinis or use top-quality baby jacket potatoes to carry the caviar. There is no point in killing this delicacy after you've spent an arm and a leg to buy the stuff. Alternatively, spoon a small portion of caviar into the hollow formed between your thumb and index finger and simply lick it up. As caviar reacts with silver and other metals, spoons made of mother-of-pearl or bone are traditionally used to serve caviar.

'Caviars' derived from lumpfish, salmon or other fish are mostly used as garnishes for other dishes rather than served by themselves.

CEVICHE

A traditional Mexican dish, ceviche [S'VEH-cheh] is basically raw, saltwater fish marinated in citrus juice (often lime) and flavourings, commonly onion, chilli, coriander and garlic. However, the fish is not served raw in the true sense of the word, as the acidic citrus juice 'pickles' the fish, changing its colour, texture and flavour. No wine will be entirely happy with so much citrus and raw onion, which are key ingredients, but a piercingly crisp Sauvignon Blanc should handle the dish fairly well.

CHARCUTERIE

See **Cold meats**, page 126.

CHICKEN LIVERS

Chicken livers, whether sautéed or deep-fried and served whole, or chopped and served with a hard-boiled egg garnish, need a medium-bodied wine and are happiest with a white. A dry or off-dry Weisser Riesling or a Pinot Gris/Pinot Grigio work very well but, amazingly, so does Gewürztraminer. You may ask if Gewürztraminer wouldn't be too fruity for the dish, but chicken livers are highly aromatic with a sweetish note, so the fruitiness of Gewürz is the perfect match.

If you ever happen to see a bottle of Gamay Noir at your local wine outlet, buy it and cellar it, ready for the day you really want to push out the boat for a perfect match of wine and chicken livers.

For **Chicken liver pâté**, see **Pâtés and terrines**, page 134.

CHILLI BITES/DHALTJIES

These spicy, deep-fried balls, which are popular in South Africa, are ideal as an appetizer or snack. At first glance, the ingredients (which include cayenne pepper, turmeric, ginger, cumin and garam masala), would suggest a cautionary approach for the wine drinker, yet these little morsels are mellow and aromatic rather than pungent. Apart from the spices, there is very little weight in the ingredients and chilli bites/dhaltjies will be happy with a lightish white wine such as a Colombard or a Sauvignon Blanc-Semillon blend to set them off perfectly.

CHILLI POPPERS (stuffed jalapeños)

Also known as jalapeño poppers, these delectable appetizers seem to be a restaurant version of the classic Mexican dish, chile rellenos. Jalapeño chillies are hollowed out, stuffed with cream cheese, then battered and deep-fried. A typical variation uses minced beef as a stuffing. This is a dish for a dry white wine and there are two that will work equally well: Chardonnay from a cool-climate and either an unwooded or a lightly wooded Viognier.

CHIMICHANGAS

There is a bit of a debate as to the origin of chimichangas. Some people claim that it originated in the Mexican state of Sonora, while others claim it is 'Tex-Mex' – the fusion of Mexican and Texan cuisines. Either way, this tasty dish is typically prepared by folding a tortilla into a rectangular package and filling it with minced beef flavoured with tomatoes, chillies and spices (or, for a vegetarian version, with guacamole, cheese, cream and diced potatoes). It is then deep-fried and served accompanied by salsa, guacamole and sour cream or grated cheese. Choose a wooded Chenin Blanc, a Sangiovese or, in its absence, a quaffable Pinotage.

COLD MEATS

When served as a starter or a light meal, a mixed platter of cold meats, such as **ham**, **salami**, **pastrami**, **cold roast beef** and **turkey roll**, is often accompanied by salads, which may include olives, pickled onions or gherkins, and assorted breads. Amazingly, this is white wine food, specifically Pinot Gris/Pinot Grigio, Gewürztraminer or off-dry Weisser Riesling (with its natural acidity to cut the fattiness and its touch of sweetness to offset the saltiness of the meat). Chenin or Sauvignon Blanc will do the trick, but should be unwooded with good acidity, as one from a cool climate would have. If you want a red wine, go for one with low tannin and some acidity. Look for a Barbera, Sangiovese or Pinotage or, if you want to push out the boat, a Pinot Noir. At all costs, avoid a wine with even a hint of sturdy tannins.

Cured hams The most famous cured hams include Parma and San Daniele from Italy, Serrano from Spain, Bayonne from France and Westphalian from Germany. The Italian word 'prosciutto' [proh-SHOOT'toh] is commonly used for raw hams in most English-speaking countries. Strictly, it should be 'prosciutto crudo' to distinguish it from 'prosciutto cotto', which is cooked ham. Many South Africans tend to call all these cured meats 'Parma ham'.

Italian and Spanish raw hams are only cured, not smoked, whereas the French and German hams are smoked after the curing process, which adds another flavour dimension. Although imported hams are readily available (if expensive) locally, southern Africa produces a range of cured hams that are similar to their European counterparts. Namibia, particularly, produces a Black Forest ham that resembles the typical German cured and smoked product.

When it comes to wine, white wines that are not too acidic are the best partners for ham served on its own. If you are serving any of the cured hams on its own, choose a full-bodied, nutty Chardonnay, provided the ham is not too salty. If it is salty, Weisser Riesling or Gewürztraminer are better choices as they have clearly defined aromatic profiles – spicy, fruity and floral. If you must have a red, you could try a medium-bodied Pinot Noir, but there should not be even the slightest hint of tannin present, as salt in food only emphasizes the tannins in red wine.

Prosciutto (such as parma ham) served with melon (spanspek) can pose a problem, as melon is not particularly wine-friendly. A medium-cream sherry, with its extra bit of alcohol and touch of sweetness, is the best match for this combination. But, if you're not into sherry, try an off-dry Weisser Riesling, Gewürztraminer or Bukettraube. Prosciutto served with fresh figs or ripe pears perfectly matches an off-dry Weisser Riesling or Colombard.

Cooked hams See **Gammon and ham**, page 200.

Cold roast beef See above, and also page 184.

Brawn See page 211.

COURGETTE FLOWERS

Courgette (baby marrow) flowers are starting to appear on menus in South Africa. They can be dipped in a batter and deep-fried, or stuffed and baked (sausage meat and Ricotta are common choices for stuffings). When deep-fried and served with a lemon wedge, they need a glass of chilled Sauvignon Blanc. The stuffed version is uncannily delicious with an unoaked Chardonnay.

CROSTINI

'Crostini' means little pieces of toast (often toasted slices of baguette or ciabatta) topped with one of many ingredients, such as seafood (squid, mussels, shrimps or prawns), tinned tuna, smoked salmon or poached fresh salmon, grilled red peppers, olive tapenade, basil pesto, sautéed chicken livers, various cold cuts including salami and prosciutto, or simply some Parmesan shavings.

Any of the wines listed under **Antipasto** (see page 120), will pair well with crostini and its endless variations.

CRUDITÉS

'Crudité' means 'rawness'. When applied to food, crudités commonly refer to raw vegetables and a dip of some description, served as a starter. In South Africa, the dip is frequently based on dairy (cream or yoghurt) or oil, and therefore rich and creamy. We might assume that the weight of the dipping sauce will determine the choice of wine, but strong, raw vegetable flavours, such as celery, radish, carrot, cucumber and cauliflower, will not be dominated by the dip, which leads us to a crisp, fresh dry white wine, not the creamy white that would match the dip. The Italian duet, Pinot Bianco/Pinot Blanc and Pinot Grigo/Pinot Gris really shine like stars next to a platter of crudités. If you have difficulty in finding these ideal partners, opt for a Crouchen Blanc (Cape, Paarl or South African Riesling) or a light-bodied, crisp Chenin Blanc.

DEEP-FRIED BRIE/CAMEMBERT

Deep-fried, crumb-coated soft cheese (traditionally Camembert or Brie) is often served as a starter, accompanied by a tangy relish made of red berries, such as cranberries. The sweet, acidic relish generally complicates the choice of wine, but a light, high-acid, low-tannin red, such as Pinot Noir or Pinotage, fits the profile.

See also **Haloumi**, page 130.

DOLMADES

In South Africa, we know dolmades as rice-stuffed vine leaves that are served cold as part of a mezze platter. Typical stuffings include nuts, dried fruit (such as currants or figs), herbs (such as parsley and mint) and spices like allspice, cinnamon and black pepper. What all of these ingredients want is a Sauvignon Blanc. If you choose a very fruity one, do not over-chill it or you will lose its flavours.

EGGS

Eggs do not pair well with wine but, if they are served in a sauce or with an ingredient the wine can latch on to, the problem is solved.

See **Eggs and egg-based dishes**, pages 159–163.

FOIE GRAS

As defined by French law, foie gras is the liver of a duck or a goose that has been specially fattened by *gavage*, a controversial, force-feeding procedure. Fattened liver can be produced by alternative methods and is referred to in France as 'fatty goose liver'. Outside France, many liver pâtés are called 'foie gras', although they do not conform to the French legal definition.

Whether you are serving fresh foie gras, pan-fried and served pink and warm, or the tinned version, both pair sublimely with noble late harvest wines. The combination of rich, nobly rotted wines and rich, densely textured, silky liver is irresistible to the cognoscenti, but it makes a substantial start to a meal, particularly in South Africa, as our noble late harvests are much fuller-bodied and sweeter than their French counterparts. Once, starting a meal with a sweet wine would have seemed odd, but nowadays, we like to drink precisely what will be the best match for the dish. A short pause and a sip of water is all that is required before the next course is served.

Alternative matches are Gewürztraminer made in a late harvest or special late harvest style, or dry (sec) to off-dry (demi-sec) sparkling wine. When foie gras is served with a robust sauce, such as a port-wine reduction or bitter-chocolate sauce, a tawny port or a white muscadel will be a successful partner.

From the sublime to the bizarre; as astonishing as it may sound, sparkling Pinotage or Shiraz are breathtakingly good partners for foie gras. No doubt the French would be aghast at this suggestion!

For **Pâté de foie gras**, *see* **Pâtés and terrines**, page 134.

FRITTO MISTO DI MARE

Fritto misto di mare is mixed seafood, battered, deep-fried and often accompanied by a garlic and anchovy dipping sauce. It is a rather light dish and, when selecting the wine, we should take our cue from the fact that fried foods are often served with a wedge of lemon and choose a wine with equally refreshing acidity. Many foods suited to deep-frying pair best with white wine but, of course, the weight of the ingredients must be taken into account. Fritto misto di mare loves unoaked Chardonnay from a cool climate, with acidity of its own, but a Sauvignon Blanc's sharpness of flavour also provides a lively contrast with fish and seafood.

FRUIT AS A STARTER

Fresh fruit is often used as a starter, particularly in summer, although it also has a place at the end of a meal. The most frequently used 'starter' fruits are melon, fig, grapefruit, litchi and pear. In general, fresh fruit is not very happy with wine but, when we want to seek out something to enjoy with our fruity starter, a wine with residual sugar and prominent acidity is the solution. Haul out a late or special late harvest made from Chenin Blanc grapes and smile all the way.

Fresh figs are often paired with cheese as a starter: for example, figs topped with blue-veined cheese, grilled and served with a citrus-based vinaigrette. Pair this combination with a late harvest or stein.

If the figs are wrapped in prosciutto crudo (such as Parma ham) and served with an egg-rich mayonnaise, you will need a sturdy wine with a bit of added alcohol – a medium cream sherry will be just the thing. If the figs are wrapped in cooked ham, a Weisser Riesling or a Colombard will work very well. These wines will also be good partners for grilled figs napped with a balsamic reduction.

Grapefruit can be served as is, with a splash of sherry or another fortified wine, or topped with sugar and cinnamon and placed under the grill – a real head scratcher, because grapefruit and wine are incompatible. Try the tartest white wine you can find, like a bone-dry Cape/Paarl/SA Riesling. Better still, chuck out the grapefruit!

Litchi is often served on crushed ice. A late harvest or special late harvest has the ideal weight in sweetness for litchis.

Melon, in all its varieties, has an uneasy relationship with wine. It responds fairly well to semi-sweet sparklers and has a certain affinity with port, especially white port. Whether served simply, as chilled slices dressed with a grinding of black pepper, soaked in sherry or port, or macerated in a light syrup flavoured with gin and mint, serve melon with a medium cream sherry. This holds true even for melon served with prosciutto crudo although there is a wider selection of wines in this instance (see **Cured hams** under **Cold meats**, above).

Pears go well with cream cheese, with prosciutto, and with blue cheese and walnuts on a bed of rocket. A medium cream sherry is just the thing to round off any of these pear starters.

For more on matching wine and fruit, see pages 254–256.

GUACAMOLE

Typically Mexican, guacamole is a contrast of colour, texture and flavour, combining the smoothness of avocado, the acid freshness of tomato and lime or lemon juice, and the keen bite of garlic, spring onion and chilli. Often served plainly, with tortilla chips or pitta bread, pair guacamole with dry Chenin Blanc, Sauvignon Blanc or a young Weisser Riesling as they will all provide good natural acidity.

See also **Nachos**, page 133.

HALOUMI

Haloumi (halloumi), a white, semi-soft cheese with a curiously rubbery texture, is ideal for frying as it holds its shape well. Pair it with a white wine such as Sauvignon Blanc or Weisser Riesling.

HUMMUS

Hummus, a purée made from chickpeas, tahini, lemon juice and garlic, is reputedly one of the oldest known prepared foods. When served as a dip with pitta bread, it is best accompanied by a very crisp, dry and aromatic white wine with no oak. Sauvignon Blanc, Chenin Blanc and dry Weisser Riesling – grapes associated with good natural acidity – are the winners here.

KEFTEDES (keftethes)

These little meatballs made from spiced, minced lamb often form part of a mezze platter (see below). When served on their own, they have a certain weight that a wine must be able to stand up to. A medium-bodied Cabernet Sauvignon, Merlot or Shiraz will have an equal weighting; avoid a heavy red wine.

See also **Kofta**, page 193.

MEZZE

In the Middle East and eastern Mediterranean, mezze (meze) is the equivalent of mixed hors d'oeuvres in western Europe. The cuisines of Lebanon, Jordan, Syria, Turkey, Cyprus and Greece have all contributed dishes to the modern mezze platter.

A selection of stuffed vine leaves (dolmades), haloumi, hummus, taramasalata, tzatziki, brinjal/aubergine purée (baba ghanoush), artichoke salad, deep-fried calamari, meatballs (keftedes), spanakopita, tabbouleh, olives and feta are served, along with pitta bread. Sometimes, individual portions of moussaka are included. It is difficult to select one wine that will cope with such a variety of flavours and textures all at once. Sauvignon Blanc or Chenin Blanc with racing acidity fare quite well until you get to the moussaka, at which point a blanc de noir or rosé would be a better overall partner. But you should avoid Chardonnay.

In the countries of origin, the accompanying drink is either wine or raki/arak/ouzo (an aniseed-flavoured alcohol that turns white when water is added). Greece has a tradition of *krasomezedes* (literally 'wine mezze'), which are bite-sized portions of food that pair well with wine, and *ouzomezedes*, which pair well with ouzo. Who said food and wine pairing is a new innovation?

See also individual listings for typical mezze dishes.

MOUSSES

A cold savoury mousse is a purée of fish, shellfish, meat, poultry, game or vegetables bound with cream, cream or cottage cheese, mayonnaise, béchamel sauce, or a combination of these. Sometimes stiffly beaten egg white is added for a lighter texture. Aspic or gelatine may be added to stabilize the mixture, particularly if the mousse is to be moulded. The angst that goes with unmoulding a mousse has led to the simpler way of serving it as individual portions or in ramekins. (In supermarkets and some restaurants you may see this preparation offered as a pâté.) Cold mousses provide Weisser Riesling's finest hour, as the wine's elegance and finesse are shown to its best advantage. Choose the best example you can find, one made from grapes ripened to full fruit flavours.

The mousses listed below, made from different ingredients, will all favour Weisser Riesling; other options are unwooded Chardonnay or Semillon. Blanc de noir or rosé could also feature.

Avocado mousse Dry Weisser Riesling.

Biltong mousse Off-dry Weisser Riesling.

Chicken, ham or other poultry mousses Dry Weisser Riesling, or unwooded Chardonnay or Semillon.

Chicken liver or foie gras mousse Off-dry Weisser Riesling.

Cucumber mousse Dry Weisser Riesling.

Fish mousses For mousses made with unsmoked fish, such as sole, canned salmon or tuna, choose a dry Weisser Riesling, or an unwooded Chardonnay or Semillon.

Smoked fish mousses For smoked fish, such as salmon, snoek, angelfish or haddock, choose an off-dry Weisser Riesling.

Roquefort or blue cheese mousse Off-dry Weisser Riesling.

Game mousse Blanc de noir or rosé.

Seafood mousses Prawn, crab or crayfish mousses pair well with off-dry Weisser Riesling, or an unwooded Chardonnay or Semillon.

MUSHROOMS

The earthy, fungal quality of mushrooms – whether white (button) or brown – can make them hard on many wines. For instance, a pairing of mushrooms with Chardonnay should be treated with caution. A better white wine choice would be Pinot Gris/Pinot Grigio. Generally, mushrooms prefer red wine and they have a pronounced affinity for Tempranillo and Cabernet Sauvignon.

Plainly grilled or fried Choose a rounded, well-flavoured, mature Cabernet Sauvignon or Bordeaux blend, or a Tempranillo.

Mushrooms with garlic butter These are sometimes called 'mushrooms with snail butter', as the pungent topping is the same as for serving snails. Go for a Chenin Blanc with good natural acidity.

Crumbed and deep-fried (1) When mushrooms are served with a creamy sauce or dip, such as sour cream and chives, an unwooded Chardonnay is tops. The weight of the dish lies in the sauce, which determines the wine choice. Mushrooms are usually no friends to Chardonnay, but they swiftly become just that when a creamy mush-room sauce wants an equally creamy white wine.

Crumbed and deep-fried (2) Served with tangy creamy sauces, such as garlic mayonnaise, choose a lightly wooded Chardonnay.

Stuffed mushrooms These come in many guises, depending on the creativity of the cook or chef. The most simple stuffing is bread-crumbs flavoured with garlic and parsley, perhaps enriched with egg and cream. Go straight to mushroom's old friends, Tempranillo or Cabernet Sauvignon. If the stuffing includes something smoky, such as ham or bacon, a Shiraz will not be out of place.

Mushrooms topped with sliced brinjal When grilled or baked under a mozzarella covering and served with tomato in some form or another (either sliced and layered into a tower, or as a relish-like sauce), and finished off with a scoop of pesto or sprigs of fresh basil, this combination will benefit from a herbaceaous, crisp Sauvignon Blanc or fruity Chenin Blanc. An unwooded Chardonnay from a cool climate, or a dry rosé or blanc de noir would also cope with the con-trasting textures and sweet-bitter flavours of this popular starter, which features frequently as a light lunch or vegetarian main meal.

NACHOS

This delightful Mexican starter is made of deep-fried tortilla chips, topped with grated cheese, guacamole, sour cream and jalapeño chillies, then grilled until the cheese melts. With so many contrast-ing flavours and textures, the wine drinker's first reaction may be to hide behind his sombrero. Fear not! A wooded Chenin Blanc provides the creamy richness and the acidity that nachos requires. Wooded Sauvignon Blanc is often successful too, but choose a lighter style, as it can easily overwhelm the nachos.

OLIVES

Olives are commonly served as a snack but, if you prefer to nibble on them in place of a starter, pour yourself a glass of pale dry (fino) sherry, which echoes the saltiness of the olives.

OYSTERS

A generation or two ago, these molluscs were cheap and plentiful for coastal dwellers. Nowadays, oysters are strictly in the luxury class, wherever you live.

Fresh oysters When served on the half-shell with lemon wedges and thinly sliced brown bread (and Tabasco sauce for some), these are ambrosia. It is hard to beat sparkling wine as an ideal partner for oysters, especially if it is made from Chardonnay and served well-chilled to match the oysters embedded in ice. However, oysters are equally happy with a high-acid white wine such as Sauvignon Blanc, provided the wine is fairly neutral and not overly fruity. Chenin Blanc and Cape/Paarl/SA Riesling (Crouchen Blanc) are excellent alternatives. But that's not all; an unwooded, cool-climate Chardonnay, grown within spitting distance of the ocean, is another appealing option. You may even find a whiff of the sea in your wine if you are feeling imaginative that day!

Oysters mornay Covered in a cheese sauce, topped with grated Parmesan and grilled, this dish calls for a full-bodied, slightly fat-textured white wine, such as a wooded Chardonnay or Semillon. It is equally happy with a Pinot Noir-based sparkling wine, and won't blink an eye if paired with a rosé or a blanc de noir.

Oysters Rockefeller Perhaps the most famous cooked oyster dish, this was not named for Mr Rockefeller, but is a reference to his pecuniary state – rich; exceedingly so. The 'richness' of the bread-thickened green sauce topping on grilled or baked oysters is said to have been the inspiration for this New Orleans dish. However, it is highly flavoured, rather than rich in the egg or cream-sauce sense. Typical ingredients are spring onions, fennel and spinach cooked in butter and given 'zhoozsh' with parsley, Tabasco, lime and Pernod. It should come as no surprise that sparkling wine goes best with this opulent dish. Billionaires-in-training who want to live up to the dish's name, can consider Krug's 1995 Clos d'Ambonnay, a limited release champagne which retails for over $3,000 a bottle! For the rest of us, a cap classique will do just fine...

Smoked oysters Tinned smoked oysters are normally preserved in oil. Serve them with an equally rich, fat, smoky Chardonnay.

PÂTÉS AND TERRINES

We normally understand pâté to mean a preparation of meat, fish or poultry that has been finely ground (minced), mixed with spices and other flavourings and then baked. In culinary terms, there is no real difference between a pâté and a terrine mixture; the latter simply takes its name from the dish in which it is baked. As pâtés have a high fat content, portions are normally modest and accompanied by toast or French bread to act as a foil for their rich flavours. This is a fine moment for Weisser Riesling, especially when the grapes have ripened into full-fruit flavours.

Chicken and duck liver pâté These call for a Weisser Riesling, Pinot Gris/Pinot Grigio or Gewürztraminer. **Pâté de foie gras** is best with a Gewürztraminer that has quite a bit of residual sugar. If the pâté contains a high proportion of duck or goose liver in relation to the other ingredients, it will be very happy wth a special late harvest or a lighter styled noble late. See also **Foie Gras**, page 128.

Fish pâté or terrine When made with unsmoked fish, fish pâté is happiest with a dry or off-dry Chenin Blanc, while pâté made with smoked snoek, angelfish or salmon will go well with a cool climate, lightly oaked Chardonnay that shows good acidity. A dry or off-dry Weisser Riesling would be a good alternative. Tuna or crab pâté is happiest with a full-bodied Semillon, as it perfectly balances the richness and texture of these fish types.

Game and red meat terrines These call for a white wine rather than a red wine. Again, it is Weisser Riesling, Pinot Gris/Pinot Grigio or a Gewürztraminer that cater for these terrines.

Mousse-type pâtés These are made with ready-cooked ingredients (chicken, ham, etc.) and mostly bound with cream, cream cheese, mayonnaise or a combination of these. They often include aspic or gelatine to help set them. The 'pâtés' you buy at the supermarket are usually of this type. See **Mousses**, page 131.

PICKLED AND SALTED FISH

These days, freezing is the predominant method of preserving food, so pickling in vinegar or salting fish is no longer a necessity. However, these traditional dishes have endured for their unique flavours.

Bokkoms Harders (mullet) are preserved with salt and then air- dried, similar to biltong. In days gone by, 'dop en dam', that is, brandy and water (the predecessor to brandy and Coke) was quaffed with this West Coast speciality. The wines available at the time were mostly full-sweet ones and, not surprisingly, they were quite a hit with bokkoms, as salty food has a pronounced affinity for wine with residual sugar. The saltier the food, the sweeter the wine can be.

With tongue firmly in cheek, we suggest that the 'correct way' to eat bokkoms is sitting on your haunches round the fire, waiting for the coals to be ready for the braai. With a bokkom in the one hand and a *knipmes* (pocketknife) in the other, you'd absentmindedly whittle slivers of bokkom and eat them straight off the blade while listening to the tale of a raconteur – another speciality of the West Coast. You may say that this is a very masculine scene. Well, yes; the womenfolk would, inevitably, be in the kitchen...

These days, we have a broader range of wines to choose from than our forebears. A medium-sweet white, with a touch of acidity to cope with the oiliness of the fish, would be a good choice; try a Chenin Blanc made in this style.

Gravlax (gravadlax) is a Scandinavian dish consisting of raw salmon cured in salt, sugar and dill. It is usually served thinly sliced and accompanied by a dill and mustard sauce, on bread of some kind or with boiled potatoes. The combination of salmon, sugar, salt, dill and mustard sounds like a tall order for any wine but, actually, there is one brilliant combination and three alternatives: Weisser Riesling is the star, as its flavours harmonize with both salmon and dill but, because of the sweet note of the dish, choose an off-dry version (or an off-dry Chenin Blanc). Also, try an off-dry Gewürz or a sec sparkling wine based on Chardonnay. A still Chardonnay is good, but it should be a top-notch wine with judicial wood treatment.

Marinated herrings and rollmops What comes to mind is a shot-glass of ice-cold aquavit, as few wines pair happily with marinated herring; those that do, need to be white, have racy acidity to cut through the oiliness of the fish, and be neutral rather than fruity. Unassertive Sauvignon Blanc, Chenin Blanc, Weisser or Cape Riesling are all options. Or try a pale dry (fino) sherry. Marinated herring is often chopped and served in a sweetish sauce, in which case an off-dry Weisser Riesling or Chenin Blanc would be a better match.

See also **Pickled fish**, page 152.

QUAIL

For wines to match these tiny birds, see page 226.

QUESADILLAS

Mexican cuisine has given us these delicious cheese-filled tortillas. Grated Cheddar cheese is laced with chopped green chilli or, for a richer version, a dollop of thick sour cream and placed on one side of a tortilla that is folded over into a half-moon shape and warmed, fried or baked until the cheese has melted. Quesadillas is a Spanish word meaning 'little cheesy thing' (from 'queso', meaning 'cheese'). An unwooded or lightly wooded Chardonnay is an excellent partner to these little morsels. Red wines that would go well are Cabernet Franc or a soft-centred Merlot.

RILLETTES OF PORK

Rillettes of pork (rillettes de porc) are one of the classic appetizers of provincial France. It is a delicate pâté made with pork that is either ground to a smooth texture or shredded so that the fat clings to the pork shreds, rather than blending into it. Cabernet Franc is its best ally but, if you want to drink a white wine with rillettes, find a cool-climate Semillon that shows some acidity.

SALMON

See **Smoked Fish**, page 138.
See also **Gravlax**, under **Pickled and Salted Fish**, page 135.

SAMOSAS

These celebrated triangular-shaped minced meat, chicken or vegetable patties, flavoured with spices and chilli and deep-fried, are a popular snack in South Africa, and often served with pre-dinner drinks. As a match for the spicy curried filling, Viognier comes out on top but, as a second choice, consider Gewürztraminer or an off-dry Weisser Riesling. A quaffable Cabernet-Merlot blend would be a good red wine choice.

SARDINES

Whether fresh and grilled in the Portuguese style, or canned, sardines cry out for a bone-dry white wine and Cape/Paarl/SA Riesling, Sauvignon Blanc and Chenin Blanc immediately come to mind. Sardines are invariably served with a squeeze of lemon, which spells the end for any fine bottle of red wine. Lemon will also flatten a Chardonnay produced in a low-acidic style with a touch of residual sugar, or any bland, neutral, low-acidic white for that matter.

If your wine store has an imported, good-quality, Portuguese estate-bottled Vinho Verde, either a white or a red (the latter being even more astringent), do not hesitate to grab it, as the combination of a bone-dry, slightly fizzy wine and sardines is legendary.

There are some South African wines produced in a similar style, called perlé, with which you can experiment. The key element to look for is that they are dry, without even a hint of residual sugar.

SEAFOOD COCKTAIL

Whether your seafood cocktail contains shrimps, prawns, crabmeat or crayfish, it will probably be dressed in a sauce based on mayonnaise, with or without tomato sauce, lemon juice, Worcestershire sauce or Tabasco, and this dressing can be very hard on wine. What it requires is the trinity of creaminess, acidity and sweetness, which is a tall order for any single wine to deliver. An unoaked Chenin Blanc with keen acidity and upfront fruit rises admirably to the challenge. Avoid an oaked Chardonnay.

SEAFOOD SALAD

Seafood salad is usually dressed in a lemony vinaigrette or sauce but, even if the sauce or dressing has been enriched with butter or cream, it will still need a white wine with racy acidity. A well-chilled Sauvignon Blanc is the obvious choice, while a dry sparkling wine will make a delectable partner. An unoaked Chardonnay from a cool climate will be very successful too.

See also **Seafood salad**, page 146.

SHISH KEBABS

Shish kebabs (from the Turkish *sis kebabi*) are brochettes of cubed lamb with cinnamon, olive oil and pepper flavouring. Served as part of a mezze platter or as a starter on their own, mini shish kebabs make a delicious feast on a stick when washed down with a glass of hearty, fruity Pinotage.

SMOKED FISH

As a starter, smoked fish may be presented in many different ways. In all instances, the accompaniments or garnishes will not affect the choice of wine, as the weight will always be in the fish itself.

Salmon spends much of its life in the sea and only returns to fresh water to spawn. **Smoked salmon**, which is imported from Norway, Scotland or Canada, has a romantic legacy of being one of the best partners for champagne or quality sparkling wine. Hmmm, it's time to rethink that one. Even when served plainly with brown bread and butter and a squeeze of lemon, smoked salmon can kill a prized sparkler as it is too smoky, oily and salty for this delicate style of wine. Rather pair it with a fat, cool-climate wooded Chardonnay or Semillon that shows some acidity, or with a Viognier or an off-dry Weisser Riesling. Even if served à la russe, that is with chopped hard-boiled egg, chopped raw onion and capers, which are so hard on a wine, the fish still dominates and the wine choices will remain the same. This also holds true for smoked salmon prepared with crème fraîche or cream cheese.

A classic way of serving smoked salmon is with creamy scrambled eggs, or other creamy egg dishes. An amazing transformation takes place when smoked salmon is enveloped in egg; it now begs for that sparkling wine. We suspect that this combination is the origin of the 'ideal' pairing of smoked salmon and champagne, but the eggs obviously got lost in the translation! If you serve scrambled eggs with smoked salmon slivers for breakfast, forgo the orange juice and have your bubbly 'neat'; you won't regret it.

Smoked trout Trout, a freshwater fish, provides a 'lighter' type of smoked fish which, predictably, does well with a dry sparkling wine or an unwooded or lightly wooded Chardonnay or Semillon, as it is not very oily or salty. (Note that although **Smoked salmon trout** is packaged in much the same way as smoked salmon, they are not the same thing. There is a big difference in the weight of the two, hence the different wine choices.)

Smoked snoek, angelfish and mackerel These naturally oily fish all have the same weight as smoked salmon (see above) and pair well with the same wines.

SNAILS (*escargots*)

Snails by themselves are rather bland, but they absorb the flavours of their accompanying sauce well. Burgundy (yip! the one in France), is famous for its snail dishes and the Burgundians have been eating them with garlic and assorted herbs since Roman times.

Snails with garlic butter (*escargots à la bourguignonne*) This classic way of serving snails is the one most often seen on restaurant menus. They are poached in red or white wine and stuffed back into their shells with butter flavoured with garlic, herbs and, sometimes, lemon juice and then baked until the butter is bubbling, before being served with bread to soak up the sauce. Remarkably, there is no single wine that is traditionally paired with this dish. On reflection, this is understandable, as the mild flavour of the snails and the equally mild garlic and herb butter are both undemanding on a wine partner. A middle-of-the-road Pinot Noir, Sangiovese, an easy-drinking Pinotage or a Bordeaux blend are all good companions. Other good matches are a dry blanc de noir or rosé, Semillon or Chardonnay, but don't choose high-end ones, keep them crisp and savoury. Cool-climate wines will provide the necessary acidity.

Snails in red wine (*escargots au vin rouge*) Snails simmered in red wine with bacon and garlic and finished off with a splash of brandy is so typically Burgundian you wonder why it isn't known as *escargots à la bourguignonne*. Choose from Pinot Noir, Pinotage or a Bordeaux blend, but keep to simple and easy-drinking versions.

Snails with truffles (*escargots à la dijonnaise*) In this version, the garlic butter includes chopped truffles. Match it with a Pinot Noir.

Snails with tomato, onions, peppers and chillies (*escargots à la gourmande*) This dish originates from Spain, where it is known as *cargols a la gormanda*. Tempranillo pairs splendidly, as the wine can handle the chilli without overwhelming the snails. Alternatively, choose a dry blanc de noir, rosé or any young, easy-drinking red.

Vigneronne The snails are first cooked in butter and garlic, then dipped in batter and fried. The wines mentioned under snails with garlic butter, above, will all pair well with this dish.

SPANAKOPITA

Spanakopita – triangular phyllo pastry pies filled with spinach and cheese – are not only delicious, but convenient as a pass-around starter. They are ideal morsels to accompany a full-bodied, fresh, dry, white wine. Choose a lightly wooded Chardonnay or Semillon.

If you really must have a red, choose a low-tannin Gamay or Pinot Noir. A dry blanc de noir or a rosé made from Cabernet Sauvignon or Pinotage grapes would be a better compromise.

TAPAS

'Tapa' means 'lid' or 'cover' in Spanish and the word is thought to originate from the bar custom of covering glasses with a plate of small morsels of food. Tapas can include almost anything: a chunk of tuna, cocktail onions, chorizo, Manchego cheese, anchovies, sardines or mackerel in olive oil, calamari, scrambled egg with shrimps or mushrooms, cubes of meat with a sauce, and then some. It is rare for a tapas selection not to include olives. Tapas are often strongly flavoured with garlic, chillies, paprika, cumin, salt, pepper or saffron, and often served in plentiful amounts of olive oil. The astonishing variety of these appetizers makes an exact wine match difficult. A chilled fino sherry copes best with the varied, salty and savoury flavours, but a good second choice is a crisp, dry blanc de noir or rosé. If you want to drink a white wine, it should have the same profile. Choose a Sauvignon Blanc that is tangy and not too ripely fruity.

TAPENADE

Tapenade is a French dish consisting of puréed or finely chopped olives, capers, anchovies and olive oil. Although tapenade's base ingredient is olives, its name comes from the Provençal word for capers, 'tapéno'. It is generally eaten as an hors d'oeuvre, spread on breads such as baguette or ciabatta. Tapenade is often flavoured with garlic, herbs, lemon juice or brandy. These spreads are as sharp as a scimitar. The one wine that will survive scot-free is pale dry (fino) sherry, but a dry blanc de noir made from spicy Pinotage, or a herby, dry rosé will also make the grade.

TARAMASALATA

Taramasalata, a paste made from fish roe, is often served with hot toast. Traditionally, it is made from the roe of the grey mullet, called tarama, but cod or carp roe is also used. The oily, garlicky texture of the dish demands a white wine with racy acidity to counteract the richness. Sauvignon or Chenin Blanc, Weisser or Cape/Paarl/SA Riesling fit the bill. Blanc de noir or rosé are also contenders, provided they are very crisp and dry. *See also* **Mezze**, page 131.

WHITEBAIT

These young or juvenile fish can normally only be purchased during or close to the netting season. They are normally coated in flour or a light batter, deep-fried, and served very hot with lemon juice and bread and butter. A crisp, dry Sauvignon Blanc is a classic match for whitebait. The grape's attractive grassiness and good natural acidity serve as a refreshing counterpoint to this slightly oily dish.

Soups

Soup is one of the simplest dishes to make, but pairing it with wine is a bit more tricky. Most soups involve very little effort to prepare and, if you make a mistake along the way, it can be corrected easily. Too thick; add water, milk or cream. Too thin; thicken with cornflour.

But what if the wine doesn't do any favours to the soup? Water and thickeners won't do the trick, so it is best to find a good match upfront, as a 'starter' soup and its accompanying wine can be considered an indication of the culinary and vinous pleasures to follow.

If you're fifty-plus you'll remember when sherry was the accepted wine to serve with soup. This came to us via Europe and the UK, along with other food and wine guidelines of the day: serve white wine with white meat, red wine with red meat. We acquiesced until we could no longer face sherry with our butternut-and-orange or curried fish soups. While the Brits and Europeans were still savouring consommé (which does go with sherry, we might add), down south, we were into fusion soups. How can you pair a medium cream sherry with a spicy curried soup? The sherry simply had to go!

Then along came a new theory. If you're in your thirties, you may remember being told that, actually, soup should not be paired with any wine (or any drink for that matter), as serving liquid with liquid is tautologous, similar to the Japanese thinking that serving sake (rice wine) with rice is tautologous. However, for the food and wine pairer, worrying about liquids and solids seems like an oddity, as his (or her) concern would be how food and wine taste together, not how liquid or solid either of them are. If a particular wine and a specific food are good matches, why not enjoy them together?

The way to go when selecting a wine to go with soup is to match the main ingredient in the soup to the wine, for example, split peas are the main ingredient in a pea soup, and oxtail in an oxtail soup. If there is no discernable single ingredient, such as in a vegetable soup, select a wine that will match the resulting composite flavour.

As most soups are a 'diluted' version of their main ingredients, you do not need a 'big' wine to make the perfect match; in fact, you need the opposite. If a wine is too complex, the subtlety will be lost from both the wine and the soup.

Some suggestions for matching wines to both cold and hot soups are given on the following pages.

COLD SOUPS

Avocado Dry Chenin Blanc or unwooded Chardonnay.

Cucumber Unwooded Chardonnay or Pinot Gris/Pinot Grigio.

Gazpacho Pale dry (fino) sherry is the best partner for most variations of gazpacho (red, white or green). However, if it is tomato-based, a young, crisp Sauvignon Blanc or Sangiovese are better choices. An unoaked Semillon or Chardonnay pair well with a white gazpacho.

Vichyssoise Unwooded Chardonnay or Pinot Blanc.

HOT FISH AND SEAFOOD SOUPS

Bisque Pick a fat, rounded, well-wooded, 'top-drop' Chardonnay or Semillon for this soup that is mainly a thick, rich shellfish purée, often made with crayfish, crab or prawns. As a shellfish bisque has about twice the weight of a shellfish soup, it requires about twice the weight in its accompanying wine. *See* **Crayfish** soup, below.

Bouillabaisse Blanc de noir, dry to off-dry rosé, lightly wooded Chenin Blanc, Chardonnay, Semillon, or Pinot Gris/Pinot Grigio – there's a whole range of wines to choose from for this main-dish soup that can contain up to ten different kinds of fish and shellfish. The traditional accompaniment, rouille (a garlicky green and red pepper purée), does not change the choice of wine, as the weight remains in the fish and shellfish.

Chowders Concentrated, rich, buttery Chardonnay is just the thing to pair with these stew-like soups.

Crayfish A fruity, lightly creamy Chardonnay with sweet vanilla-oak flavours will do well with this lightly creamy soup with its touch of 'crayfish sweetness'.

Mussel Lightly wooded Semillon with good acidity, or lightly wooded Chenin Blanc.

Provençale fish soup (*la bourride*) Lightly wooded Chenin Blanc, Chardonnay, Semillon or Pinot Gris/Pinot Grigio are the best partners for this celebrated 'fisherman's soup', and you don't have to hold back on the often accompanying aioli (garlic mayonnaise).

HOT MEAT AND POULTRY SOUPS

Chicken Unwooded Chardonnay; or a lightly wooded one when the soup is creamy.

Consommé Dry, fortified wine, such as a pale dry (fino) or medium cream sherry.

Curry (mulligatawny) Viognier or Gewürztraminer.

Oxtail Choose a light red wine, such as a quaffable Merlot, or go for a blanc de noir or rosé.

Scotch broth A quaffable Cabernet-Merlot blend, blanc de noir or rosé will go with this hearty soup based on mutton/lamb and barley.

HOT PULSE SOUPS

Bean or **Lentil** A balanced level of acidity in the wine is crucial, so choose Sauvignon Blanc, Chenin Blanc or easy-drinking Pinotage.

Pea and ham Choose a wooded Chenin Blanc or Sauvignon Blanc (blanc fumé), or a lightly wooded Chardonnay with good acidity.

HOT VEGETABLE SOUPS

Asparagus Wooded Sauvignon Blanc (blanc fumé) or Semillon.

Beetroot (borsch) Blanc de noir, dry to just-off-dry rosé or Pinot Noir.

Butternut Dry/off-dry Weisser Riesling, Chenin Blanc or Bukettraube will work, whether the soup is plain, or flavoured with curry, orange or other flavourings.

Corn Lightly wooded or unwooded Semillon is the ideal partner for all corn soups, whether plain and lightly creamy, or chunky and chowder-like with added ingredients such as chicken or shellfish. A Chardonnay with some sweet-vanilla oak flavours also works well with corn soups that tend to have a bit of sweetness of their own.

French onion Dry, fortified wine, such as a pale dry (fino) or medium cream sherry is best with this classic soup.

Minestrone Medium- to full-bodied dry white, such as a Semillon or Sauvignon-Semillon blend; light red with good acidity, such as a quaffable Pinotage, or a Sangiovese or Chianti from Italy.

Mushroom Lightly wooded Chardonnay, as the soup would most likely contain some cream.

Potato and leek Unwooded Chardonnay or Pinot Gris/Pinot Grigio.

Ribollita Sangiovese or an Italian Chianti, a quaffable Pinotage or Cinsaut or a medium-bodied Tempranillo are all well suited to this substantial, rustic, bread-thickened cannellini bean and vegetable soup. ('Ribollita' means 'reboiled' because it is traditionally prepared the day before and then heated again before serving.)

Sweet potato Dry or off-dry Weisser Riesling, off-dry Chenin Blanc or Bukettraube.

Tomato (fresh or cream of tomato) Sauvignon Blanc. Choose a wooded version for the creamy soup.

Vegetable Chenin Blanc, Pinot Gris/Pinot Grigio.

Salads

Traditionally, the French serve a simple salad after the main course, to cleanse the palate for the cheese course that is to follow. In South Africa, we serve salad either as a starter or as an accompaniment to the main course. We also serve salads as a light meal, often adding protein, in the form of eggs, fish, meat, poultry or cheese, to make the salad more substantial. Both our climate and our preference for informal entertaining lend themselves to eating outdoors; alfresco dining and salads go hand-in-hand.

The key to selecting a wine to go with a salad is the dressing. Most often, salad dressings contain an acidic element, such as vinegar, lemon or lime juice. This sour element predisposes itself to a wine with equal natural acidity, and there is a wide choice. For the whites: Sauvignon Blanc, Chenin Blanc, dry Weisser Riesling or Cape/Paarl/SA Riesling, Pinot Gris/Grigio, Fernão Pires or Pinot Blanc, or a dry blanc de noir or rosé. On the red side, the stars are Sangiovese and Gamay Noir. Forget about pairing an acidic dressing with Chardonnay, Semillon or Viognier, because none of these wines, particularly a wooded Chardonnay, can stand up to it. In the mouth, when acid meets wood, the oak separates from the wine and lies on top, leaving you with the sensation of chewing on a wooden plank.

But we do not like to be quite so prescriptive. What if you *want* a Chardonnay with your salad? Then do it! Just manage the salad; you can do nothing about the Chardonnay once the winemaker has put a cork in it. How do you 'manage' a salad? Instead of vinegar, lemon or lime juice, use a splash of the wine you are going to enjoy with the salad, and blend it with a nutty oil, such as walnut or sesame, to echo the typical nuttiness of the Chardonnay. Adding a few nuts to the salad will further enhance the wine. Yes, we must sometimes cook for the bottle; you are, after all, already cooking for guests. Cooking for the bottle is just one more little chore.

However, not all salad dressings have a sour note – some are bland and creamy and pair well with Chardonnay, especially unwooded. If you like to add a touch of sweetness to your salads, such as cubed apple, pineapple, plums or segments of orange, an off-dry Weisser Riesling, with its sweet-sour character, will come to the rescue. All is not lost for the lover of sweetish wines either. Remember those old-style dressings made with condensed milk? Resurrect them!

In the **How to pair food and wine** chapter, we deal with acidity more extensively (see pages 20–21).

BRINJAL SALAD (eggplant/aubergine salad)

Most Middle Eastern countries have a variation of grilled brinjal dressed with olive oil, lemon juice and garlic, sometimes with the inclusion of tahini, chopped tomato and/or green pepper. Often, the brinjal is mixed with yoghurt before adding a drop of olive oil and some fresh garlic. Served with other salads as a starter, eaten with flatbread, or served as a light lunch or supper dish, it is at its best with Sauvignon Blanc or dry Chenin Blanc.

CAESAR SALAD

This American classic was created during Prohibition by Caesar Cardini, who saw an opportunity and opened a restaurant in Tijuana, just south of the Mexican border, so that Americans could hop over and enjoy a drink or two without breaking the law. Egg yolk is used to make a creamy, garlicky dressing that, together with grated Parmesan cheese, coats the salad leaves and croutons (or squares of toast). Chardonnay with tropical notes, or a Viognier, should stand up well to this salad.

CAPRESE SALAD (insalata caprese)

The star of this Italian salad is the tomato. Very simply, it comprises sliced tomato interleaved with sliced Mozzarella and fresh basil leaves. Traditionally, it is served with no other dressing than a drizzle of extra virgin olive oil. But, if the tomatoes are not absolutely the best, a little balsamic vinegar will help them along. As you might guess, the tomato-wine, Sauvignon Blanc, is spot on, but dry Chenin Blanc or Weisser Riesling will also be obliging partners.

CHICKEN MAYONNAISE (chicken salad)

This salad, which is also served as an appetizer, albeit a substantial one, may have canned tuna added to shredded chicken and chopped hard-boiled eggs blended into a well-flavoured mayonnaise. Whatever the additions, the weight of the dish lies in the creamy, eggy mayonnaise, which cries out for an equally creamy white wine. An oaked Chardonnay or Semillon come out tops for 'tjicken maynays', as it tends to be pronounced in the Cape. One of the many fashionable new white blends on the market, where at least one component has been in contact with wood, would be equally good.

GREEK SALAD

The 'Greek salad' has many local interpretations. However, it is safe to expect tomatoes, olives, feta and cucumber, with or without lettuce, green peppers and sliced red onions. The traditional dressing is rather lemony, but the steakhouse or supermarket version may be less so. In any event, this salad loves a fresh, crisp Sauvignon Blanc best of all. Chenin Blanc or Weisser Riesling, the other two 'salad wines', will suffer from the combination of the saltiness of the olives and the acidity of the tomatoes and the dressing. It is best to avoid rosés and red wines.

SALAD NIÇOISE

Green beans, canned tuna, boiled eggs, anchovy fillets and boiled baby potatoes are mixed with crisp lettuce and stoned black olives to create this flavoursome main-course salad. It calls for a fairly big, unoaked Chardonnay, but is equally happy with a blanc de noir or dry rosé. The protein ingredients give this salad a weightiness that diverts attention away from the dressing.

If you use fresh tuna, either lightly seared on the grill or pan-fried, the wine match will be the same.

SEAFOOD SALAD

Unoaked Chardonnay will cope with most creamy seafood salads, but if their dressings have an acidic note, switch to Sauvignon Blanc. See also **Seafood salad**, page 137.

TABBOULEH

Tabbouleh is a salad made with cracked wheat (bulgar/burghul), tossed with tomatoes, onions and chopped mint and moistened with lemon juice and olive oil. It often forms part of a mezze platter. This Middle Eastern dish cries out for Sauvignon Blanc, but a dry Chenin Blanc or Weisser Riesling are also splendid partners.

WALDORF SALAD

This crunchy, slightly sweet salad, which was 'invented' at New York's famous Waldorf Astoria hotel, is a combination of diced red-skinned apples (traditionally), walnuts and celery, dressed with mayonnaise. You may find it served with other types of apples, depending on the season. A white wine with a touch of residual sugar, such as an off-dry Weisser Riesling or a Chenin Blanc, is the ideal partner. If the salad is not too sweet, for instance if Granny Smith apples are used and no raisins are added, a dry Weisser Riesling or Chenin Blanc is a better choice because the salad's acidity will sweeten an off-dry wine even more, which may be undesirable to you.

Fish and seafood

South Africans are fortunate to have access to a wide variety of freshwater and saltwater fish and seafood. Fish is very adaptable and there are many ways to serve it: braaied, grilled, poached, fried, baked, or in soups or stews. Seafood provides a similar canvas for the chef or cook to leave his or her thumbprint on. Every chef and home cook has his or her individual favourite preparations and interpretations for cooking this bounty from the sea, vlei or river.

So, where do we start when selecting a wine? When it comes to fish, flavour intensity is the initial consideration – just how 'fishy' is that fish? Weight is the next consideration – how much 'body' does the fish have? This is related to texture; is the flesh 'meaty' and firmly textured, or fragile and soft? For example, a sardine and a piece of fresh tuna may have the same flavour intensity, but whereas the sardine is fragile and soft, the tuna is meaty and firmly textured. A light-bodied wine would go well with the sardines, but the tuna needs something more strongly constituted. The cooking method also comes into play, while an accompanying sauce or dressing, or added ingredients such as herbs, spices or other seasonings, which might alter the flavours, could throw their weight around.

Fish

We have listed the most common fish available in South Africa. Mindful of the guidelines on sustainable seafood, we have omitted those on the 'no sale, no purchase' list, such as white steenbras, galjoen, white musselcracker, leervis and seventy-four, as it is illegal to buy or sell these species. To check the status of the fish or seafood you are planning to serve, see the SASSI recommendations on page 158.

BRAAIED, GRILLED OR PAN-FRIED

Mildly flavoured fish	
These fish can be overpowered by a wine that is too heavy or too flavourful.	
Angelfish Catfish Cob (kob, kabeljou) Elf (shad) Hake (stockfish)	*When plainly served, with nothing added:* Keep the wine as neutral as possible. Select a gentle, dry white, such as Pinot Gris/Pinot Grigio, Pinot Blanc, unoaked Chardonnay, Chenin Blanc or Semillon.

Kingklip	*With richer treatments (such as the addition*
Shark	*of butter, cream, oil, herbs or vegetables):*
Skate	Select a more aromatic wine, such as a
Sole	lightly wooded Chardonnay or Semillon.
Tilapia	*With sauces:* Sauces served with mildly
	flavoured fish will influence your choice of
	wine. *See also* **Sauces**, pages 32–43.

Medium-flavoured fish

Medium-flavoured fish pairs well with medium-bodied white wines. Unoaked versions are the tried-and-tested partners, but fruity, lightly wooded wines are also good choices.

Black musselcracker	*When plainly served, with nothing added:*
Dorado (dolphinfish)	The forward, yet subtle personality of a
Geelbek (Cape salmon)	Chardonnay is the obvious choice, with
Gurnard	Pinot Gris/Pinot Grigio, Weisser Ries-
Harder (mullet)	ling and Chenin Blanc hot on its heels.
Hottentot (sea bream)	*With richer treatments (added butter,*
John Dory	*cream, oil, herbs, vegetables):* Choose
Monkfish (mock crayfish)	richer wines. The creamy, rounded, full,
Queen mackerel	and often silky character of a wooded
Red roman	Chardonnay or Semillon will be magi-
Red snapper	cal. Viognier can also be a good choice.
Red steenbras	*When robustly flavoured, as in stews:*
Rockcod	Stay with the wooded wines, but also
Sand soldier (red tjor-tjor)	consider a Pinot Noir or Merlot.
Santer (soldier)	*With sauces:* Any sauce accompani-
Scotsman	ment will influence your choice of wine.
Silverfish (carpenter)	See also **Sauces**, pages 32–43.
Stumpnose (red/white)	
Swordfish	
Trout	

Intensely flavoured fish

With intensely flavoured fish, acidity in a wine is a plus, especially when the fish is oily, as it cuts through its strong fishy taste and acts just like a squeeze of lemon.

Butterfish	*When plainly served, with nothing added:*
Chub mackerel	Sparkling wine, with its good acidity, is
Katonkel (king	the perfect foil for oily 'fishy' fish. But so
mackerel)	is Pinot Gris/Pinot Grigio, Chenin Blanc
Maasbanker (horse	and, in the case of sardines, Cape
mackerel)	Riesling (Crouchen Blanc).

Marlin	*With richer treatments (added oil, herbs,*
Oilfish (Butterfish)	*seasonings, vegetables):* More flavour
Salmon (fresh,	in the fish will take more flavour in the
imported from	wine. Pinot Gris/Pinot Grigio is still on
Canada, Norway	the table, as is Chardonnay, preferably
or Scotland)	one from a cool climate. Merlot is a good
Sardine	choice, especially if the fish is meaty and
Snoek	firmly textured; fresh salmon and tuna go
Tuna	well with a medium-bodied Merlot.
Yellowtail	*When robustly flavoured, as in stews:* Up
	the flavour with full-bodied Merlot, Tem-
	pranillo, Gamay or Petit Verdot. Cab Sav
	will hobble along; Sangiovese is fine with
	tuna or salmon but will turn its back on
	the others. Avoid Shiraz, which can be
	thrown out of balance by a strong fishy
	taste, Pinot Noir and Viognier.
	With sauces: Any accompanying sauces
	will play a part in your choice of wine.
	See also **Sauces**, pages 32–43.

BACALHAU (bacalao)

Dried salted cod is known as *bacalhau* in Portugal, *bacalao* in Spain, *baccalà* in Italy and *bakaliaros* in Greece; there are literally hundreds of ways of serving this dried fish. What we are pairing the wine to is the stew-like Portuguese preparation, rich in olive oil, which is almost a national dish. An astringent Portuguese Vinho Verde is the traditional wine served with it, but Chardonnay and Semillon are the best all-rounders, provided they are only lightly oaked. A light, aromatic, earthy red wine with some acidity also works with the strong, hot flavours of the dish. Choose a young Tempranillo, quaffable Pinotage, Pinot Noir, Sangiovese or zesty Barbera.

BRANDADE

For this pâté-like spread, see page 122.

CAJUN-STYLE FISH

Firm-fleshed fish takes on another life when it is flavoured with a spicy Cajun-style rub of cumin, cayenne, black pepper, thyme, origanum, mustard powder and sage combined with lemon juice. Although Shiraz is not a fish wine, with this dish, a medium-bodied, quaffable Shiraz, Shiraz-Grenache, Shiraz-Malbec or Shiraz-Cab-Merlot blend are your best choices.

CEVICHE

For wines to match this raw, marinated fish dish, see page 125.

ESCABÈCHE

This dish originated in Spain as a way of preserving fish in pickling liquid and spices. Because of its high level of acidity, a white wine is essential. Sauvignon Blanc, with brilliant acidity, or Cape, Paarl or South African Riesling (Crouchen Blanc) are your best options.

FISHCAKES

Patties of flaked fish mixed with creamy mashed potatoes and subtly flavoured with lemon and herbs are gently fried until golden. You need a crisp aromatic white wine, such as a Sauvignon Blanc, an unwooded, young Chardonnay or a Semillon, or opt for a Pinot Gris/Pinot Grigio, the fall-back 'fish wine'.

FISH CURRY

A mild or spicy fish curry pairs well with Viognier. However, if there is a touch of sweetness to the curry, or it is tomato-based, an off-dry Chenin Blanc would be better.

FISH 'N CHIPS

Pour a glass straight from a box of chilled dry white wine to enjoy with your fried fish and vinegary *slap tjips*. If you are feeling a bit more formal, haul out a bottle of unoaked Chardonnay but, if you are having some tartare sauce or tomato sauce on the side, rather open a dry or off-dry Chenin Blanc.

FISH PIE

Whether it is an elaborate pie of mixed white and smoked fish, such as hake and haddock, baked under a golden puff pastry, or a more traditional Cape fish pie of flaked fish and braised onions under a topping of mashed potatoes, Semillon takes first prize. There is something quite unique about fish pie and Semillon, and tasting is believing. In the absence of Semillon, go for a full-bodied Chardonnay or Pinot Gris/Pinot Grigio.

FISH STEW OR CASSEROLE

A fish and vegetable stew in a creamy sauce is mad about Semillon, but Pinot Gris/Pinot Grigio is always happy with the fruits of the sea. A tomatoey fish stew that includes green or red peppers would prefer a lightish red, so choose a Pinot Noir, Sangiovese or Cinsaut.

FLORENTINE

Cooked fish fillets (often sole) layered on a bed of spinach, then topped with a cheese sauce and browned under the grill, will do well with an unwooded or lightly oaked Chardonnay.

GEFILTE FISH

Often, two or three varieties of fish are minced together to give gefilte fish – poached fish balls – a more distinctive flavour. This traditional Jewish dish pairs well with Sauvignon or Chenin Blanc, as the acidity of these wines gives it a lift, just as a squeeze of lemon would do.

HADDOCK

Elsewhere in the world, haddock is a sea fish similar to cod; what we call haddock in South Africa is mostly smoked hake. It is often gently poached in milk or water and served with lemon butter. You need a wine with good acidity, such as a dry Weisser Riesling, Chenin Blanc or Sauvignon Blanc. If you are serving haddock with a rich cheese sauce, a wooded Chardonnay sidles up close.

HERRING

See **Pickled and salted fish**, page 135.

KEDGEREE

This dish of rice and flaked smoked fish is either made plainly or spiced up with turmeric or curry powder. Traditionally, this brunch or supper stalwart includes sliced or quartered hard-boiled eggs. A rich, full-bodied, oak-flavoured Semillon or Chardonnay will match its weight exactly. Kedgeree also works very well in a vertical pairing when accompanied by a crisp Sauvignon Blanc, Pinot Blanc, Pinot Gris/Pinot Grigio or a bone dry (brut) sparkling wine. In this pairing, which provides a sharp contrast between wine and food, the flavours of the dish are highlighted.

KIPPERS

Kippers are smoked herrings. The raw fish are split, gutted, slightly dehydrated in brine and then smoked. The smoking process gives them their distinctive, deep yellowish-brown colour although, often, they are dyed to a deeper red shade. Served with little pats of butter, kippers go well with a pale dry (fino) sherry, which provides just the right amount of tang to the fish.

PICKLED FISH (ingelegte vis)

Traditionally made with snoek or yellowtail, the fish is preserved in a vinegary curry-based sauce with sliced onions, and often served with buttered wholewheat bread. A dry Chenin Blanc or Sauvignon Blanc without too much assertive fruit will fit the bill. A particular local quirk you may come across is when the bread is spread with smooth apricot jam, in which case it would be a good idea to switch to a semi-sweet Chenin Blanc.

SARDINES

For wines to match these, fresh or canned, see page 137.

SMOKED FISH

For **smoked salmon**, **snoek**, **trout**, **gravlax** etc., see page 138.

SMOORSNOEK (braised snoek)

In this traditional Cape dish, cooked fresh or smoked snoek is flaked and added to sautéed onions, potatoes, tomatoes and chilli, covered and simmered until heated through. Talk about comfort food... Haul out an equally comforting wine, such as a Chenin Blanc. If you've used smoked snoek, try a wooded Chenin.

TUNA, MACKEREL, PILCHARDS OR SALMON (canned)

These popular store-cupboard standbys pop up in anything from a salad to a pasta bake or quick fishcakes. If the fish is just one of many ingredients, the wine choice would depend on the final dish. Refer to an appropriate entry in this chapter or elsewhere.

Seafood

When fresh seafood is served plainly, without any elaborate preparations, its best partner is a dry white wine that is neither too heavy nor aromatic. Choose an unwooded, dry Chenin Blanc or a Pinot Gris/ Pinot Grigio, a time-honoured partner to seafood. When seafood is coated in a creamy sauce, it can take richer, fuller wines, such as unwooded or lightly wooded Chardonnay or Semillon. If you want a red wine, aim for a light, low-tannin version, ideally one that you can chill a bit, such as Pinot Noir, Cabernet Franc, Gamay or a quaffable Pinotage. Avoid heavy-bodied red wines with discernable tannins, as these can make all seafood taste metallic or tinny. Lemony sauces and dressings, which often accompany seafood, are also tough on blockbuster reds.

ABALONE/PERLEMOEN (locally farmed)

Abalone is known variously as klipkous, paarl-lemoen or perlemoen – the latter being the general term used in South Africa, whatever language we're speaking. Unless prepared with care, perlemoen can be tough and unappetizing. Consequently, it is often boiled or pressure-cooked in white wine to tenderize the flesh, which is really a muscle. Served on a bed of rice with lemon wedges and a sauce made from the tenderizing liquid, pair perlemoen with Sauvignon Blanc, Chenin Blanc or Pinot Gris/Pinot Grigio. When served in a creamy white sauce, flavoured with green peppers, a touch of curry powder and a splash of Worcestershire sauce, a Viognier would be delightful, but so would a lightly wooded Chardonnay.

See page 158 for catching restrictions.

CALAMARI (SQUID)

Calamari is the Italian name for squid. Grilled, or battered and fried, calamari is often served with lemon or garlic butter or tartare sauce. Pair it with Sauvignon Blanc, Chenin Blanc or Pinot Gris/Pinot Grigio. A frequent menu option is Cajun-spiced calamari, either grilled or pan-fried. This should be served with a spicy, light-bodied red wine, so choose a Shiraz or Pinotage for this version. A Mediterranean-type stew of calamari, stuffed with rice flavoured with fennel, saffron and chilli and simmered in a tomato and red wine sauce, needs a red wine with good acidity to cope with the robust sauce. A Pinot Noir, Barbera or quaffable Pinotage should do the trick.

CRAB

Crabs contain less meat for their size than crayfish, but the meat is a good deal sweeter. As crabmeat is rich, you need only small portions per serving. Unless you live on the Garden Route and can collect your own from the beach, fresh crabs are not readily available in South Africa. The canned version is a good substitute, though.

Crab salad With salad leaves and an oil-vinegar dressing; serve it with Pinot Gris/Pinot Grigio, Chenin Blanc or Sauvignon Blanc.

Devilled crab Crabmeat, spiced up with cayenne pepper and a splash of Worcestershire sauce, is mixed with a creamy sauce and topped with breadcrumbs and cheese before being browned under the grill. A Viognier will do splendidly.

Dressed crab As the white and dark meat of a crab have such different flavour intensities, they are kept separate when spooned back into the shell so that each type of meat can be enjoyed on its own. Pinot Gris/Pinot Grigio, unwooded Semillon and dry to off-dry Weisser Riesling are all good partners.

CRAYFISH (rock lobster)

Apart from those fortunate residents of the southwestern Cape who are able to catch their own, for most South Africans, crayfish (*kreef*) is an expensive item. If you are lucky enough to get your hands on some, make the most of this crustacean. With the exception of the stomach and the vein that runs through the body, every part can be used, although the tender and succulent tail meat is the best. And, when you've eaten, you can even boil the shell with white wine and flavourings to make a basic stock to use for soup or a sauce.

Grilled crayfish Halved crayfish are grilled, often over the coals, and served with lemon butter or a wedge of fresh lemon. Unwooded or lightly wooded Chardonnay or Semillon are the classic choices for this simple yet undeniably lip-smacking dish.

Crayfish mayonnaise Cubed, cooked crayfish meat is served with mayonnaise, sometimes garnished with strips of anchovy, sliced hard-boiled egg, olives and capers. Although all these garnishes are unfriendly towards wine, they play second fiddle, as the weight of the dish is in the crayfish and the mayonnaise. Serve it with a lightly wooded Chardonnay, a dry blanc de noir or a dry rosé.

Crayfish thermidor Crayfish meat is combined with a wine and mushroom sauce, enriched with cream and gently flavoured with mustard and cayenne pepper before being spooned back into the half shell. The filled shells are then sprinkled with breadcrumbs and grilled. Select a top-notch, full-bodied, buttery Chardonnay.

Crayfish à l'américaine This dish was created by a Parisian chef who had worked in the USA and named the dish in memory of his stay in that country. The crayfish meat and its garlic, tomato and cognac-flavoured sauce is traditionally served with rice. Choose a fruity, full-bodied Sauvignon Blanc, a top-notch, unwooded Chenin Blanc, or a dry (sec) sparkling wine.

LANGOUSTINE

This is the French name for what is also variously known as scampi, Dublin Bay prawn or Norway lobster. Preparations for langoustine are similar to those of prawns. *See* **Prawns**, page 155.

MUSSELS

Black mussels are inherently wine-friendly. They love crisp, dry white wines but, as black mussels can be cooked in umpteen ways, it is easiest to match the wines to the ingredients of the accompanying sauce. To open mussels, they are usually cooked in a little dry white wine flavoured with onion and herbs, and this cooking liquor is then used as the base for many of the sauces. As mussels don't have any natural fat, they combine particularly well with creamy sauces and oily dressings. Some of the most common preparations are:

Mussel pot (*moules et frites*) This potjie-styled dish, a Belgian classic served with shoestring chips (*frites*) on the side, loves Sauvignon Blanc, Chenin Blanc and dry Weisser Riesling.

Mussels in a coriander broth Green-lipped New Zealand mussels are often used for this Asian-influenced dish. An intensely aromatic, herbaceous Sauvignon Blanc, which has the right weight, makes the most of this succulent starter or main course.

Mussels in creamy sauces Whether in an unadorned creamy sauce (*moules à la marinière*) or one flavoured with saffron or curry, serve with Sauvignon Blanc, but seek one that is rounded out with Semillon; there is an increasing number of these blends to choose from.

Mussels with garlic butter Here, the garlic butter calls the shots, so serve the dish with an unwooded Chardonnay.

Mussels in tomato sauce Mussels stuffed with breadcrumbs and garlic and smothered in a tomato-based sauce calls for Sauvignon or Chenin Blanc. When skewered with bacon, grilled and served with a Provençale sauce, stay with Sauvignon and Chenin, choosing lightly wooded ones for an exact gastronomical match.

OYSTERS

For wines to match oysters, see page 133.

PAELLA

This internationally famous Spanish rice dish gets its name from the two-handed pan, called a *paellera*, that was used over an open fire. There are as many recipes for paella as there are fish-eaters, and sometimes a seafood paella will include poultry and spicy chorizo sausage. If the paella has been flavoured with saffron (traditional, but pricey), it pairs well with dry blanc de noir or rosé. If it contains only seafood and fish, with no saffron, a dry Chenin Blanc will come out on top; however, if saffron is present, stick to the pink wines.

PERLEMOEN

See **Abalone**, page 153.

PRAWNS

Prawns and other shellfish are often served very simply so that their delicate taste can be enjoyed to the full (see overleaf for options). To appreciate their colourful and appetizing appearance, prawns are often served in their shells. A top-notch dry white wine, such as a lightly wooded Chardonnay, is their best ally.

Deep fried Battered, deep-fried prawns are usually served with lemon wedges. A lightly wooded Chardonnay from a cool climate should have the richness and acidity to cope with the oily batter and the lemon but, if you have a heavy hand with lemon, rather choose a full-bodied, flavourful, top-notch Sauvignon Blanc.

Fried, grilled or braaied Usually served with either garlic or lemon butter or peri-peri sauce, choose a fine, lightly wooded Chardonnay from a cool climate, or a full-bodied Sauvignon Blanc.

Jambalaya This traditional Creole dish of prawns with rice, bacon and tomatoes, a cousin of paella, needs the forthright intensity of a bone-dry, unwooded Chenin or Sauvignon Blanc. The good acidity of these two wines will do this dish proud. Avoid a wooded wine.

Kebabs Skewered prawns and vegetables, such as mushrooms and green peppers, are marinated in oil, wine and soy sauce before being grilled or braaied. Grilling or char-grilling imparts slightly acrid, sweetish flavours to prawns, which already have a sweetish nature. This is the perfect moment for an off-dry Weisser Riesling, but you could also consider an off-dry rosé.

Stir-fry When prawns are stir-fried, Chinese style, with garlic, spring onions, ginger and soy sauce, a crisp white wine with fairly light body and sweetness is best, but also take into account the contrasting textures. The obvious choice is dry or off-dry Weisser Riesling, but a fruity, dryish rosé or blanc de noir would make a nice change.

Tempura *See* **Japanese cuisine**, page 240.

SCALLOPS

These small circular molluscs with their ribbed shells taste as good as they look. Their delicate flesh requires light and subtly-flavoured treatment. Scallops are always removed from the shell before cooking, but are often served on the deeper half of the shell. The flesh is simmered in white wine flavoured with herbs and onion and the poached scallops may then be finished in a sauce, served *au gratin*, or deep fried. Scallops are often referred to by their French culinary term, *Coquilles St Jacques*.

Deep-fried scallops The usual accompaniment for battered and deep-fried scallops is a tartare sauce. Serve with a crisp, full-bodied Sauvignon Blanc or Chenin Blanc.

Grilled scallops Poached scallops, tossed in melted butter and breadcrumbs, are gently grilled until golden brown. This Provençale dish is often eaten unsauced with a crisp green salad. Choose a light, crisp white wine with a touch of sweetness. An off-dry Weisser Riesling or dry Chenin Blanc is just the thing, but also consider an unwooded Chardonnay or a Pinot Gris/Pinot Grigio.

Scallops *au gratin* Poached scallops are mixed with mushrooms and a fish velouté sauce before being spooned onto the scallop shells, sprinkled with Parmesan and breadcrumbs, and grilled. A medium-bodied, moderately oaked Chardonnay or Semillon would do this dish proud.

Scallops in a tomato sauce Scallops simmered in a white wine and tomato sauce is a traditional Bordeaux dish. Serve it with a crisp but full-bodied Sauvignon or Chenin Blanc.

SCAMPI

This Italian name is often used for a miniature member of the lobster family. Other names are langoustine, Dublin Bay prawn or Norway lobster. The preparations are similar to **Prawns**, see page 155.

SEAFOOD CASSEROLE/POTJIE

The ingredients for a seafood casserole (or a potjie or stew, if you prefer) are often adapted to whatever is available, whether fresh or frozen or canned, but they are predominantly creamy or tomatoey. With a luxurious, creamy casserole, serve an equally rich, creamy Chardonnay, the best you can afford, or a Semillon. For a vertical (contrasting) pairing, you could opt for a Pinot Gris/Pinot Grigio, which is always in tune with whatever comes from the sea. More robust tomato-based fish dishes will be better with a lightish red, such as a Pinot Noir, Sangiovese, Cinsaut or Ruby Cabernet.

SEAFOOD PLATTER

A typical South African mixed seafood platter consists of a piece of 'catch-of-the-day' fish, plus grilled or deep-fried calamari and prawns, and some black mussels. Crayfish and/or oysters may be offered as optional extras. If you're having this platter with just a wedge of lemon, choose an unwooded Chardonnay, Pinot Gris/Pinot Grigio or a Sauvignon Blanc with good intensity. However, chances are that you'll opt for lemon or garlic butter or a peri-peri sauce, in which case, select a wooded Chardonnay or Semillion or a Pinot Noir.

See also **Fritto misto di mare**, page 129.

SHRIMPS

According to their scientific classification, prawns and shrimps belong to the same order, although to different suborders. In South Africa, as elsewhere, the terms tend to be used interchangeably, particularly in a culinary context. But, regardless of whether you call a shrimp a prawn, or a prawn a shrimp, their preparations are similar.

For wine partners, see **Prawns**, page 155.

A note on sustainable seafood

The South African Sustainable Seafood Initiative (SASSI) maintains a list of local fish and seafood regarded as 'sustainable' and 'vulnerable', as well as those species which it is illegal to buy or sell.

When it comes to buying fish, 'Green' species are the best choices as they come from well-managed populations that can handle current fishing pressure, although this status could change if stocks are overfished. 'Orange' species are under threat from overfishing, or the fishery may be subject to environmental damage or suffer a high by-catch of other species. Most 'Red' species are protected and may not be bought or sold, although some may be caught by recreational anglers in possession of the appropriate permits.

For easy reference, we have listed, some of the most popular local eating fish in all three categories:

Green (best choice) Anchovy, angelfish, butterfish, crayfish (rock lobster, both West coast and South coast), dorado (dolphinfish, mahi-mahi), gurnard, hake, horse mackerel (maasbanker), hottentot, John Dory, monkfish, mussels, oysters, panga, Natal snoek (queen mackerel), santer, sardine (pilchard), snoek, tuna (but not bluefin, the tuna most prized by sushi-makers), yellowtail.

Orange (caution) Bluefin tuna, elf (shad; this may not be sold in KZN), geelbek (Cape salmon), king mackerel (couta), kingklip, kob (kabeljou), langoustines and prawns, both locally caught and trawled, poenskop (black musselcracker), red steenbras, rock cod (all except potato and brindle bass), roman (red roman), skates and rays, sole, swordfish.

Red (no purchase or sale permitted) Abalone*, banded galjoen, brindle bass, Cape stumpnose, galjoen, garrick (leervis), John Brown, kingfish, Natal stumpnose (yellowfin bream), potato bass, river snapper (rock salmon), seventy-four, west coast steenbras, white musselcracker (brusher, cracker), white steenbras (pignose grunter), zebra (wildeperd), and most sharks.

(*Only cultured or farmed abalone/perlemoen may be bought or sold in South Africa.)

Eggs and egg-based dishes

As eggs marry well with most sweet and savoury flavourings, there are hundreds of ways of preparing them; you could probably serve egg dishes for a year without repeating any. Not that the wine drinker would be tempted to serve eggs for a year – of all the tricky ingredients for pairing with wine, eggs are near the top of the list. They certainly are no friends of wine! The problem is twofold: eggs coat your taste buds, preventing you from tasting the wine and, if the yolk is still runny, the wine becomes unpalatable. The recommendations below provide solutions but, generally speaking, there are just five wines that you could put into your proverbial 'basket of eggs': Pinot Blanc and Pinot Gris/Pinot Grigio as all-rounders; a dry (brut or sec) sparkling wine to go with the sort of egg dishes typically served at breakfast or brunch; unoaked or lightly oaked Chardonnay to go with creamy egg-sauced dishes; and Weisser Riesling, which can valiantly hold its own against most egg-based dishes.

CURRIED EGGS

A rather old-fashioned Sunday night supper dish that still makes an appearance. Hard-boiled eggs are served in a straightforward curry sauce knocked up from a bit of stock and fried onions flavoured with curry powder straight from the packet, with a pinch of sugar added for good measure. Viognier and Gewürztraminer are the two wines that rise in unison to this occasion. A red? Not this time.

OMELETTES

There are two ways of making an omelette. In a Spanish tortilla or Italian frittata, the filling ingredients are cooked with the eggs. In a French omelette, either flat or folded, the filling is added after the eggs have set. A soufflé omelette is a variation of the French version where the white and the yolks are beaten separately, resulting in a light and fluffy dish.

Plain omelette When served without any type of filling, an omelette instantly turns wine away as an accompaniment. The texture of the eggs coats the mouth in an unpleasant, almost glutinous, way. If you want to drink something other than water, try a dry Weisser Riesling or dry Gewürztraminer and hope for the best.

Omelettes with fillings fare much better with wine, as some kind of contrasting ingredient is added. Select a wine to match the main added ingredient (for example, ham, mushrooms or tomato).

POACHED EGGS

Adding other ingredients and garnishes to poached eggs can turn this breakfast staple into a great lunch or supper dish. Classically, poached eggs are notoriously tough on wines; they have a set white with a soft yolk that is slightly runny inside, and it is this soft yolk that instantly turns any wine on its head. However, what seems like an insuperable problem can be solved by adding other ingredients or sauces to the eggs for a make-over.

Benedict The American version of eggs Benedict is poached eggs with cooked ham and hollandaise sauce served on an English muffin or on toast. In South Africa, it is often served with smoked salmon instead of ham. *Oeufs bénédictine*, the original dish invented by Benedictine monks, was rather different, consisting of brandade (a purée of salt cod), spread on triangles of fried bread, with a poached egg on top and napped with hollandaise sauce. At first glance you might think that eggs (the poached ones) beneath more eggs (in the hollandaise sauce) spell double trouble, but the butter and lemon in the sauce come to the rescue.

Eggs Benedict is such a wonderful dish that it is worth taking time to choose a wine that will latch onto the hollandaise, which is where the weight of the dish lies, and which masks the texture of the poached eggs' runny yolks. If the sauce is markedly lemony, go for a Sauvignon Blanc; if it is more on the creamy side, a lightly wooded Chardonnay with a bit of acidity, or a lightly wooded Semillon from a cool climate, should be a sumptuous match.

Florentine This comprises a poached egg served on a bed of spinach, napped with a cheese (mornay) sauce. Although spinach is a slightly acidic vegetable, the weight of eggs Florentine lies in the sauce, to which you should match your wine. A medium-bodied, wooded Chardonnay, Semillon, or Chardonnay-Semillon blend will happily sidle up to that cheesy sauce.

Mediterranean Both the Italians and the Spanish poach eggs in a savoury tomato sauce. In Italy, they may add chicken livers, while the Spanish version might have chorizo sausage and red or green peppers. Whether you feel Italian or Spanish, select a Sauvignon Blanc with classic Sauvignon flavours and good acidity. If you lean towards the Spanish side, stay with Sauvignon, but look for a lightly wooded one (blanc fumé), although a wooded Chenin Blanc would be equally good. If you want to hop across to Italy and include those chicken livers, then choose a Sangiovese or an imported Chianti, now freely available locally. However, if you're South African through and through, chances are you're poaching your eggs in a tomato 'smoortjie' you've prepared on the skottel, with a piece of boerewors or a lamb chop on the side, so go for a quaffable Pinotage or its mama, a Cinsaut. If you prefer a white wine, choose a dry Chenin Blanc, the most planted grape variety in South Africa.

Poached in red wine (*oeufs en meurette*) If you want poached eggs for lunch or supper, then do what the French do and poach them in red wine. Use the poaching wine to make a sauce, pour it over the cooked eggs and crack another bottle of the same wine to drink with it. Talk about cooking for the bottle! This may be pairing wine with wine, but so what, it works.

Provençale In this Mediterranean version, poached eggs are served with anchovies, which partner well with egg, but make any classic still wine miserable. This combination is one of the food and wine pairer's worst nightmares. Usually, the ingredients added to poached eggs come to the wine's rescue but here, the anchovies double up the problem, and we are left with nothing to subdue the taste bud-smothering texture of the eggs or the pungent saltiness of the anchovies. Instead of admitting defeat, why not try a dry (brut or sec) sparkling wine or a pale dry (fino) sherry? Both would be ideal at a Sunday breakfast or brunch. Or consider a third possibility: a dry Vinho Verde from Portugal, which is now available in good wine stores throughout South Africa.

SCRAMBLED EGGS

Scrambled eggs are quick to prepare and invaluable when time is short or unexpected guests arrive. On their own, their creamy texture coats the mouth in a most determined way so that, when it comes to wine, any fruit flavours and other nuances will be lost with the first mouthful. But the fact that eggs marry well with other flavourings is a blessing for the food and wine pairer, because that is exactly what is needed to turn the tables – a contrasting main ingredient that the wine can latch onto; more or less similar to diverting a child's attention away from potential danger.

Scrambled eggs with asparagus Fruity Sauvignon Blanc with good acidity, or unwooded Chardonnay or Semillon are excellent matches.

Scrambled eggs with bacon, ham or mushrooms Serve any of these options with a lightly wooded Chardonnay or Semillon.

Scrambled eggs with smoked salmon A classic way of serving scrambled eggs is with slivers of smoked salmon, which is usually added once the eggs have set. When salmon, with its piercingly smoky flavours and inherent saltiness, combines with hard-to-please scrambled eggs, a wondrous transformation takes place, and this fusion of smoke, salt and creaminess is worth special treatment. Choose the best sparkling wine, either bone dry (brut) or dry (sec), that you can afford. The wine and the salmon-spiked scrambled eggs will luxuriate in each other.

Scrambled eggs with truffle shavings Serve this luxury dish with a Viognier or a deeply fruity, rich, judiciously oaked Chardonnay.

QUICHES

Classic quiche Lorraine (with bacon) has made way for many innovations. Anything from fish, meat and cheese to vegetables, such as onions, leeks, mushrooms, asparagus, broccoli and spinach, is used to fill what is, basically, an egg-based tart. Take the filling ingredients into account when selecting a wine to serve with quiche, although an oaked Chardonnay or Semillon, or a Bukettraube, will be a safe choice for most of them. You might have to taste it to believe it, but many quiches are great with Gewürztraminer. If you want to drink red, keep it light, and opt for a quaffable Merlot or Cinsaut.

SOUFFLÉS (savoury)

Soufflés are delicately flavoured and have a texture of airy lightness, so you'd think they should be served with equally delicate, light-as-air white wines. Surprisingly, this is not the case, and soufflés are an excellent way to show off both fine white and red wines. Soufflés are generally flavoured, so take the dominant flavouring ingredients into account when making a wine choice. You'll find that deeply fruity, but lightly wooded, Chardonnays and Semillons with fine balancing acidity will match most soufflés made with fish, while those made with cheese are better with a red wine. Stick with medium-bodied, light-on-tannin reds, but the choice is wide: Pinot Noir, Tempranillo, Barbera, Sangiovese or Merlot.

For **Sweet soufflés**, see pages 267–268.

STUFFED EGGS

Although you'll rarely find these on a restaurant menu, stuffed eggs are handy make-ahead appetizers for home entertaining, picnics and catered events. A variety of savoury ingredients are bound with mayonnaise and the mashed yolk of hard-boiled eggs, then piped or spooned into the whites. Go for an unwooded Chardonnay although, if pickles and capers have been included, a Pinot Gris/Pinot Grigio would fare better. When a dollop of tomato sauce is added to the stuffing mixture, the resulting sweet note calls for an off-dry Weisser Riesling, Chenin Blanc, Bukettraube or stein.

OTHER EGGS

When we think 'eggs', we generally refer to hen's eggs, but the eggs of a few other feathered species may come your way:

Ostrich eggs

You may not be in the habit of cracking an ostrich egg for a quick meal but, if you do happen upon one, you would most probably use it to make scrambled egg or an omelette. Just invite about ten mates around to help you consume that one egg, as that is how far it will take you. If you want to hard-boil your ostrich egg, you should have time on your hands as it will take more than an hour for the yolk to set. Then, haul the hammer out of your toolbox to crack the shell, quarter and slice the egg, and serve it on toast, with or without a sauce. For a wine to drink with it, just follow the suggestions for hens' eggs in this chapter. Ostrich eggs may be exotic and rich, but they still pair with the same wines as hens' eggs.

Quail eggs

The small speckled shells of boiled quail eggs look so intriguing that you rather regret having to remove them before serving. These miniature eggs are often added to salads or starter dishes or used as a garnish, but they can best be appreciated when served on their own with pre-dinner drinks or at parties. Their texture is much finer than hens' eggs and, consequently, easier to match with wine. Quail's eggs are delicious when served with a fine-quality sparkling wine, especially one based on Chardonnay, but any unwooded, crisp, light, still white wine is a good match too.

Pasta, pizza, risotto and vegetarian

The 'dough' of pasta, the rice of risottos, the crust of pizzas and the lentils, dried beans and other legumes in vegetarian dishes have one thing in common: they are neutral backdrops to carry various flavours, not only from food ingredients but also those found in wine.

BRINJAL (AUBERGINE/EGGPLANT) PARMIGIANA

We'd be forgiven for jumping to the conclusion that *melanzane alla parmigiana* hails from Parma, but apparently it does not; in fact, almost every region of Italy claims its creation. This dish of fried or grilled brinjal (aubergine/eggplant) slices, layered with pulped tomatoes, Mozzarella and Parmesan cheeses and then baked, requires a medium-bodied red to partner it. Choose from Tempranillo, Sangiovese or a Cabernet-Merlot blend. Don't be scared that the brinjal, which can be bitter, will make the Cab-Merlot taste bitter too. Tannic wines go well with bitter vegetables.

CALZONE (pizza)

The word 'calzone' means 'trouser leg', presumably because there is a resemblance. Calzone differs from traditional pizza in that the base is folded over the topping, in the shape of a half moon, but it pairs with the same wines. See **Pizza**, page 167.

CANNELLONI

For this meaty pasta dish, see page 176.

CAULIFLOWER GRATIN

This baked dish of cauliflower in a rich cheese sauce, usually made with Cheddar or Gruyère, is not only a vegetarian favourite, but also a great lunch or supper dish. Surprisingly, it requires a fairly robust red wine. Shiraz, Cab-Shiraz-Merlot blends, Shiraz-Grenache blends or a solo Merlot will all do the dish proud.

GNOCCHI

The more well-known version of gnocchi is made from potatoes but, for the Roman one, semolina flour is used. Both are traditionally served with sage-flavoured melted butter, but a pesto, tomato- or meat-based sauce are frequent options. A Pinot Gris/Pinot Grigio or light-to-medium-bodied Merlot (with its special affinity for sage) are the best wine choices here.

LASAGNE

For wines to match this baked pasta dish, see page 180.

LENTILS

Vegetarian dishes based on lentils can be quite substantial. They are generally better with red wines, provided the wines are rather hearty, such as Shiraz and Shiraz blends, but without being strident. If the dish is prepared with herbs, you can swing it towards a white wine. Sauvignon Blanc, with its young, 'green' flavours and tangy acidity can provide a good contrast in what would become a vertical pairing, especially if the dish also includes peppers, brinjal, baby marrow, asparagus or leeks.

MACARONI CHEESE

This baked dish of macaroni in a cheesey sauce with the optional additions of tomato and/or bacon is homely and very comforting. Surprisingly, it requires a rather full-bodied wine and, even more surprisingly, a red one. Choose a Merlot, medium-bodied Shiraz or Shiraz-Grenache blend.

MOUSSAKA

A vegetarian moussaka is made similarly to the meat version, except that lentils are used instead of meat. Choose a softly contoured, low-tannin red, such as a Pinot Noir, Grenache or Cinsaut. You'll find that if you serve a tannic red with a dish containing little or no protein, the tannins will appear even harsher.

NUT ROAST

Mixed nuts combined with rice or breadcrumbs, with or without the addition of legumes and flavouring ingredients, are baked in a loaf pan. The flavour of the nuts dominates, giving the roast depth and heartiness. A nut roast needs a rich white wine, such as a lightly oaked Chardonnay or Semillon, but is equally happy with a red. Choose a medium-bodied, fleshy, not-too-tannic Merlot, or a Cabernet-Shiraz blend. Or you could go to the other end of the spectrum and adventurously pair it with a Fernão Pires, which will echo its nutty flavours even as it takes a bit of a knock from this heavy dish.

PASTA SAUCES AND DRESSINGS

Pasta has evolved into an extraordinary number of varieties and shapes. The Italians, who have grown up eating pasta, have a great understanding of which sauce should be matched with which pasta to attain the best complement of flavour and texture. We list some of the more popular traditional sauces, without indicating which pasta they usually are served on (generally spaghetti or spaghettini, fettuccine, tagliatelle, penne or fusilli). Chances are, you'll have your own opinion on what makes a good combination, anyway. Pasta goes with everything, but we do not eat it on its own. We serve it with a sauce, and it is the sauce that changes the whole picture.

CREAMY SAUCES

Alfredo Although this sauce has all the makings of a northern Italian dish, it was created by a Roman restaurant owner who gave it his name. The sauce of butter and cream is garnished with a dusting of nutmeg and some grated Parmesan.

Carbonara You may come across recipes that call for cream but, traditionally, carbonara comprises crisply fried bacon (or pancetta, if you want the 'real deal') and beaten raw eggs tossed into just-cooked pasta. The heat of the pasta 'cooks' the egg, creating the rich creaminess of this sauce.

Gorgonzola Dolce, a creamy, almost runny kind of Gorgonzola, is melted in milk, butter and cream for this rich sauce.

Primavera 'Primavera' means 'spring' and, as the name suggests, this is a sauce of fresh spring vegetables and cream.

When it comes to creamy sauces, go for a medium- to full-bodied white wine with some flavour, such as Chardonnay, but select one that is neither too exuberantly fruity nor too oaky. A lightly wooded Semillon is also a very good choice.

TOMATO-BASED SAUCES

Amatriciana Named after the town Amatrice in Italy, this sauce was traditionally made with cured pig's cheek, but the version we know today uses tomato and crisply fried bacon.

Arrabbiata This sauce takes its name from the Italian word for 'angry', which infers that it is hot and spicy. The tomato, garlic and bacon sauce can have as little or as much crushed chilli as you wish, according to the intensity of your 'anger'.

Bolognese *See* **Spaghetti Bolognese**, page 185.

Butter and tomato Oodles of butter and ripe plum tomatoes are simmered until a thick sauce forms.

Marinara This robust tomato-based sauce is similar to Neapolitan (see below), but has onions and extra herbs added. The name derives from 'marinaro' and marinara sauce, loosely translated, means 'the sauce of the sailors'. This leads us to expect that it contains fish or seafood of some description, but it is just a basic tomato sauce. And thereby hangs a tale: the sauce orginated in 16th century Naples, when sailors took it on board ship with them because the high acidity of the tomatoes meant the sauce would not easily go off.

Neapolitan (Napoletano in Italian) This is a basic tomato sauce, made from fresh or canned plum tomatoes, with no other added ingredients, save for a hint of garlic and origanum.

Puttanesca With its rather curious name, derived from 'puttana', which means 'whore', this is a robust sauce of tomatoes, capers and olives. The origin of the name is debated. One theory is that it is a more flavourful version of a simple 'home-style' tomato sauce which has been 'tarted up', as the English would say. Another is that its name arose because it was a quick, inexpensive sauce for pasta that the local prostitutes could prepare between customers.

Seafood (*frutti di mare*) Mixed seafood is tossed in a tomato-based sauce, and sometimes enhanced with a touch of white wine.

Vongole Made with or without tomatoes, the flavour of this 'clam sauce' comes from the juices the clams give off as they are steamed in white wine. A touch of garlic and chilli and, sometimes, lemon zest, is added for additional flavouring.

Young, fruity, medium-bodied red wines that have quite assertive acidity, but not astringently so, are the ideal all-rounders, as they will go with the tomatoes, seafood or meat used in these sauces. The sharpness of the ingredients points towards equal sharpness in a Barbera, Sangiovese, light-bodied Pinotage or cool-climate Merlot.

WITH OIL OR PESTO

Olive oil and garlic (*olio e aglio*) Nothing could be simpler than pasta (often spaghetti) tossed with garlic-flavoured olive oil, some chilli flakes and chopped parsley.

Pesto This well-known pasta sauce is traditionally made from fresh basil, garlic, pine nuts, Parmesan and olive oil. Coriander, rocket or sun-dried tomatoes are sometimes used as a substitute for the basil.

When pasta is simply dressed with olive oil and fragrant pesto, dry white wine works better than red, but it has to be crisp and firmly textured. Pinot Gris/Pinot Grigio and Colombard are excellent choices, but you could stretch the elastic a bit and opt for an unwooded, feather-light Chardonnay or Sauvignon Blanc. If the pesto is made from sun-dried tomatoes, opt for a Sauvignon or Chenin Blanc.

PIZZA

Although pizza is found all over the world today, it began life as a 'fast-food', sold by vendors and eaten hot on the backstreets of Naples where, by the mid-19th century, pizzerias had opened in most poor neighbourhoods. When the Italian queen consort, Margherita, visited Naples in 1889, she wanted to taste this new food she had heard so much about. For her visit, a *pizzaiolo* (pizza-maker) created a pizza based on the colours of the Italian flag, using basil (green), mozzarella (white) and tomatoes (red). It was later named in her honour.

There are two styles of wine that pair well with pizza, irrespective of its topping: a fresh, fruity red with some acidity (Sangiovese or, if unavailable, a Cinsaut or easy drinking Pinotage), and a medium-bodied white (Chardonnay, provided it also has some acidity).

POTATO BAKE

A potato bake is a good vegetarian standby. For variety, any number of vegetables can be layered with the sliced potatoes. Serve with Chardonnay, or opt for a Viognier to add a bit of excitement, if the dish is not too rich.

RATATOUILLE

This famous Provençal dish shows the influence of its Mediterranean neighbour, Italy, in its mixture of tomato, brinjal (aubergine/eggplant), onion and courgette. The proportions of the ingredients can be varied according to taste, and may include green and red peppers and even slices of potato. The contrasting textures of this dish, as well as its sweet-bitter flavours, need to be taken into account when selecting a wine.

A vividly fruity, crisp Sauvignon or Chenin Blanc, an unwooded Chardonnay from a cool climate, a fruity, dry rosé, or a blanc de noir will all provide a change from the more obvious choice of an off-dry Weisser Riesling.

RISOTTO

Short-grain or medium-grain rice, normally arborio, is slowly cooked while stirring in a flavouring liquid, such as chicken stock or wine, resulting in the creamy texture of risotto. A host of extra flavours may be added: cooked peas, sliced mushrooms, seafood of all sorts, cooked sausage, bacon, ham or chopped raw tomatoes. Below, we list a few of the more commonly occurring flavours.

Risotto is fairly accommodating across a whole spectrum of wines, from dry to off-dry whites and light reds, but the added ingredients or flavourings should be taken into account. Risotto can easily be overpowered by a wine, as it is a rather delicate dish.

Asparagus This risotto is particularly flavoursome as the asparagus stems are puréed with the stock and added to the rice during cooking. Serve with a medium-bodied Sauvignon Blanc that is not too acidic, or an unwooded Chardonnay.

Meat As the meat sauce used in this risotto is quite tomatoey, a light-bodied red, with good acidity is a good match. Choose Barbera,

Sangiovese or quaffable Pinotage. You can also consider a blanc de noir or dry rosé, but either needs to show good acidity.

Milanese This traditional accompaniment to osso buco takes its yellow colour from saffron and its rich flavour from beef marrow. When served as an accompaniment, match the wine to the osso buco. If you are having risotto Milanese on its own, choose a lightly wooded Chardonnay. A Viognier may be a bit too heavy, but it would certainly love the saffron.

Mushroom Generally, mushrooms prefer red wine but the weight of this dish lies in the creamy rice. Even though strongly flavoured mushrooms, such as porcini, are normally used to flavour the risotto, a lightly wooded Chardonnay will provide the matching depth, but so would a Viognier.

Pea (*risi e bisi*) This rice and pea dish from northern Italy often includes bacon or ham. Serve with a lightly wooded Chardonnay.

Red wine As the dish is so simple, a good-quality wine, with no rough edges, is required to prepare a red wine risotto. Bring this one home, and use a Ruby Cabernet for the preparation as well as the accompanying wine afterwards.

Risotto nero Getting its name from the Italian word for 'black', this risotto is flavoured with calamari and coloured by squid or cuttle-fish ink. Serve with an unwooded Chardonnay.

Seafood Mixed seafood and fish flavour this risotto. Serve with an unwooded Chardonnay or a Semillon.

STUFFED PASTA

The various stuffed pastas, such as **ravioli** and **tortellini**, are usually served with one or other pasta sauce to complement the ingredients used for the filling, so match your wine to the sauce.
See **Pasta sauces**, page 165; **Sauces and their impact**, page 32.

STUFFED PEPPERS

Green, red or yellow peppers are filled with spicy rice and vegetables and then baked for a tasty vegetarian meal. Choose a Sylvaner or off-dry Bukettraube if you fancy a white wine, or a Pinot Noir, Ruby Cabernet or Gamay if a red is called for.

Matching meat and wine

A key factor in pairing food and wine is to match the **weight** of the wine to the weight of the food (see page 18). Red meat has 'weight', so it will not be matched by delicate, light-bodied wines. A braaied or grilled steak, for example, needs a wine that will mirror its weight. In choosing that wine, we must consider how much fruit, tannin, oak (wood) and alcohol it has, as well as its 'mouth-feel', which can be anything from soft and velvety to chunky and robust.

A second consideration is the **cooking method**, as this will change the flavours or texture of the finished dish and, consequently, affect the choice of wine. Roasting entails browning, which creates new flavour compounds, including caramelization when sugar is present, as in basting sauces. Braaiing or grilling imparts a slightly bitter carbon taste, while stewing or braising breaks down the meat fibres, resulting in a softer texture. Compare the falling-off-the-bone, melt-in-the-mouth tenderness of braised lamb neck with the heavy, chewy texture of a grilled rare steak. While both dishes have similar weight, their different textures point to different wines: a velvety Merlot to go with the melt-in-the-mouth lamb and a chunky Cabernet Sauvignon or Shiraz for the chewy steak.

The acrid flavours that develop from char-grilling (braaiing) are mirrored by the bitter edge of the tannins in a red wine, which may just be a posh way of saying 'drink red' with your *tjoppie* or braaied steak. If you drink red wine on its own, you may notice some austere, astringent tannins but, once you add red meat, these same tannins are tamed, becoming bright-eyed and bushy-tailed.

Flavours that develop in meat through different cooking methods are bounced back by flavours that are added to a wine when it is oaked (matured in wood). The similarity is quite striking. For instance, flavours developed by roasting are reflected by the toasty character of an oaked wine, while those added by braaiing will be reflected by the charry profile of the wine. When meat has been smoked, it will meet the smokiness of an oaked wine head-on, while a caramelized glaze on a roast snuggles up to the caramel character of oaked wines.

A third, crucial consideration is **seasoning** and **saucing**, which impacts on both the meat and the wine. Lamb stands out in that it positively welcomes a whole range of flavours, from herbs, garlic and vegetables to lemon juice and olive oil and, of course, spices.

But, before you head for the wine cellar, consider how you have seasoned your leg of lamb. Have you used just herbs or spices, or a combination? And what sauce do you intend to serve with that stuffed shoulder of pork? Is the sauce creamy or tomato-based, lightly lemony and acidic, or is it a rich, meat-based reduction? And with the *frikkadels* and mash, are you offering a tasty gravy like Mom used to make? When you think about it, it becomes clear that a plainly grilled steak dusted with nothing more than a twist of salt and a grind of pepper, and the same steak smothered in a creamy pepper sauce, will need two very different wines.

The final consideration is the **added ingredients** of the finished dish, although these mostly play second fiddle in terms of wine matching. Onions and carrots added to a meat stew will have no influence on the choice of wine; but juniper berries, with their strong flavour, or sauerkraut with its acidity, will have a definite say in the matter. Similarly, side dishes, such as simply cooked vegetables, rice or potatoes, seldom let out even a little squeak, as the weight of the main ingredient, the meat, determines the choice of wine.

But here's a handy hint: when the time comes to open that well-aged, rounded red wine you've been hoarding for a special occasion, serve it with an unadorned, sensitively and simply cooked piece of top-quality meat that will let the wine take centre-stage. An elaborately sauced and garnished dish might overshadow the wine, which is probably not what you had intended.

Beef

The key is to match the 'weight' of the beef, taking into account its cooking method, seasoning and saucing, to a similar profile in the wine (alcohol level, overall texture and oak influence, if any).

BEEF (BOEUF) BOURGUIGNONNE

This homely Burgundian dish is a stew of cubed beef gently simmered in a liquor of red wine, along with baby onions, mushrooms, bacon and herbs. In its native Burgundy, it is traditionally served with Pinot Noir but, for the rest of us, there is a light-hearted rule of thumb regarding pairing wine with beef bourguignonne: cook it with Pinot Noir (Burgundy), but serve it with Cabernet Sauvignon (Bordeaux). After adding all those ingredients, the dish has gained some weight and a glass of Pinot Noir, even when full-bodied, will not do it justice. A Cabernet Sauvignon-Merlot blend will do splendidly, as will an easy-drinking Shiraz.

BEEF CURRY

There are two distinct types of South African curry: a hot 'Durban' curry and a milder, more fragrant 'Cape Malay' curry. When made with beef, Durban curry happily marries with light-bodied, easy-drinking, low-tannin Cabernet Sauvignon or Cab-Merlot blends (but not a blockbuster). The Cape Malay-style curry, which has a hint of sweetness, is happier with a white wine that is bursting with flavour; Viognier is the obvious choice, as it pairs with anything curried.

To accompany curry, South Africans like to haul out their favourite sambals, including coconut, various chutneys, sliced bananas and chopped tomatoes with onions. This is a time to match your wine to the accompaniments. If you like to go wild with coconut, choose a wooded Chardonnay or a Pinot Gris/Grigio, which loves coconut in a curry. If you have a heavy hand with chutney, an off-dry Weisser Riesling is just the thing for a beef curry flavoured with aromatic spices, such as cardamom, cinnamon, cloves, cumin and turmeric. It will also not blink an eye at the acidity of a tomato and onion sambal.

BEEF OLIVES

Thin slices of lean beef are rolled around a stuffing of flavoured mince or a herby breadcrumb mixture and cooked in beef stock, perhaps with a dash of red wine added. Choose any medium-bodied red wine, but keep it simple; save your special bottle for another day.

BEEF STEW

A stew of braising steak with potatoes, carrots and onion (often with red wine added) should be matched with a fairly simple, medium-bodied red. The cooking method here plays a part in the choice of wine. Most Merlots, with their little velvet paws, are simply sublime when served with the soft, melt-in-the-mouth texture of slow-cooked beef. However, you could opt for a medium-bodied Cab or Shiraz, or an inexpensive Cab-Merlot blend.

BEEF STROGANOFF

This creamy, mushroomy stew works better with white wine than with red, because the copious amount of cream in the sauce adds weight and determines the choice of wine. Choose an equally creamy white, such as a wooded Chardonnay or Semillon. If you have slaved over this dish and want to accentuate the opulent sauce, do a vertical pairing and go for a dry or off-dry Weisser Riesling, with its inherent good acidity. The wine will suffer (so don't spend too much on it), but it will put the sauce under the spotlight.

BEEF WELLINGTON

This is a rather grand dish of beef fillet, spread with a mushroom and liver pâté mixture, and then baked in a coat of puff pastry. Beef Wellington deserves a rather opulent wine, and the first choice would be a good Bordeaux blend, where either the Cabernet Sauvignon or the Merlot dominates.

Beef Wellington can be made more regal by adding truffle shavings to the traditional pâté mixture that is spread over the fillet. This rather delicate dish is made weightier when more than a hint of truffle is added, so you may want to opt for Nebbiolo (which is wild about truffles) or a Nebbiolo blend. Pinot Noir with a bit of bottle maturation, or a top-drop Merlot are equally successful.

Beef Wellington does not insist on being paired with red wine, though. A pedigreed, barrel-fermented Chardonnay will latch onto the buttery puff pastry, while Viognier, which has a weakness for liver pâté and a musky affinity with truffles, is also sublime with this dish.

Although beef Wellington is often served on its own, the traditional accompaniment is Madeira sauce. Now here's the thing – chances are that sherry or port will be substituted for the Madeira, as this wine is not on the shelves of every liquor outlet. These substitutes are much sweeter than Madeira so, if your beef Wellington is served with this sauce, forget about all the wines mentioned except for the top-drop Merlot. However, you will need to choose one with abundant, upfront, sweet cherry flavours.

BOBOTIE

Bobotie is a wonderful example of early fusion food, of East meeting West at the tip of Africa more than two centuries ago. The dish was traditionally made with minced leftover roasted lamb or mutton and jazzed-up by Malay cooks using their favourite spices. Nowadays, you will mostly encounter the version made with minced beef. The meat is flavoured with onions, curry spices, lemon juice and apricot jam (or chutney or sugar) and then baked under a savoury custard. Bobotie is usually served with yellow rice (rice flavoured with turmeric and studded with raisins). When eaten without any sweet accompaniments, the perfect match is a Viognier, but an off-dry Weisser Riesling or Chenin Blanc are good second choices. If you want to drink red, choose a low-tannin, easy-drinking Cabernet or Merlot, *sommer* straight from the box. If you serve your bobotie with the traditional sambals of chutney, desiccated coconut, sliced bananas and chopped tomato and onion, opt for a semi-sweet Chenin Blanc, or select a stein or late harvest made from any grape variety.

BOEREWORS

What would a braai be without this national icon? There are many different recipes for making boerewors, but coriander is probably the dominant spice in all of them. However, because we should match the wine to the main ingredient of a dish (in this case, minced meat), the flavour of the spices will play second fiddle. Any young, gluggable Merlot, Pinotage, Shiraz or a blend will do fine for that *stukkie wors* hot off the coals. If you prefer white wine, a medium- to full-bodied Chenin Blanc is just the thing (if you want to splurge, pick a wooded one). However, if you're tucking into a boerewors roll slathered with tomato sauce and mustard or with a tomato and onion relish (*smoor*) or chakalaka on the side, then Pinotage would be the best bet. In this case, we suggest a boisterous Sauvignon Blanc for the white-wine drinkers. Of course, Viognier as a white wine choice and Pinot Noir as a red would work seamlessly, but these are rather opulent wines for boerewors and you may wish to save them for another day.

BOEUF EN DAUBE

A traditional Provençale dish, and one of the most ancient, boeuf en daube is an earthy beef stew flavoured with onion, unsmoked bacon, garlic and herbs, and slow-cooked in red wine. A bottle of medium- to full-bodied Shiraz, Pinotage or any Shiraz or Pinotage blend will make a clean breast of this hearty dish.

BOLLITO MISTO

This dish of 'boiled meats' is a rich stew made with several different types of meat and poultry. In grand restaurants in northern Italy, it may include up to seven different meats, but elsewhere it might be less flamboyant, with only two or three, such as chicken, beef brisket and tongue, all cooked in one pot along with vegetables. Traditionally, bollito misto is served with mustard or a sharp, pesto-like sauce of hard-boiled egg yolk, anchovies, capers and herbs. Select a robust red, especially a Nebbiolo, Shiraz or Pinotage to serve with this equally robust dish.

BRISKET

As brisket is a cut of meat unsuited to roasting, it is either braised or slow boiled (simmered), then pressed, and often served cold. The final flavours are less intense than those of roasted or grilled beef and, therefore, the accompanying sauces play an important part in the choice of wine. A wide range of medium-bodied, low-tannin, easy-drinking reds make good partners.

The Irish way of preparing brisket is with spices, saltpetre and stout (Guinness). This salty dish works better with an off-dry Weisser Riesling or Chenin Blanc. If you want to stick with red, a Gamay Noir will counterbalance the salt.

BURGERS/HAMBURGERS

Although there are many claimants to the title 'home of the hamburger', no one really knows where the first hamburger was made. A common presumption is that it travelled to the USA from Hamburg in Germany, but this overlooks the fact that Hamburg has no tradition of serving such a thing as we know it today. More likely, it derives from something called a 'hamburger steak', which was a patty of chopped or minced beef shaped into a fairly thick, round steak, cooked on a grill, and eaten with a knife and fork. With time, the 'steak' part was dropped and the name was shortened, first to 'hamburger' and now, usually, to just 'burger'. Sliced tomato, onion, gherkin and lettuce are the usual additions.

The wines that suit a hamburger best are Pinotage and Zinfandel, but not the 'monster' ones. Select versions that are light- to medium-bodied and not too fruity. These wines will pair well even if a sauce is added – barbecue, monkeygland, mushroom, chilli or creamy cheese being among the most popular sauces. A quaffable Cabernet Sauvignon, Cab-Merlot blend or Shiraz also work. If you like to slather your burger with tomato sauce, then an off-dry rosé, Weisser Riesling or stein will be better partners.

BURRITOS

Although there are many variations, beef burritos are tortillas that are filled and rolled. Fillings can include strips of 'Mexican-flavoured' grilled steak (typically cumin, cinnamon, chilli and herbs) or picadillo (a spicy minced beef, see page 182), along with any or all of sour cream, guacamole, grated cheese, shredded lettuce and salsa fresca (chopped tomato, onion and chilli with lemon or lime juice).

This is a food and wine pairer's worst nightmare come true. All those flavours and textures rolled into one, and we're looking for *one* wine to serve it with? Not wanting to admit defeat, we opt for a wine that will do nothing more than add a bit of background music. But you need one with a bit of acidity, or there will be no music at all. If you want white, choose a Sylvaner, if you can find one, or settle for a quaffable Pinot Gris/Grigio or a dry or off-dry Chenin Blanc.

However, a red wine is a better choice with your beef burrito. Again, select one with good acidity, such as a Barbera or Sangiovese. Pinot Noir will not clash either, but why do this to the wine? Rather select an unwooded or lightly wooded Pinotage, and cross your fingers.

See also **Enchiladas**, page 179.

CANNELLONI

Tubular pasta stuffed with a tomatoey, herby beef sauce (*ragù*) is laid on a bed of tomato sauce, then topped with a white sauce and baked. Although we might be inclined to think of this as a pasta dish, it is the high proportion of meat to pasta, as well as the tomato, that provides the dominant weight and flavour. A medium-bodied Sangiovese, or an imported Chianti (an Italian red wine now quite freely available in South Africa) will be spot on with cannelloni.

CARBONNADE (carbonade à la flamande)

You may think that this Flemish stew of braising beef, onions and garlic, slow-cooked in stock and beer (ale), would automatically pair with the same ale you used in the cooking. But, by the time the dish is ready, the beer that was used as a flavouring agent no longer bears any resemblance to a freshly opened bottle.

Regardless of whether it is an ale, lager or pilsner, beer is just too one-dimensional to accompany this flavoursome dish. But why worry about beer when there is a wine that rises superbly to the occasion: Cabernet Franc. So, choose the best example you can afford for an unexpectedly precise gastronomical match.

CHATEAUBRIAND

This dish is a thick steak cut from the centre of the fillet, tradition-ally grilled, rather than roasted, and served with a side sauce. This method of preparing a beef fillet was invented by Montmirail, chef to Vicomte Chateaubriand. The serious wine drinker will often choose this uncluttered dish to show off a treasured Bordeaux blend or a Cabernet Sauvignon that has been saved for a special occasion. This combination of seared, rare, soft-textured meat and the velvety texture of well-aged Cabernet is one of the best-known gastronomi-cally precise matches.

Of all the beef cuts, fillet is the least flavourful, perhaps to the point of blandness. However, it is the perfect backdrop for a luxuri-ous sauce as fillet, which has no fat or marbling, will never compete with the sauce. This cut is frequently served with chateaubriand, château or bearnaise sauces, or a *maître d'hotel* butter. Chateau-briand sauce is an emulsified butter sauce flavoured with stock and lemon juice whereas the château (or Colbert) sauce is an emulsified butter sauce flavoured with white wine and chopped fresh tarragon. Bearnaise sauce is an egg and butter emulsion flavoured with tarra-gon, while *maître d'* butter is simply creamed butter with parsley and a drop of lemon juice. Although the sauces are all on the piquant side, they are rich and a little lemony, but by no means sharp. If you insist on a sauce, then it is not the moment to uncork a matured vinous treasure, but it is certainly the time to drink a good quality younger wine. A wine with a bit of an acidic edge, like Pinot Noir, Pinotage, Nebbiolo or Malbec, will cope admirably with the piquant character of all these sauces. If you want to be a bit contrary and drink a white, choose Semillon or Chardonnay from a cool climate as you need a good dollop of acidity in the wine.

See also the sauces listed under **Steak**, pages 185–189.

CHILLI CON CARNE

There are many interpretations of this favourite Mexican dish, and debate rages as to whether the red kidney beans should be added to the minced beef or served separately. Some say that the copious chillies in a dish such as this should rule out wine as a partner, but nothing could be further from the truth. Sure, chilli burns and anaes-thetises your taste buds and will make you oblivious to a wine's finer nuances, but chilli does not change the character of a wine. The other essential flavouring of chilli con carne, ground cumin, leads us straight to a full-bodied, pedal-to-the-metal Shiraz, Shiraz-Cabernet blend, Zinfandel or Pinotage. If your choice is Shiraz, you will have a double-whammy, as it likes both legumes and spice equally.

COCIDO MADRILEÑO

This rather rich but satisfying **Madrid stew** is one of Spain's oldest national dishes. A casserole of beef, chicken, sausage, ham, chickpeas, potatoes and vegetables, it cries out for a monster of a wine. Choose a full-bodied, robust, chunky Shiraz, Zinfandel or Pinotage to accompany this hearty meal.

CORNED BEEF (brisket)

Tinned corned beef, or 'bully beef', is usually made into a hash with onions and potatoes. What we are referring to is brisket or silverside, which has first been salted or cured in brine, and is then slowly simmered in water with carrots and onions and served in the traditional English way with either dumplings or boiled potatoes.

It is often accompanied by a creamy horseradish sauce, which sets off alarm bells for the food and wine pairer. Horseradish is one of the hardest foods to match with wine, as it strips it of all fruit and flavour. Viognier copes best, but does not like the salt in the dish. If you must have horseradish sauce (and why shouldn't you?), choose a red wine with sweet fruit flavours, such as a Gamay Noir, Zinfandel or Pinotage. However, go slow on the vinegar or lemon in the sauce and double-up on the cream. White wine drinkers should choose an off-dry Weisser Riesling, Gewürz or Pinot Gris/Pinot Grigio as these will counterbalance the saltiness of the dish.

If you serve mustard with your corned beef, you have a blank cheque and can choose any of these wines as mustard (provided it's not too hot or vinegary) has an affinity for both white and red wines. However, if you opt for a bitter orange sauce (bigarade), reach for that off-dry Weisser Riesling, and pray.

COTTAGE PIE

This popular family dish of savoury minced beef baked under a topping of mashed potatoes is quite content with an everyday red wine with no sharp edges, so your choice is wide open. If you have a heavy hand with the herbs and spices, choose an early-drinking Shiraz or a Shiraz-Cabernet blend, a Merlot or a Tempranillo.

COZIDO À PORTUGUESA

'Cozido' is the Portuguese version of the Spanish 'cocido', a rich stew made from beef shin, pork, and sometimes chicken, and served with any combination of cabbage, carrots, turnips, chorizo (spicy sausage), rice, potatoes and vegetables. Like the Spanish *cocido Madrileño* (see above), it loves a rich and robust red wine.

ENCHILADAS

Beef enchiladas are tortillas, stuffed with strips of spicy beef or picadillo (a Mexican savoury mince, see page 182), then rolled, topped
with a cooked tomato sauce, baked, and finished off with sour cream.
Two wines are superb with this dish: Barbera and Sangiovese, and
it's a toss-up as to which is best. White wine drinkers should choose
Chenin Blanc, which will sit quietly alongside it.

See also **Burritos**, page 176.

ESPETADAS

From Portugal, we get the popular espetada. Cubes of steak, marinated in herbs, are skewered with onion and peppers and grilled
over an open flame. Originally, bay tree twigs were used as skewers
but, although bay leaves are still used in the flavouring, nowadays
most espetadas are presented on a metal skewer which hangs from
a hook on a stand. Go straight for a killer Touriga Nacional, Malbec,
Tempranillo, Shiraz or Pinotage. If your espetada is flavoured with
anything other than the traditional bay leaf seasoning, you're having
a kebab (in which case, see **Kebabs**, below).

FRIKKADEL

See **Meatballs**, page 181.

HUNGARIAN GOULASH

The gentle, spicy flavours of paprika, caraway and tomato in a Hungarian beef goulash require an equally gentle red wine. A medium-
bodied Merlot or Cabernet, or a blend of these, is ideal. If you want
to add a bit of spice to the pairing, choose a Shiraz-Cabernet blend
or go straight for a Grenache, if you can find one.

KEBABS

Kebab, the Turkish word for a brochette, is a commonly used term in
South Africa to describe cubed foods cooked on a skewer (although
many people call any skewered food a sosatie). The meat may be
marinated before being cooked, or simply basted during cooking.
Beef kebabs come in many forms:

Marinated in a barbecue sauce Choose a hearty, sweet-fruited
red, such as a Grenache, Tempranillo or Shiraz.

Marinated in a curry sauce We are not dealing here with beef
curry, but with complex, compound flavours that develop as the
curry marinade is exposed to char-grilling. Unsurprisingly, the wine
choice is not an easy one, as there are no fail-safe matches. To top it
all, there is even a touch of sweetness in the kebab. Soft-centred red

wines, such as Sangiovese, will not clash with curried kebabs but will be much diminished and will merely hobble along. Shiraz whispers, 'I'm all right, Jack', but the pepperiness that develops in the combination is not what the chef or wine drinker welcomes. Head for a medium-bodied, easy-drinking Pinotage and hope for the best.

For traditional South African **sosaties**, which are usually made from lamb, see page 193.

Marinated in a garlic and herb sauce Choose from a Malbec, Tempranillo, Zinfandel, Shiraz or Pinotage.

Peri-peri Bird's-eye chilli is the key ingredient in peri-peri. You may think that **chilli** is a murderous ingredient, but chilli does not ruin the taste of wine. What we are dealing with is the weight of the beef with a very distinct flavour definition; therefore, we need a young, not-too-light-bodied wine with good intensity of flavour. Pinotage, with its hidden acidic note, works with the tomato base of the marinade.

Satay When you are served an Indonesian or Malaysian-style **peanut sauce** that does not contain coconut, choose a Cabernet Franc, Pinot Noir or a medium-bodied Shiraz or Shiraz-Grenache blend. As peanuts appear in both the marinade and the often-served accompanying sauce, we can look to Fernão Pires, which has an ongoing flirtation with anything peanutty, or an oak-aged Chardonnay. The most avant garde, free-thinking wine drinker can even venture towards a *skrik-vir-niks* Gewürztraminer.

Spicy Moroccan-style with cumin, chillies and lemon: Choose a Malbec, Tempranillo, Zinfandel, Shiraz or Pinotage.

With fruit (such as Polynesian-style, with canned pineapple, soy sauce and mustard) Choose a hearty, fruity Grenache, a Tempranillo or a Pinotage.

With kidneys (lamb or game) Choose a medium- to full-bodied Shiraz, and if it has a touch of bottle maturation, so much the better. You could also try a Barbera.

LASAGNE

Strictly speaking, the sheets of pasta are known as 'lasagne' and the baked dish is called lasagne al forno, but in South Africa we use the term 'lasagne' for both the pasta and the finished dish. Layers of meat sauce (*ragù*), lasagne and béchamel sauce, baked with a cheese topping, makes for a very comforting dish. Serve lasagne with a fruity, medium-bodied Sangiovese, Barbera, Zinfandel or a very lightly oaked Pinotage or Pinot Noir. An unoaked Chardonnay with some acidity, probably from a cool climate, or a wooded Chenin Blanc are also sympathetic partners.

MARROW BONES

Roasted marrow bones, served with toast, are making a comeback after a long absence. You may have heard this referred to as 'boere caviar'. No wonder, as it is as rich and decadent as caviar. A wooded Chardonnay or Semillon slithers seamlessly into the dish. However, if you're looking for a bit of excitement, pair this immensely rich dish vertically with an overtly fruity Sauvignon or Chenin Blanc, or choose a Sangiovese or a young, quaffable Pinotage.

MEATBALLS

Where does a frikkadel end and a meatball start? We seem to call those round little balls or patties of flavoured mince 'frikkadels' when they are pan-fried, grilled or baked and served as they are, but switch to meatballs the moment they swim in a sauce. That Italian creation, 'spaghetti with meatballs', just wouldn't be the same if it was presented as 'spaghetti with frikkadels'!

Many cuisines have some form of meatballs in their repertoire. The Danes have **frikadeller**, the Italians **polpette**, the Indians **kofta**, and the Greeks **keftedes**, although they use lamb for theirs. These may sound more enticing than 'meatballs', but they all fit the same bill and, generally, they all pair well with a red wine.

However, there are many variations in flavouring and saucing meatballs (or frikkadels, if you insist), which leads us to some interesting pairings. When meatballs are delicately flavoured, they love a classy, well-matured, medium-bodied red wine of great pedigree, such as a matured Bordeaux blend or Pinot Noir. In this variant, the white-wine drinker should go for an oaked Chardonnay but, paradoxically, not an opulent one. When the meatballs are herby, they pair well with a medium-bodied Shiraz or Pinotage, or with a Viognier. If they are made in a spicy Middle Eastern or Indian style, or curried, stick to the Viognier. And meatballs in a rich tomato sauce, for which every Italian family has its own recipe, require a robust, fruity red – here, a Nebbiolo or Pinotage are hard to beat.

See also **Keftedes**, page 131 and **Kofta**, page 193.

MEATLOAF

Almost an American institution, and often parodied as an 'end of month' standby, meatloaf comprises minced (ground) beef, bound with egg and flavoured with herbs and, often, Worcestershire sauce. It is baked in a loaf tin and served, either hot or cold, in slices. Pair this rather bland dish with Gamay Noir or, if it is not the end of the month and you're feeling extravagant, a Pinot Noir. A lightly oaked Chardonnay would be the white wine drinker's choice.

MOUSSAKA

In its Turkish or Greek form, moussaka is made with minced lamb, but in South Africa, most versions are made with minced beef. Sliced aubergine is layered with a tomatoey meat sauce, flavoured with herbs and spices, notably cinnamon and black pepper, then topped with a savoury custard and baked. Although not traditional, you may find sliced potatoes in the layers, probably to make this an all-in-one dish. A full-bodied Pinot Noir or Tempranillo or medium- to full-bodied Shiraz all make a clean breast of this luscious dish.

OXTAIL

Stews and casseroles are the most common oxtail dishes: braised in beer, with root vegetables and a touch of molasses; flamed in brandy, then braised in white wine with mushrooms and onions, or the more common South African version, where the oxtail is braised or slow-cooked in red wine. From the vineyards of France comes the inventive *queue de boeuf des vignerons* or winegrower's oxtail, slow-cooked with salt pork, root vegetables, herbs and a large bunch of lightly crushed white grapes. From Italy, we get the Roman *coda alla vaccinara*, a herby, spicy oxtail stew. All these hearty dishes cry out for a powerful red wine, so go for a killer Shiraz. A Shiraz-Cab blend also leaves its calling card, while a Nebbiolo or Tempranillo will do equal justice to this dish.

PICADILLO

Raisins, almonds and, sometimes, apple, are added to tomatoey mince which is flavoured with cumin, cinnamon and chilli. Picadillo is served as a main dish with rice, or used as a filling for tortillas, enchiladas, chimichangas, burritos, taco shells or empanadas. It is also used to stuff peppers before they are baked. However you prepare it, choose a Tempranillo, Grenache or a medium-bodied Shiraz.

See also **Burritos**, **Enchiladas**, **Tacos** elsewhere in this chapter.

POTJIE

A beef potjie has many interpretations – depending on the potjiekos-maker but, in essence, it is a stew that happens to be slow-cooked over the coals, in the oven or on the hob. As with most stews, it is the main ingredient or overall flavour that will determine the choice of wine to drink with it.

For the recommended wine matches, refer to the various stew- or casserole-type dishes listed elsewhere in this chapter, such as **beef bourguignonne**, **beef curry**, **beef stew**, **bollito misto** and **oxtail**. If, while cooking your potjie, you splash in a glug of the beer you're quaffing while tending the fire, you'd be making a **carbonnade**. And, as we mentioned in that entry (see page 176), Cabernet Franc would then be an ideal partner when you finally sit down to eat your potjie, by which time you may not want another beer.

RISSOLES

The culinary term 'rissoles' can cause some confusion. In French cuisine, these are envelopes of pastry stuffed with poultry, meat, game or vegetables and either fried or baked. Locally, rissoles normally mean small rolls or patties of beef mince, sometimes rolled in breadcrumbs, that are shallow fried.

For wine matches, see **Meatballs**, page 181.

ROAST BEEF

One of the key principles for the food and wine pairer is to match the weight of the food to the weight of the wine. No dish illustrates this as clearly as roast beef. The cuts usually used for a roast are the rib roast, sirloin, fillet and topside. The sirloin and majestic rib roast can take a medium-weight or slightly heavier red wine, while a piece of rare-roasted topside or whole roasted fillet, which generally lack flavour, need a gentler, more sympathetic wine.

Another key element is to match the flavour intensity of a dish to the flavour intensity of a wine. Dry-roasting not only browns the outside layers of the meat, it also adds a new compound flavour to the crust that forms, extending the flavour range and intensity of the meat. Many of the upfront, fruity, bold red wines that can overwhelm more gently flavoured foods, will find their match in roast beef. However, the temperature at which you serve your roast beef will have an impact on your choice of wine.

Hot roast beef A 'straight from the oven' roast, flavoured with no more that a hint of herbs and garlic and served with only the meat's own juices, is the perfect partner to that vinous treasure you've been saving. Your star-quality, perfectly aged red of great finesse will be shown off to its best advantage by simply roasted beef of whatever cut. But you may not have such a wine just lying around, nor care to serve your roast quite so plainly, so adjust your wine according to the flavourings or seasoning used in the cooking.

A more liberal sprinkling of herbs on the meat and in its gravy will impact on your choice of wine. Choose an equally herby or slightly spicy red, such as Petit Verdot, Malbec, Pinotage, Zinfandel, Tempranillo or Shiraz. If you serve your roast with a port-enriched sauce or a balsamic reduction, you will need even more power, so opt for deeply fruity and spicy versions of Pinotage, Tempranillo or Shiraz. If your beef is encrusted with black pepper, it will be hard to beat a Shiraz; if it is rubbed with ground coffee, Pinotage steps in. If you're into fusion, with sweet touches creeping in, stick to the killer-versions of any of these three wines, as their ripe sweet-berry fruit will mimic the sweetness in the seasoning.

The more rare the beef, the more tannic the red wine can be, as rare meat seems to tame tannins. On the other hand, a not-so-rare roast will highlight a wine's tannins. Also, a more robust, fibrous cut of beef, such as the sirloin or rib, requires a bigger, more 'chewy' wine than the gentler texture of a fillet, which needs a well-rounded wine with soft acidity – perhaps an older vintage that will identify with the softer mouth-feel of the fillet.

Horseradish has a remarkable affinity for beef, cutting into the fat and stimulating the appetite, but this condiment is murderous on a wine, as it strips it of its flavour. Here, you have three choices: Firstly, have the horseradish, but step down on the quality of the accompanying wine. Secondly, skip the horseradish and stick to that bottle of fine wine. (In this case, you could replace the horseradish with mustard, provided it is not too hot, vinegary or sweet; Dijon is an excellent choice. Mustard has an ongoing love affair with red and white wine.) Thirdly, say *c'est la vie*, and have both the horseradish and your treasured wine, accepting that all the fine nuances and subtleties of the wine will be lost.

Cold roast beef The wine that you enjoy with your hot roast beef is not likely to be as happy with the same meat when it is served cold. Like other roasted meats, beef becomes denser when the fat in the fibres coagulates on cooling. While a Malbec may have been superb with the roast when it was hot from the oven, when the beef is cold, you need to turn to a rosé or lighter red, such as Gamay, or to a red wine with good acidity, such as Sangiovese or Pinot Noir, which seldom clashes with any cold roast meat.

This switch in wines is explained by the fact that tannic wines do not like solidified fats, whereas wines with some natural acidity will obligingly cut through the fat.

SAUERBRATEN

This wonderfully rich beef casserole originates from Germany and Austria. The meat is marinated in a spicy, sweet-sour mixture that is later used for the gravy. The dish is traditionally served with red cabbage cooked with apples, and German-style noodles (*spätzle*) sprinkled with caraway seed. The overall richness requires an equally rich, robust wine such as a Nebbiolo, a substantial Barbera or a Sangiovese, all of which have good acidity.

SLOPPY JOES (savoury mince)

A sloppy joe is an American dish of *very* tomatoey, savoury minced beef served on a hamburger bun. Enjoy this informal meal with an easy-drinking wine like a Barbera, Sangiovese or Cinsaut, or go straight for the 'tomato' wine, Sauvignon Blanc.

SPAGHETTI BOLOGNESE (Bolognaise)

Whether you use the Italian/English spelling, Bolognese, or the French Bolognaise, 'spag bol' is one of the most popular and well-known Italian dishes around the world. Interestingly, the Italians themselves would never dream of serving their traditional *ragù*, or sauce, from Bologna on spaghetti; they use tagliatelle or other pasta ribbons. Unsurprisingly, this tomatoey meat sauce is happiest with an Italian grape (a good example of regional food pairing best with regional wine), so crack open a bottle of Sangiovese, Barbera or Nebbiolo, or opt for an imported Chianti. If you can't lay your hands on one of these, Pinot Noir will always come to the rescue, as will the much-less noble Cinsaut. You could also keep it simple and reach for a boxed Ruby Cabernet, Cab Sav or Cab-Merlot blend.

If you want to drink a white wine, be prepared for your wine to take a bit of a knock. Choose a bold, packed-with-fruit Sauvignon Blanc with good acidity, or a wooded Chenin Blanc. These wines will hold the fort if the *ragù* is very herby (with origanum and basil); if there are no herbs but a touch of nutmeg instead, a Viognier could work, although it won't be all that happy with the tomato in the sauce – but that's compromise for you.

STEAK AND KIDNEY PIE

A homely, comforting dish from a bygone era, now making something of a comeback, steak and kidney pie (or pudding) requires a gently textured wine, but one that is also flavourful enough to match the gamey nature of the kidneys. Pinot Noir comes out tops, but an easy drinking Cabernet Sauvignon, Nebbiolo, Tempranillo or Malbec are also good options. These reds will pair even better if they have had a touch of bottle maturation. If you want to drink a white wine, Viognier is your best bet.

STEAK

A grilled, pan-fried or braaied beef steak is remarkably easy to pair with red wine. This holds true whether you're having a fillet, sirloin, tournedos, t-bone, porterhouse or rump steak. There are three sound reasons why red wines pair so well with steak, and it's not just because they're both red! Colour plays no part in this pairing.

Firstly, red wines are the classic choices because the weight of steak finds a match in equally heavy wines. Secondly, steak pairs well with oak flavours, and most red wines are oaked. Lastly, grilling, pan-frying or braaiing involve charring to some degree and the acrid or carbon-like flavours that develop in the steak find an echo in the bitter edge of the tannins present in red wine.

When selecting a wine, you won't go wrong with a structured Cab, Merlot, Shiraz, Pinotage, Tempranillo, Malbec, or blends of these. A pan-fried steak will be more accommodating to the lighter style of red wine, whereas a char-grilled steak, with its singed aroma, probably wants a bigger wine. And here the Oscar goes to a full-bodied, tannic Petit Verdot or Shiraz, with Pinotage close on their heels.

Steak's flexibility with red wine does not carry over to the whites, so you need to be more selective in your choice. Unsurprisingly, it prefers a white wine profile not too far removed from red; that is, good fruit intensity to give weight, wooding to give oak flavours and, instead of tannins, a wine with some acidity. This acidity acts like a squeeze of lemon on the steak, rounding off the slightly bitter grilled flavours. A top-quality, wooded Chardonnay, with concentrated, powerful fruit, buttery richness and balancing acidity is your best choice.

However, when a **sauce** is served with steak, there are variations to classic pairings and things become just a wee bit more precise. (And we do not mean a knife-tip of mustard or another condiment, but a sauce in which a specific flavour is emphatically present.)

We have listed some common steak preparations and sauces. If your personal favourite is not here, refer to **Sauces,** pages 32–43.

Béarnaise sauce, a liaison of egg yolks and butter, flavoured with herbs and lemon juice, is a great accompaniment to all grilled meats. Eggs in a sauce do not present the same problems for wine as eggs on their own do, but neither are they overly friendly. Eggy sauces are infinitely better with white wines than with reds, because the tannins in red wine are the protestors. Chardonnay or Semillon, with their creamy textures, will fit the bill, but they do need some good acidity. If you don't want to drink white wine, Pinot Noir, Gamay Noir or Sangiovese will come to the rescue.

An artichoke heart filled with béarnaise sauce and served atop a fillet medallion becomes a Tournedos Henri IV. Artichoke heads the list of tricky ingredients in food and wine pairing, playing merry hell with all wines by making them taste metallic and sweeter than they really are. Refuse to admit defeat, and stay with the Pinot Noir or Sangiovese, but ask for your Henri IV to be served with a wedge of lemon on the side to defuse the artichoke. Then pray that the lemony nature of the sauce will do the rest!

Bordelaise sauce is a meat sauce reduced with red wine and enriched with beef marrow. Pair this classic, rich sauce on a grilled steak with an equally classic rich wine, such as a Bordeaux blend. Also good would be a solo Cabernet, Merlot, Shiraz or Zinfandel.

Braaied steak with relish In South Africa, braaied meat is sometimes topped with a cooked tomato and onion relish (*smoor*) or chakalaka, a spicy African relish that includes cooked carrots, cauliflower, green peppers, chilli, onions and baked beans. Although either relish will add a sour note, the weight of the dish remains with the meat. In a case like this, it is a good idea to choose a red wine that appears to have its own acidity, such as Pinotage, Pinot Noir or Nebbiolo. For the white wine drinker, Viognier will get you by, but you must be prepared for the wine to take a knock.

Carpetbag steak Steak stuffed with fresh oysters is often regarded as a uniquely Australian dish that was popular in Sydney in the 1950s, but it most likely originated in the USA, where they call it a Carpetbagger steak. Why this strange name? Well, after the American Civil War, traders from the victorious northern states sought out commercial opportunities in the devastated south. They carried their wares in what was, literally, a 'carpetbag', a large hold-all made by saddle-makers from worn-out carpets. (However, the combination of fresh oysters and beef goes back a lot further, as the Chinese have been flavouring their beef stir-fries with oyster sauce for centuries.) Packed into their steak 'bag', the oysters add a pungent richness to the dish, so the matching wine needs to be equally rich and full. Choose a favourite red to fit this profile, or bring out one of those blockbusters you've been keeping for a 'special occasion'.

***Maître d'hôtel* butter** Butter creamed with parsley and lemon juice adds a bit of richness and a touch of acidity to steak. Stick to your favourite red but, if the chef had a heavy hand with the lemon juice, you may find that a Pinotage comes out on top.

Mexican Either marinated or dry-rubbed, this steak is flavoured with chilli, cumin, origanum or marjoram, garlic and lime juice. A Shiraz or Pinotage will add intriguing flavours to this already complex mix of herbs and spices.

Monkeygland sauce This rather imprecise sauce has many variations, depending on who is making it. However, the commonality will be fruitiness and a slight sweetness. For the best combination, you need a red wine with vibrant, sweet-fruit flavours, so think Shiraz, Pinotage, Mourvèdre, Tempranillo or Grenache. If you insist on a white wine, a Gewürztraminer, off-dry Weisser Riesling or a full, ripe, unoaked Chardonnay will match the sauce, but you may find them a bit light for the weight of the steak.

Mushroom sauce A creamy mushroom sauce is a steakhouse staple. An equally creamy white wine is indubitably the best choice. Go for a rich, ripe, oaked Chardonnay, Semillon or a Viognier, which has a special affinity for mushrooms. An easy-drinking Merlot or Merlot-Cab blend are your best red wine choices.

Pepper sauce Black-pepper sauce is a great South African favourite to accompany steak. Here, we are dealing with a combination of cream and spice, so a vibrant, full-bodied, oaked Chardonnay will pair wonderfully, although you'll also have success with *young* reds with some acidity; think Barbera, Sangiovese, Tempranillo, Malbec. Medium- to full-bodied reds, such as Shiraz, Shiraz-Cab blends, Petit Verdot and Zinfandel, will also work. If green peppercorns are used instead of black, the same wines will pair well.

Pepper steak The term 'pepper steak' can be a bit confusing. Some folk use it to mean a steak served with a pepper sauce, while others are referring to *steak au poivre*. See above and opposite for specific wine matches for both versions.

Red wine marinade Steak soaked in a simple French-style red wine marinade and then grilled or char-grilled, is unfussed, so choose your favourite red, but go for at least a medium-bodied one, as the marinade adds flavour and depth to the steak.

Roquefort butter Crumbled Roquefort (blue) cheese and freshly chopped parsley are mashed into butter with a touch of lemon juice. *See also **Maître d'hôtel** butter, page 187.*

Roquefort sauce This is a creamy sauce with depth of flavour. Choose an equally creamy wine, such as full-bodied, fruity, oaked Chardonnay or Semillon. If you want to drink a red, Pinotage or Pinot Noir work well with the salt and cream combination in the sauce.

Rossini This luxury dish consists of tournedos (small rounds of fillet) topped with foie gras (or pâté de foie gras) and a slice of truffle. These additions add weight and flavour intensity that need to be matched to the wine. While the richness of the foie gras makes its presence felt in no uncertain terms, it is the truffle that brings flavour to the party. Nebbiolo's affinity for mushrooms and truffles comes to mind, as the wine will match the combined weight of the meat and the foie gras. If you can't get your hands on a Nebbiolo, then go for a red with some bottle maturation, but stay with richness and flavour.

An aged Pinotage will be perfect, with an aged Pinot Noir, Tempranillo or top-notch Merlot hot on its heels. The white wine drinker can successfully pair a tournedos Rossini with Viognier, but it will need more than a single slice of truffle for the combination to work, and if the Viognier has a bit of bottle maturation, so much the better. A mature, oaked Chardonnay would also be a good match.

For years, the Champenoise served this grand dish with matured vintage champagne, but they must have been looking at the foie gras and truffle only, forgetting about the steak. Even at its richest, champagne does not have the weight to stand up to red meat. However, the New World has come up with an answer in sparkling Shiraz (traditionally made bubbly, that is, not sweet carbonated red fizz). Quirky as it may seem, this combination actually works. (You may have difficulty sourcing a bottle though, as only a few South African producers make méthode cap classique from red wine.)

Steak au poivre Pan-fried steak encrusted with crushed black peppercorns and served plainly with only the pan juices, perhaps finished by a splash of brandy, needs a young, boisterous red wine with slightly sweetish fruit and firm tannins. Choose a Shiraz or Petit Verdot, with Pinotage or Zinfandel as second choices, although you'll search far and wide for a better match than Shiraz with *steak au poivre*. Two fusions occur simultaneously in this match: the pepper acts as a foil to the tannins in the wine, while bright fruit downplays the hot intensity of the pepper and highlights its flavour. If you stick to a young Shiraz, nothing can go wrong with this match made in heaven. However, if you want to drink an aged wine, you may have to cut back on the black pepper which, when presented with lower tannins, can over-accentuate the alcohol of the wine. This is just a nice way of saying that the alcohol will stick out like a sore thumb.

Steakhouse barbecue sauces Not many wines will survive when swamped by sweet-spicy-sharp barbecue sauces. A concentrated, densely flavoured red wine packed with sweet fruit flavours will, however, hold its head above water. You may decide on a full-bodied, richly textured, ripe Merlot or Zinfandel, but a Shiraz with the same profile would do even better. The white-wine drinker should reach for a Gewürztraminer or a ripe, full, but not too oaky Chardonnay. Some people might swear by a semi-sweet white, but not everyone wants to drink this style of wine with steak.

Surf 'n turf There are many versions of this famous American dish, but the basic ingredients are steak served alongside seafood of some sort and, perhaps, some garlic or herbed butter. Adding fish or seafood to meat, or the reverse, adding meat to fish, is as old as the hills. The Chinese have been doing it for centuries, seasoning their beef stir-fries with oyster sauce. The Brits were not far behind when they added oysters to their steak and kidney puddings, while Europeans wrapped plain fish fillets in cured ham. When surf converges with turf, a pungent richness gets added to the dish and the accompanying wine needs to be equally rich. Red wines are the most successful, so go straight for a full-bodied Pinotage.

STEAK TARTARE

In the traditional presentation of steak tartare, raw chopped fillet steak or sirloin steak is shaped into a flat circle with a dent in the middle, into which a raw egg yolk is placed, along with chopped onion and capers. On its own, raw beef poses no problem for wine, but raw egg yolk annihilates it, especially a red wine with firm tannins. The capers are an additional headache for the food and wine pairer. A white wine is a best match here, so go for an unwooded Chardonnay or Semillon from a cool climate, which shows some good acidity. If anchovy fillets and gherkins are served on the side, stick with the Chardonnay. If Tabasco or Worcestershire sauce are added to the meat or used as a condiment, the dish will become spicier and more difficult to pair, and Viognier is the answer. If tomato sauce is used, a Sangiovese is about the best you can hope for.

STIR-FRIED BEEF

Stir-frying is a method of cooking meat and/or vegetables quickly and evenly with little added fat. Unlike roasting, it adds no additional flavours – a green pepper remains a green pepper, and a carrot a carrot. The resulting dishes tend to be light, with clearly defined flavours. Consequently, we look to lighter, sweet-fruity, low-tannin red wines. Pinot Noir is hard to beat, but you could easily enjoy a white wine, such as a lightly oaked Semillon, with your stir-fry. When the finished dish is flavoured with soy sauce or oyster sauce, the flavour intensity of stir-fried beef will be increased, so a flamboyantly fruity Pinotage would be just perfect.

TACOS

Tacos are tortillas that are deep-fried and folded in half to make a crisp shell that is stuffed with savoury fillings. To savoury minced beef (see **Picadillo**, page 182) are added salsa, refried beans, shredded lettuce, grated cheese, chillies and guacamole. Almost any wine will find it difficult to cope with such a hotchpotch. Unlike a chicken taco, where the chicken simply disappears under the avalanche of flavours, the more robust beef taco throws its weight around. We need some acidity to cope with the acidity of the cooked tomatoes in the mince and the raw tomatoes in the salsa. Go straight for a Chenin Blanc, Cinsaut, Sangiovese or quaffable Pinotage.

Lamb

Two red grapes must have been invented for lamb, in whatever form: Cabernet Sauvignon and Tempranillo.

BRAAIED, GRILLED OR PAN-FRIED

Lamb chops are a mainstay of many a South African braai. At their simplest, the chops are seasoned with nothing more than salt and pepper, which is when Cabernet Sauvignon and Tempranillo really come into their own. From there, the seasoning steps up and you could fill a shopping basket with the many spices, rubs, marinades and basting sauces on the market.

The pronounced 'browning' flavours that develop with grilling, braaiing and, to a lesser extent, pan-frying, find a match in a young Cab Sav or Tempranillo, with their flavours of ripe berry-fruit and the smokiness of oaking. When a sweet marinade or basting sauce is used, you need the bigger profile of a deeply fruity, supple wine with low tannins, such as Zinfandel, Pinotage or top-notch Merlot. This is one of the occasions when we are reminded of Merlot's flexibility; it is astounding how it copes across the spectrum of flavours, from the gentle flavours of oven roasting to the robust flavours of char-grilling. Another option is to choose the ever-accommodating Shiraz. If you can, try a sparkling version made by the cap classique method; it may be difficult to find, but will be worth it.

If you're a dedicated carnivore who enjoys that strip of browned fat on a braaied chop or ribbetjie, a smoky, oaky Chardonnay will happily take a seat at the table, but stick to potato salad and pass on any vinegar-dressed green salads.

If you like your braaied meat accompanied by pap topped with a cooked tomato and onion relish or chakalaka, choose a red wine with a touch of astringency, such as Pinotage or Barbera. Or, if you go easy on the relishes, you could stick with one of lamb's heavenly twins, Cab Sav and Tempranillo.

BREDIE

An old Cape favourite, bredie was traditionally made with mutton rib, but these days we use stewing lamb, such as knuckle or neck. The meat and onions are browned, then cooked very slowly in their own juices, with perhaps a splash of water, until nearly tender, then a vegetable of choice is placed on top of the meat, without stirring it, until all the ingredients are cooked.

Various bredies include cabbage, cauliflower, pumpkin, green bean, (dried bean versions are also known as boontjie bredie), potato, waterblommetjie and the well-known tomato (tamatie). Parsnip and quince bredies seem to have faded into history. Interestingly, some heritage recipes dating from the 1800s call for a red chilli to be added; an unusual ingredient for the time!

A bredie is a hearty dish that calls for an equally hearty red wine and you can't go wrong with Cabernet Sauvignon or Tempranillo. However, if you're making tomato bredie, a red with a touch of astringency, such as Pinotage or Barbera, would be better. Waterblommetjie bredie is a great success when paired with Sauvignon Blanc, but the wine must have enough body and flavour to stand up to the lamb.

IRISH STEW

This world-famous lamb, onion and potato dish is thick and creamy. Although the addition of carrots or other vegetables is not traditional, their inclusion will have no effect on the choice of wine. If your version of this dish is heavily flavoured with thyme, the herb normally used, a Cabernet Sauvignon would be particularly pleased. Alternatively, choose Tempranillo or Pinotage. Shiraz will also work, provided the thyme offers no more than a vague hint of flavour. If you're a dedicated white-wine drinker, just go slow on the thyme and pair the creamy texture of this dish with an equally creamy (which is just a fancy way of saying 'wooded') Chardonnay.

KEBABS

Cubes of meat on a stick or skewer are known variously around the world as kebabs, brochettes or satays (satés), but it appears that South Africans have opted mainly for the word 'kebab', which we enjoy in a variety of manifestations.

Barbecue spiced/sauced As 'barbecue' flavourings are often sweetish, a Gewürztraminer will do the trick, although it is not really suited to powerful foods and you will be better off with a red. Choose a deeply fruity, supple, oaky, low-tannin Shiraz, Zinfandel, Pinotage, or a flexible little Merlot that won't blink an eye in the presence of sweet and tangy barbecue sauces.

Moroccan If the lamb is marinated in a mixture containing ground cumin, chilli and coriander, you'll need a red wine with enough weight and breadth to stand up to the spices. Go for a Shiraz, Zinfandel or Pinotage. White wine drinkers will be delighted with Viognier.

Seehk (sheek) kebab For these Indian kebabs, see page 231.

Shish kebab Perhaps the most famous of the world's skewered meat dishes is the Turkish shish kebab. Cubes of lamb, flavoured with onion, garlic and olive oil, sometimes with a touch of cinnamon or herbs, are skewered and grilled, either over an open fire or under a grill. Shish kebabs may be served on the skewer with perhaps a rice pilaf or a salad on the side, or the meat and salad are stuffed into pockets of pitta bread. Choose a Shiraz, Pinotage or Viognier.

Sosaties Although many South Africans use the term 'sosatie' to describe any skewered meat, what we are describing here, and pair the wine to, is the traditional sosatie which originated in the Cape with the fusion of Malay and settler cuisines. Cubes of lamb are marinated in a sour, curry mixture before being skewered with some lamb fat (spek) and dried apricots. The sourness of the marinade comes from vinegar, lemon juice or tamarind. The sosaties are then grilled or braaied and, sometimes, finished off with a sauce (derived from the marinade), sweetened with apricot jam.

What a headache for the food and wine pairer! All red lights are flickering in the presence of a full-house of tripwires: sourness, sweetness, bitterness, fattiness, smokiness, chariness that's just short of charcoaliness, and curry spices to top it all off! It's murderous to a wine, but what does work is an off-dry Weisser Riesling. Gewürztraminer also comes to the rescue, but can be overbearing. Not everybody will be happy to drink these wines with barbecued lamb, though. Pinotage hobbles along, but you need one that is packed with sweet fruits, subtle tannins and good acidity. You could also try one of the Italians, such as a Barbera or Sangiovese. Having highlighted these tripwires for wine you may exclaim, as they did way back in the past, 'Why not a beer?'. Well, beer is certainly enjoyable at a braai, but wine makes a considerably more complex and gastronomically constructive match with sosaties.

KEFTEDES

For these little meatballs, see page 131 and also **Kofta**, below.

KLEFTIKO

In this Greek favourite, lamb on the bone is slow-cooked with fresh herbs, particularly thyme, to a falling-off-the-bone degree of tenderness. Cabernet Sauvignon or Tempranillo is as close to a perfect accompaniment as you can get, but you could also try a Cab-Merlot blend, as the texture of the lamb finds an echo in this match.

KOFTA

Nearly every country has some type of meatball in its cuisine. In eastern Mediterranean, Balkan, Middle Eastern and South Asian countries the name for meatballs is a variation of the Urdu term 'kofta': *köfte* in Turkey, *keftedes* in Greece, *kufta* in Israel, and *kofta* in Pakistan and India. For kofta, minced lamb is usually seasoned with spices, such as cinnamon, coriander, cumin, cloves and nutmeg. Herbs such as mint, thyme and parsley are added, and ground pine or pistachio nuts may be included. When cooked, the smallish meat-balls are often used to fill the pockets of pitta bread or piled on top of flatbreads along with salad-like ingredients.

The acidic sauces that often accompany kofta, such as a minty yoghurt, are generally hard on a wine, but the natural acidity of Sangiovese should be able to cope with this. Pinotage and Barbera are other options.

LAMB CURRY

We are all familiar with two styles of South African lamb curries: the hotter, red-coloured 'Durban' curry and the milder, slightly sweeter, yellow-coloured 'Malay' curry.

A Durban or Indian-type curry is very happy with a light-bodied, easy-drinking, low-tannin Cabernet Sauvignon or Cab-Merlot blend, but save your fine, matured wines for another day.

The slight sweetness of the Cape Malay style is happier with a Viognier that is bursting with flavour. Sambals of coconut, chutney, sliced bananas, and chopped tomatoes with onions often accompany this style of curry. If you particularly love coconut in or with curry, you can also go for a wooded Chardonnay or Semillon. On the other hand, if chutney is your thing, an off-dry Weisser Riesling or Gewürztraminer will come to the rescue.

If you don't want to drink a white wine with a Cape Malay-style lamb curry, then reach for a Mourvèdre, if you can find one. As a last resort, consider Merlot, but it will have to be packed with sweet-berry fruit and be without a hint of tannin.

LAMB STEWS AND CASSEROLES

Look no further than Cabernet Sauvignon to pair with a basic lamb stew flavoured with onions, garlic and, perhaps, some rosemary or thyme. The texture that is so unique to a full-bodied Cabernet works well with a thick, rich, slow-cooked lamb stew and its viscous gravy. Tempranillo, Bordeaux blends and solo Merlot are also naturals.

LANCASHIRE HOTPOT

Layers of potato and lamb neck, or cubes of lamb, are slow-cooked with sliced carrots, onions and, perhaps, turnips or celery. This hearty English dish is similar to an Irish stew, though not as creamy.

Choose the same wines as for an **Irish stew**, see page 192.

MUTTON (OR LAMB) PIE

A South African favourite, but perhaps from a bygone era when you didn't have to mortgage your house to buy the lamb! The pie's filling of cooked and shredded lamb is enhanced by the addition of bacon or smoked ham. This touch of smokiness is just enough to let us reach for a Shiraz instead of lamb's best chum, Cabernet Sauvignon. White-wine drinkers will enjoy a wooded Chardonnay that works well with the butteriness of the pastry and the smokiness of the filling.

NAVARIN OF LAMB

This French lamb stew is either called a navarin or a ragoût. The meat is slowly stewed in a stock with onions, turnips, potatoes, peas, herbs and a dollop of tomato purée until it is tender and aromatic. *Navarin d'agneau printanier* takes its name from the fresh spring vegetables that contribute to its delicious taste. A Bordeaux blend would be ideal, as would a solo Tempranillo or Cabernet Sauvignon.

NOISETTES OF LAMB

The 'wheels' formed from a deboned rib or loin are pan-fried, grilled or barbecued. They are often stuffed with a savoury meat mixture or, South African style, with fruit, and served with gravy or a fruit-based sauce, such as raspberry or redcurrant. If there is quite a bit of sweetness in the dish, choose a big, deeply fruited red that can handle sweetish fruit flavours, such as Mourvèdre, Shiraz, Zinfandel or Pinotage. If your version is more savoury, stick with lamb's table-mates, Cabernet Sauvignon or Tempranillo.

POTJIE

A potjie is similar to a **bredie**. *See* pages 191–192 for wine pairing suggestions for various bredies.

ROAST LAMB

Unlike beef, almost any cut of lamb can be roasted. Even some of the cheaper cuts can be plainly roasted on the bone, or stuffed with a savoury, sour or sweet mixture. The most usual cuts for roasting are leg, loin, best end of neck (rack), shoulder or breast.

With **plainly roasted lamb** served with a traditional gravy, roast potatoes and vegetables, it is hard to beat a Cabernet Sauvignon, Bordeaux blend or a Tempranillo. The classic pairing of a fine, young (or older) star-quality Cab with roast lamb is considered to be one of the most exact gastronomic matches. Cab Sav stretches its wings to reach new heights in the presence of two herbs, **rosemary** and **thyme**; try roasting your lamb plainly and with both herbs and decide which you think is the best. The same wine match applies if the lamb is roasted in the **French manner**, where the joint is spiked with thin slivers of garlic, spread with rosemary and lemon-flavoured butter and roasted until the outside is well seared, but the inside still pink and moist. And Cabernet Sauvignon or a Bordeaux blend are still the belles of the ball with a rack of lamb roasted with a **breadcrumb and herb topping** or a joint **stuffed with a savoury mixture**.

Where a fine, top-notch Cabernet throws in the towel and retreats is if the roast is served with **mint sauce** or **jelly**. 'Death by chocolate' has nothing on 'death by mint sauce'! No wine is happy in the face of that fatal combination of sugar and vinegar. Of course, this is not going to stop you from daubing these murderous add-ons on your slices of roast lamb, but just gear down to a quaffable wine, preferably one with some acidity. However, there is an excellent solution: sprinkle finely chopped fresh mint, without any liquid additions, over the lamb when you serve it; this will take care of the love-triangle between mint, lamb and Cabernet.

Cabernet Sauvignon also takes to the hills when a deboned joint is **stuffed with a sweet mixture** such as apricots or prunes. Merlot, with its higher acidity levels, fares much better with sweet and sour ingredients, although Pinotage or Pinot Noir are, perhaps, the best.

Served cold Like other meats, roast lamb takes on a different complexion when it is served cold, as its texture becomes denser when the fats in the fibres coagulate. That fine bottle of Cabernet Sauvignon that you enjoyed when the joint was served hot will now take a beating. A well-structured red wine with firm tannins is not going to be happy in the presence of solid, cold fat. Switch to a white instead, and choose a lightly wooded Chardonnay or Semillon or a Viognier. If these wines seem rather opulent in the presence of that humble little sandwich made with leftover lamb, then tap yourself a glass of quaffable red from a box.

SHANKS

Lamb shanks have become quite fashionable and appear frequently on restaurant menus. The many flavouring possibilities are essentially the same as for roast lamb or lamb stews, so refer to those listings (see above) for our pairing suggestions.

One flavouring not mentioned elsewhere is North African **harissa** paste, which is often used when preparing lamb shanks. The basis of this fiery paste (or sauce) is roasted red peppers to which garlic, chilli, caraway, coriander and cumin seeds are added. Besides the coriander and cumin, the addition of caraway gives harissa its distinctive flavour. This is a rich, slow-braised dish that, theoretically, should like the texture of a fuller-bodied Cabernet Sauvignon. However, as the spice level has stepped up dramatically, the scales are tipped in favour of Shiraz, making this an excellent example of how to force lamb to favour Shiraz.

SHEPHERD'S PIE

Traditionally, this is a cottage pie made with minced lamb instead of with beef – a distinction that may be fading in South Africa. Pair the savoury minced lamb under its topping of mashed potatoes with a soft-centred red, such as a medium-bodied, easy-drinking Merlot-Cab or Merlot-Shiraz blend, a Barbera or a Sangiovese.

SOSATIES

See **Kebabs**, page 192–193.

TAGINE (Tajine)

The dish, which gets its name from the domed clay pot in which the spicy stew is cooked, appears in the cuisines of Morocco, Algeria and Tunisia. It is the North African answer to the South African bredie.

North African foods have a clear preference for three red wines: Shiraz, Pinotage and Zinfandel, especially when the wines are big, spicy and can handle strong flavours in food. For a piquant lamb tagine made with preserved lemons, Pinotage, with its acidic edge, is just the thing. But for the more common, slightly sweeter tagines, which often include nuts and dried fruit such as dates, raisins or apricots, Shiraz or Zinfandel, both of which share the flavours of the dish, are natural partners.

Pork

As a very general suggestion, pork is happiest with a gentle red wine or a richly textured white wine.

BRAAIED/GRILLED RIBS OR CHOPS

Pork ribs and chops are often marinated in, or basted with, a sweetish mixture that has a touch of saltiness. The combination of the caramelized marinade and the grilled flavours that develop during cooking calls for a moderate amount of sweetness in the wine. An off-dry Weisser Riesling or Chenin Blanc are both good choices with sweet-salty combinations; stein comes a close second. For the red-wine drinker, the key is also a sweet-fruity core, but with moderate alcohol (below 13.5%) and low tannin. Mourvèdre, Shiraz, Pinotage or Zinfandel all fit this profile as they are 'sticky-sauce friendly'. If the wine has a touch of smoky oak, so much the better, as this will provide a complementary echo, especially to char-grilling.

CASSEROLES AND STEWS

Pork makes a good choice for slow-baked casseroles, as the flavour of the meat blends well with a range of herbs and spices to provide a wide repertoire of dishes.

Hot-pot (hotch-potch) A gently flavoured pork casserole topped with potatoes or savoury dumplings, is equally happy with a not-too-fruity white wine or an easy-drinking red with low tannins. Take your pick from Chenin Blanc, Pinot Blanc, Pinot Gris/Pinot Grigio, Colombard or an unoaked Chardonnay. For a red you can't improve on Pinot Noir, rosé or blanc de noir. Apples or pears incorporated into the stew add a sweetish note that steers us towards a wine with balancing sweetness. Stay with Chenin Blanc, but select an off-dry style, or opt for a rosé or blanc de noir with a dollop of residual sugar. Gewürztraminer's exuberance lifts this gentle dish to another level.

Oriental-style pork casserole Gently spiced strips of pork, cooked in sherry and soy sauce, with crunchy vegetables and nuts, is very good with an off-dry Weisser Riesling or Chenin Blanc which will admirably balance out the moderate levels of salt in the dish.

Pork and bean casserole Pork cooked with dried beans, onions and tomatoes makes a hearty stew. This wine-friendly dish gives you carte blanche, so choose your favourite dry white or red cultivars, but stick to medium-bodied ones. If your stew is enlivened by a touch of curry powder, a Gewürztraminer or Viognier would add a festive note.

Spicy pork casseroles When gently spiced, and with the merest hint of sweetness, this casserole will embrace a Gewürztraminer. However, when exuberantly spiced, you'll have to double-up on the spice in the wine; a medium-bodied, low-tannin Shiraz, a Shiraz-Grenache blend or a Mourvèdre will fit the bill.

CASSOULET

This classic French 'meat and bean' stew usually combines three meat types in its preparation, one of which is a fatty meat. It may be the traditional combination of pork with duck and lamb, or pehaps pork with chicken and chorizo sausage, but all cassoulets include haricot beans and require long cooking to thoroughly merge the flavours of the ingredients. What this dish needs is a young, intensely fruity red with a touch of richness-cutting acidity. Gamay, Malbec, Cinsaut, Mourvèdre or Pinotage are ideal, but a cool-climate Shiraz is also good, or try a Shiraz-Grenache blend. The dedicated white-wine drinker needs to sit this one out, or pour a glass of Cinsaut, the easiest of the 'cassoulet reds', and pretend that it is a white wine.

CHOUCROUTE

'Choucroute' is French for sauerkraut, but it is also a famous dish from Alsace in northeastern France, *choucroute Alsacienne* (often shortened to just choucroute). In this dish the preserved cabbage (sauerkraut) is simmered with diced pork, onions, white wine and juniper berries with, traditionally, the addition of frankfurter or pork sausages and, sometimes, bacon. Provided they are not too fruity, a dry or off-dry Weisser Riesling or a Gewürztraminer – both of which are grown in Alsace – will have the weight to stand up to the different meats in the dish, as well as the acidity to cut through its richness. An unwooded Chardonnay also does beautifully, as does Pinot Blanc. Sylvaner, another wine from Alsace, seems an obvious choice, but the strong aroma of the juniper berries makes it limp a bit. However, if the berries are omitted, it will be an ideal partner.

EISBEIN

Boiled, pickled pork shank is traditionally served with boiled or mashed potatoes, sauerkraut and split peas. Nothing can go wrong if you pair this hearty German dish with a classic grape from the German winelands, and a dry to off-dry Weisser Riesling makes a time-honoured table partner for eisbein. An easy-drinking, fruity red, such as a Cinsaut, Gamay or gluggable Pinotage will come to the rescue of the red-wine drinker.

GAMMON AND HAM

Unless you're in the meat trade, you may be confused about the terms bacon, gammon and ham. Are they all the same? When is gammon 'ham'? Why, if we look up 'gammon' in a cookbook, are we referred to 'boiled bacon'? Obviously a foreign publication! In South Africa, we fry the stuff and serve it with eggs for breakfast, so what are they talking about? It turns out that there is quite an easy explanation: Ham is the hind leg taken from a fresh carcass, and then cured and matured. However, if the whole carcass, with the hind legs intact, is cured and then split in two, you have two 'bacon sides'. If you remove the hind leg from a bacon side – take your pick from either the left or the right side – you have a 'gammon'. Got it?

A boiled bacon or, if you're still confused, a boiled gammon (as you now know, it would not be a 'boiled ham') studded with cloves and glazed is a favourite on buffets or at Christmas. When gammon is served hot, a light, fruity, soft red, such as Cabernet Franc, Pinot Noir, Gamay, Tempranillo or easy-drinking Shiraz, will pair happily without any confusion as to what goes with what. If you prepare your gammon the classic way, garnished with pineapple rings and glacé cherries, then Gewürztraminer, off-dry Weisser Riesling or Chenin blanc are seamless matches to the confluence of saltiness and sweetness. However, when served cold, rosé is such a good partner that we suspect it must have been invented for gammon. If you serve your cold gammon with salads, a dry or off-dry Weisser Riesling or an off-dry Chenin Blanc are options.

A rich, smooth mustard sauce is often served with hot or cold glazed gammon. As mustard, in all its incarnations, is equally happy with red or white wine, choose any of the wines mentioned above, as they will all cope with a touch of sweetness in the mustard sauce.

See also **Cold Meats**, page 126.

HAXE/HOCK

These are alternative terms for **Eisbein**. See page 199.

'KALAHARI KREEF' (pork fillets in bacon)

These bacon-wrapped fillets of pork (or venison) were designed as braai fare. The smokiness obtained by barbecuing intensifies the smokiness of the bacon and wines with equally smoky flavours provide a favourable echo. You may think that this would be too much of a good thing, but it is amazing how the smokiness in the food and wine meet each other halfway to complement, rather than overemphasize. A medium-bodied Shiraz, Pinotage, Nebbiolo or oaked Chardonnay are all good choices.

KASSLER CHOPS

These lightly smoked pork loin chops are normally gently fried or grilled and often served with red cabbage and apple, or apple sauce, and potatoes in one form or other. An off-dry Weisser Riesling, which loves everything smoked, is sublime with kassler chops. The sweet and sour combination of food and wine, especially when apple is one of the accompaniments, is magic. A rosé or light, fruity, soft red, such as Cabernet Franc, Pinot Noir, Gamay or an easy-drinking Shiraz or Tempranillo, are also good partners.

MEATBALLS

Minced pork made into meatballs (sometimes with the addition of beef or veal) are usually gently herbed or spiced, and cooked as we would a frikkadel. An example of this is Berlin meatballs (*Berliner bouletten*), which are flavoured with nothing more than fresh parsley and a dash of nutmeg. Meatballs are also often cooked in or coated with a sauce. The German savoury meatball, *Königsberger klopse*, has a creamy lemon and caper sauce. Capers are one of the ingredients that play merry hell with wine but, in the case of the *klopse*, they are a bit camouflaged in the creamy sauce. When choosing a wine that will cope with the acidity of the capers, we must rely on the creaminess of the wine to latch on to the creaminess of the sauce. Lightly wooded Chardonnay, wooded Sauvignon Blanc (blanc fumé) or wooded Chenin Blanc are time-honoured partners, but they need good acidity. Off-dry Weisser Riesling is another obliging partner, and a good example of how regional food pairs with regional wine. Light-bodied reds with good acidity, like Pinot Noir, Sangiovese, Barbera or Cinsaut are good choices too, and work equally well with both the *klopse* and the *bouletten*.

PORK CHASSEUR

The pork for this stew is simmered in white wine with mushrooms and red and green peppers, and sometimes flavoured with juniper berries. It calls for Pinot Noir, light-bodied Pinotage or Cinsaut. For a white wine, choose an unwooded or lightly wooded Chardonnay.

PORK CHOPS

There are many ways of preparing pork chops and the method will determine the wine partner.

Crumbed pork chops (baked, grilled or fried) When crumbed (breaded), pork chops are best with an unwooded or lightly wooded Chardonnay or Semillon. Pinot Noir, light-bodied Pinotage, Merlot, Cabernet Sauvignon or Tempranillo are good red wine partners.

When served with apple sauce, Gewürztraminer or off-dry Weisser Riesling are the better white wine choices, with Pinot Noir, Pinotage, Barbera or Sangiovese standing up for the reds.

Pork chops in cider In this version, pork chops are marinated in a mixture of cider, honey, juniper berries and bay leaves before being grilled. The marinade is then cooked up into a sauce with pineapple added. The sweet, fruity character of the dish will be increased if the chops are garnished with apple rings poached in cider and sugar. A rosé or white wine with marked sweetness and balancing acidity fits like a glove. Choose from Gewürztraminer, Weisser Riesling, Chenin Blanc or stein. If you'd prefer to drink red, choose one that is both light-bodied and has some sweet-fruited intensity, like Mourvèdre, Pinotage, Shiraz or Zinfandel.

Spicy grilled chops These like a spicy wine. Viognier will be hard to beat, but the dedicated red-wine drinker could opt for a medium-bodied Shiraz or Pinotage instead.

PORK CURRY

An uncomplicated pork curry will pair happily with an easy-drinking Cabernet Sauvignon or Cabernet-Merlot blend (just hold off on your prize-winning blockbusters). Viognier makes an excellent white wine choice, but if the curry has a sweet touch, perhaps from the addition of fruit chutney or sultanas, a white with some residual sugar would be better. Pitch the level of sweetness of the wine to that of the dish, and look to Weisser Riesling, Chenin Blanc or stein.

For **Vindaloo**, the famous Indian pork curry renowned for its fiery heat, see page 235.

PORK PIE

Whether you call this traditional British food simply a 'pork pie' or use its 'designated name of origin', Melton Mowbray pie, it is the same thing: succulent pieces of lean pork in a savoury jelly, encased in a raised pastry case. These pies are eaten cold, often with a lightly dressed green salad. You need a crisp, dry white wine with good acidity that will cut through the richness of the pastry while coping with the salad dressing. Think Weisser Riesling (but one on the drier side), Sauvignon Blanc or Chenin Blanc.

PORK SCHNITZELS AND ESCALOPES

Pork escalopes are often used to replace the traditional veal when making Wiener schnitzel. Dry or off-dry Weisser Riesling, Pinot Noir, Barbera, Sangiovese or Cinsaut happily step in when crumbed (breaded) escalopes are served with a wedge of fresh lemon. When the escalopes are served with a sauce, such as a creamy walnut sauce, crank up the weight of the wine and go for a wooded Chardonnay or a Viognier, which will love the nuttiness of the sauce.

See also **Escalopes**, page 206.

PORK SAUSAGES

Some pork-based sausages can be eaten cold or hot, although, when heated, their flavours tend to come to the fore. However, as the flavours of the sausages are not changed by heating, the wine pairings given below remain the same whatever their temperature.

Bratwurst These cooked German sausages are often accompanied by sauerkraut, potatoes in some form or other, and mustard. Served this way, they need a light- to medium-bodied red wine with an acidic edge to cut through the richness of both the sausage and the sauerkraut (especially if it has been prepared in the traditional way with fried onions, bacon pieces and juniper berries). In South Africa, we have no qualms about marrying an Italian grape to this oh-so-German dish, so go for a Sangiovese or Barbera, or happily settle for Pinotage, or even a Pinot Noir, if you want to splurge.

Bratwurst is not necessarily served with sauerkraut; if it is accompanied by potatoes only, Sylvaner, Colombard or Pinot Gris/Pinot Grigio will all be successful, although the rich sausages will certainly benefit more from a dry Chenin Blanc with its acidic tail.

Frankfurters or similar-styled cooked sausages only need to be heated through, or can be eaten cold. Served with potato salad, they are a good stand-by dish for lunch or supper. Before you automatically reach for the Weisser Riesling, consider also Pinot Blanc, Pinot Gris/Pinot Grigio or Sylvaner to express your free spirit.

Pork sausages, either pan-fried or grilled, are an essential component of a full English breakfast. When served as a supper dish, accompanied by mashed potatoes, they famously become 'bangers and mash'. The word 'banger' comes from their habit of exploding during cooking due to shrinkage of the tight skin. When it comes to wine, these pair similarly to bratwurst (see above).

Russians are spicy, smoked sausages in the same mould as the Italian **cabanossi** and Spanish **chorizo**. All three are generally used in other dishes to add depth and flavour. On their own, enjoy them with Shiraz, which follows them like a hound on the scent of a hare, with Pinotage at its heels.

Toad in the hole Browned pork sausages are baked in a batter and served with onions and gravy. This calls for a light- to medium-bodied red with an acidic tang to counterbalance the richness of the sausage. Choose a Sangiovese, Barbera, Cinsaut or Pinotage.

ROAST PORK

Because of their fatty outer layer, most pork cuts can be roasted, either on or off the bone, flavoured with a complementary topping or rub, filled with a variety of stuffings, or roasted plainly and served with accompaniments. The fat layer can be removed before or after cooking, or placed under a hot grill to produce crackling.

Plainly roasted Roasted pork with a crunchy crackling, served with roast potatoes and gravy, is not very demanding on wine. Many medium- to full-bodied reds will make suitably good table-mates, with Tempranillo at the top of the list. On the white side, a full-bodied, judicially wooded Chardonnay will be equally good.

When served with a traditional apple sauce, the Chardonnay still works, as the sweetness from the oaking latches onto the sweetness of the sauce. But, you've guessed it already, an off-dry Weisser Riesling or rosé will also tap-dance, even though roast pork is really happier with a red wine than with white. Compromise in the presence of that apple sauce by selecting a red that is medium- to full-bodied, but deeply sweet-fruited, such as Shiraz, Pinotage or Zinfandel.

Stuffed with dried fruit Whether the fruit is dried peaches, apricots or prunes, the effect is the same as having apple sauce with a plainly roasted joint. See above for wine recommendations.

With herbs A deboned cut of pork stuffed with a herb mixture, or a joint studded with garlic and herbs, loves most red wines. However, if you've used thyme or rosemary, Cabernet Sauvignon rules the waves, with Merlot on stand-by.

Served cold When roast pork is served cold, it does an about-face, turning its back on the reds that it liked so much when warm. Now it looks towards Chardonnay, but not the exuberant, oaky version it tap-danced with when served hot; this is the time to gear down and choose a lighter version, or opt for an unoaked Chardonnay.

Veal

In South Africa, a calf carcass weighing less than 100kg is classified as veal. We are aware of the anti-veal lobby that has emerged around the world, but this guide would not be complete without wine pairing suggestions for the best-known veal dishes. Pork is often used as a substitute but when these dishes are made with veal, fine white wines are king. It is a full deck of cards, from Pinot Gris/Pinot Grigio through Weisser Riesling, Chenin Blanc, Gewürztraminer and Chardonnay. Although the final choice will depend on the preparation of the dish, you cannot go wrong with any of these wines. Red-wine drinkers don't have to take a back seat though, as this is the time to haul out a well-aged vinous treasure that has had its rough edges knocked off it during the long time spent in the bottle. Dust off that mature Bordeaux blend or Pinot Noir, and fly.

BLANQUETTE DE VEAU

For a blanquette, cubes of veal are first soaked in acidulated water to whiten the meat, before being simmered in a light stock flavoured with onions, carrots, cloves and nutmeg. A velouté sauce is made from the cooking liquid, then thickened and enriched with egg yolks and cream. White wine will be the best choice, but one with some character and concentration. A wooded, full-bodied Chardonnay will echo the buttery, creamy complexity of this stew, which is made slightly sweet by the onions and carrots and has a touch of spice from the cloves and nutmeg.

CHOPS

When veal chops are plainly grilled or sautéed in a bit of butter, an aged Cabernet Sauvignon, Bordeaux blend or Pinot Noir would be decadently good with this straightforward dish. When the chops are crumbed (breaded), the chances are that a wedge of fresh lemon will accompany them, and this will spell death to a fine red wine. In this case, rather choose a white wine with some acidity; a lightly oaked Chardonnay from a cool climate will not blink an eye at that squeeze of lemon juice. For chops done in the Normandy-style, with the addition of cream and apples (*côtes des veau normande*), stick to Chardonnay. Here, you can happily up the ante and go for a lush, rich, deeply fruited, oaked version.

ESCALOPES

An escalope is simply a thinly sliced piece of meat. It is a popular way of preparing veal (and pork).

Parmigiana Escalopes are coated with Parmesan-flavoured breadcrumbs, fried and served with a raw tomato sauce and melted Mozzarella cheese. The acidity of the tomatoes replaces the traditional squeeze of lemon juice on breaded escalopes. You need a wine with crisp acidity, which is more than Chardonnay can deliver, so choose from Sauvignon Blanc, Chenin Blanc or Pinot Gris/Pinot Grigio for the whites. For a red, choose a Barbera or Pinot Noir.

Piccata Gently fried veal escalopes are served with a sauce made from reduced white wine and stock, flavoured with lemon juice and capers. When the gentle flavour of veal is spiked up to maximum voltage, as in this case, a Sauvignon Blanc shows up beautifully.

Saltimbocca Veal escalopes are topped with, or rolled in, slices of prosciutto crudo (such as Parma ham) and lightly fried in butter. A reduced white wine and butter sauce is usually spooned over the veal. As the traditional herb used in this dish is sage, this is the time for a blanc de noir with good acidity to click its heels.

Scaloppine These small escalopes can be prepared in various ways, but generally, they are gently fried and served with a buttery sauce lifted with lemon juice or white wine and sprinkled with herbs. An unoaked Chardonnay from a cool climate will be just the thing to pair with this gently flavoured dish. An oaked Chenin Blanc is a worthy second choice.

Wiener schnitzel Often called just schnitzel, these crumbed and fried escalopes are usually served with lemon wedges. This gentle dish suits a variety of medium-bodied white wines with a streak of acidity. Dry Weisser Riesling comes first to mind, then a moderately fruity Pinot Gris/Pinot Grigio, Chenin Blanc, or an unoaked or lightly oaked Chardonnay. For the reds, a light-bodied red, such as Pinot Noir or Sangiovese, would do splendidly.

With a Calvados cream sauce Calvados is an apple brandy from Normandy, in northern France. A number of apple varieties are used to make a traditional dry cider that is distilled and aged in oak casks for at least two years, often longer. As with French wines, Calvados is controlled by legislation related to its methods of production and place of origin. Choose a lightly wooded Chardonnay for this sauce.

With a creamy mustard sauce For this, you need a rich white wine, such as a buttery Chardonnay, but one that shows good acidity, as the mustard sharpens the sauce. Do not overlook Weisser Riesling or Gewürztraminer as alternatives. Mustard has an uncanny talent for making any dish love both red and white wine, so consider a gluggable Merlot, or stick with tried and tested Pinot Noir, which will be an ideal match to the veal.

With a mushroom sauce A lightly wooded Chardonnay would be hard to beat for a creamy sauce incorporating mushrooms, but a Viognier comes a close second.

With a sweet wine sauce Traditionally, Madeira was used, but since this imported wine is not widely available, port or sherry make good alternatives. An off-dry Weisser Riesling or Gewürztraminer will cope with the sweetness of the sauce, but battles with its weight. Red wine fares much better, but not just any old red. You need a deeply sweet-fruited red, so choose a Shiraz, Mourvèdre, Pinotage or Zinfandel made in this style, keeping it medium-bodied.

FRICASSEE

Very similar in appearance to a blanquette, for a fricassee the meat is first lightly seared to seal it before being simmered until tender. Thereafter, the process is the same as for a blanquette, as is the wine match. See **Blanquette de veau**, page 205.

MEATBALLS

Veal mince is used to make patties (and, in Scandinavia, *frikadeller).* These small, delicate little meatballs are often made with a mixture of veal, beef and pork mince. A not-too-heavy-bodied, lightly wooded Chardonnay, or an aged, medium-bodied red showing some finesse, such as a Bordeaux blend, are good choices.

OSSO BUCO

There are two ways of preparing a classic osso buco: with or without the addition of tomatoes. (In Italian, 'osso' means 'bone' and 'buco' means 'hole'. Osso buco literally means 'the bone with a hole in it'.)

Osso buco alla Milanese In this classic dish of braised veal shanks, the delicate flavour of a gremolata (a lemon rind, garlic and parsley mixture) features prominently, and tomatoes are not included.

Osso buco with tomatoes This is the version with which many of us are familiar. With the robust flavours of tomato and white wine in the cooking liquid, a gremolata is not necessary to flavour the dish, but is often added as a garnish.

Neither version is easily matched with wine, but both have white wine in the cooking liquid and both include the white wine-loving vegetables, onion, carrot and celery.

Osso buco is often served with risotto alla Milanese, which is also made with white wine and flavoured with white-wine loving saffron. In addition, the risotto is enriched with beef marrow. The cooking wine, the vegetables, the saffron and the creamy, rich rice seem to call for a rounded, full white wine with good acidity, and the dish reaches out to a full-bodied, luscious, well-oaked Chardonnay. And yet, there are red wines that will shoulder the whites into second place. Nebbiolo crosses the finishing line first, with a young Pinot Noir and medium-bodied, freshly fruity Pinotage short on its heels.

If osso buco is served with tagliatelle or a similar pasta, instead of risotto, you could opt for a light red with good acidity, such as a Barbera or Sangiovese, or go for a powerful Sauvignon Blanc.

ROAST VEAL

This uncomplicated dish must have been invented purely to show off an aged Pinot Noir. This is the time to showcase that vinous treasure you have been carefully cellaring for years.

VITELLO TONNATO

Slices of roasted veal are served with a tuna and anchovy sauce, and topped with capers. In the Milanese version, the sauce is thinned with cream, while in the Piemontese dish, the sauce is mayonnaise-based. A full-bodied, dry white, like a Chardonnay, immediately comes to mind, but one also thinks of a dryish Gewürztraminer. However, the flavourful ingredients of the sauce result in a dish with enough substance and zing to serve a medium-bodied red with it. Choose from Pinot Noir, Barbera or Pinotage.

Hunting is a great South African tradition. Those who are into it usually have many tales to tell when they offer a dish made from one of the antelope species (springbok, kudu, gemsbok/oryx) or perhaps from crocodile or warthog. If you don't hunt, and can't persuade your hunting friends to part with some of their bounty, many butchers and supermarkets stock vacuum-packed farmed venison all year round.

As a meat, venison is not that different from beef, although it is less fatty and has a drier texture. While venison can be described as 'gamey', it does not have the wild flavours that many people ascribe to it. However, what the animal ate or was fed, and the length of time it was hung for, can play a part in the eventual flavour of the meat.

The wines that match venison best are impressive, heavy-weight reds, especially Shiraz, Mourvèdre and Pinotage. Although the depth and complexity of these wines suit more robustly flavoured venison cuts, such as from a wildebeest or impala, a top-notch Pinot Noir can be just as successful.

Some folk swear by the contrasting sweetness of a late harvest wine with venison, very much in line with the sweet-berry sauces that often accompany it. However, we cannot endorse this pairing. For us, a late harvest is not at its best with plainly roasted venison. Even if the meat is accompanied by sweet sauces and condiments, the wine won't perform, as its sweetness cannot make up for its lack of weight. Rather match venison served with sweet trimmings to the 'venison wines', namely Shiraz, Pinotage or Mourvèdre, which are packed with their own generous berry fruit.

Venison

ROAST HAUNCH OF VENISON

A roasted haunch, leg or saddle of venison requires a big, burly red wine. When your roast is served with one of the traditional sauces, such as *poivrade* (made with game stock to which vinegar is added, and seasoned with peppercorns) or *grand veneur* (a *poivrade* sauce with added redcurrant jelly and, sometimes, cream), go straight for Shiraz, Pinotage and Mourvèdre. The wine choices remain the same if the meat is served with a red berry sauce, or if juniper berries feature. If a Cumberland sauce accompanies the roast, go for a full-bodied Pinotage. See also **Sauces**, pages 32–43.

STEWS, CASSEROLES AND POTJIES

Stewed or casseroled venison dishes often include red wine, bacon, mushrooms and cream. These dishes require a full-bodied Shiraz to pick up the smoky flavours of the bacon and the earthy flavours of the mushrooms. If juniper berries are added, the wine will not change, but also consider a Tempranillo or Cabernet-Merlot blend. When dried fruit, such as apricots or prunes, are incorporated into a casserole, select from Mourvèdre, Shiraz or Zinfandel, as these rich-textured wines are packed with their own sweet fruit.

VENISON PIE

Like a casserole, the filling of a venison pie often includes red wine, bacon and mushrooms. Serve with Tempranillo, Shiraz, Mourvèdre or a Bordeaux blend, but also consider a full-bodied Pinot Noir, which would be an exact flavour match.

VENISON STEAKS

Pan-fried or grilled venison steaks can be served with any sauce used for beef steaks, see pages 185–189. If your venison steak is accompanied by a red berry sauce, choose Mourvèdre or Shiraz. If it is served with a traditional game-stock sauce, such as *poivrade* or *grand veneur*, stay with Mourvèdre or Shiraz, or head for Pinotage, Pinot Noir, Tempranillo or a Cab-Merlot blend. See **Sauces**, page 32.

Ostrich

Ostrich, which is gaining in popularity due to its low-fat and low-cholesterol attributes, is freely available in South Africa. It is most commonly sold as steaks, mince, 'goulash' cubes and sausage. The meat is dark and 'beefy' and is therefore treated much like beef in terms of preparation and cooking. Cabernet Sauvignon is a prime candidate for pairing with plainly cooked ostrich steaks but, if you are using ostrich in dishes that would typically use beef, refer to the wines listed under the relevant entries in **Beef**, pages 172–190.

A note for hunters If you have made mince, sausage, biltong, droëwors or smoked fillets from your venison or ostrich, take the preparation method, added ingredients and accompanying sauces into account when it comes to wine matches. Chances are, you'll opt for a Pinot Noir, Shiraz, Mourvèdre or Pinotage.

Offal

The English word offal is derived from 'off fall' which, like the more descriptive Afrikaans term *afval*, describes those parts of animals that are cut away when the carcass is dressed. Offal (also called variety meat or organ meat) is nutritious and easily digested as there is little fat or gristle. Kidneys and liver are perennial favourites and tripe, which disappeared from restaurant menus for a while, seems to be making something of a comeback. The rich, assertive flavours of offal generally call for a rich and assertive wine, in fact, a big and rather opulent one.

BRAINS

Lamb's and ox brains are most commonly shallow-fried in butter, or crumbed and deep-fried. Whether they are served plainly, on curried rice or in a tomato or red wine sauce, brains display a savoury flavour that can be matched with a well-structured, dry white wine. Choose a lightly wooded Chardonnay, as too much oak in the wine makes the dish overly rich.

The pungency that develops in a wooded Chardonnay with some bottle maturation makes the match even better. If you want to add some oomph, go for a Viognier and, if you can find one with bottle age, don't think twice. The mildly spicy, apricot flavours that develop when the Viognier has been cellared for two or more years make for a perfect pairing with this rich and savoury dish. If you serve your shallow-fried brains à l'indienne, that is, on curried rice, that glass of aged Viognier will make an exact gastronomic match.

BRAWN

Sheep's trotters or pig's heads are boiled with aromatic herbs, such as cloves and peppercorns. The deboned, cubed meat is then set in a mould using the natural jelly (aspic) that forms from the cooking liquid. A light lunch or supper dish from yesteryear, brawn is served cold, with bread and butter and a plain salad. If you don't want to rock the boat, choose a Sylvaner or Colombard.

In South Africa, brawn is often curried, which adds both depth and flavour. In this case, you can choose a wine with more flavour, such as an unwooded Chardonnay or Semillon. If you've decided to rock the boat after all, go for a Viognier and ride the waves.

KIDNEYS

Kidneys are very lean, but they have a rich flavour that, like liver, is emphasized by the addition of piquant flavours such as herbs, spices, mustard and wine, or when softened by cream, yoghurt or butter.

Devilled kidneys The 'devil' sauce is prepared with Worcestershire sauce, French mustard, cayenne pepper, tomato purée and lemon juice and poured over the pan-fried kidneys. A soft-hearted red, such as Pinot Noir, Tempranillo or Barbera, or a quaffable Pinotage, are excellent matches. If you want to drink a white wine, choose a lightly wooded Chenin Blanc.

Grilled or pan-fried kidneys When finished with a knob of butter and served with the pan juices on buttered toast, these call for a softly centred, softly contoured Merlot or Cabernet Sauvignon, or a blend of the two.

Kidneys Dijonnaise Here, lamb's kidneys are served in a white wine and mustard sauce. Unless mustard is overly sweet or acidic, it is equally fond of red and white wines, but the kidneys are the main ingredient in this dish, so choose a Merlot or Pinotage. If you want to drink a white wine, go for a Chardonnay or Semillon.

Kidneys stroganoff This richer preparation combines onion, mushrooms and cream with sliced kidneys. Pair it with a lightly wooded Chardonnay, Semillon or Viognier.

LIVER

Liver, which contains very little fat, becomes solid and unpalatable if it is overcooked, so it is normally gently fried, grilled or casseroled. As the flavour of liver is rather rich, it benefits from the addition of salty or piquant ingredients. Quick sauces, made in the pan with the juices left over after frying the liver, make good accompaniments, flavoured with wine, lemon or orange juice, mustard, soy sauce or herbs. The liver dish most of us know best is fried lamb's or calf's liver accompanied by masses of soft, golden onion rings.

The sweetness of pan-fried liver can lead you down the garden path. Resist the temptation to match its sweetness with a wine that is also sweetish. What you need here is a deeply fruity, spicy and quite rustic red, and one that is fairly young. Take your pick from Pinotage, Nebbiolo, Tempranillo, Shiraz or Grenache; a supple Merlot is an excellent option too and is particularly good when partnered with liver in caul fat (*skilpadjies*) and liver patties.

For **Chicken livers**, see page 125.

SWEETBREADS

Sweetbreads, which come from the thymus gland and pancreas of an animal, are considered a great delicacy. They can be braised, shallow-fried or grilled. When braised and served with a sauce made from the braising stock, with mushrooms added, an unwooded Chardonnay or a Semillon are good partners. When shallow-fried, sweetbreads are often served with a tomato-based sauce. Stick to Semillon, but select one from a cool climate, with good acidity. Grilled sweetbreads are usually served in a butter and parsley sauce. Creamy textures need gently creamy white wines so, to match a rich, buttery sauce, crank up the richness a notch or two and go for an oaked Chardonnay, Chardonnay-Semillon blend, Viognier or a Colombard. Avoid reds, as they will taste metallic.

TONGUE

The front part of an ox tongue is rather lean and bland in flavour, so the sauces served with this part tend to be rich and either slightly sweet or piquant. Meltingly tender tongue, served hot with a robust sauce, pairs well with a gentle red wine such as a Gamay or Merlot.

Pressed ox tongue, sliced and served cold with Cumberland sauce or mustard, is very happy with a Sauvignon or Chenin Blanc.

TRIPE

Tripe is the stomach lining of a steer, cow, sheep or goat. There are different types of tripe, depending on which of the animal's stomachs it comes from. Good butchers and supermarkets usually offer tripe ready cleaned and trimmed. Pair 'English-style' tripe and onions with a slightly acid-edged white wine, such as a Chenin Blanc. A favourite South African dish, tripe and trotters (*pens en pootjies*) is often flavoured with a touch of curry. For this, you'll need a seriously fruity red, such as a Grenache, Nebbiolo, Malbec or a Cabernet-Merlot blend.

Chicken and other birds

'What do frogs' legs taste like?' 'Oh, a bit like chicken.' 'And croco-dile?' 'Also like chicken...' Chicken is often used as the reference for describing other, more exotic meats because it is so neutral in flavour. It is, indeed, the one ingredient that, at the chef's whim, can be turned into any creation. Chicken lends itself to herbs, spices or any flavouring imaginable. From Latin America to the Mediterranean via Africa, Southeast Asia and the Far East, chicken is indiscriminate – you can throw almost any ingredients at it and it will carry it off!

When it comes to the rest of the poultry family, there are more definitive characteristics. Turkey meat is denser than chicken and its flavour is more pronounced. Duck, which has a high fat content, does not have much meat, but its dark-coloured legs are rich and succulent, with a distinctive flavour. Goose, which is popular in parts of Europe, is not well known in South Africa, while guinea fowl and quail are most often encountered on restaurant menus.

Chicken

BRAAIED CHICKEN (barbecued chicken)

With the health consciousness of the times, braaied chicken – whether in portions or a whole spatchcocked (butterflied) bird – with its crispy, slightly blackened skin, is almost more popular than our traditional *wors* and chops. When it comes to wine, choose a red or a white, as you please, although with char-grilled meat, red wine is usually more appropriate. A fruity Merlot or Pinot Noir will be an ideal choice. If you've used a spicy marinade, up the ante and go for a red with some body and the same degree of flavour as the marinade, such as a Shiraz or Pinotage. If you want to stick with white, Viognier or a wooded Chardonnay or Semillon will do well.

See also **Devilled chicken** and **Grilled chicken**, page 222.

CAJUN-STYLED CHICKEN

Since the 1980s, when South Africans became Cajun-*mal*, any food that has been dusted with hot Creole spices and then blackened is referred to as 'Cajun'. But our restaurant offerings are often a far cry from the authentic cuisine that originated in the southern US state of Louisiana. When flavoured with a typical Cajun spice mix of chilli, cumin, thyme, origanum, sage, mustard and black pepper, chicken goes well with light- to medium-bodied reds. Pinotage, Mouvèdre, Malbec or Shiraz would all be a good choice, as would a Zinfandel or Tempranillo, if you're fortunate to find one of these. However, if the chicken is 'blackened' (spiced, then cooked over a high heat and finished off with a squeeze of lemon), Sauvignon Blanc would be a better option.

See also **Chicken jambalaya**, page 218.

CHICKEN À LA KING

In case you've ever wondered, this has nothing to do with those regal men whom you address as 'Your Majesty'. Instead, it is an American dish created by a brown-nosing chef who named it for his boss, a Mr. King. Consequently, the 'k' in King is always written as a capital. There are as many versions of this dish as buffet dinners you might attend but, traditionally, it consists of diced cooked chicken (preferably breast meat), mushrooms and sliced green peppers, cooked in cream and bound with sherry and egg yolks. This creamy, eggy version calls for a wooded Chardonnay or Semillon. The everyday version, made with cooked chicken in a white velouté sauce, needs an unwooded version of these wines.

CHICKEN BREASTS

Each breast consists of two pieces, the large suprême and the small fillet. Chicken breasts are generally rather bland and tasteless, and depend on the cook or chef to give them some life.

Breast in a cream sauce Chicken breasts poached in a bit of white wine, with perhaps a touch of garlic and some mushrooms, and finished with thick cream to make a rich sauce, need an equally rich white wine. Choose a wooded Chardonnay or Semillon. Better yet, opt for a Chardonnay blend (with Semillon, Sauvignon Blanc or Viognier). Variations of this dish, incorporating delicate herbs such as tarragon, will not affect the wine choice. If the herbs are either rosemary or thyme, a Pinot Noir would do better.

Breast with mango In this example of nouvelle cuisine, sautéed sesame seed-encrusted breasts are served with a lime-flavoured cream sauce and sautéed sliced mango (or any other fruit). This dish cries out for an off-dry Weisser Riesling or a Chenin Blanc with a touch of residual sugar.

Breast with prosciutto crudo and tomato Breasts are wrapped in Parma ham or pancetta and topped with a herb-infused tomato sauce. Medium-bodied reds with an acidic note, such as Pinot Noir or Pinotage, will work very well, but Sangiovese is the ideal choice. Avoid white wines, especially Chardonnay, with this dish.

Breast with prosciutto crudo, cream cheese and Parmesan Any combination that incorporates cream cheese sends us back to the whites, with a wooded Chardonnay as the obvious choice.

CHICKEN CACCIATORA

In cooking, the French term 'chasseur' and the Italian 'cacciatora' [kaht-chah-TOR-ah] mean 'hunter's style'. Both chicken chasseur (see below) and chicken cacciatora include sautéed chicken pieces, onions, mushrooms, perhaps some bacon (or pancetta) and tomatoes, all cooked in white wine. Where the Italian dish differs from the French version is in the quantity of tomatoes used. Cacciatora is more tomatoey than chasseur and, consequently, it needs a wine with good acidity, like a Sauvignon or Chenin Blanc, or a red wine, such as Pinot Noir or Pinotage, that has a hint of acidity on the finish. But why not stay with the Italians and find yourself a bottle of Sangiovese, which is the perfect match?

CHICKEN CHASSEUR

Any dish, chicken or otherwise, with the word 'chasseur' in the name indicates that it is 'hunter's style' (see also **Cacciatora**, above). You would therefore expect to find mushrooms, onions and a touch of tomato, with white wine as the cooking liquid. Perhaps not *haute cuisine*, but it certainly is a comforting and tasty dish. As the chicken pieces are cooked in white wine, it seems logical to drink white wine with it, but a Pinot Noir, light-bodied Pinotage or even a Cinsaut will be a better match. If you prefer white, an unwooded Chardonnay comes to the rescue. At all costs, avoid a wooded white wine.

For a similar dish made with red wine, *see* **Coq au vin**, page 221.

CHICKEN CORDON BLEU

The combination of cooked, smoked ham and melting cheese, normally Gruyère or Emmenthal, tucked inside a crumbed and fried chicken breast, is a perennial favourite on local restaurant menus, even if we ask for it as 'Gordin blue'. On the wine side, a wooded, buttery Chardonnay wins hands down, as it loves melted cheese. Melted hard cow's-milk cheeses also pair well with red wines, so you could opt for an inexpensive, fruity Cab-Merlot blend, but keep your prize-winning reds for another occasion.

CHICKEN CURRY

South Africans serve two distinct types of curry: a hotter 'Durban' curry and a milder, fragrant 'Cape Malay' curry, which uses more turmeric in the spice mixture, giving it a characteristic yellow colour.

The Durban-type curry marries happily with a light-bodied, easy-drinking Cabernet Sauvignon or Cab-Merlot blend (but don't waste your prize-winning blockbuster).

The Cape Malay style, on the other hand, will be happier with a white wine that has some residual sugar, as sweetish ingredients – like raisins, almonds and chutney – are either included when cooking the curry or served separately as sambals. Pitch the level of sweetness of the wine to that of the dish (but bear in mind that a dessert-type wine, such as port or muscadel, will be too sweet for most Cape Malay curries). If the curry contains coconut, a wooded Chardonnay or Semillon will work very well.

And what about the tradition of 'beer with curry'? Well, yes, but wine just works so much better, so give it a try.

For **Indian** and **Thai** curries, refer to the relevant chapters.

CHICKEN ENCHILADAS

Tortillas, rolled and stuffed with cooked chicken, grated cheese and sour cream or yoghurt, are smothered in a hot tomato sauce and baked. A medium-bodied Chenin Blanc is just the thing but, if you're more into red wine, choose a Sangiovese or Barbera if these are available. If not, Pinot Noir, with its natural acidity, is the obvious alternative, or simply go for a gluggable Pinotage or Merlot.

CHICKEN FRICASSEE

A fricassee (French *fricassée*) is a 'white' stew. Sautéed chicken pieces are cooked in a white stock which is enriched with egg yolks and cream. Croutons of various shapes, crisped in butter, are often used as a garnish and provide a contrast to the velvety smoothness of the sauce. This dish needs an equally smooth white wine, such as a wooded Chardonnay or Semillon. Avoid red wines.

CHICKEN GOUJON

Goujon are strips (fingers) of solid breast meat that are crumbed and fried. This is more a manner of preparing chicken than a dish.

See **Chicken schnitzel**, page 220.

CHICKEN IN A CHOCOLATE-CHILLI SAUCE

Mole poblano, made with chicken, is perhaps a more common dish than *mole poblano de Guajolote*, made with turkey, and which is Mexico's great festival dish, served at any special occasion. 'Mole' (pronounced mo-lay) means 'sauce', while 'poblano' indicates it comes from the Mexican state of Puebla. But, whether it is served in Mexico or Maritzburg, *mole poblano* is a dish of poultry, a variety of dried chillies, spices, nuts and dark, spicy chocolate, tradition-ally accompanied by rice, beans or tortillas and guacamole. Before chocolate-chilli sauces became the rage in the 1990s, many South Africans were surprised – and some still are – that the combination of chocolate and savoury ingredients could be desirable. Although foreign to us, the use of chocolate in savoury dishes is an older tradi-tion than its use in sweet dishes. And not just in Mexico, either; for centuries, dark chocolate has been used in Spain and Italy to enrich savoury casseroles.

At last wine finds its niche in chocolate, and we can finally claim that the echoing chocolate flavours in Shiraz, Pinotage, Cabernet Sau-vignon, Merlot and Nebbiolo marry with a chocolate dish, but it has to be a savoury dish. The delicate ripe-fruit sweetness in a red wine cannot compete with the high level of sweetness in, for instance, a chocolate dessert. Anything sweeter than a mole will hammer every bit of sweet-fruit flavour out of these wines.

CHICKEN JAMBALAYA AND GUMBO

Jambalaya, a cousin of paella, reflects the Spanish influence on what is now the southern US state of Louisiana after France ceded the land to Spain in 1762. A typical chicken jambalaya might include ham, smoked sausage or shellfish and, certainly, cayenne pepper.

Although 'gumbo' refers to the okra that was traditionally used in that dish, the essential difference between a jambalaya and a gumbo is in the cooking method. In a jambalaya, the rice is cooked with the meat (or fish) in a stock so that the rice absorbs the flavour as it cooks, whereas a gumbo is served on a bed of pre-cooked rice. In either case, serve a herby, flinty Sauvignon Blanc.

See also **Cajun-styled chicken**, page 214.

CHICKEN KIEV

Chicken Kiev, the most famous of all the deep-fried chicken dishes, has nothing to do with the cuisine of the Ukraine or its capital city, Kiev (although it might well have originated in Moscow). A 'Kiev' is a flattened chicken breast, wrapped round a pat of cold garlic- and lemon-flavoured butter, breaded and then fried. In an episode of the popular TV series *Friends*, the character Rachel refers to it as 'that chicken where you poke it and all the butter squirts out'!

The natural acidity of a Chenin Blanc suits this dish to a T, as it balances the richness of the butter. Equally good are Semillon-Sauvignon Blanc blends and unwooded Chardonnays.

CHICKEN MARENGO

This dish was created by Napoleon's chef in 1800, following the Battle of Marengo in Piemonte, Italy. Chicken portions are cooked in a tomato-based sauce which is then reduced. The original creation was elaborately garnished with crayfish and fried eggs; nowadays, it is accompanied by croutons or slices of fried bread. The tomatoey sauce calls for one of the two 'tomato wines' *par excellence;* reach for a Sauvignon Blanc or Sangiovese.

CHICKEN MARYLAND

Fried, breaded (crumbed) chicken, served with fried bananas and corn fritters and, sometimes, fried bacon and tomatoes. This is a dish for an off-dry Weisser Riesling (but, if it is served with its traditional accompaniment, horseradish sauce, the wine will suffer).

CHICKEN PAELLA

The ingredients for this Spanish dish can vary, but the basics are rice, olive oil and saffron. In a typical chicken paella, the poultry is joined by seafood, such as calamari and prawns, and other flavoursome ingredients, like chorizo, onion, red and green peppers, green beans and peas. Although the wine options range from aromatic whites to light reds, the prize here goes to pink. You'll find that a dry, full-bodied blanc de noir or rosé is an exact match.

CHICKEN PICCATA

Scaloppine (escalopes, thin slices of flattened chicken breast) are sautéed with capers, lemon juice and white wine. Do not hesitate; choose a Sauvignon Blanc with racy acidity.

CHICKEN PIE

This quintessentially British dish has become so popular that every pie shop, supermarket, café and highway pit-stop inevitably has a version of chicken (or chicken and mushroom) pie, pre-baked and ready for immediate consumption. Originally, home-made English-style chicken pies included ham (or bacon) and sliced hard-boiled eggs (as in a traditional South African hoenderpastei). The sauce is usually flour-thickened, but cream is sometimes added for a richer version. If you are serving chicken pie as a main meal, go for a buttery, rather than a citrusy, Chardonnay. Alternatively, a light red will work, particularly if the pie contains mushrooms; a Grenache or Shiraz-Grenache blend will make a good partner.

CHICKEN PILAF (pilaff, pilau)

A pilaf is a one-pot rice dish. Basic chicken pilaf has browned chicken portions, onions, green peppers and tomatoes cooked together with rice and saffron in chicken stock. An aromatic white, a light-bodied red or a dry blanc de noir or rosé are all very suitable partners for a basic pilaf. When the dish is spiced up with cumin, cardamom and cinnamon, a medium-bodied Shiraz works perfectly. However, when curry powder is added, Pinotage wins hands down.

CHICKEN POTJIE

There are probably as many variations of chicken potjie as there are aspirant potjiekos-makers, each with his (or her) own 'secret recipe'! Basically, the key ingredients are chicken, browned with onions and other vegetables, then simmered slowly in a cooking liquor. If your potjie is not heavily spiced, you need the tangy, buttery intensity of an unwooded or lightly-wooded Chardonnay from a cool climate. If your potjie is heavily spiced, a spicy, light-bodied red, such as Pinotage or Pinot Noir, will be a good partner. For a potjie with a touch of sweetness, you need the same degree of sweetness in the wine, so opt for an off-dry Weisser Riesling or Chenin Blanc. And, Mr Potjiekos-maker, if your image can handle it, with those sweeter potjies, it's rosé all the way!

CHICKEN SCALOPPINE

Scaloppine (escalopes) is an Italian dish consisting of thin slices of meat (often veal, although chicken is frequently used), dredged in flour, sautéed, and served with a white wine sauce and a wedge of lemon. A wine with a streak of refreshing acidity is the one to search for here and, as there is a weightiness to chicken scaloppine, we need a wine with an equal weight to stand up to the sauce. Either a Sauvignon Blanc-Semillon blend or a stylish, unwooded Chardonnay will fit the bill, as would an oaked Chenin Blanc. If you want to intensify and sharpen the flavours, choose Sauvignon Blanc as a single variety to provide a vivid contrast.

CHICKEN SCHNITZEL

Chicken schnitzel comes to us via Wiener schnitzel which, in turn, originated in Italy as cotoletta alla milanese, a dish made with veal. Flattened chicken breasts are coated in breadcrumbs, pan-fried and traditionally served with parsley potatoes and a wedge of lemon. Schnitzel favours white or red wine; choose a Weisser Riesling or Chenin Blanc with good, natural acidity, or a light-bodied Pinot Noir or Pinotage. If you can lay your hands on a Sangiovese, grab it.

CHICKEN TAGINE (tajine)

This Moroccan slow-cooked stew combines chicken with olives, the sourness of preserved lemons, and a whole basket of spices and flavourings, such as garlic, ginger, cumin, saffron, paprika, cinnamon and, for good measure, chopped fresh coriander. An off-dry Weisser Riesling, with its sour-sweet and spicy profile, will provide a perfect backdrop for this slightly sour and salty dish. Red wine drinkers can head straight for Pinotage.

Another version of chicken tagine omits the lemons and olives and uses sweet ingredients, such as dates, instead. The off-dry Weisser Riesling is still a good match, but a Gewürztraminer or off-dry Chenin Blanc can now take a seat at this table. Pinotage will continue to do nicely, but choose one that is deeply fruity and spicy. A Shiraz or Zinfandel would perform equally well.

COQ AU VIN

This dish evolved in Burgundy as a way to use the tough old birds that strutted around the farmyard. Nowadays, coq au vin is made with any chicken, not specifically the cockerel or capon that the name implies. Chicken portions are flamed in brandy, then cooked on the bone in red wine with onions, garlic, bacon, mushrooms and herbs. In Burgundy, the red wine was traditionally a Gevrey-Chambertin (a top-notch Pinot Noir) for both the pot and the glass but, given the price of imported Burgundies, we hasten to say that you needn't go this far! A humbler wine will suffice for the pot. When it comes to the accompanying wine though, choose the best Pinot Noir you can afford. But this ultimate comfort food will also stand up to a much sturdier wine, such as a Pinotage or Cabernet Sauvignon, thanks to the presence of the bacon and mushrooms.

CORONATION CHICKEN

This cold dish was created in 1953 for the coronation of Queen Elizabeth II. Cooked chicken is bound in a sauce made with mayonnaise and cream, flavoured with curry paste, tomato purée, red wine and puréed apricots. (As an aside, in the 1980s, the good ladies of the Stellenbosch Fynproewersgilde chucked out the apricots, added a dollop of Mrs Ball's chutney, renamed the dish 'Eikestadhoender', and claimed it for themselves – in defiance, we imagine, of anything British!) But back to food and wine pairing, Viognier must have been invented for Coronation chicken but, if you don't happen to have a bottle handy, choose an unwooded Semillon-based blend or a fruity, aromatic white with good acidity, such as Sauvignon Blanc, Weisser Riesling or Chenin Blanc. Avoid a wooded wine.

DEVILLED CHICKEN

Versions of devilled chicken feature in the cuisine of many countries. For example, the French have *poulet à la diable*, the Italians have *pollo alla diavola* and, closer to home, South Africa has given the world Nandos! A whole chicken is spatchcocked or butterflied (colloquially called a 'flattie') and grilled with a tangy marinade or basting sauce containing chillies or, as often in the local version, peri-peri. A crisp white wine that is not-too-light-bodied and has good natural acidity, such as Sauvignon or Chenin Blanc, will do fine.

See also **Grilled chicken**, below.

GRILLED CHICKEN

Whether you grill your chicken in portions or as a whole or half spatchcocked bird (a 'flattie'), you probably marinate it first and/or flavour it with a basting sauce while cooking. A few favourite local flavours, and their wine matches, include:

Barbecue A number of wines are successful matches: Viognier, wooded Chardonnay and Semillon for the whites; Pinot Noir, a fruity Merlot or a medium-bodied Shiraz or Pinotage for the reds. The prize would go to Viognier for a white and Pinot Noir for a red.

Chilli or peri-peri To a wine drinker, chilli may seem a murderous ingredient in a dish but, like fresh ginger, chilli does not ruin the taste of wine. What we are dealing with here is sheer flavour definition; therefore, we need a young, fresh, crisp, not-too-light-bodied wine with good intensity of flavour and acidity. Almost invariably that means Sauvignon Blanc, but Pinotage, with its hidden acidic note, also does splendidly. Pinot Noir is a match made in heaven, but save your expensive bottle for another day as your tastebuds will undoubtedly be somewhat bullied by the chilli.

Honey and mustard baste A wooded Semillon is an exact match.
Lemon and herb baste Sauvignon Blanc or Chenin Blanc.
See also **Braaied (barbecued) chicken**, page 214.

JERKED CHICKEN

Jerk is a style of cooking native to Jamaica in which meat (traditionally pork and goat, but now including chicken, fish, beef, sausage, even tofu) is dry-rubbed with a fiery spice mixture called Jamaican jerk spice before being grilled. Jerk seasoning principally relies on two items: allspice (pimento) and Scotch bonnet chillies (among the hottest chillies). Other ingredients include cinnamon, spring onion, thyme and ginger mixed together to form a paste which is rubbed onto the meat. At last! Here is a chicken dish that loves Shiraz. Spice meets spice, and you could not wish for a better pairing.

ROAST CHICKEN

A whole roasted chicken won't mind whether you drink a red or a white wine with it. If it is being served as a traditional Sunday lunch dish, with a rich gravy and roast potatoes, a red wine is usually better than a white. This is when you can haul out your best Pinot Noir and *laat waai*! If you have prepared a traditional sage and onion stuffing, your chicken *kraais* out for Merlot. If your preference is for white wine, a wooded Semillon or Chardonnay are both brilliant partners. Viognier can work, although its fruity character may get in the way.

If you are serving cold roast chicken, as we tend to do in summer, forget the red wine and go for a well-structured, lightly oaked Chardonnay that is not too exuberant.

SOUTHERN-FRIED CHICKEN

Deep-fried coated chicken portions have been popularized the world over by KFC. By itself, the chicken will happily pair with either white or red wine. Choose an easy-drinking Chardonnay or a Cab-Merlot blend. If there is a fair amount of pepper in the coating, select a Shiraz-Merlot blend instead. The Colonel would approve!

SPATCHCOCKED CHICKEN

See **Grilled chicken**, page 222.

STIR-FRIED CHICKEN

Stir-frying allows chicken to be cooked quickly and evenly with little added fat. It is a cooking method that allows ingredients to speak for themselves, without introducing cooking flavours, so the resulting dish tends to be light, with clearly defined flavours; a green pepper remains a green pepper, and a carrot a carrot.

Plainly cooked chicken stir-fries are best matched with fairly light-bodied white wines. A dry Weisser Riesling is the flag-bearer, and even an off-dry one has the right sweetness and weight to complement the dish. Beyond this, any additional flavourings, ingredients or sauces used in the cooking will affect the pairing. Both soy sauce and sweet-and-sour sauce can make the wine choice more difficult; stick to off-dry Weisser Riesling, choosing one with ripe sweetness and subtle spiciness. Gewürztraminer is usually too powerful for a basic stir-fry, but you can consider it when the flavours have been intensified by the addition of ingredients such as lemon grass, lime juice and Eastern sweet and spicy sauces.

When it comes to red wines to accompany your stir-fried chicken, a lightly chilled, low tannin, light-bodied, soft and fruity Pinot Noir should have what it takes.

But do also consider a sec (dry) or demi-sec sparkling wine. A brut is almost as successful, because it is, after all, not totally bone dry. Huh? you might say, but yes, by law, a brut (bone-dry) sparkling wine can have up to 15g per litre of residual sugar, and many of them do, whereas a dry still white wine may only have up to 5g per litre. Anyone on a low-sugar diet might wish to bear this in mind.

TACOS

Tacos, which have been called the 'Mexican sandwich', are soft or crisp tortillas that are filled with a variety of ingredients, folded or rolled up and eaten by hand. A chicken taco may include tomato-based salsa, refried beans, shredded lettuce, grated cheese, chillies and guacamole or fresh avocado – plus shredded chicken. No wine could possibly satisfy every flavour in this conglomerate, so just take a step back and choose any quaffable white or red wine that will sit quietly, thumb-in-mouth, alongside it.

Other birds

TURKEY

South Africans are most familiar with the Christmas turkey and its stuffings and sweet trimmings. Turkey meat is dense, but as bland as chicken and, therefore, equally adaptable to similar accompanying wines. Turkey breast is often roasted plainly. In this preparation, it is kind to red, white and rosé wines. Choose a Pinot Noir, Cabernet Franc or an opulent Chardonnay. When the whole bird is prepared with sage and onion stuffing, a medium-bodied Merlot, Pinot Noir, Grenache, softly contoured Shiraz or an intensely fruity Cabernet Sauvignon would work admirably. When it is served with sweeter trimmings, such as cranberry sauce or jelly, stick to Shiraz, or have fun with a sparkling Pinotage or Shiraz.

DUCK

The proportion of meat to their frame is less in ducks than in chicken or turkey, but the fat content is higher. The dark-coloured flesh is deliciously rich and succulent, with a distinctive flavour.

Cassoulet A long-cooked stew, usually containing pork, duck and lamb, with haricot beans and spicy sausages. For our wine pairing suggestions, see Cassoulet in the **Pork** chapter, page 199.

Duck à l'orange Now here's a dish that runs screaming from a red wine. The sweetness and acidity of orange sauces combined with savoury food doesn't do wine any favours. The best solution is to serve an off-dry Weisser Riesling or Chenin Blanc. Sometimes the cook or chef will add a splash of Grand Marnier or another orange liqueur to the sauce, increasing the level of sweetness. In this case, the finished dish will need a white wine with discernable sweetness as well as acidity. A late harvest, especially one made from Chenin Blanc, works well, but is more in tune with the sauce than with the meat. You may find this quite agreeable, though.

Duck confit (confit de canard) A confit is a preserve in French culinary terms. Confit de canard would translate as 'potted duck' in English. Served cold with a green salad, or hot with a light meat sauce, it pairs best with a rich, soft-tannin red, such as Tempranillo, Cabernet Sauvignon, Merlot or Shiraz.

Duck with cherries Whether it is duck with an accompanying cherry sauce, or duck and cherry pie, the black cherries inevitably come from a can, as fresh black cherries are not readily available in South Africa. Wines with plenty of ripe berry fruits of their own, such as Pinotage, Zinfandel or Merlot, are all good partners.

Duck with olives Adding either pitted or stuffed green olives to roasted or casseroled duck moves away from the fruity treatments so often seen with this bird. Either way, the dish is sharp, but not aggressive, and pairs well with a Pinot Noir.

Duck with sauerkraut This recipe, which originates from Strasbourg in France, reflects the Germanic influence on the cooking of Alsace. The duck flesh is permeated with wine-flavoured juices from a bed of sauerkraut on which it is baked. Two wines make excellent partners: an off-dry Weisser Riesling or a Pinot Noir.

Roast duck Roasting is a favourite method of cooking duck as it gets rid of the excess fat. A simply roasted duck needs a robust, firm red with some spiciness and a Shiraz, Shiraz-Cabernet blend, Merlot or Zinfandel are the obvious choices. However, gentler reds, like Pinot Noir, a Bordeaux blend or Tempranillo, are equally good. If you prefer a white wine, Viognier would be your best choice.

Roast duck is traditionally served with tangy fruit, like oranges or black cherries, to cut the richness of the meat, or with fruit sauces that have noticeable acidity. Sauce bigarade (a bitter orange sauce) is a classic. To match this sauce, you'll need a white wine that has both sweetness and acidity, and a late harvest produced from Chenin Blanc immediately comes to mind. Avoid red wine, as it will clash headlong into sauce bigarade.

Other non-citrus fruit sauces, such as black cherry, plum or the voguish pomegranate, are much kinder to a red wine though. Choose a ripely fruit-filled Pinotage, Zinfandel or Shiraz, or a Pinot Noir, which is a fail-safe standby.

GOOSE

Geese are very fatty, with creamy white flesh that becomes light brown when cooked and has a faint gamey flavour. Although goose is not often found on menus in South Africa, roast goose is one of the 'classic' Christmas dishes in the UK. Goose is also popular in both Poland and Germany, where red cabbage or sauerkraut is the traditional accompaniment. When roasted and served with redcurrant jelly, serve your goose with a Gewürztraminer or an off-dry Weisser Riesling to match both the richness of the bird and the sweetness of the jelly. If the goose is cooked or served with sweet fruits, serve a late harvest, a gamey, full-bodied Pinot Noir, a sweet-fruited Merlot or a Shiraz with enormous depth and flavour.

GUINEA FOWL

Although guinea fowl are game birds, their flesh isn't gamey at all. They can be roasted or braised like chicken or turkey. When roasted plainly, they are very kind to all red, white and rosé wines – from the humble to the exalted. However, you are perhaps marginally better off with reds. An elegant Pinot Noir is always hard to beat, especially when there is an aromatic, herby, meaty stuffing with copious amounts of onion. Also try a spicy, peppery wine, such as Shiraz or Petit Verdot. If your guinea fowl has been braised with bacon, onion, mushrooms and cream, it needs a rich and rounded dry white, such as Pinot Gris/Pinot Grigio, or a wooded Semillon or Chardonnay.

OSTRICH

Although ostrich is a 'bird', the meat is more akin to beef and game. See **Ostrich**, page 210.

QUAIL

Quail, the smallest of the game birds, can be roasted, sautéed, grilled or cooked in a casserole. Quail is a dark meat and, when plainly roasted, it can be paired with a fine, but not too heavy red, such as Pinot Noir, a medium-bodied Merlot or a Sangiovese. When prepared with fruity stuffings or sauces, as quail frequently are, you need to bring in a white with some acidity and sweetness. An off-dry Weisser Riesling or Chenin Blanc, or a full-bodied, deeply fruity, aromatic Sauvignon Blanc are all excellent choices.

Indian cuisine

For decades, it has been a widespread and popular belief that beer is the only drink that goes with curry. Some people think it is impossible to partner Indian cuisine, with its intricately flavoured and spicy dishes, with wine. Another whinge is: 'Why waste money on a good wine when your mouth is on fire and you can't taste it?' Curry-lovers are told to 'reach for a lassi (a yoghurt drink) or a lager' instead of wine. If you defiantly insist on wine with your curry, you'll be given further 'advice' to stick to something simple, almost insipid, to keep it white, and to chill your wine to within an inch of its life to knock the last vestige of flavour out of it. Behind this epicurean 'wisdom' was our long-held notion that curry was curry, just as we believed that red wine was red wine and white was white. When we thought of Indian cuisine, we only thought 'curry.'[1]

The reason for this was that we simply did not know what authentic Indian cuisine was, so how could we tell the difference between a Kashmiri lamb dish and a Madras one? But how the tables have turned in recent years! Just as we now know the difference between a Shiraz and a Cabernet, so we can now also tell a korma from a vindaloo. To bypass wine as an accompaniment to Indian cuisine is to miss out on, and deprive ourselves of, some of the most delectable food and wine combinations that exist. Furthermore, while the West caught up on India, that country caught up on winemaking, and now makes Shiraz and Cabernet wines, among others. Even they must have grown tired of all those beers...

The vast Indian subcontinent has many climatic variations and, naturally, the cooking reflects the different produce of each region. Northern dishes make liberal use of butter or clarified butter (ghee) and cream while those from the south use coconut extensively in all its forms: flesh, milk and oil. The northern dishes are milder than those from the south, which tend to be very fiery. Furthermore, the cooking traditions are varied: no two Indian cookery books will prepare the same dish with the same ingredients in the same way, and neither will any two Indian chefs.

Indian cooking is remarkably flexible but, if there is a common denominator in all Indian foods, it is the imaginative use of spices. The process of blending, grinding and frying spices in hot oil, called

---

1 The word 'curry' does not exist in any of India's many languages. Its origin is in dispute, but it appears to be an English corruption, from the days of the British Raj, of the Hindi word 'karahi' (a wok-like frying pan), or the Tamil word 'kaari' (a spicy sauce).

the 'bhoona', is an important part of curry preparation, removing the rawness of the spices and creating an intense flavour profile that influences the final taste of the dish.

Not all Indian dishes are hot, as Westerners tend to think, but all of them are flavourful. Similarly, not all dishes are eaten with rice. It is quite intriguing what clear ideas Indians have of which bread should go with which dish: chapati, naan, paratha and puri are just a few. Slow cooking is another common thread; although India has its 'fast foods', such as tandoori chicken or stir-fries, a great many dishes have slow simmering in common.

When selecting a wine to accompany any dish, the food and wine pairer's main consideration is the complexity of flavour of that dish. Within Indian cuisine, some spices certainly send warning signals to the pairer, notably fenugreek, mustard and fennel seeds, cumin, cardamon, asafoetida, coriander, tamarind, turmeric and, to a lesser extent, black pepper, cinnamon, and cloves. Other ingredients that can be, or apear to be, tricky, include chilli, ginger, raw (palm) sugar, dried fruit and nuts, lime, yoghurt and coconut.

Although chilli numbs the taste buds and can burn the palate, it does not destroy the taste of wine; it merely strips it of some of its flavours. The same applies to fresh ginger. Coconut is never a problem and, although raw yoghurt is extremely hard on a wine, most moderately-spiced, cooked yoghurty dishes are easily matched by a good quality, wooded Chardonnay that also has some acidity.

With few exceptions, the food and wine pairer always begins by considering the main ingredient of a dish, followed by the flavourings used, as these will determine where the weight of a dish lies. Indian cuisine is one of those exceptions; here, the pairer must look at the end result – the final dish – in order to select a wine. There are endless variations, with the spices being differently composed to produce different dishes, irrespective of the poultry, meat, fish, seafood, vegetables, pulses or grains used. Just one spice may be added to a simple potato dish, or up to fifteen might be used to make an elaborate meat dish. The result could be mellow and aromatic, pungently sharp, creamy with yoghurt, or sweetish with onions.

In summary, what the food and wine pairer needs to know is how light or heavy the finished dish is, and how sweet, sour, bitter or 'hot' it will be, in order to select a wine with enough spunk to stand up for itself against these odds. This eliminates light-bodied, lightly flavoured wines, fragile, old wines and quietly subtle ones. Flavour is the order of the day, so head straight for the grape varieties that can deliver ripe, fruity wines. If they have sweetish vanilla oak, rather than toasty flavours, so much the better.

In general, Indian dishes prefer white wines. South Africa's fruit-driven sparkling wines are also very compatible, and the off-dry ones are best with highly spiced dishes; they even help to tame the heat.

With red wines, low tannin and moderate alcohol are the keys, especially with fiery dishes, so as not to further bully the taste buds. Upfront fruity Cabs, Merlots and Zinfandels hold their own, but Pinot Noir is likely to be blown out by spices and heat, losing its gentle aromas and fruit. Shiraz can be very good with the richer North Indian dishes, but choose one that has low tannins and is fruity, rather than spicy or peppery. This may appear to be a contradiction, as we usually match spice with spice, but the Indian blend of spices strips Shiraz of its fruit and emphasizes its peppery character. Imagine pepper on pepper. Who wants to burn to death?

You may recall when we drank sweet fortified wines with Indian curries: sherry, jerepigo, hanepoot, muscadel and port. Although we appreciate the principle of pairing highly flavourful wines with highly aromatic foods, there are better options. When these wines are paired with curries, they become overbearingly spirity and alcoholic (or 'hot' in wine-speak).

BIRIANI (biryani/breyani)

Biriani, also written as biryani, and in South Africa, as breyani, originated in the Middle East, from where it was spread to the Indian subcontinent and South and Southeast Asia by Muslim traders and travellers. It reached South Africa via Indians who settled in Natal and the Malays of the Cape. This festive, rice-based casserole is a meal in itself. Part-cooked rice is layered with poultry, meat, seafood or vegetables. Saffron-infused milk is dribbled over the top, thereby colouring some grains yellow while leaving others white. In order to conserve the flavours, the pot was traditionally sealed with a flour paste to prevent even a drop of steam from escaping.

Unlike most Indian dishes, with biriani you should match the wine to the main ingredient added to the rice, rather than the end result. When poultry is added, a mellow-textured, lightly wooded Chardonnay makes a clean breast of it; with lamb, opt for a light-bodied red with prominent berry fruit; with beef, a quaffable Cabernet or Cab-Merlot blend is delightful, as is a Barbera or Gamay Noir. If seafood, fish or vegetables are used, a fruity Chenin Blanc with good acidity will make an ideal match.

BUTTER CHICKEN

See **Makhani**, page 232.

CHICKEN TIKKA (tikka masala)

See **Tikka**, page 235.

DHANSAK (dhan sakh)

Western Indian cuisine was greatly influenced by the Parsees. These refugees from Persia brought with them dhansak, a spicy stew that combines vegetables, notably pumpkin, with various types of lentils, pulses (dhal), and lamb or chicken. The mixed pulses give the dish a rather mealy texture, which leads us to the choice of wine. The way to go here is to avoid anything too fruity; meet it half-way with an unoaked Chardonnay, Sylvaner or Colombard.

DO PIAZA (dopiaza/do-piazah)

The meaning of the name of this meat and onion curry remains un-certain. In Urdu, one of India's many languages, 'do' means two and 'piaza' means onion. Some maintain 'do' refers to the fact that it contains twice as much onion as other curries, while others say it is because onion appears twice in the cooking process. Whether prepared with chicken, lamb or beef, this elegant dish can be made as mild or hot as you like. Although conventionally spiced, it also contains whole spices (cloves, cardamom, cinnamon) that are not meant to be eaten, just pushed aside when encountered. Match this savoury, sweetish dish with an off-dry Weisser Riesling or lightly wooded Semillon with sweet vanilla flavours. If the spicing is on the hot side, a Gewürztraminer or even an off-dry sparkling wine would hit the right note. If you'd rather drink a red wine, choose a medium-bodied Cabernet-Merlot blend with low tannins and upfront sweet-fruit flavours. A Shiraz that is spicy rather than peppery, or a Zinfandel, would also make a fine match.

JALFREZI

This dish was created during the British Raj as a way to use up left-overs. The remains of Sunday's lamb roast and veg were chopped and sautéed, or 'jal frezi'ed', in a curry sauce. Nowadays, a jalfrezi can be made from any marinated meat or vegetables seasoned with curry spices and cooked in a thick tomato and onion sauce, along with green chillies and red and green peppers. The dish can range from medium to very hot. Head for the good acidity of an off-dry Weisser Riesling or off-dry local sparkling wine to tone down the heat a bit. If the dish is fire-alarm hot, choose a Gewürztraminer. Sauvignon Blanc is another option, although it will be stripped of some of its flavour; better still, a wooded one (blanc fumé) will have the depth to complement the weight of the sauce.

KASHMIRI CURRIES

Many dishes that originate from Kashmir are red in colour from the extensive use of the herbal food colouring *rattanjog* (or *rattan jot*). Another feature is the use of saffron and nuts, which are grown in this mountainous northern region. Some Kashmiri dishes are fiercely hot, others mild and soothing, such as Kashmiri *yakhni* (mutton) or *gosht* (lamb). These are really stews flavoured with fennel (and no chillies) that are thickened with yoghurt to achieve a creamy tartness.

The chicken dish, **Kashmiri murgh**, combines yoghurt, almonds, pistachios, saffron, fresh coriander and mint in a mild, aromatically flavoured dish. Look for a wine packed with fruit and with good acidity: Chenin or Sauvignon Blanc, Pinot Gris/Pinot Grigio and Weisser Riesling are all good matches, while Gewürztraminer or dry sparkling wine will do wonders for the dish. If you want a red, choose a soft-textured, fruity Cabernet Sauvignon, Barbera or Gamay.

See also **Rhogan Josh**, page 233.

KEBABS

Kebabs originated in the Middle East, from where they were spread far and wide by Muslim traders. In the West, we tend to think that all kebabs are grilled on skewers. However, on the Indian subcontinent, there are two types of kebabs: **Shami kebabs** are flat, round cakes of minced meat mixed with cooked lentils and spices and fried so that the outside is crisp and the inside soft, like our frikkadels. They are usually served accompanied by burani, a minty yoghurt sauce.

Sheek kebabs (seekh kebabs) are spiced minced or cubed meat on a skewer, generally flavoured with or marinated in an onion, ginger, garlic, chilli and yoghurt mixture before being grilled. These are served with lemon or lime wedges and a salad.

A red wine with a savoury edge is the best match for both shami and sheek kebabs. Choose a gluggable Pinotage, but go slow on the burani. Equally good choices are Shiraz, but one with low tannins that is fruity rather than peppery, or Zinfandel. A white-wine drinker will be quite content with Viognier.

KOFTA

Meatballs, either grilled or fried, are often finished off in a tomatoey curry sauce. A Sauvignon Blanc-Chardonnay blend or a Semillon are ideal partners. If you want a red, choose a Barbera, Gamay or an easy-drinking Pinotage with very little oak flavour. When kofta are served in a creamy nut sauce, either a Viognier or a full-bodied oaked Chardonnay is an excellent match. A Cabernet Sauvignon-Merlot blend, with good fruit concentration, will also do the trick.

KORMA

Although there is some debate as to what 'korma' actually means, with some people maintaining that it is a cooking technique, to most of us it is a rich, mild and creamy curry. Meat, chicken or vegetables are cooked in liberal quantities of cream or yoghurt with nuts, often almonds or pistachios, added. The dish, which owes its ancestry to Persian food, is typical of an era when a just moderate amount of mustard seeds and black peppercorns were the commonly used spices. It is easy to forget that chillies were only introduced to Asia and the Indian subcontinent in the 16th century by the Portuguese, who had discovered them in the Americas. This fragrantly spiced dish is well-partnered by an unoaked or lightly wooded Chardonnay, but Viognier takes the cake.

MADRAS

Citizens of the city of Madras would probably not recognize 'Madras curry', which is a Western restaurant creation. The dishes of southern and southeastern India are typically flavoured with coconut and lots of chillies, which explains why many restaurateurs label any very hot curry as 'madras'. Old Madras, or Chennai, as it is now known, on the southeast coast of India, is in the heart of a region where vegetarian meals predominate, but the Madras curries served in Western restaurants mostly incorporate chicken, beef or lamb in a tomato-and-coconut curry sauce with options as to the heat level (mild, medium or hot). One wine stands head and shoulders above others as a partner to Madras curry – a mellow, aromatic Cabernet Sauvignon. Although we don't understand the alchemy, these two sure can boogie. A Merlot, Cab-Merlot blend or a Malbec will also play along to the same tune.

MAKHANI

'Makhani' is a Hindustani word meaning 'with butter'. It is used in the names of several dishes originating in Punjabi cuisine; perhaps the best known being **chicken makhani** or murgh makhani, which translates as **butter chicken**. In the classic version, a spicy tomato and cream-based sauce is enriched with butter to which chopped tandoori chicken is added. Nuts may be incorporated into the dish or used as a garnish. Match this gentle, but rich, dish with an unwooded or lightly oaked Chardonnay. Semillon takes to butter chicken like a duck to water as it amplifies its nutty flavours; or, if you'd prefer to add a bit of zest to contrast the richness, choose a wooded Chenin Blanc. Avoid red wines with this dish.

MOLEE/MOULI

Fish or seafood dishes from southern India are cooked in coconut milk with mustard seed or oil and chillies. Sometimes referred to as a Goan fish curry, a molee is a bit tart from the addition of vinegar and lemon or lime juice. A Sauvignon Blanc-Chardonnay blend is ideal, but an unoaked Chardonnay, with good acidity, also works well.

PASANDA

This curry differs from others in that the meat is sliced, not cubed. 'Pasanda' indicates small pieces of boneless meat, flattened as thinly as possible. It is a legacy of the Mogul courts where, centuries ago, Indian cuisine reached a refined peak. Beef was originally used, although lamb has become better known. The curry sauce includes ground almonds and the dish is garnished with flaked almonds. This gently flavoured dish, with its nutty, creamy texture, needs an equally softly textured white wine. A lightly oaked Chardonnay is just the thing, but Chenin Blanc, especially when oaked or with a touch or residual sugar, comes out on top.

PILAU (pullao/pulao/pilaf)

Rice-based dishes have their origin in Persia, from where they spread during the time of the Persian Empire, hence the many variations in spelling. The difference between this dish and a biriani is that, in a pilau, the rice is boiled along with the vegetables, poultry, meat or seafood until tender, whereas in a biriani the various ingredients are par-cooked and then assembled in layers. Many restaurants refer to spiced rice as pilau rice. A famous pilau from the Kashmir, Shah Jahani pilau, a festive dish of lamb, yellow rice and peas, is named after the prince who built the Taj Mahal. Wine matches for pilau are the same as for **Biriani**; see page 229.

PHAL

This chilli-laden restaurant creation is the hottest curry of all – its incendiary heat is for fire-eaters only! Keep your 'better' wines under lock and key. Now is the time to go for boxed wines labelled 'light'. Avoid any wine that has the faintest hint of acidity. If you're not into boxed wines, consider a gentle Sylvaner or Colombard to provide just a bit of background music to your fire eating. If the heat really gets to you, reach for a refreshing lassi or a piece of bread.

RHOGAN JOSH (gosht)

'Rhogan josh' means 'red gravy'. The characteristic red colour of this Kashmiri lamb dish was traditionally provided by the use of a natural dye called *rattanjog* (or *rattan jot*), but nowadays, food colouring or tomatoes and tomato purée provide a more readily available, and less expensive, alternative. Unlike many other forms of curry, this one is cooked with very little liquid; the creaminess comes from the yoghurt in which the lamb is marinated. A full-bodied Sauvignon Blanc, lightly wooded Chardonnay, or a blend of the two varieties are good partners. A big-fruited Pinot Noir is a fine red match to this elegant dish, although it will take a bit of a beating. If one is not at hand, choose one of the 'Indian cuisine' standby reds: Pinotage, Barbera or Malbec.

See also **Kashmiri curries**, page 231.

SAAG GOSHT

'Saag' means spinach. It is used with ginger and garlic to make the fragrant sauce for the lamb or 'gosht'. This robust, home-style dish from the northern state of Punjab, is beloved by families all over India. Spinach is often combined with potatoes, as in saag aloo, and with the Indian cheese, paneer, as in saag paneer. Some restaurants also make versions that include chicken or beef. Spinach is a naturally acidic vegetable, which is why it makes a good salad ingredient. An acid-edged white wine will make a clean breast of any saag, and Weisser Riesling, Sauvignon Blanc or Chenin Blanc are all good choices. Red-wine drinkers will be content with a medium-bodied Pinotage or Barbera.

TANDOORI

The tandoor is a vat-shaped clay oven, heated with charcoal or wood. Originally, the tandoor was confined to cooking chicken, lamb and naan bread, but nowadays, it is used to cook other foods as well.

The build up of heat in the tandoor is immense, way beyond the maximum of a home oven. A whole chicken, skewered and thrust into the tandoor, cooks in about 20 minutes flat! It is very difficult to make tandoori chicken (tandoori murgh) without a tandoor, but it is not necessary to sink a tandoor into your back garden, as there are ways around the problem.

The best approximation at home is to portion the chicken and use a kettle braai (or heat the oven to its maximum setting). Marinate the deeply scored chicken portions in yoghurt that has been flavoured with onion, garlic, ginger, chilli and spices, and coloured with red or orange food colouring. (The colour was originally obtained from alkenet root, but artificial colouring tends to be the norm these days.) Once baked, the chicken portions are served hot with lime or lemon wedges, or with a butter sauce. See also **Makhani**, page 232.

Gewürztraminer, off-dry Weisser Riesling or lightly wooded Chardonnay with sweetish vanilla oak flavours are appetizing matches as their sweetness latches onto the charry crust of the chicken. A medium-bodied Pinotage with sweetish, spicy fruit is sympathetic to charred flavours and makes an excellent red alternative, as do Shiraz or Zinfandel. If you particularly enjoy the tang from the lemon or lime wedges, you could consider a Barbera or Malbec.

TIKKA

Tikka is marinated chicken, meat or seafood that is skewered and then barbecued or baked in the tandoor. The marinade is a spicy tomato and onion or a spicy yoghurt mixture. It is typically eaten with a yoghurt-based side dish made with chopped mint or coriander.

Chicken tikka masala started life in a British restaurant, some say a London one, while others swear it was in Glasgow. One story goes that, when a customer found regular chicken tikka (murgh tikka) too dry and asked for 'gravy', the chef improvised by making a sauce from tomato soup, yoghurt and spices. Irrespective of its origins, this dish has become so popular that it has spread all over the world, even to India! There is no standard recipe for chicken tikka masala but, for pairing purposes, we will go with a very common version: chicken pieces in a sauce incorporating tomato, cream and mixed spices (masala). Lightly wooded Chardonnay with good acidity, or lightly wooded Semillon give a good account of themselves. A Sauvignon Blanc-Chardonnay blend will add some zip to the creamy sauce and latch onto the tomato. On the red side, a medium-bodied Cabernet Sauvignon or Cab-Merlot blend with ripe, sweetish berry fruit is more than an arranged marriage; it is love at first sight.

VINDALOO

A vindaloo curry is hot, sour, garlicky and usually made with pork. There is quite a tale to the origin of its name, which derives from two Portuguese words; 'vin', a shortened form of the word for 'vinegar', and 'alho', meaning 'garlic'. A Portuguese name for an Indian dish? This is easily explained, as Goa, on the west coast of India, was a Portuguese colony until as recently as 1956. When the Portuguese made the long sea voyage to their colony, they took with them pork preserved in wine vinegar, garlic and pepper. The local Hindus and Muslims, who did not eat pork, were unimpressed with this foreign food brought to their shores. However, a Konkani-speaking group of converts to Christianity had no such qualms and saw a future for this new ingredient. They jazzed up the preserved, garlicky pork by spicing it to suit their Indian tastes and, *voilà!* vindaloo was born.

Many people, looking at the word, misinterpret *aloo* as the Hindi word for potato, which is written in the same way. This led to even more confusion, as many restaurants started to serve the dish with some potatoes chucked in. Traditional vindaloos, however, do not include potatoes and the name found its roots long before restaurants added vindaloo to their menus. A third leg to the tale is that, as the type of chilli originally used in Goa is particularly hot, many restaurateurs refer to any very hot curry as a vindaloo. But, however it is made, this hot, tart, garlicky curry (made nowadays from pork, chicken, beef or lamb) calls for Gewürztraminer, Weisser Riesling, a Sauvignon Blanc-Semillon blend or Viognier, which particularly takes to the spicing of this dish. A quaffable Pinotage or Barbera are good red wine choices, but they should have bold fruit flavours.

At a glance: wines to accompany Indian dishes	
White: Mellow-textured wines (such as Chardonnay). *Red:* Low-tannin wines with moderate alcohol, not too oaky, and young and fruity (such as Cabernet Sauvignon with this profile). Generally speaking, these are the 'Indian food wines'. However, some other wines would be a 'touch better' with specific foods:	
Acidic dishes that are strong on tamarind, lemon or lime	*Any of the above wines or, a touch better:* *White:* Sauvignon Blanc, Chenin Blanc, dry or off-dry SA sparkling wine *Reds with acidity:* Pinotage, Barbera, Gamay, Malbec
Creamy and coconutty dishes	*White:* Chardonnay, Semillon, off-dry Weisser Riesling, dry or off-dry South African sparkling wine *Medium-bodied reds:* Cab Sauvignon, Cab-Merlot blends, Gamay
Delicately spiced dishes and curries, but not too rich	*White:* Viognier *Medium-bodied reds:* Pinotage, or stay with Cabernet Sauvignon, Cab-Merlot blends, Gamay
Highly spiced dishes which are difficult to match; very rich dishes	*White:* top-notch Chardonnay, Gewürztraminer, off-dry sparkling wine *Upfront fruity reds:* Pinotage, Cabernet Sauvignon, Cab-Merlot blends, Malbec

Japanese cuisine

Japanese food appears to be gloriously light and elegantly simple, but beware! The force of some of the flavours can slaughter any accompanying wine. Japanese cuisine often delivers a powerful punch, with sharp acidic notes, hot pungent flavours and, like Chinese cuisine, a hint of sweetness in the savoury dishes. Of all the ethnic cuisines covered in this guide, the Japanese one presents the greatest challenge to the wine drinker.

As most Japanese food is eaten with wooden chopsticks, it is cut into bite-sized pieces and presented in bowls or small, flat dishes. A main meal would typically include rice, a soup (most often miso), a vegetable salad or pickles, fish or shellfish, and a beef, pork or poultry dish, all served in small portions. A simple meal may be just a bowl of noodles. What a picture of innocence to the wine drinker!

However, Japanese seasonings and dipping sauces are anything but innocent, even when they seemingly resemble their Chinese equivalents. These seasonings and dipping sauces pack a whopping punch. Japanese cuisine features light and dark soy sauces, wasabi (a tear-jerking horseradish-like paste), pickled ginger, radish (daikon or mooli), rice vinegar, spring onions, mirin (a spirit-based rice liquid used as a sweetener), the yeasty, salty, fermented soya bean paste called miso, sesame seeds, an incredibly sharp-sour plum paste, citrus fruits, especially lime, and sansho, the Japanese equivalent of pepper. Chillies are added to some dipping sauces. These flavours are very, very hard on wine. Wasabi, especially, should be used with great care if you want the flavour of any wine to survive.

Saki (sake), an alcoholic rice wine, which is often used in cooking, is one of the best all-round matches for Japanese food. It is quite readily available but, if you can't find any, the closest local equivalent is dry (fino) sherry, which also mirrors typical Japanese flavours.

For the Western wine drinker, a general guide to follow with Japanese cuisine is to match the intensity of the food to that of the wine. Because of the predominance of vinegar and citrus in the dishes, the wine should have good acidity in order to cope, so white wine is the answer. Light- to medium-bodied white wines have the perfect weight to match the weight of Japanese food. They must also have intense flavours (but not oak), to match the flavours of the food. In this respect, dry sparkling wine and Weisser Riesling are the two stalwarts when it comes to pairing wine with Japanese food.

CHAWANMUSHI

Chawanmushi is a savoury, steamed egg custard flavoured with soy sauce, **dashi** (a stock made from either edible kelp, shiitake mushrooms, or dried seafood and fish flakes) and mirin, and eaten as an appetizer in the West. Ingredients such as shiitake mushrooms or shrimp can be added to the custard, which is served in a tea-cup-like container and eaten with a spoon, which is unusual for a traditional Japanese dish. Chawanmushi is madly in love with Weisser Riesling.

GYOZA

Gyoza is the Japanese version of Chinese dumplings. It typically consists of a ground meat (mince) and/or vegetable filling wrapped into a thinly rolled piece of dough, then pan-fried (sometimes boiled or deep-fried). Without a dipping sauce, dumplings are rather bland and will pair well with an unoaked Chardonnay. If served with a soy-based dipping sauce (*tare*), perhaps seasoned with rice vinegar or chilli-flavoured sesame oil, the wine picture changes completely and you will need a Weisser Riesling or dry sparkling wine, especially a Chardonnay-based version.

MISO SOUP

This famous soup is flavoured with miso (fermented soya bean paste) dissolved in dashi (stock, *see* **Chawanmushi**, above) and usually includes two or three solid ingredients, like seaweed, tofu, or vegetables such as shiitake mushrooms and spring onions. This acidic soup cries out for saki, the traditional drink with Japanese cuisine, or a pale dry (fino) sherry, which is the closest Western equivalent to saki.

NABEMONO (nabe)

'Nabe' is the Japanese word for 'pot' and nabemono (or nabe) dishes are all one-pot stews served at the table. It works a bit like a fondue; diners gather round a large, deep ceramic dish filled with stock, bubbling away over a burner in the centre of the table. Ingredients such as raw beef, chicken, seafood and fishcakes, as well as tofu, and vegetables like mushrooms, leeks and Chinese cabbage, are added to the stock by individual diners. When the ingredients are cooked, it's time to fish out what you want and drop it in your dipping sauce before eating. Once the meat and vegetables have been eaten and the stock has become richly flavoured, noodles or cooked rice are added to make a delicious soup.

The food and wine pairing will depend on the ingredients of the dipping sauce. See the table on page 241.

RAMEN

This dish of noodles in soup is originally from China, but the Japanese have made it completely their own and it is now something of a fast-food institution. A typical ramen shop will have a large pot of meat bones and vegetables constantly bubbling away to supply the stock for hundreds of bowls of steaming soup every day. Ramen noodles are boiled separately and added to the soup along with toppings such as bean sprouts, spring onions and slices of roast pork.

In Japan, there are four main flavour versions of ramen: *shio* (salt), *shoyu* (soy sauce), *tonkotsu* (pork soup) and *miso* (fermented soybean paste). Pair the shio with a Weisser Riesling; with the shoyu, choose either a Weisser Riesling or Sauvignon Blanc (you may find the latter a touch assertive, but if there is a hint of wasabi present, it will be ideal). With the tonkotsu and miso ramen, either saki or a dry, yeasty fino sherry would be delightful.

ROBATAYAKI

Grilled food, whether vegetable, poultry, meat, fish or seafood is called robatayaki, which takes its name from the Japanese words 'ro' and 'yaki'. The former refers to the hearth, while 'yaki' means grilled. Ingredients for robatayaki are treated simply, and lightly flavoured with perhaps teriyaki sauce, a dollop of miso or even a drizzle of melted butter, especially in its more Western format. But most of the fare is seasoned solely with salt. The 'robata' sauces offered by some restaurants are usually of their own creation.

For our wine pairing recommendation, see the table on page 241.

SASHIMI

Sashimi is raw, thinly sliced fish or seafood, served with soy dipping sauces. Served on its own, with perhaps just some daikon (Japanese radish) and shiso (the Japanese name for perilla, an aromatic herb of the mint family) on the side, an unwooded Chardonnay or Weisser Riesling pairs exceptionally well. When sashimi is accompanied by wasabi paste and pickled ginger root, as is often the case, a Sauvignon Blanc or dry sparkling wine is preferable.

SUSHI

Of all the foods associated with Japan, sushi is the most famous. Technically, the term 'sushi' refers to the rice. Nigiri sushi are pieces of fish, shellfish or fish roe on vinegared rice. Maki sushi is vinegared rice plus a filling, rolled up in Japanese seaweed (nori). If it is an inside-out roll, with the nori on the inside, it is called uramaki (California roll). If the nori is cone-shaped, it is called temaki (hand-roll).

As the rice is always vinegared and the pieces dipped in soy sauce, don't even think of pairing sushi with red wine. We recall a rather delightful voyeuristic experience in a sushi restaurant at Cape Town's Waterfront. A dapper, older man was entertaining three young ladies and he was obviously out to impress. He chose the most expensive, whoppingly robust Cabernet Sauvignon on the wine list. Staying in command, and with great panache, he ordered a full-house of sushi and sashimi for the table. Knowing what was going to happen, we surreptitiously watched for the reaction. It came almost immediately after they started eating, as the 'stomp-tande' effect kicked in. Red wine in combination with soy sauce (which is rich in **umami**, see page 24) seems to strip teeth of their enamel. At one point, when the three ladies left the table *en masse*, as ladies tend to do, the gentleman, under cover of his left hand, used his serviette to scrub his teeth to rid them of this unpleasant effect... You have been warned!

Besides saki, there are four styles of wine that perfectly fit the demands of sushi: Weisser Riesling, dry sparkling wine, pale dry (fino) sherry and, in the presence of wasabi, Sauvignon Blanc.

TEMPURA

Tempura is a Japanese culinary institution that rivals sushi in fame and popularity. The basic principle is taking fresh ingredients, coating them in a light, airy batter, frying them quickly and eating them immediately. Tempura menus are based primarily on seafood, but popular vegetables include brinjal (aubergine/eggplant), peppers, pumpkin and onion. The morsels of cooked food are served with a dipping sauce whose most important ingredient is dashi, a stock made from dried seaweed (kelp). As the tempura dipping sauce will be intensely savoury (umami), in flavour, a wine with good acidity, like Sauvignon Blanc or Weisser Riesling, is the ideal choice, especially for seafood tempura. Vegetable tempura calls for a slightly bolder wine, and a Chardonnay, with just a hint of oak, will do splendidly.

TEPPANYAKI

Teppanyaki is a type of Japanese cuisine that uses an iron griddle (a *teppan*) to cook food. Typical ingredients are beef, shrimp, scallops, crayfish, chicken and assorted vegetables. Soybean oil is typically used to cook the ingredients. Side dishes of mung bean sprouts, baby marrows, garlic chips or fried rice usually accompany the meal. Some Western restaurants provide a variety of sauces in which to dip the food; in Japan, usually only soy sauce is offered. Wines with good acidity, such as Sauvignon Blanc or Weisser Riesling, pair well with the savoury, or umami, dipping sauces.

TERIYAKI

Teriyaki is grilled or pan-fried meat, fish, chicken or vegetables glazed with or marinated in *tare* (soy sauce sweetened with sugar or honey and blended with saki or mirin). Apart from sweetness, the wine also has to cope with a sour note to the dish. The weight of teriyaki points to a heavier wine than the usual whites that pair so well with Japanese cuisine. We suggest a light-bodied red with an acidic note, such as Pinot Noir, dry Pinotage-based rosé or blanc de noir. We'll raise an eyebrow or two by suggesting that a Sangiovese or Italian Chianti would be equally successful.

TONKATSU

Tonkatsu is breaded, deep-fried pork eaten with a thick Japanese Worcestershire-like sauce and generally served with shredded cabbage. It is interesting that tonkatsu sauce contains more than a hint of apple, echoing the Western tradition of serving apple, in whatever style, with pork. An off-dry Weisser Riesling will go splendidly with this dish because of the inherent sweet touch of the tonkatsu. An off-dry or dry Chenin Blanc are worthy alternatives, because of the otherwise savoury character of the sauce.

YAKITORI

Yakitori takes its name from the Japanese words for 'grilled' (*yaki*) and 'chicken' (*tori*). This dish is normally served with a dipping sauce, which will determine your choice of wine. See the table below.

At a glance: wines to accompany Japanese dishes	
Japanese cuisine in general	Weisser Riesling; fino sherry; sparkling wine; saki
Dishes with some acidity and a sweet note: sashimi; sushi; savoury soup custards; vinegared rice; *nabemono*; poultry dishes	Weisser Riesling; sparkling wine
Miso-flavoured dishes	Fino sherry
Lime-based sauces and bastings; wasabi; vinegared rice; sushi; sushi with pickled ginger; tempura	Weisser Riesling, sparkling wine or, as an alternative, Sauvignon Blanc; or saki
Beef dishes; teriyaki-flavoured beef and chicken dishes	Pinot Noir; dry Pinotage-based rosé; blanc de noir

Chinese cuisine

At the heart of all Chinese cooking lies the harmonious blending of flavours, textures and aromas that produce a well-balanced cuisine. As you would expect of this vast country, there are many regional variations in both cooking methods and ingredients; for instance, the delicate flavours of Cantonese cooking, the rich, sweet dishes of Shanghai, and the hot, spicy style of Sichuan (Szechuan).

Texture and contrast are important, as evidenced by the variety of dishes served at a typical Chinese meal, as well as the ingredients used for each dish. Freshness of flavour is paramount. Flavourings and sauces also play an important role, but these are generally used in moderation, never overwhelming the main ingredients, even in Sichuan cooking.

The use of aromatic fresh ginger, garlic and spring onions is a common feature to all the regional cooking styles. Other popular flavouring ingredients include soy sauce, fermented black (soya) beans (pungent and salty), salt, sugar and, depending on the region, rice wine, sharp and spicy Sichuan pepper (which is not a pepper at all), five-spice powder, and both fresh and dried chillies. Fresh Chinese chillies are normally less hot than the varieties used in Southeast Asia. The common sauces used in cooking and/or for dipping are chilli-bean sauce (hot and spicy), oyster sauce (rich and savoury, rather than fishy) and hoisin (a sweetish sauce).

Herbs are few and far between in Chinese cooking. The dominant herb is fresh coriander, which has a bitter-sweet character. It is used mainly as a garnish, but also appears in sauces and stuffings.

Chinese cooks have mastered all the major cooking techniques: steaming, roasting, deep-frying, baking, grilling, poaching, stir-frying, stewing and braising; basically everything, except microwaving.

Vegetables are cooked lightly and quickly to preserve their crispy, crunchy texture, and pickled or raw vegetables are used for the same reason. The most commonly used vegetables include cabbages of every description, including the well-known bok choi variety, yard-long (snake) beans, mangetout, brinjal (aubergine/eggplant) and mushrooms. Pork is the favourite meat, although beef and lamb also feature, along with duck, chicken and all types of fish and seafood.

These main ingredients are served with a neutral starch, such as rice, noodles, dumplings or pancakes. Tofu (soya bean curd) is used as a substitute for both dairy products and meat.

This overview of Chinese cuisine may lead us to think that their dishes are relatively easy to match with wine. At first glance, the fresh, mild flavours and balanced textures do not present a problem, but we must remember that, at a typical Chinese meal, several contrasting dishes are served simultaneously. Choosing one wine to suit everything calls for the delicate art of compromise.

Many wines, especially from New World producers, and most reds, are too brash for gentle Chinese flavours. As there is often a touch of sweetness in Chinese savoury dishes (not only in sweet-and-sour sauces), we should veer towards wines with some residual sugar. The sour element of the sauces adds a further complication.

BANG BANG CHICKEN

From the Sichuan (Szechuan) province in the heart of China, the classic bang bang chicken is an example of the use of sesame, which is typical of that region's cooking. A platter of cold chicken, cucumber and noodles is coated in a sesame dressing that has both a sour and a sweet note. Although a sesame dressing is the authentic one, a peanut dressing is often also used. Wines that echo the nutty character of the dish are the most successful, especially if they have a touch of sweetness. A lightly wooded Chardonnay, with its sweetish vanilla oak, is the ideal choice, but a lightly wooded Semillon also works beautifully.

BARBECUED PORK (char siu)

Char siu, or barbecued pork, is a Cantonese speciality. The meat is seasoned with a mixture of sugar or honey, five-spice powder, fermented bean curd, soy sauce, hoisin sauce, red food colouring and Chinese spirits. The strips of seasoned, boneless pork are skewered onto forks or hung from hooks and grilled in a covered oven or over a fire. Char siu is typically accompanied by a starch, whether inside a bun (char siu bau), with noodles or with rice (char siu fan). When it comes to choosing a wine, we immediately think of sweetness and acidity but, for once, the delicacy of Weisser Riesling is not suited to the powerful flavourings of the marinade. Three elements create a tripwire: smokiness, caramelization and spices. Our first reaction is to roll out a Gewürztraminer, but this Chinese-food standby can be a bit overbearing. A very fruity, supple, low-tannin, modern-style red will come to the rescue, especially if it has a smoky character. Pinot Noir or Pinotage fits the bill, as does a rosé made from Pinotage grapes. If you'd like to drink a white wine, choose a very spicy Viognier or a huge Chardonnay (provided it has been given the full wood treatment).

CHICKEN AND BLACK BEANS

On the whole, Cantonese dishes are neither highly seasoned nor peppery-hot. In this typical stir-fried dish, the black beans add a bitter, salty element that responds very well to a wine with a touch of sweetness. Beside the obvious choice of an off-dry Weisser Riesling, you could go for a Chardonnay with pronounced sweet-vanilla oak or even a spicy Viognier.

CHICKEN WITH CASHEW NUTS

With its mixture of crunchy vegetables, flash-fried chicken, ginger, garlic and spring onions, this dish typifies Chinese cuisine. Up to this point, we are inclined to go for a Weisser Riesling, which is Chinese-food friendly, but the addition of cashew nuts steers us towards a lightly wooded Chardonnay, a wooded Chenin Blanc or the lesser known, but nut-friendly, Fernão Pires.

CHOP SUEY

Chop suey is not a traditional dish; in fact, it was created by Chinese immigrants to California in the mid-1800s. There is some debate as to how the dish got its name, but it is generally accepted that it means 'bits and pieces' or 'leftovers' and, indeed, it can be prepared with chicken, beef, pork, prawns or vegetables. Irrespective of the ingredients, though, chop suey loves unwooded white wines produced from Chenin Blanc, Semillon or Chardonnay grapes. For once, they beat Weisser Riesling hands down.

CHOW MEIN

Chow mein is a generic term for a dish of stir-fried noodles. Like many other Chinese dishes, it can be made with either chicken, beef, pork, vegetables or seafood. As this is not a highly flavoured dish, you have a wide choice of suitable wines to pair with it. Keep it white though, and choose from Chenin Blanc, Semillon, unwooded Chardonnay and, of course, Weisser Riesling.

CRISPY DUCK

A simpler version of the more famous **Peking duck**, see page 246, crispy duck is no less delicious. The gamey flavour of the duck cries out for an equally gamey red wine. Pinot Noir certainly fits the bill, but its offspring, Pinotage, is a winner. Merlot and a medium-bodied Shiraz are also in the race, though. If you'd like to enjoy a glass of white wine, choose a ripe, spicy Viognier.

CORN SOUP

This chicken and corn-based soup has egg white and sesame oil stirred in just before serving. You've guessed it: Semillon is the flag-bearer, but Chardonnay, either on its own or blended with Semillon, will be equally good with this Cantonese classic.

DIM SUM

In China, dim sum is part of *yum cha* (tea drinking), where bite-sized portions of foods are served alongside the tea. However, in Western restaurants, it is often offered as an appetizer. The variety of foods served as dim sum is wide. For instance, char siu bau (steamed buns filled with barbecued pork), har gau (shiny, translucent sea-food dumplings), lor mai gai (sticky rice and meat wrapped in lotus leaves), rice noodle rolls, bean curd rolls, spring rolls, stuffed veg-etables and fung jeow (chicken's feet in black bean sauce) are just a few of the tasty morsels in the dim sum repertoire. As quite a few of these have a sweet note, the safest wine choice is an off-dry Weisser Riesling. However, a Chenin Blanc with quite a bit of residual sugar is not to be sneezed at as a pairing partner.

FISHCAKES

Battered and fried fishcakes, often made with calamari, are rather oily. They need something similar to the refreshing wedge of lemon that is often served with fried foods; a Chenin Blanc with good acid-ity, and not too fruity, would be the answer.

FOO YOUNG

Foo young (fu yung) is an egg dish with either fish, seafood, poultry, meat or vegetables added. An unwooded Chardonnay should cope with all versions of this dish.

HOT AND SOUR SOUP

Unlike other Sichuan recipes, this popular dish gets its heat from white pepper, while the sour taste comes from vinegar. Almost any ingredient can be used for the soup, but white pepper and vinegar are the two flavouring ingredients always present. Even if we were blindfolded, we would automatically reach for a Weisser Riesling to pair with hot and sour soup.

KUNG PAO

Kung pao chicken, a classic Sichuan dish, consists of marinated chicken, diced and stir-fried with roasted peanuts, red peppers, rice wine, hoisin sauce, oyster sauce and chillies. Although chicken is traditionally used, seafood, such as shrimp or scallops, or meat (beef or pork) sometimes feature. The sweet and hot flavours of kung pao cry out for an off-dry Weisser Riesling or a Gewürztraminer. Pinot Gris/Pinot Grigio is a worthy alternative if you want a change from the ever-handy Weisser Riesling.

LEMON CHICKEN

Strips of battered and fried chicken in an intensely lemon-flavoured sauce requires a wine that can cope with the sourness of the lemon and the otherwise sweetness of the dish. Gewürztraminer, which copes well with fruity sauces, *loooves* lemon chicken. Medium- cream sherry is also surprisingly good, provided it is served well-chilled; the reason being that it has the ideal weight, in both sweetness and flavour, to match the sauce.

MA PO TOFU

This famous Sichuan dish, Ma po tofu (mapo doufu), is supposedly named after an old woman whose pockmarked complexion led to the dish being called 'pockmarked grandmother's tofu'. True or not, this dish of minced beef and bean curd (tofu) is flavoured with the trinity of Chinese flavours: garlic, ginger and spring onions. It is made spicy with the addition of Sichuan peppercorns and chilli bean paste (*toban jiang*). The spiciness of this dish is happy with an equally spicy blanc de noir made from Pinotage grapes or a dry rosé. An easy-drinking Pinotage would also work, but be prepared for the wine to lose some of its flavour.

PEKING DUCK

Peking duck is famous not so much for the way it is cooked, but rather for the theatrics of the way it is served. The appeal of the dish is biting into crispy duck skin, juicy meat, crunchy vegetables and a piquant sauce, wrapped in a pancake, and all in one mouthful! The sweetness of the sauce leads us to select a white wine with residual sugar, such as Chenin Blanc, Colombard and Bukettraube. A rosé with a hint of sweetness would also be good.

See also **Crispy duck**, page 244.

SICHUAN BEEF

At last, a Chinese dish that will pair with a bold, spicy red wine! Both Shiraz and Pinotage leap to the fore alongside spicy Sichuan beef, which is made with the famous Sichuan 'pepper' that is not pepper at all, but the berry of a thorny bush of the Rutaceae family.

SPARERIBS

These rather messy, but delightful, roasted ribs in sweetish-savoury sauce are normally served as a starter dish. The hoisin sauce in the basting leads us to a semi-sweet white or rosé wine. Also consider a stein, or any other wine that comes in one of those cute little bottles with broad hips (known as a bocksbeutel, in wine-speak).

SPRING ROLLS

A perennial favourite starter in Chinese restaurants, spring rolls are normally offered with a chicken or a vegetarian filling. Both can be rather bland, so the predominant sensation comes from the crisp casing. A wine with good acidity – it can even have a touch of sweet-ness – is a good partner whether you have spring rolls on their own or with a sweet-and-sour dipping sauce. Although Gewürztraminer immediately comes to mind, it could be a touch overbearing, so rather go for Weisser Riesling.

STEAMED FISH

Cantonese dishes – which are neither highly seasoned nor peppery-hot – demand the freshest ingredients. Frozen or canned items are never substitutes. For Cantonese steamed fish, the fish should still be swimming in a tank while you are building up some steam in the wok. It should be that fresh! Once the fish has been steamed for a few minutes, it is sprinkled with shredded garlic and spring onions. Smoking-hot oil is then slowly poured over the fish, causing the skin to crisp and cooking the garnish. A dry Weisser Riesling is the obvi-ous choice, but an unwooded Chardonnay will be unobtrusive.

STIR-FRIED DISHES

Although the Chinese use all cooking techniques, stir-frying is their speciality. There is a four-step process to be followed in quick and uninterrupted sequence: Firstly, to 'awaken the wok', it is heated until a wisp of smoke rises; a small amount of oil is poured in to coat the inside and garlic, ginger and spring onion are added; as these sizzle in the hot oil, they release their fragrances – the wok is now 'aroused'. In the second step, the main ingredients of the dish, already cut up and perhaps marinated, are added in rapid succes-sion and stirred until partially cooked. Thirdly, a dash of rice wine is poured along the rim of the wok so that the sizzling alcohol inter-acts with the other ingredients, enhancing their fragrance. Finally, a small amount of sauce, pre-prepared with a thickening agent, is stirred in to bind the mixture.

Crisp white wines with fairly light body, sweetness and weight suit most stir-fries, but we must take into account the ingredients used. Stir-fried calamari, prawns, bean sprouts, chicken or noodles, irrespective of the accompanying sauce, will be happy with dry or off-dry Weisser Riesling, whereas stir-fried beef with oyster sauce will be happier with a dry or off-dry rosé or a blanc de noir.

SWEET-AND-SOUR DISHES

It hardly matters whether the main ingredient is prawns, battered pork or chicken; the sauce in these dishes is what the wine has to cope with. Pineapple, carrots and red peppers, together with a touch of sugar, provide sweetness, while vinegar adds a sour note. Not surprisingly, it is crisp, off-dry Weisser Riesling that partners best with all sweet-and-sour dishes.

At a glance: wines to accompany Chinese dishes	
Chinese cuisine in general	Weisser Riesling (the 'indispensable Chinese-food wine')
To match the sweetness and subtle spiciness of sweet-and-sour dishes	Weisser Riesling *Alternative:* Sparkling wine (off-dry or medium-dry)
Spareribs Hoisin, plum and other sweet fruity sauces	*Any of the above wines or, a touch better:* Gewürztraminer; medium-sweet Chenin Blanc
Dishes where the beef flavour is prominent	Pinot Noir *or* an easy-drinking red

Thai cuisine

Thai cuisine is hot, sour, salty and sweet all at the same time. It is typified by seriously intense and vibrant flavours, to the point of being explosive. Indian influences are noticeable, especially in the hot curries, to which chilli is added but, essentially, Thai cuisine is completely different to that of India, in which roasted dry spices and herbs form the flavouring backbone.

Thai curries make use of fresh herbs and other fresh ingredients such as galangal (a spicy root, similar to ginger), Thai holy basil, lemon grass, lime leaves (makrut lime), citrus juices, chillies, and coriander (both the root and leaves). Consequently, Thai food is never bland, even when the flavours are subdued with coconut milk.

Other flavourings used by the Thai chef include fermented fish paste and fish sauce (nam pla), pungently aromatic dried shrimps or prawns, and hot and spicy relishes and dipping sauces, such as nam prik, which are made from chillies, garlic and shrimp paste, fish sauce and lime. Also in the repertoire are pickled fish, sour lime pickles, roasted peanuts and ground roasted rice. Palm sugar is used to sweeten both savoury dishes and desserts.

When added to meat, poultry, fish, seafood and vegetable dishes, all these upfront flavours may seem threatening to wine but, amazingly, Thai ingredients, such as ginger and chilli, do not ruin the taste of wine. In fact, lemon grass, coriander and Thai basil are extremely happy with crisp, dry white wines. Even coconut is not a problem. The salty fish sauces and pastes, as well as the pickled items, need a wine with racy acidity, and Sauvignon Blanc is ideal, especially when it is young, fresh, crisp and not too light-bodied.

In fact, Sauvignon Blanc, in all its incarnations, whether classic, pungent, minerally, grassy, fruity, figgy, green peppery or blended with other grape varieties, like Semillon or Chardonnay, is Thai food's best wine partner.

As to other wine options: sparkling wine, which goes well with Japanese dishes, is a mismatch with Thai food, particularly when the wine is semi-sweet. (Thai food makes a bubbly taste sweeter and blander than it actually is.) Weisser Riesling is also totally overwhelmed by Thai flavours, except the mildest of noodle dishes. Red wines usually suffer as well, except with Thai curries where beef is the prominent ingredient.

THAI CURRIES

Around the world, the most easily recognized Thai dishes are the richly scented red and green curries. Although Thai families all have their own special recipe, patiently grinding and pounding the ingredients from scratch, we are fortunate in that just about every supermarket and convenience store has at least one brand of pre-prepared Thai curry paste to choose from.

Dry curry (panaeng) The word 'dry' in this curry appears strange at first glance. However, when you consider that most Thai curries are almost soup-like (and need to be served in bowls), panaeng is more like a Western stew in consistency. Traditionally made with beef, it is not too hot, but has a sweet-and-sour taste. Although most red wines lose out with Thai food, this dish, in which the beef flavour is prominent, works with a medium-bodied Cabernet Sauvignon, but you must be prepared for the panaeng to strip the wine of some of its character and flavour.

Green curry (gaeng khiew wan) Whether made with chicken, beef, fish, seafood or vegetables, the ubiquitous Thai green curry tap-dances in the company of Sauvignon Blanc. However, if you want to tango instead, try a spicy Pinot Gris/Pinot Grigio. Sauvignon Blanc-Semillon blends, in which the Semillon is lightly oaked, or wooded Chenin Blanc are also good dance partners.

Massaman curry (gaeng masaman) Taking its name from the Thai Muslims who originally made this dish, Massaman is an Indian-style curry, made with roasted dried spices. It is most commonly made with beef, but duck or chicken are options. It usually contains coconut milk, roasted peanuts, potatoes, cardamom, cinnamon, palm sugar, fish sauce and tamarind. It comes as no surprise that a chicken or duck Massaman curry needs Sauvignon Blanc to accompany it. Beef Massaman is good with a medium-bodied, soft-fruited Cabernet Sauvignon. If the dish is served with ajaad, a relish made with cucumber and peppers macerated in vinegar and sugar, head straight back to Sauvignon Blanc.

Red curry (gaeng phed) This medium-hot red curry is made distinctly pungent with the addition of Thai fish sauce (nam pla), lime, ginger and chillies. Gewürztraminer is an exact match, as its own spiciness echoes the spice combinations of gaeng phed. Viognier is almost as good. If your red curry is made with beef, choose a medium-bodied, supple Cabernet Sauvignon (but not a jammy one), as the characteristics of stir-fried beef will change the perception of the dish. You can go easy on your pocket, as a good bottle of Cab Sav will inevitably lose some of its character and flavour, which would be a waste.

FISHCAKES (tod man)

Fried fishcakes, made with white fish or seafood, are often served as an appetizer, accompanied by a sweetish chilli dipping sauce and, perhaps, a cucumber relish. Instead of the Western tradition of chopped parsley, the Thais use chopped or sliced green beans in their fishcake mixture. As fishcakes are rather delicately flavoured, the dipping sauce will determine the choice of wine. There are four possibilities: any white blend incorporating Sauvignon Blanc, a Colombard, a Colombard-Chardonnay blend, or an off-dry Chenin Blanc, which seems to have the exact weight for the dish.

FRIED RICE (khao pad)

Rice is a staple of Thai cuisine, and fragrant jasmine rice is indigenous to Thailand. Fried rice can be made with chicken, beef, pork, shrimp or prawn, or in a vegetarian style with coconut or pineapple. A plain and simple, crisp, light-bodied white wine, especially a blend, will suffice for any version of khao pad.

NOODLES (pad thai)

Rice noodles and bean sprouts fried with chicken, beef, pork, seafood or vegetables is sharply flavoured by the addition of fish sauce, lime juice or tamarind pulp and requires a Sauvignon Blanc with good acidity to accompany it. However, if you want a change from always drinking Sauvignon Blanc with Thai food, and provided there are no peanuts in the dish, select a dry, spicy rosé or blanc de noir produced from Pinotage grapes.

PAWPAW SALAD (som tam)

The pawpaw (papaya) used in this salad is green, not ripe. The main ingredient, be it chicken, pork or seafood, is first coated in a chilli paste mixture and then tossed with the grated pawpaw and lime juice. If your first instinct is to have Sauvignon Blanc with this dish, you'd be spot-on. However, if you're having the salad with pork, you'll have to re-think. Perhaps you can find a bottle of Gamay Noir, the softer and fruitier cousin of Pinot Noir. Its naturally low-tannin levels will avoid a clash with the lime juice in the salad. Another easy-to-drink red, like Cinsaut, would be an alternative.

SALADS (yum)

Yum, or yam, is the general name for any type of sour Thai salad. The dressing typically contains lime juice (in South Africa, frequently lemon juice), chilli, ginger (galangal), Thai fish sauce (nam pla) and fresh coriander. Tomatoes are not traditional, but you may find them in the salads offered by some Thai restaurants. Whether you have the famous glass noodle salad (yum wun sen/yum woon sen) or a seafood salad (yum talay/yum talae), the ideal wine for all sour Thai salads is Sauvignon Blanc.

SATAY

Satay (saté) is actually of Indonesian origin, but it has become an international dish and features on many Thai restaurant menus. Grilled skewered meat, usually pork or chicken, is served with a peanut sauce that has a sweet and piquant note. Satay pairs well with four wines. The first three are Semillon, Gewürztraminer and Fernão Pires, the peanut-friendly wine (provided you can lay your hands on one). The fourth choice, an oaked Chardonnay, is generally not associated with Thai food, but it is delicious with satay, even beef satay, as the oaky, fruity and buttery character of the Chardonnay complements the coconutty peanut sauce.

SPRING ROLLS (po pia)

Spring rolls, whether filled with vegetables, seafood or meat, are usually served with a dipping sauce. If it is a plain soy sauce, go no further than Sauvignon Blanc, Thai food's best friend. But, if there is a touch of sweetness present, as in a sweet chilli sauce or peanut sauce, any white wine with some residual sugar will be ideal.

STIR-FRIES

Stir-frying forms the mainstay of Thai cooking. Although there are many stir-fried foods, the commonality is the pungency of the dish. Whether made with chicken, pork, fish or seafood, the best wine partners are Sauvignon Blanc, Chenin Blanc, Pinot Gris/Pinot Grigio or Gewürztraminer. The exceptions are stir-fries using beef and Thai basil; for these, choose a light- to medium-bodied, supple, soft-centred red wine. Avoid a robust, fruity red.

SOUPS

Tom yum (tom yam), perhaps the most famous Thai soup, is characterized by its distinct hot and sour flavours. The basic broth or stock is made with ingredients such as lemon grass, lime juice, fish sauce, tamarind, galangal, onions, mushrooms and crushed chillies.

Tom yum is usually made with prawns (tom yum goong or kung), chicken (tom yum gai), fish (tom yum pla), or mixed seafood (tom yum talay or talae). A variation, tom yum nam khon, where coconut milk is added to the broth, is almost always made with prawns.

Another famous soup is tom kha or tom kha gai, where the flavour of galangal (a 'root' resembling ginger) dominates the soup.

In all instances, a pale dry (fino) sherry works very well. But, guess what? If you have no qualms about fusing a Japanese drink with Thai food, then saki is actually quite delicious with sour soups.

At a glance: wines to accompany Thai dishes	
Thai cuisine in general	Sauvignon Blanc, the 'all-rounder' wine for Thai cuisine
Creamy, coconutty dishes (even the hottest and creamiest!)	Sauvignon Blanc
Satay (pork, chicken or beef)	*Sauvignon Blanc or, a touch better:* Oak-influenced white wines (such as wooded Chardonnay or wooded Semillon)
Milder, aromatic curries, where the beef flavour is prominent	*Any of the above wines or, a touch better:* Medium-bodied Cabernet Sauvignon, or an easy-drinking red

Desserts

To state the obvious, desserts are predominantly sweet, and sweet food is best matched with a wine that is equally sweet, or just a touch sweeter (see page 19). If the food is sweeter than the wine, it will make the wine taste thin and sour; if the wine is the sweeter element, the food will be overwhelmed, with the wine becoming virtually a dessert in itself, and whatever effort went into preparing the dessert will be lost. Given this, it is hard to understand why we persist in serving dry champagne or sparkling wine with dessert. Perhaps this habit, which started years ago, came from the sense of occasion and indulgence that a sparkling wine brings to the table. It certainly was not based on the torturous combination that these two divergent tastes can bring about – pairing a brut sparkling wine with chocolate mousse is pure agony!

But matching sweetness with sweetness can be complicated. It is only a starting point, albeit a good one. Here's the thing: desserts not only vary in their levels of sweetness, but also in their weight and flavour intensity. Furthermore, they are distinguished by the combinations of their ingredients and their varying textures. Clearly then, not any old sweet wine will do with any old dessert – fine-tuning is the order of the day. Yet, how often don't we take our eye off the ball when it comes to the finale of a meal? Unwittingly, our return shot often slams into the net.

There are many sweet wines to choose from, and South Africa produces the full range, from late harvest (the least sweet) through special late harvest to noble late harvest, detouring via the fortified wines: hanepoot, 'cream' and 'old brown' sherries, jerepigo, port and muscadel. Oh, and let's not forget liqueurs, even if they are not wine-based. For more on the sweetness and sugar content of still wines, see page 73.

At this point, you might be thinking: 'Not another wine with this meal!', but ending a meal with a 'dessert wine' is not as expensive as you may think, as a little goes a long way. The most pricey wines in this category, the noble late harvests, usually come in a 375ml bottle, which is more than enough to serve ten dinner guests. And, if you don't finish that little bottle, the wine will last for up to a month in the fridge. Fortified wines have an even longer shelf-life.

Another way to economize is to serve the same wine with both the dessert and the cheese. It requires a bit of menu planning but, by using the dessert categories that follow, and the wine and cheese pairing suggestions in the next chapter, you can select both a dessert and cheese(s) to suit the same wine.

The key is to choose your wine first. Let's say you want to drink a noble late harvest: select cheeses from the noble late harvest listing (see page 303) and search this chapter for desserts that go well with noble late harvest wines (such as creamy or egg-based desserts). That way, you'll have the ideal food **and** wine match for your single bottle without compromising on either the food or the wine.

Basic dessert categories

We have categorized desserts according to their main ingredients and their textures, and given our wine recommendations based on these. For suggestions of wines to accompany specific desserts, consult the alphabetical entries that begin on page 257.

FRESH FRUIT-BASED DESSERTS

Berries When served on their own, most berries are very good with sweet sparkling wines and late harvest or special late harvest wines, depending on their level of acidity and sweetness. For example, **Cape gooseberries**, with their inherent tartness, are quite happy with a late harvest, whereas fully ripe **strawberries** prefer the sweeter special late harvest. Berries are unhappy with most fortified wines, especially port. The one exception is hanepoot, which can be fun, provided the berries are completely ripe.

When berries are served with cream, a special late harvest or sweet sparkling wine still works very well, but when ice cream is the accompaniment, the wine suffers. See **Ice creams**, page 263.

When berries are used to garnish desserts such as Bavarian creams or baked custards, they share the stage with components that carry more weight, and a weighty wine, such as a noble late harvest, makes a good match. However, when berries are used to decorate a chocolate dessert, match the wine to the chocolate and go for port; the berries are only adding an accent to the dish.

Deciduous fruit When served fresh and on their own, deciduous fruits have an affinity for special late harvest and sweet sparkling wines. If the fruit is poached with the addition of sugar or honey, or has been canned or preserved in syrup, a noble late harvest is a very good choice, especially with quinces and apricots, as these have a high level of acidity that latches onto the marked acidity of a noble late harvest. Stick to noble late harvest when poached fruit is served with custard or fresh cream but, if it is served with ice cream, then change your tune. See **Ice creams**, page 263.

Citrus and tropical fruit Citrus fruits and tropical fruits are in their element when served with a noble late harvest. They are not happy with port or sweet sherries but, when accompanied by caramel in any form, or sweet spices, such as cinnamon and nutmeg, they leap at a red muscadel with its own citrussy overtones. Do chill it a bit, though, especially if the fruit is served chilled on a summer's day.

See also **Fresh fruit**, page 262.

DRIED FRUIT-BASED DESSERTS

This is the time to bring out the fortified wines, especially tawny ports and sweet sherries. An old brown sherry is particularly good with that old-fashioned boarding school favourite, stewed mixed dried fruit and custard. To give it a modern twist, add a tot or two of brandy to the poaching liquid, omit the custard and serve it with a cream-based liqueur, such as Cape Velvet. Alternatively, double up on the custard and go for a noble late harvest.

Mince pies and Christmas pudding are very well matched with red muscadels, but tawny ports are equally good. When served with thick cream, brandy butter or brandy sauce, you can add noble late harvest to your list of options, provided it is in the richest noble late harvest style. See **Noble late harvest**, pages 78–80.

CREAMY OR EGG-BASED DESSERTS

The creamy textures of these desserts demand viscous wines, and noble late harvest rises to the occasion. Not all creamy desserts are equally rich, so match their weight to the weight of the wine. For instance, a creamy mousse or crème caramel, neither of which are as weighty as a crème brûlée, will be happy with a special late harvest or sweet sparkling wine, especially if fresh fruit is used to decorate the dessert.

With heavy, rich cream and egg-based desserts, full of vanilla or sweet spices, a mature brandy is an excellent option (for a seasoned brandy drinker); the faint-hearted should stick to noble late harvest or a liqueur with a complementary flavour, such as Grand Marnier (for citrus) or Frangelico (for nuts).

CHOCOLATE, COFFEE, FUDGE AND TOFFEE DESSERTS

Fortified wines, such as the 'dark' dessert wines – red muscadel, jerepigo, port and old brown sherry – are just the thing to pair with the richest chocolate, coffee, fudge or toffee creations. A full cream sherry or tawny port that has been well-aged in wood will be particularly good with toffee or butterscotch desserts, while red muscadel is brilliant with an orange and chocolate combination.

Liqueurs, particularly orange, naartjie and mint-flavoured ones, are also excellent partners with chocolate desserts, provided you like the contrasting flavours.

Unfortified, upfront fruity wines, such as noble late harvests, have a hard time standing up to chocolate desserts. However, if the dessert contains fruit with an acidic edge, the acidity of the fruit will latch onto the natural acidity of the noble late harvest. This is a risky pairing, though, as chocolate 'flattens' wine to varying degrees.

With chocolate and chocolate-based desserts, it is best to avoid all sparkling wines and special late harvests, especially when the latter are young. If you are serving chocolate in place of dessert, take a leap of faith and try the combination of top-quality milk chocolate and top-quality brandy. Dark, bitter chocolate prefers something sweeter, such as a ruby port. Dark chocolate also goes with noble late harvest, as the sweetness of the wine and its good acidity are able to counterbalance the bitterness of the chocolate.

The French have a solution for the problem of matching wine with chocolate. They make port-like wines, such as Maury, from Grenache Noir, which match chocolate delectably. This comes as no surprise – it is simply a matter of matching chocolate with chocolate.

NUTTY DESSERTS

Nut-based desserts go well with fortified wines, such as red muscadel and cream sherry, and are particularly good with nut-flavoured liqueurs, such as Frangelico (hazelnut) and Amaretto (almond). Tawny ports also have their own nutty character that echoes these desserts. While almond-flavoured liqueur served with an almond-flavoured tart may sound like too much of a good thing, it is astounding how the flavours meld. However, a liqueur with a contrasting flavour, such as chocolate, could add a welcome flavour dimension.

An A–Z of popular desserts and their wines

Some of the most popular South African desserts are listed alphabetically in this section.

APPLE PIE/STRUDEL/BAKED APPLES

Apple pie and strudel, with a hint of cinnamon or cloves and, perhaps, some sultanas or raisins, is often served with custard or thick cream, as are baked apples. A noble late harvest, but especially one made from Chenin Blanc, Sauvignon Blanc or Weisser Riesling, will be a success with any apple dessert. If you have a heavy hand with the cinnamon, a noble late harvest made from Gewürztraminer is even better, as the grape's spicy overtone is not lost when the wine is nobly rotted. If your dessert is not overly sweet, a late or special late harvest might have a matching level of sweetness.

BAKED ALASKA

The French call this dessert an 'omelette surprise' or 'Norwegian omelette' (*omelette à la Norvégienne*), while the Brits call it 'Mount Vesuvius' or by its American name, 'baked Alaska'. It was very popular in the 1960s and 70s, when it was often brought to the table topped with a lit sparkler. This remarkable dessert, with its centre of cold fruit and ice cream on a sponge base surrounded by a hot meringue crust that is browned in the oven, is a gastronomic paradox – a ball of ice in a piping hot casing... When it comes to wine, it is also a head-scratcher; to what do you match the wine? The fruit, the meringue, or the **ice cream** (which in itself presents a problem, *see page 263*). No wine will be happy with so many textures, flavours and temperatures, but try a hanepoot, white muscadel or white port, all well chilled, of course.

BAVAROIS (Bavarian cream)

Smooth and creamy, rich and decorative, these cold, set desserts have a custard base, enriched with thick cream and flavoured with coffee, caramel, chocolate or fruit such as apricots, berries or pineapple. When fruit-flavoured, a special late harvest is just the thing (a noble late harvest is best with citrus flavours). With coffee, caramel and chocolate flavours, a white muscadel or white port work well.

BERRIES AND CREAM/ICE CREAM

Fresh, hulled berries, with a light dusting of castor sugar and lashings of whipped cream, are a great summer favourite. Special late harvest or sweet sparkling wines are good accompaniments but, if **ice cream** replaces the cream, the wine suffers (*see page 263*).

It may seem like a novel idea, but serving Pinot Noir with a bowl of ripe, fresh **strawberries** or **raspberries** is delicious, but there is a rider to this; it only works when no sugar or cream are added and when the berries are fully ripe. Previously in-vogue ways of serving strawberries have included freshly ground black pepper and, more recently, drizzlings of balsamic vinegar. These fashions should not change the choice of special late harvest or sweet sparkling wine as an accompanying wine. The pepper enhances both the food and the wine flavours, while balsamic vinegar with sugar intensifies what is already in the strawberries, namely sweetness and acidity.

BREAD AND BUTTER PUDDING

Making something of a comeback, this dessert of sliced buttered bread, layered with raisins or sultanas and almonds, and with a subtle hint of orange, is baked in custard. It simply cries out for noble late harvest. If you have a light hand with the sugar, a special late harvest will have the exact weight. The wine matches remain the same if you prefer a more contemporary approach, swopping plain bread for brioche, panettone or raisin loaf.

CAKES/GÂTEAUX

Cakes (or *gâteaux*, as they are known in French) are often served as a dessert. They may be rather plain or very elaborate.

Black Forest cherry cake This is a rich combination of chocolate cake, black cherries and kirsch (cherry liqueur) with decadent amounts of cream. Pair your *Schwarzwalder kirschtorte* with a noble late harvest in the richest of styles, or a red muscadel. For a combination that reveals a bit of your bohemian nature, serve a well-chilled sparkling Shiraz, which gives a 'bubbly' contrast, but has enough sweet fruit to hold its own against so much voluptuousness.

Cream cake A simple sponge cake filled and topped with whipped cream will be delicious with either a special late harvest or a sweet sparkling wine.

Chocolate cake Whether finished with a dusting of icing sugar or a butter icing, serve with a fortified dessert wine, such as a red muscadel. The muscadel may overpower a light chocolate cake, but it is always better to have too heavy a wine with cake than too light.

Fruit cake See **Fruit cake**, page 263.

Orange or lemon cake Serve with a noble late harvest, particularly one made from Chenin or Sauvignon Blanc.

Panettone This light Italian yeast cake, flavoured with sultanas and candied citrus peel, is traditionally eaten at Easter and Christmas. A special late harvest has just the right weight for it.

Pithiviers A rich almond cream (frangipane) is spread on a single layer of puff pastry or used to sandwich two layers together. You won't go wrong with a noble late harvest.

Sachertorte This rich Austrian chocolate cake, coated with chocolate fondant, is normally served with whipped cream. Reach for a red muscadel, the key to chocolate.

Savarin/rum baba Generally, a yeast cake baked in a ring mould, soaked in flavoured syrup and decorated with fruit and cream, is called a savarin. A version incorporating currants and sultanas and soaked with rum-flavoured syrup is known as a rum baba. Choose a fortified dessert wine, such as red muscadel, for either version.

CAPE BRANDY PUDDING (tipsy tart)

The date and nut sponge is soaked in a buttery, brandy-flavoured syrup when it comes out of the oven, and usually served with pouring or whipped cream or custard. If brandy is not your thing, reach for a fortified wine, such as a port or a red muscadel.

CARAMELIZED ORANGES

Caramelized oranges, or sliced oranges in a caramel sauce, require a wine with good acidity. A special late harvest, particularly made from Chenin Blanc, or a lighter-styled noble late harvest made from Weisser Riesling, would be ideal. An orange- or naartjie-flavoured liqueur may sound like too much of a good thing, but their flavours are indisputably harmonious.

CHEESECAKE

There are two types of cheesecake: baked and 'fridge'. Both are made with cream and cottage or Ricotta cheese, with or without the addition of eggs and/or other flavourings.

Baked cheesecake, with its pastry crust, is quite plainly flavoured. Match this rich, dense dessert with a noble late harvest.

'Fridge' cheesecake has a biscuit base and is usually set with gelatine. When plainly flavoured, it is often fruit-topped and pairs well with a special late harvest. However, the cheese mixture can be flavoured with dark, milk or white chocolate, or with coffee. For most 'fridge' cheesecakes, stick to special late harvest. If flavoured with lemon or orange, opt for noble late harvest, as its good acidity gives the cheesecake another dimension, just as the citrus flavours do.

CHOCOLATE BROWNIES

The ever-popular chocolate brownies, with their pecan nuts and fudge-icing topping, make a great dessert when served with a dollop of cream or ice cream. A red muscadel, the food and wine pairer's key to all chocolate desserts, is the obvious choice, but most 'dark', fortified wines would be good partners too.

CHOCOLATE MOUSSE

The classic chocolate mousse consists of dark chocolate, eggs and sugar. A richer version includes butter and perhaps a 'flavour booster' such as a splash of strong black coffee, or a dash of brandy or rum. A 'dark', fortified wine, such as red muscadel, is the ideal choice for this decadent dessert. Depending on the added flavours, a snifter of brandy or rum would not go amiss, and neither would an orange- or naartjie-flavoured liqueur.

CHRISTMAS PUDDING

Christmas pudding, laden with dried fruit, is traditionally served with brandy butter, brandy sauce, custard or cream. Although 'dark' fortified wines, such as ruby or tawny port, muscadel or old brown sherry, work with Christmas pudding, after a lengthy, rich meal, we often need a wine to refresh the palate. No wonder sparkling wines are often served at this stage. However, even the sweetest bubblies are seldom sweet enough for Christmas pudding. A much better choice is a well-chilled noble late harvest, whose good acidity does work with Christmas pudding, especially when it is served with cream or custard. Another ideal companion is a splash of brandy or a liqueur of your choice (do consider a ginger-flavoured one). South Africans often serve ice cream with this pudding, as with everything else! Ice cream is hard on any wine but it soon melts on a hot Christmas pudding and becomes more like a cream sauce, which does not bully the wine as much.

CRÈME BRÛLÉE

The French name for this desert translates as 'burnt cream', but that doesn't adequately describe these individual rich custards, made with thick cream and egg yolks and flavoured with a hint of vanilla, then baked until firm before being topped with sugar that is caramelized by grilling or blow-torching. A variation is to place fresh fruit, such as grapes, raspberries or strawberries, at the base of the dish before pouring over the custard and baking. This is definitely noble late harvest time, especially if fruit is present. Herb-infused crème brûlée is very voguish at the moment, but don't let this change your choice of wine. Remember that you need to match not only flavour, but also weight and degree of sweetness, and these will not change, even if the crème brûlée is infused with herbs.

CRÈME CARAMEL

This combination of a smooth, creamy egg custard and golden caramel sauce, deserves a special late harvest, which has the exact weight to match it. Don't be tempted to reach for a noble late harvest, as it will overpower this ever-popular dessert.

CRÊPES SUZETTE

Orange-flavoured crêpes (pancakes) are heated in butter, orange and lemon juice, sugar and an orange liqueur, traditionally Grand Marnier, and then flamed with brandy or orange liqueur before serving. The alcohol in the sauce steers us towards fortified wines. Red muscadel and old brown sherry love flambé aromas, or simply drink a glass of the same orange liqueur you used in the preparation of the sauce. This may seem like a citrus overload, but it is merely an extension of what you are already eating. The blandness of the pancake is a platform to showcase both the sauce and the liqueur. A seasoned brandy drinker might like to reach for a quality brandy with good caramel flavours.

A noble late harvest, with its citrus profile, should highlight the orange flavours of this dessert, but the wine is likely to be flattened by the alcohol present in the sauce.

FLOATING ISLANDS

Floating islands (île flottante) is an appropriate name for this dessert of soft meringue 'floating' in a sea of custard. The meringue is traditionally drizzled with caramel syrup or decorated with spun sugar.

A similar dessert, snow eggs (oeufs à la neige), has small poached meringues served on custard. Both versions are simply splendid with a noble late harvest.

FOOLS

A cold dessert of puréed fruit, whipped cream or custard and, often, additional flavourings. An apple fool may have a hint of cinnamon, a mango fool a hint of lemon, and a strawberry fool a splash of dry white wine. You need some good balancing acidity and a matching level of sweetness, as these desserts are rather sweet, but with an acidic sting in the tail. Choose a noble late harvest, which has these characteristics, or sweet sparkling wine.

FRESH FRUIT

As fresh fruit is so freely available in South Africa, we often prepare fresh fruit in some form or another as a dessert. We grew up with mixed **fruit salads** and, more recently, 'designer' **fruit platters** have appeared where the fruit is fanned, stacked, spiked and artistically arranged before being powdered and puffed with icing sugar. Fruit platters and salads vary greatly, depending on the fruit used. They may be dressed with fruit juice, or with a simple sugar and water syrup, all with different sweetness levels, but acidity and sweetness will always be present to varying degrees.

Choose a wine with good acidity, such as a Weisser Riesling or Chenin Blanc, or climb the steps of sweetness – from late harvest to special late and even noble late harvest – to find a wine that has the same level of sweetness as the dish. An alternative is a sweet sparkling wine. There is something enchanting about fruit and bubbles, provided the sweetness level of the fruit and the wine is in harmony.

The sparkler will not even blink an eye when the fruit is covered in cream. When fruit salad is served with ice cream, on the other hand, the ice cream will dominate, removing every nuance and fine characteristic of the wine and pushing the fruit into the background.

See also **ice creams**, below.

FRUIT CAKE

A dark, rich, moist cake, packed with dried fruit, cherries and nuts, flavoured with spices and brandy, and traditionally covered with marzipan and icing, often appears as a **Christmas** or **wedding** cake. A nutty, tawny port, ruby port or old brown sherry are the best choices.

FRUIT TARTS AND FLANS

Berries or poached deciduous fruit, such as pears or apples, are layered on a custard cream filling in a pre-baked pastry case. Unexpectedly, fruit flans are quite tricky to match as their sweetness levels hover between that of special and noble late harvest wines, matching neither. The acidity level of the chosen fruit contributes to this quandary. Only trial and error can identify the sweetness level of a wine to serve with your signature flan. If it is very sweet, you could consider a hanepoot with its lively, honeyed fruit flavours. At the other end of the spectrum, a late harvest offers the balancing sweetness level for tart tarts, such as an apricot one.

HALVA

Appearing across the Middle East, Central and South Asia, and the Balkans, this relatively dense confection is either semolina- or tahini-based and is sweetened with sugar or honey. It often includes pistachio nuts. Predictably, it is the 'dark' fortified wines that perform well here, so reach for a nutty tawny port, an old brown sherry or a red muscadel.

ICE CREAMS AND SORBETS

Quality **ice cream** is based on a rich egg custard mixture and the flavourings vary from plain vanilla to fresh fruits, nuts or more robust flavours such as rum and raisin or chocolate. Sorbets are ices made without cream or milk (but sometimes include egg whites) and are mostly fruit-flavoured. Less expensive ice creams do not have the richness of the home-made or 'luxury' versions. All these frozen desserts are exceedingly difficult to pair with wine. You might think that ice cream's creamy texture would pair well with the same wines that go with cream- and custard-based desserts, but it is the temperature that is the key. Coldness literally anaesthetises the taste buds, reducing their ability to function. When it comes to frozen desserts, the more you eat, the more numb the mouth becomes, and wine is a casualty. It is not as if wine and ice cream are unhappy with each other, it is just that, when challenged by extreme coldness, wine 'disappears' and you are only aware of some form of liquid passing by.

The solution is to head for the old dessert standbys: red or white muscadel and jerepigo, served chilled in midsummer. They remain intact in the face of this severe temperature onslaught and work even better if you splash some over the ice cream. A food and wine pairer may consider this cheating as you are then pairing wine with wine rather than with ice cream, but if it works, why not? Pair chocolate ice cream with a full cream or old brown sherry. For that ubiquitous standby, ice cream with chocolate sauce, stick with red muscadel or jerepigo.

However, when it comes to **sorbet** and wine, the combination of frozen fruit and alcohol can stop you in your tracks, leaving an unpleasant taste in your mouth, which is amplified when the sorbet does not contain any egg white or is made in a granita style (with a coarse, icicle-like texture).

'INSTANT' PUDDINGS

Open a packet, add milk, beat and eat. Full marks for convenience. Irrespective of the flavour of these packet versions or those that come ready mixed in tubs, grab a glass of special late harvest, preferably straight from the box for maximum convenience.

LEMON MERINGUE PIE

This melt-in-the-mouth pie, with its deliciously tangy lemon curd filling and frothy meringue topping, has been a favourite for years. A special late harvest wine is just the thing, especially when produced from Chenin Blanc, which has good natural acidity. When the filling is made with condensed milk, as it often is in South Africa, the sweetness level increases significantly. A noble late harvest, irrespective of the grape used, rises to the occasion.

LEMON TART

As can be expected, a simple lemon tart needs a wine with good acidity. Reach for a noble late harvest. If the tart has a low sweetness level, a special late harvest will provide the desired balance.

MALVA PUDDING

This delicious and indulgent local favourite is essentially a rather homely, baked, cake-like pudding, with a hint of the apricot jam that flavours it and a pleasing, almost caramelly overtone. It is soaked in a rich cream sauce when it comes out of the oven and is often served with a drizzle of extra cream or dollop of vanilla ice cream. Only the sweetest of wines won't taste thin and sour in the presence of this dessert and, once again, muscadel comes to the rescue (it will even take care of the ice cream!). If served without ice cream, a full cream sherry works just as well.

MILK TART (melktert)

Pair this heritage tart, with its light dusting of cinnamon, with a special late harvest, a glass of hanepoot or a white port.

MINCE PIES

These little pies, with their filling of spicy fruit-based mincemeat, are not only served with coffee or tea at Christmas, but also as a hassle-free dessert with a dollop of whipped cream. Mince pies are very well matched with red muscadels, tawny or ruby ports and full cream sherries.

MOUSSES

Mousses are made from an egg and sugar base, often enriched with cream and lightened with beaten egg white, and set with gelatine. Flavourings include fruit such as apricot, orange, lemon, pineapple or berries, but also chocolate, coffee or whatever. These light desserts pair very well with special late harvest and sweet sparkling wines. When referring here to a 'light' chocolate-flavoured mousse, we do not mean the chocoholic's favourite dessert, 'chocolate mousse', which is rich and dense. The weights of these two 'mousses' are poles apart and the choice of wine reflects this clearly.

See also **Chocolate mousse**, page 260.

PANNA COTTA

Panna cotta or 'cooked cream' is a Tuscan dish that is now very much in vogue worldwide. Cream and sugar is set with a touch of gelatine and served with a caramel sauce or fresh berries. A special late harvest or sweet sparkling wine (especially when fresh berries are used as a garnish) have the exact sweetness levels we are looking for to accompany this light dessert.

PAVLOVA

This dessert, believed to have been named after the famed Russian ballet dancer, Ánna Pávlova, who toured Australia and New Zealand in the 1920s, is now an important dish in the national cuisines of both countries. As cornflour and vinegar are added to the meringue mixture, the outside shell of the Pavlova is crisp and crunchy, while the interior remains soft and moist. This marshmallow-like inside is thus completely different from that normally associated with meringue, which is crisp throughout. Pavlova is traditionally topped with whipped cream and fresh fruit, which leads us to richness, acidity and sweetness. First choice is a noble late harvest, which will echo all three tastes, but a sweet sparkling wine is also delightful, as it is very happy in the company of the fresh fruit.

PEACH MELBA

The famous French chef, Auguste Escoffier, invented this dessert at London's Savoy Hotel in the early 1890s, to honour the visiting Australian soprano, Dame Nellie Melba. It combines peaches and vanilla ice cream with a raspberry sauce. According to rumour, Nellie Melba loved ice cream, but did not dare eat it often, believing it would affect her voice. So, Escoffier created peach Melba, in which the ice cream, being only one element in a whole, would not be as cold and thus not so threatening to her vocal cords. A special late harvest, although it is also threatened by the coldness of the ice cream, has the right weight and sweetness for this dessert. Thus Escoffier unknowingly solved two problems at the same time, by rescuing both vocal chords and wine. *See also* **ice creams**, page 263.

PEARS BELLE HÉLÈNE

This 19th century French dessert is a combination of pears, vanilla ice cream and a garnish of hot chocolate sauce. Chocolate and ice cream are both wine-unfriendly, but the innocuous pear becomes a catalyst and saves the day, steering us away from the dark fortified wines that inevitably come to the rescue with chocolate or ice cream desserts. A noble late harvest will be superb with this dessert.

PEARS IN RED WINE

In this classic French dessert, pears are poached in a light sugar syrup, made with red wine, cinnamon and lemon, until they are tender and have taken on a beautiful red colour. This is a potential tripwire for pairing, as the inclination is to assume that, because red wine was used for poaching, it will be a good accompaniment. But the wine in the poaching liquid underwent a change when sugar was added and it was reduced. If you serve the pears on their own, a medium cream sherry has just the right level of sweetness but, if you offer cream or a creamy custard with them, switch to a ruby port or red muscadel.

PECAN PIE

This southern USA speciality, sometimes called 'New Orleans pecan pie', is popular in South Africa. Pair this sticky, rich and nutty dessert with a 'dark' fortified wine, such as a tawny port, full cream or old brown sherry, or a red muscadel.

PEPPERMINT TART

This tart, made with boiled condensed milk (caramel), whipped non-dairy 'cream' and flavoured with grated Peppermint Crisp chocolate, is a perennial 'old school' favourite. It pairs wonderfully with coffee-flavoured liqueurs, especially with Tia Maria, but a coconut-flavoured one will also be delightful. If you're madly into mint, you may opt for a mint-flavoured liqueur (crème de menthe), but be prepared for an instant peppermint overload!

PROFITEROLES AND CROQUEMBOUCHE

Profiteroles are small choux pastry buns filled with whipped cream and topped with a rich, velvety chocolate sauce. They are similar to their tea-time version, chocolate eclairs. In croquembouche, the choux buns are filled with crème pâtissière, covered in caramel and stacked into a tower on a shortcake base. For a more elaborate version (sometimes chosen as a wedding cake), the tower is decorated with a delicate web of fine spun sugar. White muscadel is a very good choice for either version, but a red muscadel will also be very accommodating, especially with profiteroles and their hint of chocolate. A brilliant alternative is sweet sparkling wine, as bubbles simply adore choux pastry.

RHUBARB

Whether stewed and served with custard or baked into a pie or crumble, the tart-sweet rhubarb dominates and needs to be matched with a wine of marked acidity and sweetness. Noble late harvest works beautifully, especially one made from Chenin or Sauvignon Blanc.

SORBET

See **Ice creams**, page 263.

SOUFFLÉS

Sweet soufflés can be either hot or cold. However, a **cold soufflé** is not really a soufflé at all, but a mousse of egg, sugar and cream. It acquires its name simply because it is set in a soufflé dish and moulded to stand above the rim, to look like a soufflé that has risen in the oven. See **Mousses**, page 265.

Hot, sweet soufflés, on the other hand, are egg-based and must be eaten the moment they come out of the oven. Typical flavourings include chocolate, orange or lemon. These light desserts are very happy with special late harvests. Even a chocolate soufflé remains special late harvest's territory, as the chocolate flavouring is quite tame and does not result in the usual havoc that chocolate can wreak on a wine.

STEAMED PUDDINGS

A light, steamed sponge can have some of the flavouring added to the bottom of the pudding basin before steaming, or be served separately. Golden syrup is a firm favourite, but ginger and jams, such as apricot, fig or berry, are also popular. A tangier version uses lemon curd, with a sweet lemon sauce as the accompaniment. Noble late harvest is an excellent choice for all, as steamed puddings are often served with custard or cream. A boozier version, with a brandy sauce on the side, or a chocolate steamed pudding, with extra chocolate sauce, are happier with a red muscadel.

STICKY TOFFEE PUDDING

This British classic is a favourite in South Africa. A date and nut sponge is soaked with a toffee sauce, made of cream, butter and dark brown sugar, when it comes out of the oven. Variations on the theme include **Cape brandy**, **malva**, and **vinegar pudding**. They all pair with the same dark fortified wines, such as port, red muscadel, jerepigo and sweet sherries.

STRAWBERRIES (OR RASPBERRIES) AND CREAM

See **Berries and cream/ice cream**, page 258.

TARTE TATIN

Tarte demoiselles Tatin is a French upside-down apple tart. It was named after the proprietors of the hotel that made it famous in the 19th century, *les demoiselles Tatin*, the misses Tatin. Crisp, light pastry is placed on top of sliced, caramelized apples, then reversed after baking. This now voguish dessert simply cries out for a noble late harvest, especially one made from Chenin Blanc, which has a special affinity for anything appley. If the tart is not too sweet, a special late harvest also works well.

TIRAMISU

'Tira mi su' means 'pick me up' in Italian, but a more idiomatic translation would be 'cheer me up'. It is made of lady or sponge finger biscuits dipped in a mixture of strong coffee and brandy or a sweet wine, layered with a whipped mixture of eggs, mascarpone and sugar, and dusted with cocoa powder or grated chocolate. A tot of brandy adds even more cheer, but if you're not quite that low, a glass of noble late harvest would also do the picking up.

TRIFLE

Light sponge cake laced with sherry, covered with fruit, nuts and creamy custard, topped with lashings of whipped cream, has long been a South African favourite. At Christmas, sherry trifle is often decorated with angelica and glacé cherries to echo the traditional yuletide colours of red and green. One suspects that, having used sherry in the trifle, a glass of the same sherry would be just the thing to accompany the dessert, but you may find this a bit overwhelming as it competes with the custard, cream and fruit. Our suggestion is to have a *soupçon* (or more) of brandy, if you are feeling brave! The rest can get by just fine with hanepoot, white muscadel or a noble late harvest.

VACHERIN

Choose a special late harvest with upfront fruit flavours for these layers of nutty meringue sandwiched together with whipped cream and fresh fruit.

ZABAGLIONE (zabaione)

This Italian dessert is commonly spelled 'zabaglione' although the modern Italian spelling is 'zabaione' and, when a menu is written in French, 'sabayon'. However you spell it, it remains a frothy creation made by combining egg yolks, sugar and a sweet wine. In Italy, they make it with marsala, but white muscadel would be more common in South Africa. Either that same white muscadel or a hanepoot would be excellent choices to drink with zabaglione, but a sweet sparkling wine is even better, as the lightness of the bubbly echoes the sweet nothingness of the dessert.

Cheeses and cheeseboards

Where does the myth that cheese and wine are good companions come from? We suspect that the perfect partnerships that exist between, say, Roquefort and noble late harvest wines, or goat's-milk cheese (Chevin) and Sauvignon Blanc, made us believe that all cheeses go well with most wines. They don't. In fact, cheese is one of the trickiest foods to match with wine.

But why are we surprised? Many cheeses have a strong taste and are pungently aromatic; they can have a high fat, salt or acid content, and some have a sticky texture that coats the taste buds. All these challenging features spell 'trouble' when it comes to pairing cheese with wine. What makes matters worse is that cheeses differ from cheese-maker to cheese-maker. A lot also depends on whether they are 'young' or 'old', as many cheeses take on a different personality when matured; for example, a young Gouda is poles apart in flavour, texture and aroma from a matured one. To crown it all, the tried and tested principle of matching the weight of the food to the weight of the wine no longer applies when it comes to cheese; alas, the theory of pairing a 'big' cheese with a 'big' wine flops more often than it succeeds. Head for the hills if someone pours you a full-bodied, powerhouse Cabernet Sauvignon to drink with a wedge of Roquefort; to put it rather mildly, this is not a pleasant match. Contrary to popular belief, white wine performs best with cheese. And, generally speaking, it is the sweeter white wines that make the best matches.

In Old World countries, with their long history of winemaking and their culture of drinking wine with food, cheese and wine *are* looked upon as bedfellows. Italians or Spaniards wouldn't dream of serving cheese without an accompanying glass of wine, while the French have very interesting, sometimes very definite, ideas of which cheeses match which wines. Of course, these pairings are mostly based on regional wines matching regional foods. However, many cheeses come from areas where no wine is made, and regional matches are not always the best ones.

In the 1970s, when cheese and wine parties were popular in South Africa (and other countries without a tradition of drinking wine with food), it was semi-sweet white wines (the order of the day at the time) that led us to believe that wine and cheese were natural partners. For most of us, this was our introduction to matching food and wine. Unsurprisingly, though, once sweet wines started to wane in popularity, the cheese and wine party started to die out. But South Africans still love a glass of wine with cheese, even if they are not natural 'taste' partners. And why not? The trick is knowing *which* wine to serve with *which* cheese. Reading the back labels on wine bottles is usually no help: the suggestion 'serve with cheese' leaves unanswered the crucial question of 'which cheese?'.

Key points to note when pairing cheese and wine

- **Acidity** Cheese and wine both have acidity. When you serve a cheese with pronounced acidity, such as goat's-milk cheese (Chevin), match it with a wine of equally firm acidity, such as a Sauvignon Blanc, Chenin Blanc or Sangiovese.
- **Texture** Consider the texture of the cheese and then match or contrast it to the wine. For instance, match a smooth, creamy textured cheese with a full-bodied, velvety Chardonnay, Semillon or Viognier. Or, for contrast, pair it with the exact opposite – a palate-cleansing, dry sparkling wine that will highlight the texture of the cheese.
- **Protect the wine** Whether you are choosing a wine to accompany a cheese, or selecting a cheese to serve with a favourite wine, the objective is the same: to let 'no harm' come to the wine. A wine should taste just as good with cheese as it does on its own. When we talk about a successful cheese and wine match, we are actually saying that the cheese did not subtract from our enjoyment of the wine. Cheese is the dominant taste element, so we seldom have to think about how a wine will affect a cheese.
- **Tannin** Because cheese objects to the tannins in red wine, wines with soft tannins are the most successful matches. But don't haul out your carefully matured vinous treasures, as they will be overwhelmed by the complex flavours of most cheeses. Save your best wines for another day (or serve them earlier in the meal). If you want to serve cheese with a red wine that has strong tannins, opt for hard cow's-milk cheeses, provided they are not too strong in flavour, too salty, or matured for months on end. Salt emphasizes tannins and the wine will taste bitter.
- **Blue cheese** The veins of mould in blue cheeses strip many dry white and red wines of their fruit. A sweet wine is almost always a better choice. The saltier and more pungent the cheese, the sweeter and richer the wine should be. Sparkling wines stand up well to many blue cheeses, which seems quite surprising, until you remember the theory of matching acidity with acidity!
- **Mild cheese** There are some mild cheeses, such as Emmenthal, Edam, Caerphilly or Jarlsberg, which you may think should pose

no threat to wine, that are quite pernickety and not at all easy to match to wine.

- **Soft cheese** Soft cheeses made in the style of a Camembert or Pont l'Evêque are the trickiest to match, especially when they have matured. For the sake of the wine, serve them before they become too runny and pungent!

- **Sweet accompaniments** A well-made cheese needs no accompaniment to enhance it. It is easy to understand, though, why we often serve cheese with green fig or watermelon preserve, dried or crystallized fruits, fresh grapes or sweet relishes. Salty food loves sweetness, which is why it is a good match with sweet wines. When cheese is served with sweet accompaniments, you need to match sweetness with sweetness, as the cheese is no longer the dominant factor in determining the wine choice. Consider serving a brilliant cheese without accompaniments, letting both the cheese and the wine speak for themselves.

- **Bread and biscuits** Many people prefer eating cheese, especially soft, creamy cheeses or a pungent blue, with biscuits or bread. Choose unsalted, unflavoured biscuits that will not interfere with the taste of the cheese or the wine. You can't go wrong with a plain baguette or a non-sourdough loaf made simply of flour (brown or white), yeast, water and salt. Breads containing herbs, olives, sun-dried tomatoes, sugar, added fats and other embellishments are not good choices. There is one exception, though: walnut bread with Camembert, served with a glass of nutty Chardonnay.

- **Temperature** Cheese always tastes best with wine when the cheese is served at room temperature. When the cheese is too cold, its flavours are muted and cannot latch onto the flavours of the wine. A small wedge requires about an hour to reach room temperature after you have taken it out of the fridge; larger pieces need more time.

- **Cheese in cooking** Pairing wine with cheese in cooked dishes is no problem at all. In fact, cheese soufflés are a very good way to show off your finest red and white wines.

Matching cheese and wine

Very few cheeses in the world are sure of their ancestry, or even their early associations. In this alphabetical list, we indicate under 'origin' which country is most often associated with a particular cheese, but this does not mean that the one you buy under that name is an import. Many locally produced cheeses are named for the style in which they are made, for example: 'Cheddar' (origin: England) or 'Gorgonzola' (origin: Italy). In South Africa, therefore, the chances are that your piece of 'camembert' comes from KwaZulu-Natal and not from the place in France where it was (probably) first made.

In the past, South Africans' choice of cheese was very limited, but now we are spoilt for choice. Not only is a greater number of imported cheeses available, but the budding cheese-making cottage industry is growing by leaps and bounds, giving us many local versions of the world's best-known cheeses, as well as their own new creations. The descriptions below are based on the classic styles of cheeses, but cheeses are never exactly the same. If the Cheddar you bought does not fit the description below, bear in mind that cheese will differ from one purchase to the next, varying as they do in age, condition and quality. A 'factory' cheese simply does not have the distinctive taste or texture of the hand-crafted version. But then, like wine, cheese doesn't have to be the rarest or most expensive to be enjoyed to the full.

APPENZELL(ER) [APP-en-zell-(er)]

Hard cow's-milk cheese; origin: Switzerland.
This is a compelling cheese, smooth and dense, with aromas of browned butter, nuts, spice and a touch of the barnyard. It is worth looking out for because, although not as well known or freely available as Switzerland's Emmenthal or Gruyère, it is a worthy member of this country's great cheese triumvirate. When young, it is butter-coloured, turning a light gold as it matures. The best way to enjoy Appenzeller is to shave it thinly and let it melt on your tongue, releasing sweet-spice flavours galore. It is such a good match with Shiraz that you would suspect Appenzeller was created for it, but it has too long a lineage – dating back to the time of Charlemagne, well before Shiraz was paired with anything in that part of the world! Pinotage is also good with it, and a dry (fino) sherry complements the nutty flavours of the cheese.

APPLEWOOD

See **Smoked cheeses**, page 296.

ASIAGO [ahz-YAH-goh]

Hard cow's-milk cheese; origin: Italy.

A butter-coloured, full-cream cheese with a semi-firm paste and grassy, fruity, nutty and butterscotch aromas. South African-made Asiago usually hits the supermarket shelves at medium maturity (aged between eight and nine months), so expect a cheese that dissolves easily in the mouth, leaving a distinct, high-acid tang on the finish. Serve with full-bodied, grassy Sauvignon Blanc, Pinot Gris/ Pinot Grigio or Chenin Blanc, or an unwooded cool-climate Semillon or Chardonnay that shows some acidity. Among the reds, look to Sangiovese, Cinsaut, a quaffable Pinotage or Merlot. If you feel like pushing out the boat, a top-notch Pinot Noir matches it to a T.

BEAUFORT [BOW-for or BOW-furt]

Hard cow's-milk cheese; origin: France.

Inside the hard rind is a firm, deep-yellow paste that may glisten with fat at room temperature. It has a velvety texture, similar to matured Cheddar, with a few tiny protein crystals and aromas of browned butter, roast meats and nuts. As its flavour is so concentrated, it is best to shave it thinly with a cheese plane and let the slices melt in your mouth. Beaufort's sweet finish and buttery texture calls for a white wine with some viscosity: Viognier, a creamy, wooded Chardonnay or Semillon, or an off-dry Weisser Riesling are all excellent partners. A medium cream sherry will happily echo the cheese's nutty notes. Beaufort also tastes wonderful with soft-centred Cabernet Sauvignon or Bordeaux blends.

BEL PAESE [bel pah-EH-seh]

Soft cow's-milk cheese; origin: Italy.

An ivory-coloured cheese mostly used for spreading. Although it is primarily a table cheese, its fatness makes it good for melting and it can be used instead of fresh Mozzarella in cooking. The name, which means 'beautiful country', was used when referring to Italy in Dante's *Inferno* and in a sonnet by Petrarch – which is not only a good topic when making small talk over Bel Paese on water biscuits, but gives the cheese a bit of flair; there's nothing like poetry to make us look at a cream cheese differently! The delicate, buttery flavour and soft, yielding texture calls for a white wine, and an unwooded Chardonnay has just the right weight. Most red wines, even the soft-centred ones, are too heavy for Bel Paese, but Sangiovese and Cinsaut will come to the rescue of the committed red-wine drinker.

BLUE CHEESE

Blue cheeses are not all alike, and the differences between them can be so subtle you may not easily be able to tell one from another. However, differences do exist, and they are the reason why Roquefort may be happy with a particular wine while Stilton may not. As you get to know the blue cheeses, the distinctions between them and the reasons for their varying wine partners will become apparent.

See entries for **Bleu d'Auvergne, Danish Blue, Gorgonzola, Roquefort** and **Stilton**, below.

BLEU D'AUVERGNE [bleu do-VER-nyeh]

Blue cheese from cow's milk; origin: France.
Bleu d'Auvergne, probably the 'second best-known' French blue cheese, is creamier and less salty than Roquefort, its more famous neighbour in the Auvergne region. The blue veining adds a strong, pungent flavour, call it a steel fist in a velvet glove, but although it may be robust, even spicy, it is never overly piquant. You need a wine with sweetness, and a special late harvest fits the bill, working particularly well when you serve Bleu d'Auvergne alongside fresh figs or ripe pears. A quaffable red (look no further than a little boxed version) also works, but you'll have to give up the figs and pears. If your Bleu d'Auvergne has been matured, thereby increasing its pungency, it needs a more concentrated sweet white wine, so switch to a noble late harvest, muscadel or tawny port.

BLUE BRIE/BLUE CAMEMBERT

Blue cheeses from cow's milk; origin: take your pick.
The popular soft cheeses, Brie and Camembert, also come in blue-veined versions. German Cambozola, known in English-speaking countries as Blue Brie, is produced locally under various names, such as **Winelands Blue**. Similarly, blue-veined Camembert-styled cheeses also appear with proprietary names, such as **Bleu en Blanc** or **Blue & Blanc**, a play on languages, cheeses and imitations. The paste of these cheeses resembles the honeyed cream within a ripe Brie or Camembert, but the little lumps of blue cheese add another dimension. They are among the mildest of the blue-veined cheeses, and are best served with special late harvest wines or, for a red, a quaffable sweet-fruited, lightly wooded one that shows no tannins.

BOERENKAAS

Hard cow's-milk 'farmer's' cheese; origin: the Netherlands.
Often described as a 'Dutch farmhouse Gouda', when young (under four months), Boerenkaas is golden-coloured, with a dense, creamy

texture. As the cheese matures, the colour darkens and the flavours become more concentrated. Although no cheese is literally sweet, we perceive Boerenkaas as having a sweet or caramel-like finish as if it contains some measurable sugar. A nutty, medium cream sherry is a particularly pleasing partner, but if you're 'just not into' sherry, match it with Gewürztraminer, off-dry Bukettraube, Viognier or a deeply fruited Merlot, Shiraz or Zinfandel.

If your Boerenkaas has added mustard seeds, your wine choice will remain unchanged, but if you hit upon Boerenkaas with cumin, then stick with Gewürz, Viognier or Shiraz.

BOURSIN [bur-SAH]

Soft cow's-milk cheese; origin: France.
A plain, triple-crème cheese, with or without added chives, garlic and herbs, or pecan nuts. All three versions are best matched with crisp, herbaceous, fruity white wines like Sauvignon Blanc, and dry or off-dry Weisser Riesling. Red wines suffer too much, unless you choose the gentlest of quaffers.

BRIE [bree]

Soft cow's-milk cheese; origin: France.
No cheese is more celebrated than Brie, and with good reason. It is the ultimate cheese; one of the greatest achievements in cheese-making, with a taste like no other: part mushroom, part cream, part brandy, part earth. Finding good Brie, whether local or imported, is no easy matter. Four out of five times it will let you down by being either a hard piece of cake, which shows it is too young, or at the over-runny stage, which means it is too old. But, when you strike Brie number five, ripened to just the right delicate creaminess, with the colour of butter glowing in the light, and hesitantly spreading itself like heavy honey, no other cheese can compare with it. And, just as difficult, is the search for its perfect wine match.

Soft cheeses, whether they have a bloomy rind (like Brie) or a washed rind (Pont l'Evêque), are tricky to pair with wine. Brie is one of the trickiest; it needs a white wine with some texture, or a red wine that is rustic and no more than medium-bodied. Finding wines that slot seamlessly into this match is easier said than done; an unwooded Chardonnay, Colombard, Gamay or Pinot Noir are your best choices.

CAERPHILLY [ke-FILLY]

Hard cow's-milk cheese; origin: Wales.
There is a saying that those who like buttermilk will happily help themselves to Caerphilly, while those who don't will leave it alone.

This serves either as a warning or an inducement but it is, at any rate, a fair statement. Snow-white Caerphilly, with its crumbly, slightly granular texture, does indeed have a distinct flavour of buttermilk. Together, the granular texture and the flavour make a good wine-match difficult. A crisp, herbaceous Sauvignon Blanc works and, because of the slight saltiness of the cheese, so does an off-dry Weisser Riesling, but the best choice is a top-notch, fruity, judicially wooded Chardonnay. Red-wine drinkers could choose a medium-bodied Merlot or Cabernet Sauvignon, or a blend of the two.

CAMBOZOLA

See **Blue Brie**, page 275.

CAMEMBERT [KAHM-oh-bare]

Soft cow's-milk cheese; origin: France.
Camembert, France's favourite, most plentiful and least expensive cheese, is also one of the most popular and widely imitated cheeses in South Africa. At its best, it has mushroom aromas and a supple, seductive texture. Its flavour when it is at its prime – neither hard at the centre nor runny to the point of collapsing when you cut into it – is such that we can believe the tale that Napoleon kissed the Normandy waitress who first served it to him. The story goes that the cheese was nameless at the time, so after he had finished eating and kissing, Napoleon, rather unimaginatively (the kiss obviously didn't inspire him), named it after its place of origin, Camembert.

With a flavour and texture rather similar to that of Brie (see above), Camembert calls for similar wine choices, although the ones to serve with Camembert can afford to be fuller bodied and more intense. Stay with Chardonnay, as for Brie, but go for a wooded, buttery one. Pinot Noir is an excellent red-wine choice, as is a medium-bodied, softly contoured Merlot. This is also the time to take out that Pinotage you have cellared for five years or more. It will be a combination that dreams are made of.

Should you eat the Camembert rind? That is a matter of taste. If it is not ammoniated and you like the contrasting textures, then eat it by all means, but if it is strong with an ominously 'rusted' look and a slightly bitter taste, then cut it away for the sake of the wine. And, if you are opening a treasured, mature Pinotage for a decadent cheese and wine pairing, then definitely cut the rind away, even if the cheese is in mint condition.

CANTAL [kahn-TAHL]

Hard cow's-milk cheese; origin: France.
In all probability, Cantal was one of France's first cheeses. It most certainly preceded all their other hard cow's-milk cheeses and is far, far older than the soft-ripening ones, such as Camembert, with which France is more usually associated. Cantal is the only Cheddar-like cheese that the French make in any quantity. It is considered to be mature at six months when it has developed rich flavours and a smooth, butter-coloured interior. Pair it with a rich white wine, such as a Viognier or a wooded Chardonnay or Semillon. The more mature and full-flavoured the cheese, the bigger the wine should be. There is a whole range of red wines to choose from: a Bordeaux blend, solo Cab Sav, Merlot or Tempranillo.

CHAVROUX

See **Goat's milk cheeses**, page 283.

CHEDDAR

Hard cow's-milk cheese; origin: England.
The designation 'Cheddar' covers a multitude of sins; from mass-produced, shrink-wrapped blocks to hand-crafted artisanal versions and even blue-veined creations, such as **Boland Blue**. Additionally, some varieties are pepped up with Madagascan green peppercorns or jalapeño and red peppers for a Mexican touch.

That said, good quality Cheddar has pronounced acidity and a firm texture that is crumbly yet creamy at the same time. Its aromas are equally pronounced: nutty, grassy and fruity with a hint of caramel. As a sliver of Cheddar dissolves on the tongue, sweetness, acidity and saltiness mingle before ending in a long finish. You need a red wine with some intensity to stand up to Cheddar. A Bordeaux blend is the classic partner, but a solo Cabernet Sauvignon, Merlot, Pinotage or Tempranillo are equally successful. Pinotage's slight acidic grip has the added benefit of neatly cutting through the dense texture and richness of the cheese. Another traditional match that is very satisfying is with a late bottled vintage port. The white-wine drinker should select a wooded, full-bodied Chardonnay and enjoy the fusion of a buttery wine with a buttery cheese.

CHESHIRE

Hard cow's-milk cheese; origin: England.
Cheshire is probably the UK's oldest cheese. What is mostly seen on the shelves today is the medium-ripened variety, which has a rather crumbly texture. It also has a pervasive saltiness that you only detect

after about the fifth bite as it is not at all intrusive. It is this saltiness that makes Cheshire the perfect cheese to eat with celery, radishes, tomatoes and cucumbers – in fact, with any vegetable that needs salt and can be eaten raw. The saltiness influences the choice of wines: Sauvignon Blanc for the white-wine drinker and Pinot Noir, Pinotage or Cabernet Franc for the red.

A well-aged Cheshire is a good investment for a dinner party; if you come across one, buy it immediately, and pair it with Shiraz, which it is wild about. In addition, you can offer a tawny port for guests who prefer to drink something sweet at the end of a meal.

CHEVIN

See **Goat's-milk cheeses**, page 283.

CHÈVRE

See **Goat's-milk cheeses**, page 283.

COLBY

Hard cow's-milk cheese; origin: locally produced.
Cheddar has many imitations; Colby is one of those cheeses that could be called 'near-Cheddars'. It is much lighter in flavour, softer and more open in texture, with less of a salty-acidic tang and a higher moisture content. The result (as with all high-moisture cheeses) is that it perishes more quickly than Cheddar. Colby prefers red wine, and Pinotage, Sangiovese or Tempranillo suits it well. It may be a 'red wine please' cheese, but the white-wine drinker will be fine with Viognier, which has the ideal texture for softly contoured Colby.

COMTÉ [kohm-TAY]

Hard cow's-milk cheese; origin: France.
Named after the Franche-Comté region, this cheese has been made since ancient times. When young, its interior may be ivory but, with age, the colour darkens to gold and the aromas of hazelnut and browned butter become more intense. At any age, a Comté's texture will be smooth, never granular, and its flavours are impeccably balanced between sweet, salty and acidic. Look to the rich, spicy white wines: Viognier, Weisser Riesling and Bukettraube. A Chardonnay with a creamy texture, but without obvious oak, is also a very good choice, as is a dry (fino) sherry if you want to serve something different. Pinotage, Merlot and Zinfandel are good red-wine matches.

COTTAGE/CURD CHEESE (plain and flavoured)

Soft cow's-milk cheese; origin: various.
The curds in this cheese are formed when the milk is heated and the resulting cheese may be chunky or smooth. Both types contain a high percentage of liquid whey, which makes them very soft and spreadable. Cottage cheese is often enjoyed as a light meal with fresh salad ingredients and/or bread. Tap a glass of Sauvignon Blanc from your favourite box to complete this informal meal.

CREAM CHEESE (plain and flavoured)

Soft cow's-milk cheese; origin: various.
Cream cheese sold in 'brick' form is denser and richer than the tub versions. Whether you are serving it as a spread or dip, plain or flavoured, the wine choice remains the same: an unwooded Chardonnay from a cool climate that shows some acidity to cut through the richness. The red-wine drinker could choose between a Cinsaut and a Sangiovese. If you unmould it and cover the cheese with a sweet chilli sauce to serve as a pre-dinner snack, switch to a late harvest; if you can find one made from Gewürztraminer, so much the better. *See also* **Mascarpone**, page 288.

DANISH BLUE

Blue cheese from cow's milk; origin: Denmark.
Danish Blue (Danablu in its country of origin) was invented in 1914 by a cheese maker called Marius Boel, to create an alternative to French Roquefort. Denmark went seriously into the business of reproducing French and Italian cheeses during World War I, when exports from those countries came to a standstill. It is more buttery than Roquefort and even stronger tasting, and the pencillings of blue are so legible and dense throughout that you may think the Danes were out to receive accolades for drawing as well as cheese making. Danish Blue is a lovely cheese, but it does cause a spot of trouble when paired with wine. Its sharp flavour has a tingle of peppermint that turns a sweet dessert wine into a metal bar. Instead of admitting defeat, choose one of our great muscadels or jerepigos, chill it thoroughly, and open a jar of green fig preserve. You cannot inhibit a Danish Blue, so go all out. The sky is the limit!

DOUBLE GLOUCESTER [GLOSS-ter]

Hard cow's-milk cheese; origin: England.
The name refers to the Gloucester breed of black cattle whose milk was originally used, as well as to the extra-large size of this cheese. But surely the name 'Double Gloucester' implies that there must

be a 'Single Gloucester'? And so there is. Both cheeses have the same diameter but they differ in girth and age. The Single one is only about half as thick and two-thirds as heavy, and is eaten when it is about six weeks old, whereas the Double is aged from four months to a year. In South Africa it is the latter you will come across, not only in speciality cheese shops, but in supermarkets as well. And they are most likely to be small cheeses that are individually packed or sealed in a wax coating.

Double Gloucester is a bright orange cheese (often coloured with annatto, a natural food colouring) with a hard, satiny texture. 'Put a crumb no bigger than a pinhead on your tongue,' says a Gloucester cheese lover, 'and the flavour will fill your whole mouth.' If you are buying cheese to order, ask for a sliver to taste before you buy a piece cut from a big wheel, because it will immediately give you an idea of the weight of wine that will match it perfectly. Gloucester cries out for a red wine, and Pinotage is the star here, but Cabernet Sauvignon, Merlot and their blends are excellent partners, too.

DRAKENSBERG

See **Goat's-milk cheeses**, page 283.

DRUNKEN PECORINO

See **Pecorino**, page 292.

EDAM

Hard cow's-milk cheese; origin: the Netherlands.
Edam and Gouda are both smooth, mellow cheeses that are similar in flavour. The main difference between them arises from the difference in their butterfat content; Edam is made from *partly* skimmed milk, whereas Gouda is made from whole milk.

Edam is not a 'big' cheese and, for people who like cheese with a light, attractive, buttery taste and conventional texture, it can hardly be improved upon. We can learn from the Dutch and serve Edam for breakfast – it is just as satisfying as a bowl of muesli or *mieliepap*. You would probably have only a cup of coffee to drink with it then, but if you opt for an Edam and ham sandwich at lunchtime instead, consider a beer (Dutch or otherwise) or a tot of Jenever (Dutch gin), although you'd miss out on other excellent cheese and wine combinations, such as a well-chilled blanc de noir, rosé, Colombard or Bukettraube, or a Cinsaut if you'd prefer red.

EMMENTHAL(ER)

Hard cow's-milk cheese; origin: Switzerland.

Emmenthal, with its melt-in-the-mouth texture and mild, distinctly sweet and nutty flavour, is always instantly recognizable by the round holes distributed throughout its dense, golden interior. Emmenthal is not only difficult to make, requiring superior milk and special skills, it is also tricky to find a good wine match for it. It has the tendency of making most red wines seem more tannic than they are, while playing havoc with whites that show the least bit of acidity. Look for a really, really light-bodied Merlot, or a Cinsaut, blanc de noir, Bukettraube or Colombard.

ÉPOISSES [ay-PWAHZ]

Soft cow's-milk cheese; origin: France.

This centuries-old washed-rind cheese, named for its Burgundy birthplace, is one of the greatest soft cheeses of the world. The ivory-coloured interior of a ripe Époisses should be supple and soft, and smell of mushrooms, garlic and meat. Like most washed-rind cheeses, it is milder than its fragrance would suggest. Do eat the crunchy, orangey-rust-brown rind as it provides a lovely contrast to the creamy interior, and won't do a thing to your wine! Pour yourself a glass of the richest, creamiest, most opulent and intensely fruity, wooded Chardonnay money can buy, and tuck right in... If you fancy red, choose a light and obliging Pinot Noir with soft tannins, but proceed with caution, as this cheese can easily overwhelm a red wine.

FETA [FEH-tah]

From sheep's milk; origin: Greece.

Although 'real' Feta is made exclusively from sheep's milk, many are a blend of sheep's and goat's milk, while mass-produced commercial Feta is made from cow's milk. The word *feta* means 'slice', typically the form in which it comes. To make Feta the traditional way, slabs of fresh cheese are layered with salt for a day or more to draw the moisture out of them. After this first seasoning, the cheese is rinsed and packed into barrels (the old way) or sealed tins (the modern way). In these containers it forms its own brine in which the cheese is matured. Feta should be white or off-white, with a moist, creamy, yet crumbly texture. Because of the seasoning, Feta, which is naturally acidic, also takes on a salty character. It is often used to add interest to plain salads of tomato, greens, cucumbers and peppers (as the Greeks discovered years ago), but is also very pleasant when eaten on its own. Feta needs lean white wines with good acidity – it's time for the trio again: Sauvignon Blanc, Chenin Banc and

Weisser Riesling. Pinot Gris/Pinot Grigio, and a dry blanc de noir or rosé are good choices too, provided they show good acidity.

FONTINA [fon-TEE-nah]

Hard cow's-milk cheese; origin: Italy.

Delicate, smoothly textured Fontina has a compact, straw-coloured interior, broken here and there by tiny holes. The aroma is nutty and slightly herbaceous, and the taste silky and slightly sweet. Look to white wines that are creamy, nutty and rich, or have a bit of residual sugar to complement Fontina's touch of sweetness. Viognier, wooded Chardonnay or Semillon, off-dry Weisser Riesling and Bukettraube are all harmonious partners, as is an off-dry blanc de noir. Red wines with soft tannins, such as Cinsaut, Pinot Noir or Barbera, or a quaffable Merlot or Pinotage, will work too, while a dry (fino) sherry echoes its nutty notes.

GOAT'S-MILK CHEESES

Goat's-milk cheeses are one of the oldest forms of cheese; they are made worldwide wherever 'goats do roam'!

Chevin/Chèvre South African versions of this chalky cheese, with its dry texture, are excellent. Nowadays, these little logs are available in the most astounding flavour additions; anything from honey and dukkah to chakalaka. Whether served on its own, or warmed and accompanied by a dressed salad, or melted over vegetables as a starter, goat's-milk cheese, or Chevin, is best with crisp, dry white wines. Sauvignon Blanc is the classic match, as it equals the cheese in intensity and weight, and has tangy acidity of its own. Choose Sauvignon Blancs with herbal aromas rather than those with prominent fruity notes. Chenin Blanc, Weisser Riesling, Cape, Paarl or South African Riesling and dry sparkling wine are also good matches. Cabernet Franc is the star red wine with goat's-milk cheese.

Chavroux/Drakensberg This fresh goat's-milk cheese, whether a French import or the local version, stands out for its eye-catching shape: a pyramid with its top sliced off (which is also the classic shape of a Valençay cheese produced in the Loire Valley in France). Why the strange shape? Legend has it that the cheese was originally a conventional pyramid with a pointed top, until one day, as misfortune would have it, the little pyramid of cheese was served to Napoleon, who became very angry when he set his eyes on it, as it reminded him of his failed campaign in Egypt. He promptly pulled out his sword and lopped off the pyramid's peak. Like most food lore, the tale stretches the line between fact and fiction, but it's a good story anyway. Stick with Sauvignon Blanc.

Goat's-milk cheese rolled in ash After moulding and draining, this local beauty is turned out and coated with ash, which encourages beneficial moulds to develop on the surface. The cheese is creamy, becoming progressively firmer towards the centre. The aroma can be faintly nutty and, when well made, this variation delivers just the right amount of salt and tangy acidity that Sauvingon Blanc takes to like a duck to water.

Goat's milk Gouda has a creamy texture and mild flavour after being ripened for one month only. Choose a Sauvignon Blanc.

Goat's milk Pecorino-style, matured for three months, has a tangy flavour. Same refrain, choose a Sauvignon Blanc.

Goat's milk Caprino Romana reaches its full flavour after a maturation period of six months. The song remains the same: Sauvignon Blanc is the ideal partner.

GORGONZOLA [gohr-gohn-ZOH-lah]

Blue cheese from cow's milk; origin: Italy.

Gorgonzola, Roquefort and Stilton form a 'triumvirate' that dominates the world of marbled (blue-veined) cheeses. Gorgonzola is as richly creamy as Stilton, semi-soft when young, becoming slightly firmer and developing a grittiness as it ages.

Named for a village near Milan, in Italy, Gorgonzola is centuries old, although production methods have been modernized. Not that a method for developing the blue veins existed right at the beginning because, according to local lore, Gorgonzolas were originally uncured, unveined cheeses made by farmers who sold them at a market near the town's wine shop. Townsfolk who didn't have enough money to pay for their wine gave the owner cheeses instead. He accumulated so many that they had to be stored in his cellar, where they eventually developed a green mould and, *voilà!* Gorgonzola entered the stage. We could say that both cheese and wine work in mysterious ways... Very gentle red wines, such as Barbera or Cinsaut, can cope with the creamy richness, pungency and lingering saltiness of Gorgonzola, but sweet white wine, such as a ripe, full-bodied special late harvest with juicy fruit, is more at ease in its company. A medium-cream sherry will accentuate Gorgonzola's spiciness, but this may not appeal to everyone.

GOUDA

Hard cow's-milk cheese; origin: the Netherlands.

Gouda and **Edam** (see page 281) date from the Middle Ages and were exported from Holland to other countries in Europe as early as the 13th century. Today they are found around the world, and these smooth and mellow cheeses rarely disappoint. Gouda, which has a firmer texture than Edam, distinguishes itself as a red-wine cheese. Pinotage comes out on top, with Sangiovese in second place. When matured for six months or more, Gouda becomes one helluva cheese, turning drier and nuttier, and developing a caramel-like sweetness. Partnering a matured Gouda with Cabernet Sauvignon or a Bordeaux blend is one of the proverbial matches made in heaven, and will hold your attention taste after taste.

See also **Mimolette**, page 288.

GRANA PADANO

See **Parmesan**, page 291.

GRUYÈRE [grew-yare]

Hard cow's-milk cheese; origin: Switzerland.

Gruyère production began in the 12ᵗʰ century in the Swiss town of the same name. Used both at the table and in cooking, this is a solid, dependable and memorable cheese, densely textured, firm and smooth, with an attractive balance of salt and sweet on the tongue. Its pronounced nutty and browned-butter flavours are happy with white and red wines, but marginally prefer the reds. Shiraz, Cab Sav and Bordeaux blends are all good partners, as is Pinot Noir, especially if the wine is more earthy than fruity. If you'd prefer to drink a white wine with your Gruyère, choose a Pinot Gris, off-dry Weisser Riesling, semi-sweet Chenin Blanc, or a creamy, lightly wooded Chardonnay or Semillon. A dry (fino) or medium-cream sherry plays off its nuttiness beautifully.

HALOUMI [gggah-LOO-mee (with a guttural 'g')]

Goat's-milk or cow's-milk cheese; origin: Cyprus.

Haloumi (halloumi), a white, semi-soft cheese with a curiously rubbery texture, is ideal for frying as it holds its shape well. Although more common as a starter, it also makes an ideal nibble at the end of a meal, especially when you've had a very sweet pudding and feel like something savoury afterwards. Pair it with white wine, such as Sauvignon Blanc or Weisser Riesling.

HAVARTI [hah-VAR-tee]

Hard cow's-milk cheese; origin: Denmark.

Golden-yellow Havarti is a mild, creamy, slightly sweet cheese with a moist body. It is not only a table cheese of considerable quality and appeal, it also makes a good snack with a packet of pretzels, or use it as a sandwich filling with fresh dill on rye bread. On its own, Havarti cries out for an unoaked or lightly oaked Chardonnay or Semillon, but choose one from a cool climate, showing some balancing acidity. It is also happy in the company of Bukettraube, off-dry Weisser Riesling or Chenin Blanc. A Pinot Noir is decadently enjoyable with it.

JARLSBERG [YARLZ-berg]

Hard cow's-milk cheese; origin: Norway.
This is a well-textured, mild, buttery cheese, with characteristic large holes, similar to Emmenthal(er). With its sweetish flavour, Jarlsberg pairs best with white wines that have ripe fruit flavours. Look to Viognier, Weisser Riesling and Bukettraube.

LANCASHIRE [LANG-kuh-shir]

Hard cow's-milk cheese; origin: England.
Although it has a fine, grainy, crumbly texture, Lancashire is the softest of the hard-pressed cheeses. Softer does not mean milder, though, and Lancashire is stronger in flavour than matured Cheddar! It is an excellent table cheese, but also eminently suitable for cooking, as it toasts well and turns all custardy when melted (ideal for making a cheese sauce). Match its strength and sharp, acidic flavour with tangy white wines – Sauvignon Blanc, dry or off-dry Weisser Riesling, Cape, Paarl or South African Riesling, and a brut or demi-sec sparkling wine are its best allies. Lancashire is eaten when only two or three months matured. When it reaches its peak, it should have a dense texture and pungent aroma. We hesitantly suggest partnering it at this stage with a full, spicy Shiraz, although the combination is *definitely* not for the faint-hearted.

LEICESTER [LESS-ter]

Hard cow's-milk cheese; origin: England.
Known in the trade as Red Leicester, you would wonder if Leicester comes in other colours as well? But no, 'red' merely refers to the cheese's flamboyant orange colour. Although the added colouring has no effect on its flavour, it succeeds in its original purpose: to suggest to the buyer that Leicester's deep colour is synonymous with a rich flavour. And, indeed, the buyer is not misled, for when you put a sliver in your mouth, it dissolves into a rich creaminess that also has an attractive lemony tang. This immediately points to a white wine with corresponding lemony (or what can be only imperfectly described as 'citrusy') flavours. And yes, an unwooded Chardonnay showing some acidity not only works, but copes with the creaminess of the cheese as well.

But red wine is also a match for a hard cow's-milk cheese. Cinsaut, Sangiovese, Pinot Noir and soft-centred Merlot rise to the occasion. If you have a favourite boxed-red, it will probably be good too.

LEIDEN [LAY-din]

Hard cow's-milk cheese; origin: the Netherlands.
Gouda and Edam's mild little cousin, Leiden, is often flavoured with caraway or cumin seeds, both of which are extremely hard on any wine. Caraway, which seems to impart a pleasant sourness to the cheese, even though it is not itself sour, is best matched with white or red wines with noticeable acidy. Look to Sauvignon Blanc, Cape, Paarl or South African Riesling, Weisser Riesling, Cinsaut, Barbera or Sangiovese. Cumin, on the other hand, adds a strong, pervasive, almost turpentiney taste. All white wines suffer, even the spicy, fruity ones, so turn to the lifeguard-reds: Shiraz and Pinotage. Go down, down, down in quality, though, and keep it quaffable and inexpensive. Or open the good bottle and put the cheese back in the fridge to eat tomorrow morning, at breakfast, on rye.

LIVAROT [LEE-vah-roh]

Soft cow's-milk cheese; origin: France.
Cheese does not get much more strongly flavoured than this Normandy specimen. Named for the small town near Caen where it has been made for hundreds of years, it is one of the region's most important cheeses. Like two others in this group, Munster and Maroilles, Livarot is aged in ripening rooms where fresh air is not allowed to enter which, of course, accounts for its pungent, slightly overbearing aroma. Yet, it has a certain finesse, so don't be put off by its smell. If you pick up an appetizing, sound-looking Livarot from a speciality cheese shop, you'll be glad you bought it. Remove the dark, reddish-brown crust and spread the soft, ripe, yellow cheese on Melba toast or good French bread. Then pour yourself a glass of full-bodied, wooded Chardonnay, Semillon, Viognier or Pinot Noir. When you cut your second helping of Livarot, consider drinking a Calvados* with it. Or coffee. Livarot is excellent with coffee. But who wants to drink Calvados or coffee if you can have wine?

(* Calvados is a strong brandy made with cider apples; like Livarot, it comes from Normandy, where it has been made for centuries.)

MANCHEGO [mahn-TSHAY-go]

Sheep's-milk cheese; origin: Spain.
Made in Don Quixote territory on the high plains of La Mancha, this ivory-coloured sheep's-milk cheese not only has a long, distinguished

history, it is also Spain's most famous cheese, with reason. It is an excellent product, firm-textured, hard and dry, with the glistening surface typical of cheeses made from high-fat sheep's milk. A young Manchego has the aroma of sour cream or cheesecake but, as it matures, the fragrance becomes nuttier, and the tangy flavour more mellow and full, with a pronounced saltiness on the long aftertaste. Manchego is a red-wine cheese; Tempranillo, which originates from Spain is, naturally, one of its closest allies, as are the Italian trio of Nebbiolo, Sangiovese and Barbera, and our own Pinotage, all of which have, or seem to have, refreshing acidity. If you have bought a cheese with the concentrated flavours that come with age, you may be tempted to reach for that 'big red', but don't; it will likely have an impressive tannin structure, which the cheese will turn into a metal bar. Rather, treat yourself, and nibble on cubes of Manchego with a dry (fino) sherry, which echoes the saltiness of the cheese – a cheese and wine fusion that must be tasted to be fully appreciated.

MASCARPONE [mahs-cahr-PAW-neh]

Fresh cream cheese from cow's milk; origin: Italy.
This delectable, 'spoonable' cheese tastes like whipped cream and is, indeed, made from fresh cream. It is used like any other cream cheese, either as a spread on crackers or in cooking (to enrich pasta sauces, for example), but most of the time it is eaten with sugar, fruits and nuts, with or without the addition of brandy or liqueurs.

It is probably best known as the main ingredient in the well-known tiramisu dessert. If you are serving Mascarpone as a table cheese, you will find no better match than a full-bodied, lightly wooded, creamy Chardonnay. If you are spooning it onto fruit for dessert, its role changes and you should select a late harvest or special late harvest, depending on the level of sweetness you are matching.

MIMOLETTE [mee-moh-LET]

Hard cow's milk; origin: France.
This French cheese, which falls somewhere between English Cheddar and Dutch Gouda or Edam, is a real head-turner at the cheese counter thanks to its butternut colour, which comes from annatto, a harmless vegetable dye. According to legend, the French devised Mimolette in the 17th century when a ban on imports made Gouda and Edam unavailable. Although France has never been much of a market for 'foreign' cheeses, the Bordelaise appreciated these particular ones, as nothing matches a Bordeaux blend quite as well as a matured Gouda. It simply *had* to be copied, and Mimolette landed on the dining table.

The French mature this cheese anywhere from 3–24 months. As it ages, it becomes drier and saltier and its taste intensifies, picking up a slightly sharp edge, with butterscotch aromas, while its colour deepens to that of dried mango. When fully matured, not a hint of its role-models, Gouda or Edam, remains and yet, in spite of its waxy, somewhat brittle texture, it continues to echo them, happily latching on to Cabernet Sauvignon or a Bordeaux blend in which Cabernet dominates. Mimolette complements Cab Sav and its blends as few other cheeses do. It is also very good with a full-bodied, buttery Chardonnay or Viognier, while a pale dry (fino) or medium-cream sherry picks up the cheese's caramel flavours.

See also **Gouda**, page 284.

MORBIER [MOR-bee-yay]

Hard cow's-milk cheese; origin: France.

Morbier is a semi-firm, dense and creamy cheese, with a few small eyes and a thin line of grey ash running through the middle, dividing it horizontally in two. This line of ash is a remnant of the days when cheese was made on isolated farms in eastern France. When the winter weather turned harsh, it was impossible to get milk to the village dairy and the farmers had to make the cheese themselves. Traditionally, the milk used for making Morbier came from both the morning and evening milkings. In winter, the farmer would curdle the evening's milk over a wood fire, transfer the curds to their moulds and sprinkle some wood ash over them to prevent a skin from forming on top. The next morning's milk would be curdled and added to the mould by spreading it evenly over the layer of ash. The wheel would then be pressed, sealed and matured for about 45 days.

Nowadays, Morbier is mostly made in large cooperative dairies. The dividing layer is vegetable ash now, and the practice of separating evening and morning curds is a thing of the past, but the faintly earthy, meaty aroma has remained and the flavour is still a little sweet. A brut or sec sparkling wine provides textural contrast to Morbier's creaminess. Alternatively, a lightly wooded Chardonnay or Semillon, or a Pinot Gris with some viscosity, echoes its dense texture. A dry (fino) sherry is another good option, as it complements the nutty notes of the cheese.

MOZZARELLA [moht-tsah-REL-lah]

Soft buffalo- or cow's-milk cheese; origin: Italy.

At its best, Mozzarella is presented either as a single round cheese or in small, walnut-sized balls. It is very tender, creamy, dripping with fresh whey as you bite into the sweet, milky paste. Traditionally it is made from buffalo milk*, as the original name, *Mozzarella di Bufala*, indicates. Nowadays, however, Mozzarella is mostly made from cow's milk; not only in South Africa, but in Italy too. Apart from the price (buffalo-milk Mozzarella is frightfully expensive), there is no big difference between the two – although some people would disagree. Either way, they speak the same language; both are mild, but buffalo-milk Mozzarella contains almost twice the fat content of cow's-milk Mozzarella and its flavour is more pronounced and a little gamier. Both should have a thin, tight skin and a compact interior, allowing you to make a neat slice that holds together, perfect for layering with tomatoes and basil, as in a traditional Caprese salad. If you are having this salad, the tomato will play a big role in the choice of your wine; reach for a crisp white wine with good acidity, such as Sauvignon or Chenin Blanc, Weisser or Cape, Paarl or South African Riesling. However, if you decide to eat it on its own (and it is a good antipasto cheese), you need a very light dry white wine that does not shout from the rooftop; a Colombard is just the thing, but also try a dry blanc de noir or a rosé.

Mass-produced cow's-milk Mozzarella, either cylinder-shaped and vacuum-packed or shrink-wrapped in blocks, is different in texture and taste to the balls stored in whey. It is mostly used in cooking, particularly on pizzas. However, if you do use this style of Mozzarella in a caprese salad, the wine choices remain the same.

(* The domestic Asian water buffalo, which has been imported into South Africa to produce a local buffalo-milk Mozzarella; the buffalo we see in our game reserves couldn't come up with the goods!)

MUNSTER [MUHN-ster]

Soft cow's milk cheese; origin: France.
With a history that goes back to the 7th century, Munster is one of France's oldest and most famous cheeses. Powerful when it has been aged, strong and highly aromatic, with a slightly sticky, palate-coating texture and barnyard fragrance, it is not a cheese to nibble while on the run or to make a quick sandwich from! Don't trim away the rind, as its salty crunch provides a contrast to the cheese's creamy interior. Serve Munster with baguette or with new potatoes boiled in their skins and pour yourself a glass of Sylvaner if you wish to highlight the cheese. But, if you want a more exciting combination, reach for an equally aromatic wine with viscosity, such as a Viognier, Weisser Riesling, Gewürztraminer, Grenache, Shiraz or Shiraz-Grenache blend, any of which will add to the unsurpassed robust flavours of the cheese.

OLD AMSTERDAM

Hard cow's-milk cheese; origin: the Netherlands.
This extra-matured Dutch-style cheese is renowned for its rich, robust and tangy flavour. Old Amsterdam pairs well with the same wines as **Mimolette**; see page 288.

PARMESAN

Hard cow's-milk cheese; origin: Italy.
Italy produces two major cheeses that are similar to one another and belong to a group known by the generic name of 'grana cheeses' (the word *grana*, meaning 'grain', refers to the grainy texture of the properly aged cheeses). One is **Parmigiano-Reggiano** [pahr-mee-djAH-noh red-djAH-noh] and the other is **Grana Padano** [GRAH-nah pah-DAH-noh]. In South Africa – and the rest of the world for that matter – both are commonly called **Parmesan**.

Do not confuse these trademark cheeses with the little sachets and shakers of grated pasta cheese that are sometimes labelled Parmesan-style. Parmigiano-Reggiano and Grana Padano are legally protected names of origin and the cheeses must be fully produced within restricted areas in Italy to be labelled as such.

There are few differences between these two imported grana cheeses: Parmigiano-Reggiano is produced in a small, restricted area around the Italian towns of Parma and Bologna. The milk used for making the cheese must be absolutely uniform, and cheese production is restricted to seven months of the year, through spring and summer only. The cheese must be at least two years old before it can be sold, and only first-grade cheese may be exported.

Grana Padano, on the other hand, is produced throughout northern Italy, from Turin to Verona. The milk differs, for better or worse, from one place to another, and the cheese can be made all year round. (It is simply a fact that cheeses made in winter are not as good as those made during the rest of the year.) The ripening time for Grana Padano may range from one to two years and the standards for export are not as strict.

The difference, in short, is that with Parmigiano-Reggiano, you can be certain of getting a superlative cheese. On the other hand, if you buy Grana Padano, you may get a superlative cheese, or one that is very good, but it will not be the best.

For the cheese and wine pairer, the flavours of these cheeses are the most important thing. Although Parmesan is used extensively in cooking, it is just as successful as a table cheese when freshly cut and moist. To match its sweet, nutty, toasty and browned-butter flavours (and that ever-present hint of orange peel and savoury meat broth), choose a fruity, sweet-oak style of red, such as Shiraz, Zinfandel, Merlot, Tempranillo or Nebbiolo. Avoid a tannic wine because Parmesan, like other hard, sharp or pungent cheeses, will give it a metallic character. Whites such as Pinot Gris, lightly oaked Chardonnay or semi-sweet wines are other good matches. Serve chunks of Parmesan before dinner with dry sparkling wine, or at the end of a meal with a glass of dry (fino) sherry.

PARMIGIANO-REGGIANO

See **Parmesan**, page 291.

PECORINO [peh-koh-REE-noh]

Sheep's-milk cheese; origin: Italy.

Pecorino is a generic name for all Italian cheeses made with sheep's milk (the Italian word *pecora* means 'sheep'). Pecorino is produced in various styles, including table cheeses that are mild with a sweet flavour of fresh milk. The best-known Pecorino in South Africa is probably the hard-grating Pecorino Romano used mainly as a condiment on pasta and in other foods. It is designed to be ripened and spends at least four months in a maturation cellar where it develops a thin, golden rind and a firm, smooth interior with nut and caramel flavours. Choose your wine according to the age of the cheese; when young, mild and moist, it is happiest with a crisp dry white such as Sauvignon or Chenin Blanc, or a dry or off-dry Weisser Riesling. When the cheese is more mature with nutty notes, look to Viognier, unwooded Chardonnay or Semillon, or Sangiovese. A rounded, medium-bodied Shiraz or Pinotage are both complementary, if rather powerful, while a sparkling Shiraz or sparkling Pinotage are the very latest, very fashionable, off-beat options!

Drunken pecorino is made from white pecorino heads that have been immersed in a special must to allow the fermented zest and tang to permeate the cheese. This is a red-wine cheese, so stick to Shiraz or Pinotage, or the funky sparkling variations of both.

PONT L'EVÊQUE [POHN luh-VEK]

Soft cow's-milk cheese; origin: France.

One of France's most important cheeses, Pont l'Evêque traces its roots back to the 12th century. Perfect specimens are small, plump and square, their bright orange rinds marked by the mats of rye straw on which the cheese has lain. No cheese could be more French! The butter-coloured paste inside is soft but not runny, with tiny, glistening holes throughout. Pont l'Evêque is not as strong or outlandish as it smells; in fact, it is only moderately flavourful, slightly salty and savoury, with agreeable mushroom notes. A medium-bodied Pinot Noir matches the cheese in intensity and complements its mushroom flavour, but Gamay, Barbera or Sangiovese are equally appetizing matches. For a white wine, choose a velvety Chardonnay or Semillon (one without a lot of alcohol, oak or lively fruit) or a Sauvignon or Chenin Blanc. If you are serving cheese instead of dessert, opt for a tawny port instead; it works with the cheese and provides the touch of sweetness that is so satisfying at the end of a meal.

PORT-SALUT [POR sah-LEW]

Soft cow's-milk cheese; origin: France.
Port-Salut represents the perfect meeting place between the buttery cheeses and those whose strength is almost electrifying. Though not as strongly flavoured as you would expect from a soft, washed-rind cheese with French roots, it is creamy but firm, with a little edge that sets it apart from the bland, buttery camp. Soft white wines are its biggest allies: unwooded Chardonnay or Semillon, Pinot Blanc, Colombard or Colombard-Chardonnay blends.

PROVOLONE (unsmoked) [proh-voh-LOH-neh]

Hard cow's-milk cheese; origin: Italy.
In the past, Provolone came onto the market when well matured. As it increasingly resembles sheep's-milk cheeses as it ages, it was sharp, pungent and salty with a characteristic hot sting that was very hard on a wine. Today, most Provolone is sold at a younger stage, when it is creamy and mildly flavoured, with the result that we can easily find white and red wines to enjoy with it. Provolone is happiest with gentle reds that have a touch of sweet-berry fruit and balancing acidity, such as Cinsaut, Barbera or Sangiovese. Your favourite boxed dry red would suit it to a T. White-wine drinkers should select an equally gentle wine, such as an unwooded Chardonnay or Semillon, or a Colombard or Bukettraube.

RACLETTE [rah-KLET]

Hard cow's-milk cheese; origin: France and Switzerland.
Both the French and the Swiss side of the Alps produce a washed-rind cheese called Raclette, which is used in a stick-to-the-ribs dish that bears its name. The Swiss claim Raclette, which is derived from the French verb *racler* ('to scrape'), as practically their national dish. Classically, a whole cheese is cut in half vertically and placed in front of an open fireplace. As the cheese melts, it is scraped onto a plate and eaten immediately with potatoes boiled in their skins,

pickled onions, gherkins and other vegetables. The French tradition is different; they pan-fry *their* Raclette. Nowadays, most homes and restaurants use an electric device for preparing Raclette. Raclette can also be eaten just as it is, with no melting required, and it is easy to see why. It fits the mould (no pun intended) of many washed-rind cheeses enjoyed at the table; it has the fully rounded, meaty, roast-peanut and peaches-with-honey flavours associated with the washed-rinds that simply melt in the mouth. Don't remove the slightly tacky, coarse, natural rind when you help yourself to a portion of Raclette. A little bit of its saltiness helps you to enjoy the delicate, buttery, but quite firm cheese to the full. Before you reach for a wine, taste some Raclette on its own, just to experience how it cries out for Shiraz. When you are *raclett-ing* with friends, stick to Shiraz or one of the Shiraz-blends. If you need to accommodate your 'white-wine-only' friends, choose an aromatic dry or off-dry Weisser Riesling with some body and spice or, if you want to push out the boat, the best Viognier you can afford.

REBLOCHON [ruh-bloh-SHOHN]

Soft cow's-milk cheese; origin: France.

Reblochon, one of the most superior of all cheeses has, for centuries, been produced in the Alps of the Savoy region in eastern France, from milk of exceptional character. *Reblochon* means 'second milk-ing' and the name derives from the traditional practice of making cheese from the day's second yield of milk, which was richer than the first. And thereby hangs a tale: The Savoy cowboys (in the old sense of 'herdsmen') leased their pastures from wealthy landown-ers, paying in proportion to the amount of milk their Tarentais cows produced. Once a year, the landlord would drop by to have the cows' daily output measured in order to figure out what he should charge as annual rent. Legend has it that, on that day, the cow's owner would not extract all the milk from the udder while the landlord was watching, so the yield would be low. Only when the landlord had left, sniffing and wiping his nose with his lace handkerchief, did the ten-nant finish the milking, using that second batch, which appeared nowhere 'on the books', to make some cheese for himself. In due course, this became known as 'reblochon' or the second-milking cheese. It just shows what can happen if you're in the dairy business but do not understand the mechanics of milking a cow...

But to the present: Reblochon, as we know it today, has a smooth, chestnut to orange rind with a dusting of white mould, while the cheese within is pale cream, moist, supple and semi-soft, with a few small eyes. At its prime, there are plentiful aromas of mushrooms and garlic. The best wines for Reblochon are rich, top-notch, barrel-aged Chardonnay or Semillon, or medium-bodied Pinot Noir. The pungency of a dry (fino) sherry also works beautifully with the earthy flavours of the cheese.

RED LEICESTER

See **Leicester**, page 286.

RICOTTA

Soft cow's-milk cheese; origin: Italy.

We are familiar with Italian Ricotta, but similar cheeses are made in other countries, for instance, Myzithra in Greece. They are made from the leftover whey when the milk-fats have been removed to make other cheeses. Ricotta is white and creamy with a bland, almost sweet flavour. It has much in common with cottage cheese, although it has a different texture, being much smoother and with no solid curds. It is mostly used in cooking. If you have it on its own, pair it with the same wines as for **Cottage cheese**, page 280.

ROQUEFORT [rock-FORE]

Blue cheese from sheep's milk; origin: France.

According to legend, Roquefort was discovered centuries ago, in the rocky country of southwest France, when a shepherd boy left his lunch of bread and curd cheese in one of the cool caves of the district, thinking to come back for it later in the day. But, with one thing and another, it was weeks before he returned to find his abandoned lunch still in the cave. Then, with the typical curiosity of those who cannot throw something bad away without peeking first, he looked, he smelled and then he tasted. At which point there must have followed one of the greatest 'Aha!' moments in gastronomic history.

Thousands upon thousands of Roqueforts have been made since – not the way the shepherd boy went about it, but by inoculating the cheese curd, made from sheep's milk, with *Penicillium roqueforti* (a mould-producing substance made from rye breadcrumbs) and then ripening it in the damp, draughty limestone caves where the shepherd left his lunch. It is these caves, with their unusual mineral composition, that account for the unique flavour of Roquefort, and they are the reason why France's famous *bleu*, the most imitated cheese in the world, is impossible to duplicate. At least once in your life, do try an imported Roquefort, just to taste the difference.

Quality Roquefort-style cheeses are produced in South Africa, making use of the same penicillium powder and ripening the cheese in a variety of ways. (Amazingly, no local cheese maker has thought of ripening his product in the Cango or Sterkfontein caves just to see what might happen...)

Roquefort is traditionally made with sheep's milk, but most large-scale producers use goat's or cow's milk; the reason will be clear to anyone who has ever tried to milk a sheep... A well-made Roquefort has evenly distributed veins in a moist, ivory-coloured paste. It should be smooth, and not crumble when sliced. Roquefort is always bold and spicy, but should not be harsh or excessively salty.

When it comes to wine, it cries out for a noble late harvest. Yes, mould meets mould or rot meets rot, you could say; so nothing could possibly go wrong. This is one of those classic food and wine combinations described as a marriage made in heaven.

If you want to spend less on an accompanying wine, try a rich, full-sweet dessert wine or a bold special late harvest but, of course, you will lose a bit in the translation. If you are a 'red-wine-only' person, then select a deeply-fruity, mellow Merlot or Merlot-Cabernet blend that does not have a drop of tannin in the bottle. There may be a hiccup when you take your first sip with the cheese, but Roquefort often rises to the occasion.

SAGE CHEESE

Hard cow's-milk cheese with sage; origin: England.
Adding sage to natural cheese is by no means original, having originated about 300 years ago in Derbyshire, an English county known for its flavoured and herb-streaked cheeses. Why sage? Well, since antiquity, sage has been considered to be good for health; in the 18th century, it was added to meat and other food to make it safer to eat. A natural progression was to add it to cheese in the hope of making it more digestible. We no longer rely on sage's therapeutic effects in cheese today, but we may still fall for the romance of it.

In the excellent local cheese, **Natal Green Sage**, the combination of the herb's sharp, clean sage flavour with a bland cheese is a good one, assuming that you like sage, which can be an acquired taste. When selecting a wine, proceed with caution, as sage is a domineering herb with a direct impact on wine. Sage-flavoured cheese goes well with Merlot and Cabernet Franc, and happily latches on to the herbal character of Pinot Noir, but it is Sangiovese, with its inherent herbal edge, that makes it sing. The white-wine drinker should go for Pinot Gris/Pinot Grigio or Sauvignon Blanc.

SMOKED CHEESES

It is difficult to find wines to match this style of cheese, as it is often so heavily smoked that the taste completely dominates the wine.

Provolone and **Mozzarella** are the cheeses that are mostly used for wood-smoking, but you will come across others too. With all smoked cheeses, try Gewürztraminer, a special late harvest or a full-bodied Shiraz.

Smoked Applewood Cheddar, an English import, is excellent with full-bodied, wooded Chardonnay, as the attractive flavours of the charred oak barrels in which the wine is matured, perfectly match the smoky flavours of the cheese.

ST-NECTAIRE [SAHN neck-TARE]

Hard cow's-milk cheese; origin: France.
One of the finest cheeses from the Auvergne, in central France, is the mellow, buttery St-Nectaire, which has been made there since the Middle Ages. Like **Reblochon** (see page 294), it is produced from the uncommonly rich milk of Tarentais and Salers cows, which French cheese makers consider to be the 'aristocrats of milk-givers'. So, look to aristocratic wines that are mellow and buttery too and pair St-Nectaire with top-notch, wooded Chardonnay, Semillon or Viognier. Softly contoured, gentle red wines are equally successful; choose from Grenache, Tempranillo and light- to medium-bodied Merlot.

STILTON

Blue cheese from cow's milk; origin: England.
Stilton, England's best-known blue cheese, remains one of the world's finest. Immortalized in the poetry of Alexander Pope and the prose of Jane Austen, it appeared on the scene in the early 18th century. There is no evidence that it was made at Stilton, a village in the English midlands, although it probably derived its name from there; it has been recorded that travellers and coach passengers stopping at the Bell Inn could not get enough of the local cheese with 'rivers of blue' running through it.

So much time, skill and care go into making Stilton that cheese makers maintain they are more trouble than babies; just quieter! Stilton is made from the richest of milk, to which the cream of other milk is added. Unlike many other blues, which are ripened in cool caves, Stilton matures without refrigeration, natural or otherwise. It is quite different in flavour and appearance to other blue cheeses; what sets it apart is its distinct nutty, meaty, smoky and bacon-like character. Where some blue cheeses are pungent, Stilton is mellow, and where some blues are soft with butterfat, Stilton retains, even at room temperature, the consistency of aged Cheddar. Its rind is dark, crusty and wrinkled, while the cheese itself is ivory, deepening to yellow-brown around the edges.

Port has probably been Stilton's tablemate since its debut at the Bell Inn. Some people swear by a late bottled vintage, others by a tawny port but, if the budget is tight, any port will do – as long as it fits port's description, because Stilton digs its heels in if you try to pair it with the sweet white wines that go so well with other blue-veined cheeses. An unusual, but enjoyable, choice is a medium cream sherry. On the red side, a deeply fruity, mellow and rounded Cabernet Sauvignon, Merlot or Zinfandel are appetizing partners. Sauvignon Blanc does well for a white (if you think this is impossible, just remember the principle of matching acidity with acidity).

TALEGGIO [tah-LED-djoh]

Soft cow's-milk cheese; origin: Italy.
Named for the town in Lombardy in which it is believed to have originated, Taleggio is one of Italy's few washed-rind cheeses. It used to be ripened in natural caves, but today most producers use temperature- and humidity-controlled rooms. Locally produced Taleggio, which closely resembles the imported version, is mellow and mild when young, with just the slightest edge to it, providing a faintly aromatic quality that is very attractive. Pair it with an unwooded Chardonnay or Semillon.

As Taleggio matures, the slight edge will sharpen and pronounced aromas of meat, mushroom and earth will develop, although the flavour will be milder than you might expect from the smell. If you have bought a ripe Taleggio, switch from unwooded Chardonnay and Semillon to a spicy, medium- to full-bodied white or red wine; choose from Viognier, Gewürztraminer, Weisser Riesling, Shiraz, Grenache, Pinot Noir, Pinotage or Nebbiolo.

TOMME/TOMME DE SAVOIE [TOHM de sah-VWAH]

Hard cow's-milk cheese; origin: France.
The French name, *Tomme* (or *Tome*), is applied to a number of different cheeses. There are so many, and they differ to such a degree, that it is impossible to give a description of what a French *Tomme* actually is, except to say that it is usually small, round and individually packed, but not always! They all *do* have a hard, natural rind and are made all over France, as well as in Italy where they are referred to as *Toma*. Virtually every village in a cheese-producing region has its own *Tomme*, which carries the village or region's name, such as Tomme de Savoie, the version you are most likely to come across in speciality cheese shops in South Africa. This is a sturdy and reliable cheese, with a deeply coloured paste and a nutty flavour. When freshly cut, it smells pleasantly of roasted meat and moist earth,

with just a touch of the cowshed. Tomme de Savoie needs a wine with aromatic intensity and body, so reach for the Viognier, Shiraz, Shiraz blends or Pinotage.

VINTERSHOEK

Soft cow's-milk cheese; origin: South Africa.
This very good local cheese resembles French Munster.
See **Munster**, page 290, for wine-pairing suggestions.

WENSLEYDALE

Hard cow's-milk cheese; origin: England.
When sold after maturing for three to four months, Wensleydale has a well-developed rind and a semi-soft, creamy, smooth and moist interior with a crumbly, mouth-coating texture. Its aromas of buttermilk, cream cheese and caramel, and its tart, lactic finish mean it is not an easy cheese to find a matching wine for. Match its acidity with a Sauvignon Blanc with equally good acidity or opt for an off-dry Weisser Riesling or Chenin Blanc. An unwooded Chardonnay from a cool climate would also work, provided the wine does not have a high percentage of alcohol or sprightly fruit flavours. The best choice, however, is a brut, sec or demi-sec sparkling wine. Give the reds a miss on this occasion.

WITZENBERGER

Hard cow's-milk cheese; origin: South Africa.
This excellent local product is so similar to Swiss Appenzell that we imagine it to have been its inspiration.
For wine matches, *see* **Appenzell(er)**, page 273.

CHEESES WITH ADDED INGREDIENTS

Adding things to cheese is probably as old as cheese making itself. In ancient times, herbs with medicinal value were often added; spices and brines were used as a means of preserving or pickling cheeses, or to hide 'off' flavours or salvage a cheese that did not come out right; and spices or plants that provided colouring were used to impart a richer look. Even today, there is still a considerable number of cheeses that have 'something added' to them – mostly ingredients to enhance the taste of a cheese which would be considered too bland without a bit of flavouring. What often happens, though, is that the cheese takes on the character of whatever is added to it, forsaking its own identity and almost becoming the ingredient that it is hosting. The cheese snob would tell you that cheese should be left alone, so that you can experience its character more fully when you enjoy it unadorned. But people who like the cheeses to which flavourings have been added, eat them because, at that moment, they want the taste of flavouring, not the taste of cheese. Although flavoured cheeses are often not great, not every cheese needs to be great. Many are very good and, moreover, they meet a need. In any event, the cheese and wine pairer is more interested in which wines to match to flavoured cheeses than in how great they are. In general, it is the added ingredient, rather than the cheese itself, that will determine the wine match. Some popular favourites are:

Biltong (blended into cream cheese, for example): Off-dry Weisser Riesling, Bukettraube;

Black peppercorns: Viognier, Shiraz;

Fruit pieces (pineapple, fig, citrus, berries): Off-dry Weisser Riesling, semi-sweet Chenin Blanc;

Garlic and herbs: Sauvignon Blanc;

Walnuts: wooded Chardonnay or Semillon.

The cheeseboard

Do you remember the traditional mixed cheeseboard that was once served with pride in good restaurants or at a smart dinner party? The sort that displayed a piece of blue, Cheddar, Gouda, goat's-milk and/or cream cheese, Brie, Camembert, and something smoked or rolled in walnuts, or in green herbs and black pepper to add a touch of colour... Finding a wine that would go with such elaborate diversity was simply impossible, so we invariably ended up settling for port, which more or less worked with the blue cheese and the Cheddar, but hated everything else.

Many people like to follow the French example of serving only one splendid cheese and matching it to a wine that is its most pleasing partner. It is considered rather chic to do this and you can't get closer to a successful wine and cheese match than with this option.

However, there's still much to be said for serving a board or platter of 'mixed cheeses' with its enticing variety of aromas, textures and tastes, but finding a wine to accompany a selection of widely differing cheeses is not possible.

Fortunately, there is a relatively simple solution: Decide whether you want to have your cheese instead of dessert, before you serve dessert, or right at the end of the meal, after dessert.

The order really doesn't matter because, if you are following the principle of serving a wine that is the best match for each dish, you'll find that you can go comfortably from a port or noble late harvest to Cabernet or Sauvignon Blanc. If the food demands that we make such a switch, we'll switch!

Say, for instance, you want to serve cheese straight after the main course. Start by deciding on a wine that you'd like to drink at that stage of the meal; for example, a full-bodied, wooded Chardonnay. Then, simply select a few Chardonnay-friendly cheeses and serve them in the same way that you would a 'mixed cheeseboard'.

If you would prefer to serve cheese after dessert, follow the same ritual: Decide on the wine first, let's say Shiraz this time, then gather some Shiraz-friendly cheeses and indulge! Or, here's another scenario: Let's say you want to serve a noble late harvest along with your crème brûlée and you'd like to keep the same wine for the cheese; simply choose cheeses that work well with noble late harvest, and *voilà*! Once you have chosen the wine, you can move onto selecting which cheeses to serve with it.

The following suggestions should make it simple for you to put together a cheeseboard that will match seamlessly with the wine of your choice.

BARBERA

Bel Paese, Camembert, Cantal, Fontina, Gorgonzola, Gouda (young and mild), Leiden with caraway, Manchego, Parmesan, Pecorino, Pont l'Evêque, Provolone (unsmoked).

BLANC DE NOIR or ROSÉ

Dry, with good acidity: Emmenthal, Feta, Gouda (young and mild), Mozzarella.
Off-dry: Boerenkaas, Fontina.

BUKETTRAUBE

Comté, Edam, Emmenthal, Fontina, Gouda (young and mild), Havarti, Jarlsberg, Provolone (unsmoked).

CABERNET FRANC

Cheshire, Goat's-milk cheese (Chevin), Manchego, Sage cheese.

CABERNET SAUVIGNON/BORDEAUX BLEND

Beaufort, Caerphilly, Camembert (a *young* one), Cantal, Cheddar, Double Gloucester, Gouda (matured), Gruyère, Mimolette, Mozzarella (buffalo or cow's milk), Old Amsterdam, Raclette, Stilton (only with a matured or soft-centred Cab Sav).

CAPE RIESLING (Paarl/South African Riesling)

Boursin (plain or with herbs), Caerphilly, Cheshire, Feta, goat's-milk cheese (Chevin), Jarlsberg, Lancashire, Leiden (with caraway) , Pont l'Evêque, Wensleydale.

CHAMPAGNE

See **Sparkling wine**, page 305.

CHARDONNAY

When it comes to Chardonnay, avoid pungent cheeses and those high in acid, such as goat's-milk cheeses.

Unwooded Asiago, Bel Paese, Brie, Havarti, Leicester (Red Leicester), Pecorino (matured), Port-Salut, Provolone (unsmoked), Taleggio (when young and mild), Wensleydale.

Wooded Beaufort, Brie (smooth, not matured), Caerphilly, Camembert, Cantal, Cheddar (young or matured), Comté, Emmenthal, Époisses, Fontina, Gruyère, Havarti (with lightly-oaked Chardonnay), Livarot, Mascarpone (plain, used as a table cheese), Mimolette, Morbier, Old Amsterdam, Parmesan (Parmigiano-Reggiano or Grana Padano), Pont l'Evêque, Reblochon, Smoked cheeses (especially Applewood Cheddar), St-Nectaire.

CHENIN BLANC

Asiago, Boursin (plain or with herbs), Caerphilly, Cheshire, Feta, Goat's-milk cheese (Chevin), Gruyère (with a semi-sweet Chenin), Havarti (with an off-dry Chenin), Jarlsberg, Lancashire, Pecorino (when young, not matured), Pont l'Evêque, Wensleydale.

CINSAUT

Asiago, Bel Paese, Boursin (plain, without herbs), Edam, Emmenthal, Fontina, Gorgonzola, Leicester (Red Leicester), Leiden (with caraway), Manchego, Pont l'Evêque, Provolone (unsmoked).

COLOMBARD

Boerenkaas, Brie, Edam, Emmenthal, Mozzarella (buffalo or cow's milk), Port-Salut, Provolone (unsmoked).

GEWÜRZTRAMINER

This is one of the few wines that can hold its own against strongly flavoured or pungent cheeses.

Boerenkaas (plain, or with cumin or mustard seed), Munster, Smoked cheeses (such as smoked Mozzarella or Provolone), Taleggio (ripened), Vintershoek.

GRENACHE

Appenzell(er), Cheshire, Goat's-milk cheese, matured (a rather powerful combination!), Gruyère, Munster, Raclette, St-Nectaire, Taleggio (ripened), Tomme de Savoie, Vintershoek, Witzenberger.

MERLOT

Asiago, Boerenkaas, Caerphilly, Camembert, Cantal, Cheddar, Comté, Double Gloucester, Emmenthal, Fontina, Leicester (Red Leicester), Natal green sage, Parmesan (Parmigiano-Reggiano or Grana Padano), Roquefort (at a push), St-Nectaire, Stilton.

MUSCADEL, RED

Bleu d'Auvergne (when pungent and matured), Cheddar (matured), Danish Blue-style cheeses.

NEBBIOLO

Manchego, Parmesan (Parmigiano-Reggiano or Grana Padano), Pecorino, Taleggio.

NOBLE LATE HARVEST

Bleu d'Auvergne (when pungent and matured), Roquefort.

PINOT BLANC

Goat's-milk cheese (Chevin), Mozzarella (buffalo or cow), Port-Salut.

PINOT GRIS/PINOT GRIGIO

Asiago, Comté, Emmenthal, Feta, Fontina, Gruyère, Morbier, Parmesan (Parmigiano-Reggiano or Grana Padano), Sage cheese.

PINOT NOIR

The best cheeses for Pinot Noir are the milder and creamier ones.

Asiago, Boursin (plain or with herbs), Brie, Camembert, Cheshire, Époisses, Fontina, Gruyère, Havarti (best with well-matured Pinot Noir), Leicester (Red Leicester), Livarot, Pont l'Evêque, Reblochon, Sage cheese, Taleggio (ripened).

PINOTAGE

Avoid blue cheeses. Go for Appenzell(er), Asiago, Camembert (with a well-matured Pinotage), Cheddar, Cheshire, Colby, Comté, Double Gloucester, Fontina, Gouda (young and mild), Leiden (with cumin), Manchego, Parmesan (Parmigiano-Reggiano or Grana Padano), Pecorino and Drunken Pecorino, Taleggio (ripened), Tomme de Savoie (or other Tommes), Witzenberger.

PORT

Ruby: Salty blue-veined cheeses.
Tawny: Bleu d'Auvergne (when pungent and matured), Cheddar (matured), Cheshire (matured), Pont l'Evêque, Stilton.
Vintage, Vintage Reserve and Late-bottled Vintage: Cheddar (matured for at least 12 months), Stilton.

SANGIOVESE

Asiago, Bel Paese, Camembert, Cantal, Colby, Gouda (young and mild), Leicester (Red Leicester), Leiden (with caraway), Manchego, Parmesan (Parmigiano-Reggiano or Grana Padano), Pecorino, Pont l'Evêque, Provolone (unsmoked), Sage cheese.

SAUVIGNON BLANC

Asiago, Boursin (plain, or with herbs, nuts or chives), Caerphilly, Cheshire, Feta, Goat's-milk cheese (Chevin), Haloumi, Lancashire, Leiden (with caraway), Pecorino (young, not matured), Pont l'Evêque, Sage cheese, Stilton, Wensleydale.

SEMILLON

Unwooded: Asiago, Bel Paese, Brie, Havarti, Pecorino (matured), Provolone (unsmoked), Taleggio (young and mild).
Wooded: Beaufort, Brie, Caerphilly, Camembert, Cantal, Cheddar (young or matured), Époisses, Fontina, Gruyère, Havarti (best with lightly wooded Semillon), Livarot, Morbier, Parmesan (Parmigiano-Reggiano or Grana Padano), Pont l'Evêque, Reblochon, St-Nectaire.

SHERRY

Pale dry (fino): Appenzell(er), Comté, Fontina, Gruyère, Manchego, Mimolette, Morbier, Old Amsterdam, Reblochon, Witzenberger.
Cream sherries: Beaufort, Boerenkaas, Cheddar (matured), Gorgonzola, Gruyère (with medium cream sherry), Mimolette, Old Amsterdam, Parmesan (Parmigiano-Reggiano/Grana Padano), Stilton.

SHIRAZ

Avoid soft, creamy, mild or blue-veined cheeses. Shiraz pairs best with hard, strong cheeses; pungency in a hard cheese is a plus.

Appenzell(er), Boerenkaas (plain, or with cumin or mustard seed), Cheshire, Goat's-milk cheese (matured; this is a powerful combination!), Gruyère, Leiden (with cumin), Munster, Parmesan (Parmigiano-Reggiano or Grana Padano), Pecorino (a powerful combination!), Drunken Pecorino, Raclette, Smoked cheeses, Taleggio (ripened), Tomme de Savoie (or other Tommes), Vintershoek, Witzenberger.

SPARKLING WINE

Because of its good acidity, sparkling wine likes acidic, really rich or salty cheeses.

Brut or **sec** (or **blanc de blanc champagne**): Cream cheeses (especially double- or triple-cream), Feta, Goat's-milk cheese (Chevin), Lancashire (with brut, sec or demi-sec), Morbier, Parmesan (Parmigiano-Reggiano or Grana Padano), Roquefort, Wensleydale.

Sparkling Shiraz or Pinotage: Mature goat's-milk cheese, Pecorino and Drunken Pecorino.

SPECIAL LATE HARVEST

Bleu d'Auvergne, Blue Brie (Winelands Blue), Blue Camembert, (Bleu en Blanc, Blue & Blanc), Gorgonzola, Roquefort (but only at a push), Smoked cheeses.

TEMPRANILLO

Cantal, Cheddar, Colby, Gouda (young and mild), Manchego, Parmesan (Parmigiano-Reggiano or Grana Padano), St-Nectaire.

VIOGNIER

Salty cheeses are Viognier's forte, but its viscosity makes it an ideal partner for other cheeses too.

Beaufort, Boerenkaas (plain or with cumin or mustard seed), Cantal, Colby, Comté, Feta, Fontina, Jarlsberg, Livarot, Mimolette, Munster, Old Amsterdam, Pecorino (when matured), Raclette, Roquefort-style blue cheeses, St-Nectaire, Taleggio (ripened), Tomme de Savoie (or other French Tommes), Vintershoek.

WEISSER RIESLING (dry or off-dry)

Beaufort (with an off-dry), Boerenkaas (with an off-dry), Boursin (plain or with herbs, nuts or chives), Caerphilly, Cheshire, Comté, Feta, goat's-milk cheese (Chevin), Gruyère (with an off-dry), Haloumi, Jarlsberg, Lancashire, Leiden (with caraway), Munster, Pecorino (when matured), Pont l'Evêque, Raclette, Vintershoek, Wensleydale.

ZINFANDEL

Boerenkaas, Cheddar, Comté, Gouda (matured), Mimolette, Parmesan (Parmigiano-Reggiano or Grana Padano), Stilton.

Glossary of wine and cheese terms

Acid/acidity Naturally present in grapes and essential to wine, which would taste flat and flabby without it. Acidity gives white wines their zing and reds their appetizing grip, and is critical to a wine's ability to pair with food.

Ageing The maturation of wine that can take place in tank, barrel or bottle. Not every wine has the capacity to age, though. Many white wines, and a few reds, are intended to be drunk young. Most red wines, however, do benefit from varying periods of maturation.

Alcohol content The alcoholic strength of a wine, or any alcoholic beverage, depends on the amount of alcohol it contains, expressed as a percentage of the total volume of the wine. For natural wines, this is in the 8–15% range. Fortified wines are between 17 and 22%.

Balance A well-balanced wine is what all winemakers strive for: the sense that all the components – fruit flavours, acidity, sweetness, alcohol, oak and tannin – are in place and in complete harmony. If one characteristic dominates, or is deficient, in the bouquet, flavour or aftertaste, the wine may be described as being out of balance.

Barrel-aged This simply means that the wine was aged (matured) in wooden casks, usually made of oak.

Blend/blended In this guide, the term 'blend' is mainly used for a mix of two or more grape varieties. In winemaking, it could also be the art of mixing wines of different origin, style or age.

Bloomy rind Cheeses with a bloomy rind are covered in a coat of white mould that helps to ripen the cheese from the outside in, softening the texture and enhancing flavour. (They are also known as 'mould-ripened' cheeses.)

Body The weight and texture of a wine as observed when you swirl it in the glass, and as it feels in your mouth when you taste it. A wine's 'body' is described as ranging from light to medium or full. When full-bodied, it is mouth-filling and contains a high quantity of soluble solids referred to as 'extract'. A light-bodied wine is the opposite.

Botrytis/botrytized wine These are rich, sweet wines made from grapes that have been beset by the fungus, *Botrytis cinerea*, called 'noble rot' to distinguish it from other kinds, such as 'sour rot', that only ruin the grapes. When the botrytis fungus attacks ripe white grapes, it dehydrates the grape berries and intensifies their sugar while adding a distinctive flavour.

Bottle-ageing/maturation The mellowing process that takes place after bottling and which can be detected in the bouquet of a wine and in its smoothness on the palate. Certain wines have the ability to develop in the bottle, while others, made for early drinking, do not.

Brut French word for 'dry', as applied, in particular, to dry champagne and other sparkling wine.

Buttery A characteristic that develops through barrel-fermenting or barrel-ageing white wines, such as Chardonnay. When describing a wine, 'buttery' means 'rich, creamy, smooth'.

Complex/complexity The presence of multiple layers of aromas and flavours, often developed over varying periods of barrel and/or bottle maturation.

Cool-climate The prevailing cool-weather conditions of a vine growing area. The term is applied to the coolest areas used successfully for growing wine grapes, such as the southernmost vineyards in South Africa: Cape Point, Constantia, Durbanville, Helderberg, parts of Stellenbosch, and the cool coastal strip of Elgin/Walker Bay. Light, delicate table wines with good acidity are, in general, best produced in cool viticultural climates, while full-bodied, sweet, fortified wines need warmer, sunny climates.

Creamy Used to describe wines that are smooth and silky in texture. This tasting term comes from the description used for the smoothness of sherry, which is often likened to cream.

Crisp This describes a refreshing wine with good, welcoming acidity.

Cultivar A term used by professional botanists to mean a cultivated variety (see **Variety**, below). It is widely and generally used in South Africa, unlike in other vine-growing countries where it does not have a following outside botanist's and horticulturist's circles.

Demi-sec A French term meaning not quite dry; or 'medium'-dry.

Depth A tasting term referring to richness with layers of flavour, all interlocked and supportive.

Dry/dryness A measure of the sweetness in a wine. South Africa is one of only a few countries that has legislated the terms used for varying degrees of sugar content in wine. A dry wine must contain less than five grams of residual sugar per litre (5g/*l*).

Extract Soluble solids, excluding sugars, which add to a wine's body and substance.

Finish The sensation that is left in your mouth when you swallow, that is, the aftertaste. When a wine's aftertaste lingers on the palate, it is said to have 'a good finish'.

Firm A tasting term mainly used to denote the impact of tannins in red wine.

Fortified wine Wines that have had grape spirit added to them, such as port, sherry or muscadel.

Fruity Description of a wine with a clearly recognizable aroma of fruit – either one fruit only, such as Granny Smith apple or guava, or a combination, for instance, of citrus or tropical fruit.

Generous This description is usually applied to red wines with warm, ripe-fruit flavours.

Grassy A wide term used for many of the 'green' flavours detected in wine. It can refer to the varietal character of Sauvignon Blanc (a 'freshly mown lawn') or the under-ripe aromas of Chardonnay.

Herbaceous A term used to describe aromas of crushed green leaves, freshly cut grass, drying hay, fynbos or herbs in general, but none prominent enough to be identified.

Lees During fermentation and maturation, sediment (called lees) sinks to the bottom of the tank or barrel and the clear wine is drawn off the top before bottling. Frequently, wines are left on the lees for various periods to impart more flavour to the wine. Like tea leaves in a pot, a frequent stirring is necessary to keep the sediment in suspension to extract that extra flavour. Wines treated in this way are labelled *sur lie*, a French term for the process.

Light The opposite of full-bodied or heavy, light wines usually contain less alcohol than full, rich ones. Although they do not have the complexity of great wines, they have charm and pleasing characteristics of their own.

Maturation The beneficial aging of a wine.

Medium-sweet A wine with residual sugar of between 5 and 30 grams per litre, but often more than 12 grams per litre (g/*l*) – tasting quite sweet but not fully sweet.

Natural rind Cheese exposed to air develops a natural rind over time. This acts as a hard, yet permeable, wrap around it, protecting the cheese from drying out too much and too fast, while allowing it to 'breathe' and mature at the same time.

New World In the wine industry, this term denotes the wine-growing regions of North and South America, Australia, New Zealand and South Africa. When used to describe a wine, it means the wine is bold and full, and often accessible when young. (*See also* **Old World**.)

Noble rot *See* **Botrytis**, above.

Nutty An aroma and flavour identical to that of almonds, hazelnuts and other nuts. Mostly used to describe sherries, but it also pops up frequently with regard to Chardonnay, certain red wines and brandy.

Oak/oaked Oak is the wood of choice used almost exclusively to make barrels for fermenting and ageing wine. Oaked wines are those that have been matured in oak barrels; or have undergone their initial fermentation in barrels as well. To add the same oak flavour to wine without maturing it in expensive barrels, some producers add oak staves or chips to a stainless steel vat of wine.

Off-dry In South Africa a wine that is labelled 'off-dry' is semi-dry, containing 5–12g/*l* (grams of sugar per litre).

Old World A term originally used for wines made in Europe. They were supple, complex, had less oak flavours and took longer to ease out and mature. Such wines are now made in the New World too – including South Africa. (*See* also **New World**.)

On the lees *See* **Lees**, above.

Residual sugar During fermentation, yeast converts the naturally occurring sugar in grape juice into alcohol. As there may not be an even distribution of yeast and sugar present in the juice, some sugar remains unconverted, a bit like dividing an even number into an odd number and getting a remainder. The sugar that remains in the wine is called 'residual sugar'.

Robust This term indicates that the wine is full of flavour, but implies that this flavour is not very subtle.

Rounded/rounded out A wine that is smooth and ready to drink.

Semi-sweet A very South African term for wines containing between 5 and 30 grams of residual sugar; usually around 20g/*l*. They are usually white, stein or rosé wines.

Soft Mainly used for red wines that have no harsh tannins or noticeable acidity.

Structure This refers to the make-up of the wine and its ability to age. If a wine has the essential characteristics of alcohol, tannin and acidity, in balance with generous fruit and flavour, it has the structure to develop further with bottle maturation.

Supple A term that goes hand in hand with 'mouthfeel' and which is used for red wines, to indicate that they are smooth, fruity, juicy, lively and well balanced.

Sur lie *See* **Lees**, above.

Sweetness Literally the amount of sugar as perceived. Sugar levels in wine range from non-perceptible (as in dry wines) to slightly sweet (from off-dry to semi-sweet) to very sweet (as in dessert wines). In South Africa, regulations exist that clearly define the claims made on a label as to the wine's degree of dryness or sweetness.

Sweet-fruited Some wines smell and taste like ripe fruit, when it is said that the wine is deeply 'sweet-fruited'.

Tannin/tannic The harsh, bitter and, often, mouth-puckering element in red wine. Tannin derives from grape skins, seeds and stems, and also from oak barrels. Tannins soften with age and are essential for the long-term development and colour of red wines. They must be taken into account when matching food and wine.

Terroir A French term (with no precise English translation!) used to describe the complete natural physical environment of a viticultural site, that is, the combination of its soil, climate, geographical profile, the direction in which it faces, and its exposure to the sun – all of which determine the eventual character or signature of a wine.

Texture A sensation in the mouth that can range from smooth and velvety to hard and acidic.

Triple cream Cheeses that have at least 75% fat in their dry matter (the cheese minus its water) are categorized as 'triple-cream'; 'double-cream' cheeses contain 60–70%.

Unoaked Wines that have had no contact with oak (wood) at all during their production.

Variety and its adjectival form, **varietal** A vine-type that produces its own characteristic wine that is unlike any other. A wine made from, and named after, a single grape variety is called a varietal wine.

Velvety Smooth on the tongue because of lower acidity and a high glycerol content.

Vinification The conversion of the grape's natural juice into wine by fermentation.

Vintage The year that the grapes were harvested and the resultant wine made. However, when used in the context of 'vintage port' or 'vintage champagne', it means that the particular wine so labelled is outstanding, as these styles of wines are only given a vintage date in years of exceptional quality.

Viscosity The quality of being viscous; the ease with which a liquid flows. Viscosity is what wine tasters call 'body' and it can be sensed on the palate in the form of resistance as the wine is swirled around the mouth. A light, dry white wine has low viscosity and flows freely, while heavy, thick, sweet wines have high viscosity and flow more slowly.

Volatile Vaporization of liquids, carrying with it flavours and aromas, which are picked up when we smell a wine.

Washed rind 'Washed-rind cheese' is washed repeatedly during its maturation with water, brine or a mixture of brine and selected bacteria. This creates a moist, salty surface that is inhospitable to mould but favourable to certain flavour-enhancing bacteria.

Weight This is a wine-tasting term used to describe the sensation on the palate of fullness or weightiness resulting from low viscosity in a wine. The higher the alcohol and dissolved solids (extract) in a wine, the heavier the wine is said to be. Although a weighty wine makes an instant impression, it does not necessarily imply that it is a wine of quality.

Yield The production of a given area of vines, expressed in tons of grapes per hectare, or the amount of wine produced from a vineyard, measured in hectolitres per hectare.

Selected bibliography

Baljekar, Mridula, *Curry Bible* (Bath: Parragon Books, 2008).

Barrett, Christine, *The Book of Mexican Foods* (London: Salamander Books, 1991).

Barthélemy, Roland and Sperat-Czar, Arnaud, *Cheeses of the World* (London: Hachette UK, Octopus Publishing Group, 2004).

Bateman, Michael, *The World of Spice* (London: Kyle Cathie, 2003).

Beckett, Fiona, *Wine Uncorked* (London: Mitchell Beazley, 1999).

Benson, Jeffrey and Walton, Stuart, *The Right Wine with the Right Food* (Surrey: Elliot Right Way Books, 2003).

Braimbridge, Sophie and Glynn, Jo, *The Food of Italy* (Sydney: Murdoch Books, 2000).

Carrier, Robert, *Robert Carrier's Kitchen* (London: Marshall Cavendish Partworks, 1980).

Chapman, Pat, *The Curry Club Indian Restaurant Cookbook* (London: Piatkus, 1984).

Clarke, Oz, *Oz Clarke's Pocket Wine Book 2003* (London: Time Warner Books, 2002).

Dale, Rodney, *Dictionary of Culinary & Menu Terms* (Hertfordshire: Wordsworth Editions, 2000).

Duckitt, Hildagonda, *Hilda's 'Where is it?' of Recipes* (London: Chapman & Hall, 1891).

Goldstein, Evan, *Perfect Pairings*, (University of California Press, 2006).

Hands, Phyllis and Hughes, Dave, *Wines and Brandies of the Cape of Good Hope* (Somerset West: Stephan Phillips, 1997).

Hazan, Giuliano, *The Classic Pasta Cookbook* (Cape Town: Human & Rousseau, 1994).

Jaffrey, Madhur, *Madhur Jaffrey's Indian Cookery* (BBC Books, 1982).

Montagné, Prosper, *New Larousse Gastronomique, The World's Greatest Cookery Reference Book* (London: Hamlyn, 1977).

Ortiz, Elisabeth Lambert, *Taste of Mexico* (London: Hermes House, 2002).

Pellaprat, Henri-Paul, *L'Art Culinaire Moderne* (London: Collins, 1967).

Robinson, Jancis, *The Guide to Wine Grapes* (Oxford University Press, 1996); *The Oxford Companion to Wine* (OUP, 1997).

Simon, Joanna, *Discovering Wine* (London: Reed International Books, 1994).

Steer, Gina, *Woman's Own Classic Cookery* (London: Hamlyn, 1994).

Van Wyk, Magdaleen, *The Complete South African Cookbook* (Johannesburg: Central News Agency, 1980).

Index

Page numbers in **bold** represent
key entries.

A

Abalone **153**, 158
Acidity, pairing guidelines 20–21
Anchovies 111
Antipasto 111, **120–121**
Aperitif, wine as an 112–113
Appenzell(er) **273**, 299, 303, 304
Applewood **297**, 302
Artichokes 46, 100, **121**
Asiago **274**, 302, 303, 304
Asparagus 46, 64, 100, **121**
  quiche 93
  risotto 168
Aubergine see Brinjal
Avocado 121–122
  guacamole 130
  mousse 132
  Ritz 102
  salad 110

B

Baba ghannouj 123
Baby marrow 94
  flowers 127
  stuffed 66
Bacalhau 149
Beaufort **274**, 301, 302, 304, 305
Beef 172–190
  bobotie 174
  boerewors 174
  boeuf en daube 97, **174**
  bollito misto 175
  bourguignonne 172
  brisket 175
  burgers 175
  burritos 176
  cannelloni 176
  carbonnade 60, 75, **176**
  chateaubriand 60–61, **177**
  chilli con carne 177
  chimichangas 126
  cocido Madrileño 178
  corned 178
  corned beef hash 74, 75, 84
  cottage pie 178
  cozido à Portuguesa 178
  curry 172
  enchiladas 179
  espetadas 179
  frikkadel see meatballs 181
  grilled (see also roast) 65, 73, 92

  Hungarian goulash 179
  kebabs 179–180
  lasagna 180
  ma po tofu 246
  marrow bones 181
  meatballs 181
  meatloaf 181
  moussaka 182
  olives 172
  oxtail 182
  picadillo 182
  potjie 182
  red wine, cooked in 98
  roast 69, 92, 104, **183–184**
  satay 97
  sauerbraten 184
  Sechuan (Sichuan) 246
  sloppy joes 185
  steak 185–189
  steak and kidney pie 185
  steak tartare 190
  stew 91, **173**
  stir-fried 190
  Stroganoff 173
  tacos 190
  Wellington 173
Bel Paese **274**, 301, 302, 304
Berries see Fruit
Biltong **122**, 210
Biscotti 104
Bitterness, pairing guidelines 22–24
Blanquette de veau 65, 82, **205**
Bleu d'Auvergne **275**, 303, 304, 305
Blue Brie **275**, 305
Blue Camembert **275**, 305
Blue cheeses 271, **275**, 280, 284,
    295, 297, 300, 303, 305
Bobotie 174
Boerenkaas **275–276**, 301, 303, 305
Boerewors 87, 97, **174**
Boeuf bourguignonne 61, **172**
Boeuf en daube 97, **174**
Bokkoms 135
Bollito misto 175
Boursin **276**, 301, 302, 303, 304
Braaied food 65
Brains 211
Brandade 66, **122–123**
Bratwurst 105, **203**
Brawn 211
Bread, as a palate scrubber 31
Bredie, lamb 191–192

Breyani 229
Brie 84, **276**, 302, 303, 304
  deep-fried 128
Brinjal
  alla parmigiana (melanzane)
    56, **164**
  purée 123
  salad 145
Brisket 175
Bruschetta 123
Buffalo wings 123
Bully beef see Corned beef
Burgers 175
Burritos 176
Butter chicken (makhani) 232
C
Cabanossi see Sausage 203
Cacciatora 216
Caerphilly **276-277**, 301, 302, 303,
    304, 305
Caesar salad 64, **145**
Cakes 259
  Black Forest cherry 259
  brownies, chocolate 260
  lemon 259
  orange 259
  panettone 104, 259
Calamari see Seafood
Caldo verde 107
Calzone 164
Cambozola see Blue Brie
Camembert 84, 272, 273, 275,
    277, 301, 302, 303, 304
  deep-fried 128
Canapés 100, 102
Cantal **278**, 301, 302, 303, 304, 305
Cannelloni, beef 176
Capers 46
Caprese salad 145
Caprino Romana 284
Carbonada criolla 73-74
Carbonnade 176
Carpaccio 92, **123-124**
Casseroles, see Stews
Cassoulet 74, **199**, 224
Cauliflower gratin 72, 77, **164**
Caviar 100, **124-125**
Ceviche 110, **125**
'champagne breakfast' 103
Char siu 243
Charcuterie 60, 75, 77, 84
  see also Cold meats 126-127
Chateaubriand 60-61, **177**
Chavroux 283

Chawanmushi 238
Cheddar **278**, 297, 300, 301, 302,
    303, 304, 305
Cheese fondue 60
Cheeseboards 300-305
Cheeses 270-305
  see also individual entries
Cheshire **278-279**, 301, 302, 303,
    304, 305
Chevin 94, **283**, 301, 302, 304, 305
Chèvre 94, 283
Chicken 214-224
  à la King 83, **215**
  and black beans 244
  bang bang 243
  barbecue 59, 71, 91, **214**
  braaied, see barbecue
  breasts 77, **215-216**
  buffalo wings 123
  butter (makhani) 232
  cacciatora 216
  Cajun-style 111, **214-215**
  chasseur 216
  chilli 222
  cold 59
  coq au vin 221
  cordon bleu 219
  coronation 221
  curry 216-217
  devilled 222
  enchiladas 217
  fricassee 217
  goujon 217
  grilled 92, 111, **222**
  honey and mustard 59, 86, 222
  in a cream sauce 215
  in chocolate-chilli sauce 217-218
  in fruity sauces 104
  jambalaya 218
  jerked 97, **222**
  Kashmiri murgh 231
  kebabs 65
  Kiev 218
  kung pao 245-246
  lemon 246
  lemon and herb 222
  liver mousse 132
  liver pâté 134
  livers 125
  Marengo 219
  Maryland 219
  mousse 132
  paella 219
  peri-peri 222

piccata (escalopes) 219
pie 219
pilaf 220
plainly cooked 100
potjie 220
roast 58, 69, 75, 86, 92, 106, **223**
salad 145
scaloppine 220
schnitzel 220
Southern-fried 84, **223**
spatchcocked 222
stir-fried 83, 105, **223–224**
tacos 224
tagine 221
tandoori 234
tikka 235
with cashew nuts 244
with mango 215
with prosciutto crudo 215
yakitori 241
see also Indian, Japanese cuisine
Chile rellenos 126
Chilli 47, 222
bites 125
con carne 72, 97, **177**
poppers (stuffed jalapeños) 126
sauces 40, 43, 252
Chimichangas 126
Chinese cuisine 100, 105, 107, 110, **242–248**
bang bang chicken 243
– barbecued pork (char siu) 243
chicken with black beans 244
chicken with cashew nuts 244
chop suey 244
chow mein 244
crispy duck 244
dim sum 245
fish, steamed 247
fishcakes 245
foo young 245
kung pao 245
lemon chicken 246
ma po tofu 246
Peking duck 246
Sichuan beef 246
spareribs 247
spring rolls 247
stir-fried dishes 247
take-away 68
sweet-and-sour dishes 71, **248**
Chocolate, fear of 47
chocolate-chilli dishes 97, 217
see also Desserts 254–269

Chop suey 244
Chorizo 67, 72, 107, 140, 178, 199, **203**, 219
Chow mein 244
Choucroute 71, **199**
Chutney 47
Citrus fruits 256
grapefruit 49, 130
lemons and limes 50
Classic food and wine pairings 12
Cocido Madrileño 97, 178
Cocktail parties 113
Colby **279**, 303, 304, 305
Cold meats 59, 82, **126–127**
Colour-coding rule 13–16
Comté **279**, 301, 302, 303, 304, 305
Contrast in food and wine pairing 28
Confit de canard 225
see also Duck confit
Consommé 142
Cooking methods 26
Coq au vin 221
Cordero en chilidrón 106
Corned beef 75, **178**
Coronation chicken 221
Cottage cheese (curd) **280**
Cottage pie 60, 67, 75, 84, 92, 98, 106, **178**
Courgette flan 82
see also Baby marrow 66, 94, 127
Couscous salad 82
Cozido à Portuguesa 178
Crab 65, 107, **153**
mousse 104
risotto 65
Cranberry sauce and jelly 37, 48
Crayfish 107, **154**
thermidor 64, 101, 154
Cream cheese **280**, 288, 300, 305
Crostini 127
Crudités 82, **128**
Cucumber mousse 132
Cured meats see Cold meats 126–127
Curries see also Indian cuisine 227–236
beef 172
Cape (Malay) 66, 91
chicken 216–217
coconutty 100
do piaza 230
dry 250
eggs 159
fish 150

Indian 95, 106, 107, 111
Kashmiri 231
korma 95, 107, **232**
lamb 194
Madras 232
Massaman 250
molee 233
pork 202
rhogan josh (gosht) 233–234
Thai green/red 107, 110, **250**
Vietnamese chicken 95

D

Danish Blue **280**, 303
Desserts 254–269
almond-flavoured 77, 80, 104
apple
    -based 80
    crumble 80
    pie (strudel) 257–258
    puddings 110
    tarte Tatin 80, 104, **268**
apricot tart 104
baked Alaska 258
baked custard 104
banana split 77
Bavarian cream 80, **258**
berries and cream 100, 258
Black Forest cherry cake 77, 259
bread and butter pudding 80,
    104, 259
cakes 100, 259
Cape brandy pudding 260
cheesecake 80, 104, **260**
chocolate cake 77, 89, **259**
chocolate brownies **260**
chocolate-flavoured 77, 80, 89,
    90, 111
chocolate ice cream 96
chocolate mousse 80, **260**
chocolate, toffee and fudge 256
Christmas cake 89
    pudding 89, **261**
coffee-flavoured 80, 256
cream-based 256
crème brûlée 80, 261
crème caramel 104, 110, **261**
crêpes Suzette 80, **261–262**
croquembouche 267
egg-based 256
floating islands 262
fools 262
fruit-based, dried 80, 89, **256**
fruit-based, fresh 255–256
fruit cake 262

fruit, mincemeat 76
fruit platters and salads 100, 262
fruit salad, orange and sultana 80
fruit tarts, flans 80, 104, 110, **263**
fudge 96
ginger 76, 80, 107
halva 263
hazelnut-flavoured 80
Hertzogkoekies 90
ice cream 50, 76, 77, 107, 255,
    258, **263–264**
île flottante 80, **262**
'instant' puddings 264
lemon- and lime-based 80
lemon
    caramelized, tart 110
    meringue pie 80, 104, **264**
    tart 264
macaroons 90
malva pudding 96, **264–265**
marzipan 104
milktart (melktert) 90, 104, **265**
mince pies 89, 96, 256, **265**
mousses 265
nougat pudding (torrone molle) 104
nut-based/flavoured 76, **257**
orange-flavoured 76
oranges, caramelized 80, 89, **260**
pancakes 80 see also Crêpes
    Suzette 261–262
panna cotta 265
Pavlova 265
peach Melba 266
peach tarts 104
pears belle Hélène 80, 110, **266**
pears in red wine 266
pecan pie 96, 104, 110, **267**
peppermint tart 267
profiteroles 110, **267**
raspberries 84, 258
rhubarb 267
Sachertorte 77, **259**
savarin 259
sherry trifle 77, 96, **269**
sorbet 264
soufflés, sweet 267–268
steamed puddings 110, **268**
sticky toffee pudding 96, 256, **268**
strawberries 84, 100, 258
tarte Tatin 80, 104, **268**
tipsy tart 110, **260**
tiramisu 269
toffee-flavoured 256
trifle, see sherry trifle 269

vacherin 269
vanilla-flavoured 80
zabaglione 269
Devilled
  chicken 222
  kidneys 212
Dhaltjies see Chilli bites 125
Dhansak 230
Dim sum 66, **245**
Do piaza 230
Dolmades 128
Double Gloucester **280**, 301, 303
Drakensberg 283
Droëwors 122
Drunken Pecorino 292
Duck 224–225
  à l'orange 64, 100, **224–225**
  confit 58, 74, **225**
  crispy 244
  liver paté 134
  Peking 246
  roast 97, 110, **225**
  with black cherries or grapes 111
  with fruity sauces 84, 104

E
Echo factor 26
Edam 271, **281**, 284, 288,
  301, 302
Eggplant see Brinjal
Eggs 48, 128, **159–163**
  eggy sauces/dishes 35, 64
  ostrich 163
  quail 163
Eisbein 105, **199**
Emmenthal(er) 271, 273, **282**, 286,
  301, 302, 303
Enchiladas, beef 179
  chicken 217
Époisses **282**, 302, 303, 304
Escabèche 150
Escalopes 202, **206–207**, 219, 220
Escargots 139
Espetadas 179

F
Famous wine/food partnerships 12
Fennel 48
Feta **282**, 301, 302, 303, 304
Fish **147–152**, 158
  and chips 150
  bacalhau 149
  bisque 142
  bokkoms 135
  bouillabaisse 142
  braaied, grilled, pan-fried 147–149

brandade 122–123
Cajun-style 149
canned 152
casserole 150
ceviche 125
creamy sauces, in 66, 71, 107, 110
curry 150
escabèche 150
Florentine 151
gefilte 151
gravadlax (gravlax) 135–136
grilled, braaied, pan-fried 147–149
haddock 151
hake 110
harders 148
    see also bokkoms 135
herrings and rollmops 136
kippers 151
maasbanker 81, 148
mackerel 94, 110, 148
marlin 81
molee (Goan fish curry) 233
monkfish 82, 95, 148
mousse 82, 132
pan-fried, braaied, grilled 147–149
pâté and terrine 82, 110, 135
pickled and salted 135–136, 152
pie 95, **150**
plainly cooked 64, 66
poached in red wine 69
salmon, fresh 65, 69, 103, 149
    smoked 82, 103, 138, 161
sardines 95, **137**
sashimi 239
smoked 104, **138**
smoorsnoek (braised snoek) 152
snoek 81, 109, 149
sole 148
  poached 110
steamed 247
stew 150
taramasalata 140
tilapia 66, 148
trout 66, 82, 104, 105, 110
tuna, fresh 81, 149
tuna, canned 152
yellowtail 95, 149
whitebait 140
  see also Chinese cuisine
Fishcakes 150, 245, 251
Flavour intensity 19
Foie gras 71, 100, **128–129**, 132
Fontina **283**, 301, 302, 303,
  304, 305

Foo young 245
Food and wine pairing, going
      too far 16–17
Frankfurters 203
French onion tart 66
Fricassee, chicken 217
      veal 205, 207
Frikkadel see Meatballs 181
Fritto misto di mare 129
Fruit
      berries 70, **255**, **258**
      figs, fresh 129
      grapefruit 49, **130**
      melon 130
      mixed platters 262–263
      salads 262–263
      starter, as a 129–130
      see also Desserts
Fusion food 108
G
Game (venison) 87, 92, **209–210**
      birds 110
      mousse 132
      terrine 135
      see also Guinea fowl, Ostrich,
          Quail, Venison
Gammon 66, 104, **200**
Garlic 49
      sauce 36
      snails with garlic butter 139
Gazpacho 142
Gefilte fish 151
Ginger 49
Gnocchi 164
Goat's-milk cheese 93, **283**, 301–
      302, 303, 304, 305
Goose 74, **225–226**
      foie gras 128–129
Gorgonzola 104, **284**, 301, 302,
      304, 305
Gouda 270, 281, **284–285**, 289,
      301, 303, 304, 305
Goulash 75, 86
Grana Padano see also Parmesan
      291–292, 301, 302, 303,
      304, 305
Grape varieties see Wines and
      wine styles
Gravadlax (gravlax) 66, 102, 110,
      135–136
      see also Smoked salmon 138
Greek salad 145–146
Grilled or braaied food 71, 77, 81,
      86, 97

Gruyère **285**, 301, 302, 303,
      304, 305
Guacamole 64, 101, **130**
Guinea fowl 69, 100, **226**
Gumbo 218
Gyoza 238
H
Haddock 151
Haloumi **130**, **285**, 304, 305
Ham 65, 69, **200**
      mousse 132
Hamburgers 175
Harders 135
Havarti **285–286**, 301, 302,
      303, 304
Haxe (pork shank) see Eisbein 199
Herbs and spices 49–50
Herrings and rollmops 136
Hock see Eisbein 199
Honey-and-mustard flavouring
      95, 111
Horizontal pairing 28
Horseradish 50
Hot-pot 75, 198
Htapothi krassato see Octopus
      stew 62
Hummus 130–131
Hungarian goulash 179
I
Ice cream see Desserts
Indian cuisine 110, **227–236**
      breyani 229
      butter chicken, see Makhani 232
      curries 61, 71, 74
      dhansak 230
      do piaza 230
      jalfrezi 230
      Kashmiri murgh 231
      kofta 108, 193–194, **231**
      korma 64, 95, 107, **232**
      lamb dishes 72
      Madras curry 232
      makhani (butter chicken) 232
      molee (Goan fish curry) 233
      pasanda 233
      pilau 233
      phal 233
      rhogan josh (gosht) 233–234
      saag gosht 234
      tandoori murgh (chicken) 234
      tikka 235
      yoghurt as an ingredient in 60
      vindaloo 66, 107, **235–236**
Irish stew 58, **192**

J
Jalfrezi see Indian cuisine 230
Jambalaya, chicken 218
Japanese cuisine 110, **237–241**
  chawanmushi 238
  dipping sauces 237
  gyoza 238
  miso 95, **238**, 241
  nabemono 238
  ramen 239
  raw-fish dishes 100, 102
  robatayaki 239
  sashimi **239**, 241
  sushi 100, **239–240**
  tempura 240–241
  teppanyaki 240
  teriyaki 57, 72, 84, 97, **241**
  tonkatsu 241
  yakitori 241
Jarlsberg **286**, 301, 302, 305
K
Kashmiri murgh see Indian
  cuisine 231
Kassler chops 201
Kebabs 106
  beef 179–180
  barbecue-spiced lamb 192
  chicken 65
  Moroccan 192
  pork 65
  shami kebab 231
  sheek kebab 231
  shish kebab **138**, **192–193**
  sosaties 193
Kedgeree 151
Keftedes 131
Khao pad 251
Kidneys 56, 58, 106, **212**
Kleftiko 193
Kofta 108, 193–194, **231**
Korma 232
Kudu 87, 97, 111
Kung pao 245–246
L
Lamb 191–197
  braaied, grilled or panfried 191
  bredie **191–192**, 195
  chops 60, 81
  curry 194
  Irish stew 192
  Karoo, braaied, fatty 65
  kebabs 138, **192–193**, 231
  kidneys 212
  Lancashire hotpot 194

liver 56
  mutton (or lamb) pie 194–195
  navarin (ragoût) 195
  noisettes 195
  potjie 97, 195
  pré-salé 58
  roast 58, 106, **195–196**
  shanks 196
  shepherd's pie 197
  shish kebabs 138
  sosaties 193
  stews and casseroles 106, **194**
  tajine 197
Lancashire **286**, 302, 304, 305
Lancashire hotpot 194
Langoustine 154
Lasagne 180
Leek and ham bake 71
Leicester, Red **287**, 302, 303
Leiden **287**, 301, 302, 303, 304, 305
Lemon and lime juice/flavouring
  50, 110
Lentils 165
Likeness in food and wine pairing 28
Liqueurs 225, 254, 256, 259,
  267, 288
Livarot **287**, 302, 303, 304, 305
Liver 91, **212**
  calves' 69 75
  chicken 125, 134
  lamb's 56, 58, 61, 75, 87
  mousse, chicken 132
M
Ma po tofu 246
Macaroni cheese 165
Madrid stew see Cocido
  Madrileño 97, 178
Makhani (butter chicken) 232
Manchego 77, **287–288**, 301, 302,
  303, 304, 305
Marrow bones 181
Mascarpone **288**, 302
Massaman curry 250
Matambre 73
Meat risotto 168–169
Meatballs, beef 181
  pork 201
  veal 207
  kofta 231
Meatloaf 84, **181**
Mediterranean dishes and Merlot 75
Melanzane alla parmigiana 56, **165**
Mexican refried beans 107
Mezze 131

Mieliebrood 95
Mimolette **288**, 291, 301, 302, 304, 305
Mint sauce/jelly 41, **50-51**
Miso 238, **241**
Mole (Mexican) 97, **217-218**
Molee/mouli (Indian) 233
Morbier **289**, 302, 303, 304, 305
Moroccan tajines/kebabs 97, 192
Moussaka 56, 75, 86, **165**, **182**
Mousses, savoury **131-132**, 135
Mozzarella 274, **289-290**, 297, 301, 302, 303
Munster 105, **290**, 299, 302, 303, 304, 305
Mushrooms 69, 75, 77, 98, 106, 107-108, **132-133**
    ravioli 82
    risotto 169
Mussels 94, 95, **154-155**
Mustard 51
Mutton bredie, tomato-based 93
    pie 195

N
Nabemono 238
Nachos 133
Navarin of lamb 195
Nut roast 82, **165**
Nuts 102, 104

O
Octopus stew 62
Offal 77, **212-213**
    brains 211
    brawn 211
    kidneys 56, 58, **212**
    liver 56, 58, **125**, 132, **212**
    pens en pootjies (tripe and trotters) 213
    sweetbreads 213
    tongue 213
    tripe 213
Old Amsterdam **291**, 301, 302, 304, 305
Olives 51, 111, **133**
    tapenade 140
Onion tart/flan 71, 82
Omelettes 159
Osso buco 207-208
Ostrich 87, 97, 111, **210**, 226
    eggs 163
Oxtail 72, 74, 97, 142, **182**
Oysters 64, 94, 100, 101, **133-134**

P
Paella 56, **155**, **219**

Pairing of wines,
    acidity 20
    bitterness 22-24
    considerations 18-25
    five primary taste sensations 19-25
    flavour intensity 19
    horizontal and vertical 28-29
    likeness and contrast 28-29
    old serving guidelines 30-31
    saltiness 22
    sauces, impact on wine choices 32-34
    secondary considerations 25-27
    sweetness 19-20
    umami **24-25**, 240
    weight 18
Pad Thai 251
Parma ham see Prosciutto crudo 56, 82; Cured hams 126-127
Parmesan **291-292**, 301, 302, 303, 304, 305
Parmigiano-Reggiano see Parmesan
Pasanda 233
Pasta
    cannelloni 92, **176**
    gnocchi 164
    lasagne 180
    linguine 82
    macaroni cheese 165
    ravioli see stuffed pasta 169
    tortellini see stuffed pasta 169
Pasta sauces/dressings 165-167
    all'Alfredo 69, **166**
    Amatriciana 166
    anchovy 77
    arrabbiata 166
    Bolognese 16-17, 56, 67, 92, **185**
    broccoli 77
    carbonara 56, **166**
    creamy 64, **166**
    gorgonzola 166
    marinara 166
    meaty 77
    olio e aglio (olive oil and garlic) 82, **167**
    pappardelle al coniglio 92
    pesto 64, 82, **167**
    porcini mushroom 92
    primavera 167
    puttanesca 166
    seafood 167
    tomato-based 75, 92, 93, **166**
    vongole 167
    see also Pizza

Pâté de foie gras 134
Pâtés & terrines 59, 71, 102, **134–135**
Pecorino (Romano) 77, 284, **292**, 301, 302, 303, 304, 305
Peking duck 66, **246**
Pens en pootjies (tripe & trotters) 213
Pepper 26
Pepperoni 67, 72
Peppers, stuffed 71, 83, 104, 105, 106, 111, **169**
Perlemoen **153**, 158
Phal 233
Picadillo 182
Piccata 206
Picnic dishes 57
Pies
  chicken 219
  fish 150
  lamb or mutton 194–195
  pork 202–203
  steak and kidney 185
  venison 210
Pilau 233
Pilchards (canned) 152
Piperade 56
Pithiviers 259
Pizza 67, 92, 164, **167–168**
Po pia 252
Pofadders 87
Pont l'Evêque 272, 276, **292**, 301, 302, 303, 304
Porceddu 62
Pork 198–204
  and bean casserole 107
  bangers and mash 69, **203**
  barbecued pork (char siu) 243
  casseroles & stews 65, 105, **198**
  cassoulet 74, **199**
  chasseur 201
  chops with mustard sauce 69
  choucroute 199
  curry 202
  eisbein (pork shank) 199
  escalopes 202
  fillets in bacon 200
  gammon 200
  ham 200
  haxe (hock), see Eisbein 199
  Kalahari kreef see Fillets in bacon
  Kassler chops 86, **201**
  kebabs 65
  meatballs 201
  pie 203–204

ribs, braaied 198
rillettes 71, 136
roast 59, 92, 106, 110, **204**
sausages 203
stir-fried 83
suckling pig 62
toad in the hole 203
tonkatsu 241
Port-Salut **293**, 302, 303
Potato bake 168
Po pia 252
Potjie
  beef 182–183
  chicken 220
  lamb 195
  venison 210
Prawns 95, **155–156**
  tempura 94, **240**
Prosciutto crudo 56, 65, 68, 70, 82, 91 see also Cured hams 126
Provençal fish soup 142
Provolone **293**, 297, 301, 302, 304
Puff-pasty dishes 102
Pumpkin fritters 109
Q
Quail 61, 74, 86, 92, 97, 100, 104, 110, **226**
  eggs 163
Quesadillas 136
Quiche 64, 82, **162**
  Lorraine 59
R
Rabbit 60, 77, 97
Raclette **293–294**, 301, 303, 304, 305
Ragoût see Lamb, navarin 195
Ramen 239
Ratatouille 56, 111, **168**
Ravioli 169
Reblochon **294–295**, 302, 303, 304
Red meat rule 13–17
Rhogan josh (gosht) 84, 93, **233–234**
Rice, fried 251
Ricotta **295**
Rillettes de porc 60, 136
Risotto 64, 82, 92, **168–169**, 207
  alla Milanese **169**, 207
  asparagus 168
  crab 108
  meat 168–169
  mushroom 95, 101, 107–108, 169
  nero 169
  Parmesan/truffle 95, 101

pea 169
red wine 169
seafood 169
Rissoles 183
Robatayaki 239
Rollmops 136
Roquefort 12, 270, 280, 284, **295–296**, 303, 305
  mousse 132
Rules of colour coding 13–17
Russian sausage 203
S
Saag gosht 234
Sage cheese **296**, 301, 303, 304
Saki 237
Salad Niçoise 146
Salads **144–146**, 251
Salami 126
Salisbury steak 61
Salmon, smoked 138
Salsa 52
Saltimbocca 206
Saltiness, pairing guidelines 22
Samosas 137
Sashimi 82, **239**, 241
Satay 69, 97, 180, **252**
Sauces and their impact 32–34
Sauces 35–43, *see also* Pasta sauces
  almond-based 100
  anchovy 37, 208
  apple 37, 202, 204
  avocado 35
  barbecue 42, 179, 189, 192, 222
  berry 37, 195, 209, 224
  butter and wine 35
  cheese 35, 134, 188
  cherry 37, 225
  chicken stock/wine and cream 35, 215
  chilli 40, 43, 180, 222, 252
  chocolate-chilli 43, 217–218
  citrus 35, 38
    lemon 201
    orange 178, 224
  coconutty 232, 236, 253
  crayfish 37
  creamy and acidic/tangy 39, 133
  creamy tomato 39
  curry 179, 230, 231
  eggy, buttery or creamy 35, 121, 177, 186, 205, 215
  fish (nam pla) 249
  garlic 36
  herb 38, 81, 180, 222

hollandaise 64
horseradish 35, 41, 178
Japanese dipping 237
lemon butter 35, 121
Madeira 36, 173, 207
mayonnaise 36
mint 41, 196
mushroom 35, 81, 188, 207
mustard 35, 41, 135, 200, 206
onion 35, 36
peanut 38, 180, 252
pepper 36, 188
pepper, red and green 81
peri-peri 42, 180, 222
plum 37, 248
port 36, 183
raisin 42
red wine 36, 37, 187, 211
soy 43, 190, 198, 223, 237, 242
spice-based/spicy 39
sweet-basting 111
tomato-based 40
truffle and crayfish 37
vinegar 123
walnut 64, 100
white 35
wine 37, 81, 207, 220
yoghurt 40
Sauerbraten 92, **184**
Sauerkraut 71
    see also Choucroute 199
Sausages
  bangers and mash 98, 106
  boerewors 174
  bratwurst 203
  cabanossi 203
  chorizo 140, 178, 199, 203, 219
  frankfurters 105, 203
  merguez 97
  pork 203
  smoked 71, 218
  Russians 203
  with red cabbage 111
Savoury mince 60, 179
    see also Sloppy joes 185
Scaloppine 206, 219, 220
Scallops 65, 104, 110, **157**
Scampi *see* Langoustine 154
Schindlbraten 64
Scrambled eggs 161–162
Seafood 152–158
  abalone **153**, 158
  calamari 62, 105, 110, **153**
  casserole/potjie 157

cocktail 137
crab 153
crayfish 154
in light creamy sauces 100
langoustine 154
mussels 154–155
oysters 133–134
paella 155
perlemoen (abalone) **153**, 158
platter 102, **156**
prawns 155–156
risotto 169
salad 100, **137**, **146**
scallops 65, 104, 110, **157**
scampi 157
shrimps 100, **157**
tempura 240
Sechuan beef see Sichuan beef **246**
Shami kebab 97, **231**
Sharing wine in a restaurant 117–118
Shellfish 59, 64, 66, 94, 100
Shepherd's pie 197
Shish kebab 138
Shrimps 100, **157**
Sichuan beef 72, 97, **246**
Skilpadjies 87, 212
Smoked cheeses **296–297**, 302, 304, 305
Smoked fish 59, 64, 65, 77, 82, 86, 100, 103, **138**, 161
Snails 64, 92, 106, **139**
Som tam (Thai pawpaw salad) 251
Sosaties 193 see also Kebabs
Soufflés, savoury 64, **162**
sweet 267–268
Soups 141–143
asparagus 143
avocado 142
bean 143
beetroot (borsch) 143
bisque 142
bouillabaisse 56, **142**
butternut 143
carrot and orange 108
chicken 142
chowder 65, **142**
consommé 142
corn 95, **143**, **245**
crayfish 142
cucumber 142
French onion 143
gazpacho 142
garbure 74
goulash 74

hot and sour 245
lentil 74, 143
minestrone 143
mulligatawny 142
mushroom 143
mussel 142
Japanese miso 95, **238**
oxtail 142
pea and ham 74, **143**
potato and leek 143
Provençal fish 142
ribollita 143
Scotch broth 143
seafood 142
sweet potato 59, **143**
Thai (tom yum) 95, 252
tomato 93, **143**
tourin 74
vegetable 143
vichyssoise 142
Spanakopita 139
Spanish stews and casseroles 76
Spareribs 67, 97, 111, **247**, 248
Spicy dishes 71, 95, 111
Spring rolls **247**, **252**
Springbok 75, 87, 97
St-Nectaire **297**, 302, 303, 304, 305
Starters 120–140
Steak and sauces 61, 65, 74, 92, 98, 102, 111, **185–189**
Steak and kidney pie 61, 75, **185**
Steak tartare 190
Stews, bredies and potjies
beef **173**, **182–183**
beef Bourguignonne 172
boeuf en daube 97, **174**
bollito misto 77, **175**
carbonnade 176
cassoulet 74, **199**, 224
cocido Madrileño 97, **178**
cozido à Portuguesa 178
dhansak 230
duck 224
Irish 192
lamb **191–192**, **194**, **195**
Lancashire hotpot 194
nabemono 238
navarin of lamb 195
osso buco 77, **207–208**
oxtail 97, **182**
pork 198–199
pulse-based/thickened 75, 86
rabbit 77
sauerbraten 77, 92, **184**

soutribbetjie 97
stifadho 92
tagine (tajine) 97, **197**
tomato bredie 92
venison/wildspotjie 77, **210**
waterblommetjie-bredie 97
Stilton 12, 284, **297-298**, 301, 303, 304, 305
Stir-fry
   beef 190
   chicken 83, **223-224**
   Chinese 247-248
   pork 83
   Thai 252
Strawberries see Berries 258
Sweet-and-sour dishes 248
Sweetbreads 213
Sweetness, pairing guidelines 19
Suckling pig, spit-braaied 62
Sushi 59, 68, 108, 110, **239-240**
T
Tabbouleh 146
Tacos **190**, **224**
Taleggio **298**, 302, 303, 304, 305
Tandoori chicken 234
Tapas 96, **140**
Tapenade 140
Taramasalata 140
Tartare sauce 52
Taste sensations, five primary 19-25
Technological developments 15
Teriyaki 241
Thai cuisine 93, 100, 102, 110, **249-253**
   curries (green, red, other) 71, 82, **250**
   fishcakes (tod man) 68, **251**
   fried rice (khao pad) 251
   Massaman curry 250
   noodles (pad thai) 57, **251**
   salad, pawpaw 251
   satay **252**, 253
   soup (tom yum) 252
   spring rolls (po pla) 252
   stir-fries 252
Tikka 235
Toad in the hole 203
Tomato 53, 55, 93
   sun-dried 104-105
Tomme **298-299**, 303, 304, 305
Tongue 213
Tonkatsu 241
Tortillas see Tacos
Tripe 213

Truffles 75, 77, 100, 106, 107
Tuna 69, 149
   canned 152
Turkey 58, 61, 74, 95, 98, 102, **224**
U V
Umami 24-25
   pairing guidelines 25
Varietal wines see Wines and wine styles
Veal 205-208
Vegetables 56, 64, 68, 83, 84, 86, 101, 104, 110, 111
Vegetarian 56, 64, 72, 83, 84, 86, 101, 104, 126, 133, **164-169**
Venison 70, **209-210**
   larding, to serve with Pinotage 87
   pie 97, **210**
   roast 209
   steaks 75, 210
   stews, casseroles and potjies 210
   see also Game
Vertical pairing 28-29
Vietnamese cuisine 107
Vinegar 53
Vintershoek **299**, 302, 303, 304, 305
Vitello tonnato 208
W
Waldorf salad 146
Wasabi 50, 237, 241
Weight, of food and wine 18
Wensleydale **299**, 302, 304, 305
White with white rule 13-16
Wiener schnitzel 206
Wines and wine styles
   pairing with cheese 301-305
   pairing with food 54-111
   (**bold** entries indicate a pairing reference to cheese)
   Barbera 55, **301**
      food to pair with 55-56
   Blanc de Noir 56, **301**
      food to pair with 56-57
   Blanc Fumé 57
   Bordeaux blend 57
      food to pair with 58
   Bukettraube 59, **301**
      food to pair with 59
   Cabernet Franc 59, **301**
      food to pair with 60
   Cabernet Sauvignon 60, **301**
      food to pair with 60-61
   Cape blend 62
   Cape Riesling **302**
      see Crouchen Blanc 68-69

Cape Ruby see Port 68
Cape Vintage see Port 68
Carignan 62
　food to pair with 62
Chablis see Chardonnay 63
Champagne see sparkling wine 98
Chardonnay 63, **302**
　food to pair with 64–65
Chenin Blanc 65, **302**
　food to pair with 66
Cinsaut 66, **302**
　food to pair with 67
Claret 67
Colombard 67, **302**
　food to pair with 68
Crouchen Blanc 68–69
　food to pair with 68–69
Fernão Pires 69
　food to pair with 69
Gamay Noir 69
　food to pair with 69–70
Gewürztraminer 70, **302**
　food to pair with 70–71
Grenache 72, **303**
　food to pair with 72
Hanepoot 72
　food to pair with, see Muscadel 76
Jerepigo 72
　food to pair with, see Muscadel 76
Late Harvest 73
Malbec 73
　food to pair with 73–74
Merlot 74, **303**
　food to pair with 74–75
Mourvèdre 75
　food to pair with 75–76
Muscadel, white 76, red **303**
　food to pair with 76–77
Natural sweet 77
　food to pair with, see Late
　　Harvest/Special Late Harvest
Nebbiolo 77, **303**
　food to pair with 77
Noble late harvest 78, **303**
　food to pair with 79–80
Paarl Riesling **302**
　see Crouchen Blanc 68–69
Petit Verdot 81
　food to pair with 81
Pinot Blanc 81, **303**
　food to pair with 81–82
Pinot Gris 82, **303**
　food to pair with 82–83
Pinot Noir 83, **303**

food to pair with 83–84
Pinotage 85, **303**
　food to pair with 86–87
Port 88, **304**
　food to pair with 89–90
Primitivo see Zinfandel 110
Rhine Riesling see Weisser
　Riesling 108
Riesling 90 see also Crouchen
　Blanc 68–69
Rosé 90
　food to pair with, see Blanc
　　de Noir 56
Ruby Cabernet 91
　food to pair with 91
Sangiovese 91, **304**
　food to pair with 92
Sauvignon Blanc 92, **304**
　food to pair with 93–94
Semillon 94, **304**
　food to pair with 95
Sherry 95, **304**
　food to pair with 95–96
Shiraz 96, **304**
　food to pair with 97–98
South African Riesling **302**
　see Crouchen Blanc 68–69
sparkling wine 98, **305**
　food to pair with 100–103
Special Late Harvest 104, **305**
　food to pair with 104
Steen 104, see Chenin Blanc 65
Stein 104
　food to pair with 104–105
Sylvaner 105
　food to pair with 105
Syrah 105, see Shiraz 96
Tempranillo 105, **305**
　food to pair with 106
Tinta Barocca 106
　see also Touriga Nacional 107
Touriga Nacional 107
　food to pair with 107
Viognier 107, **305**
　food to pair with 107–108
Weisser Riesling 108, **305**
　food to pair with 109–110
Zinfandel 110, **305**
　food to pair with 111
Witzenberger **299**, 303, 304
X Y Z
Yakitori 241
Yoghurt 53
Yum (Thai salads) 251–252